MORAL KNOWLEDGE?

MORAL KNOWLEDGE?

New Readings in Moral Epistemology

Walter Sinnott-Armstrong

Mark Timmons

New York   Oxford
OXFORD UNIVERSITY PRESS
1996

To Liz
W. S-A.

To John, Bryan, and Andy
M.T.

Oxford University Press

Oxford   New York
Athens   Auckland   Bangkok   Bombay
Calcutta   Cape Town   Dar es Salaam   Delhi
Florence   Hong Kong   Istanbul   Karachi
Kuala Lumpur   Madras   Madrid   Melbourne
Mexico City   Nairobi   Paris   Singapore
Taipei   Tokyo   Toronto

and associated companies in
Berlin   Ibadan

Library of Congress Cataloging-in-Publication Data
Moral knowledge? : new readings in moral
epistemology / edited by Walter Sinnott-Armstrong, Mark Timmons.
p.   cm.
Includes bibliographical references.
ISBN 0-19-508989-8 (pbk.)
ISBN 0-19-508988-X (cloth)
1. Ethics.   I. Sinnott-Armstrong, Walter, 1955-
II. Timmons, Mark, 1951-
BJ1012.M633.1996   170—dc20
95-44287

1 3 5 7 9 8 6 4 2

Printed in the United States of America
on acid-free paper

Preface

In moral philosophy classes, professors usually explain many different moral theories, and then their students ask, "But how can I know which theory to accept?" or "How can I be justified in believing one moral claim instead of another?" These persistent questions are addressed in the field of moral epistemology and in these pages. No single answer is given by this volume. Instead, the editors gathered contributors who represent a wide variety of perspectives. Without assuming any background beyond an introduction to ethics, each contributor discusses a general kind of answer to the questions of moral epistemology and then defends his or her own particular answer within that general kind. Together, these essays should serve both to introduce the field of moral epistemology and to stimulate and contribute to its growth and development.

A general introduction is provided by sections 1–4 of the first chapter, by Walter Sinnott-Armstrong. Sinnott-Armstrong goes on to develop his own account of justification and his own limited version of moral skepticism. Theories of knowledge and justification depend crucially on the notion of truth, which is discussed in the following chapters, by Peter Railton and Simon Blackburn, who argue for and against moral realism, respectively.

The remaining essays can be seen as various responses to the skeptical regress argument. This argument is described in more detail in Sinnott-Armstrong's chapter, but the basic problem is simple: If a moral belief cannot be justified without depending on an inference from other beliefs, and if those other beliefs must also be justified, then justification of a moral belief seems to require a vicious infinite regress of one justification after another. In response, Robert Audi defends a version of moral intuitionism that claims that moral beliefs can be justified independently of any inference. Geoffrey Sayre-McCord then defends a version of coherentism that makes justification depend on inferential relations throughout the believer's system of beliefs, including the very belief to be justified. Richard Hare next tries to reconcile coherentists with foundationalists (including intuitionists), and also discusses the importance of understanding moral language for justifying moral beliefs. Richard Brandt then attempts to show how moral claims can be justified by appealing to science, especially cognitive psychology. Christopher Morris follows by defending a contractarian justification that grounds morality in a nonmoral notion of individual rationality; and David Copp develops a related approach that instead refers to rationality in choices by societies. Margaret Walker also emphasizes the social dimension of morality, although from a feminist perspective, and argues that a certain kind of negotiation within society can lead to justification for some moral claims. Finally, Mark Timmons defends the contextualist view that some moral beliefs can be justified by reference to unjustified moral assumptions in certain contexts. Although there are other possible moves, these essays cover most of the main approaches to moral epistemology. Further readings in these and other theories about moral epistemology can be found in the annotated bibliography prepared by Mitch Haney.

Despite the contributors' disagreements, this book is truly a collaborative effort. Early versions of each essay were mailed to each contributor. We then held a conference at Dartmouth College, where everyone had a chance to comment on everyone else's work. A flurry of written exchanges followed. We all benefitted from the close scrutiny of the other contributors, as well as of the other participants at the conference.

Many others have also contributed to this project. Generous funding for the Moral Epistemology Conference at Dartmouth College was provided by the National Endowment for the Humanities, the Mellon Foundation, the Eunice and Julian Cohen Professorship for the Study of Ethics and Human Values, and the Gramlich lecture fund administered by the Philosophy Department at Dartmouth College. Barbara Hillinger and Julie Wright of the Dartmouth Institute for Applied and Professional Ethics helped to organize the conference. Research assistance was provided by Malia Brink through Dartmouth's Presidential Scholar Program. We are extremely grateful to all of these supporters.

Hanover, N.H.   W.S-A.
October 1995   M.T.

Contents

Contributors

Robert Audi
University of Nebraska, Lincoln

Simon Blackburn
University of North Carolina at Chapel Hill

Richard B. Brandt
University of Michigan, Ann Arbor

David Copp
University of California, Davis

Mitchell R. Haney
University of Memphis

R. M. Hare
University of Oxford

Christopher W. Morris
Bowling Green State University

Peter Railton
University of Michigan, Ann Arbor

Geoffrey Sayre-McCord
University of North Carolina at Chapel Hill

Walter Sinnott-Armstrong
Dartmouth College

Mark Timmons
University of Memphis

Margaret Urban Walker
Fordham University

MORAL KNOWLEDGE?

1

Moral Skepticism and Justification

Walter Sinnott-Armstrong

In 1993, Dr. Jack Kevorkian helped Ali Khalili commit suicide. Many people believe that this act was morally wrong, but others believe just as strongly that it was not. More generally, many people believe that sodomy is immoral, but others do not. And Kantians and utilitarians disagree about whether it would be morally wrong to lie or break a promise to someone just to make someone else happier. Such moral disputes raise many questions. If I have not yet formed any opinion about the morality of capital punishment, for example, how should I decide what to think? If I come to believe that capital punishment is immoral, is this belief justified? Can other people be justified in believing the contrary? Can anyone know whether capital punishment is immoral? How?

Similar questions arise even when there is no disagreement. Almost everyone agrees that torturing babies just for fun is immoral. But is this common belief justified? Do we know that it is true? What could we say to someone who did disagree? Could we show them that their beliefs are false or unjustified? How?

Such issues lie at the heart of moral epistemology. Whereas substantive ethics is about what is morally right or wrong, moral epistemology asks whether and how anyone can know or be justified in believing that something is morally right or wrong. These questions lead into deep issues about the nature of morality, language, metaphysics, and justification and knowledge in general. All of these issues can be illuminated by studying their implications for moral epistemology.

But the issue of moral justification is not just theoretical. It also has practical importance. Debates about when, if ever, an employee health plan should pay for abortions often turn on disputes about whether someone can know that abortion is morally wrong. Also, many legal theorists argue that judges should not overturn laws on the basis of their own moral beliefs, because those moral beliefs should not be trusted when the majority disagrees. And

3

educational policies often depend on views about whether values can be justified well enough to be taught in the public schools of a free society. In these and other ways, our public debates and institutions are deeply affected by our views on whether moral beliefs can be justified.

Even in our personal lives, we often need to decide which moral claims to believe, how much confidence to place in them, and what to think of people who believe otherwise. Suppose a friend has a secret affair with a married man. If you believe that the affair is morally wrong, you have to decide what, if anything, to do about it. Your decision might hinge on whether you think that your moral belief is justified well enough.

In general, when a moral problem is serious, most people want to have some belief about it, and they do not want this moral belief to be arbitrary or unjustified. So they want to form justified moral beliefs. The question is whether they can get what they want. This is the basic question for moral epistemology.

What Is Meta-Ethics?

In order to better understand the field of moral epistemology, it is useful to locate it within the larger territory of moral theory. Any division of moral theory is bound to be controversial, but some framework can help in comparing various views. For this purpose, moral theory is often divided, first, into substantive ethics and meta-ethics.

Substantive ethics or normative ethics includes nontautologous claims and beliefs about what is morally right or wrong, what is morally good or bad, what morally ought or ought not to be done, and so on. These claims and beliefs might be about acts, states of character, persons, policies, institutions, laws, and so on. They might be about particular cases or about general kinds; and they might be combined into systems, such as utilitarianism. Anyone who makes or implies any such claim is to that extent within substantive ethics.

Meta-ethics then asks about the nature or status of substantive moral claims and theories. One prominent area of meta-ethics has been the study of moral language. When a speaker says, "Abortion is immoral," one might ask what this sentence *means,* what *effect* this utterance causes or is intended to cause, or what *speech act* is performed. Such questions fall under *moral semantics* or, more broadly, *moral linguistics.* The focus on moral language has produced some disdain for meta-ethics, but there is much more to meta-ethics than moral linguistics. Meta-ethics also includes *moral ontology,* which asks about the metaphysical status of moral properties and facts, if any. There are also debates about how to *define* morality as opposed to self-interest, religion, law, custom, and so on.

Moral epistemology is yet another area of meta-ethics. Moral epistemologists study justification and knowledge of substantive moral claims and beliefs. Of course, one cannot determine whether a claim is justified or known to be true if one has no idea what that claim means, so moral epistemology depends in some ways on moral semantics. It also depends on moral ontology and on the definition of morality. Nonetheless, moral epistemology differs from other areas of meta-ethics in that it focuses directly on justification and knowledge of morality and brings in other theories only insofar as they are relevant to these central concerns.

Moral epistemology is also distinct from substantive ethics insofar as theories in moral epistemology are supposed to be neutral among competing substantive moral views. When people disagree about the morality of abortion, they often want a method to resolve their dispute or a test of whether either view is justified. Moral epistemologists study and sometimes propose such methods and tests. In order to avoid begging the question, these methods and tests must be neutral among the views under dispute. Of course, some theories in moral epistemology are not really so neutral; and maybe no theory in moral epistemology can be neutral among all possible substantive moral views. Even so, some theories in moral epistemology can be neutral among the competitors in a particular dispute; and then they might help in choosing among those alternatives.

These divisions of moral theory remain questionable, but they provide a rough picture of some of the various issues that arise about morality:

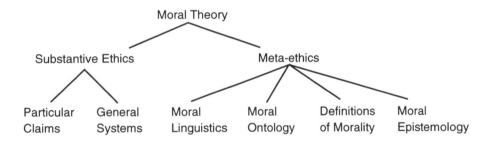

What Is Moral Epistemology?

Moral epistemology is simply epistemology applied to substantive moral claims and beliefs. Epistemology is the study of knowledge and justification in general. It asks whether, when, and how claims or beliefs can be justified or known or shown to be true. Moral epistemology then asks whether, when, and how substantive moral beliefs and claims can be justified or known or shown to be true.

To determine whether moral knowledge is possible, we need to determine what is necessary for knowledge. I don't know where President Clinton is right now if I do not have any belief about where he is, or if I believe that he is somewhere other than where he is, or if my belief is true but just a guess. Examples like these have led many philosophers to define knowledge as justified true belief. If this also holds for morality, one cannot know that stealing is immoral unless it is true that stealing is immoral, one believes that stealing is immoral, and one's belief is justified. This tradition has been questioned because justified true belief does not seem sufficient for knowledge in some cases,[1] and some philosophers argue that justification is also not necessary for knowledge.[2]

But regardless of how knowledge is analyzed, justification remains a distinct and important issue for epistemology. In moral epistemology in particular, many theories study the conditions under which moral claims or beliefs are justified or under which a person is justified in believing a moral claim. Other theories focus on processes and procedures that are supposed to justify moral beliefs and claims, or to be epistemically responsible ways to form moral beliefs. Some philosophers also develop methods for showing that moral claims or beliefs are true or justified. All of these issues about justification are important, but this essay will focus on the questions of which conditions must be met for a person to be justified in believing a substantive moral claim; and when, if ever, those conditions are met.[3]

What Is Moral Skepticism?

The main challenges in moral epistemology are posed by moral skeptics. However, many different views have been described as moral skepticism. The best way to explain the particular kind of moral skepticism that will be our topic is to contrast it with the other views that sometimes go by the same name.

Two kinds of moral skepticism are directly relevant to moral epistemology, so they can be seen as versions of epistemological moral skepticism. The first is the claim that nobody is ever justified in believing any substantive moral claim. This will be called *moral justification skepticism*. The second is the claim that nobody ever knows that any substantive moral claim is true. This can be called *moral knowledge skepticism*. If knowledge implies justification, as is often assumed, then moral justification skepticism implies moral knowledge skepticism. But even if knowledge requires justification, it does not require only justification, so moral knowledge skepticism does not imply moral justification skepticism.

Both of these views must be distinguished from the meta-ethical claim that no substantive moral belief or claim is either true or false. Some philosophers argue that claims like "Cheating is morally wrong" are neither true nor false, because they resemble expressions of emotion (such as "Boo Nicks") or prescriptions for action (such as "Go Celtics"), which are neither true nor false. Such theories rest on linguistic analyses, so I will call them *linguistic moral skepticism,* although a more common name is *noncognitivism.*[4]

Such analyses of moral language face serious problems. Critics argue that moral judgments do not simply express emotions or prescribe acts but also or instead make claims about the moral properties of those actions. When Ronald Reagan said, "Abortion is morally wrong," he wanted to say something true about abortion. He did not want only to express personal emotions or only to tell people how to act. Moreover, it would be difficult to explain the role of moral claims in logical inferences if moral claims were analyzed solely as expressions or prescriptions.[5] In response to such arguments, most recent defenders of emotivism and prescriptivism grant that moral beliefs can be true or false at least in some minimal way, possibly captured by a semantic or redundancy theory of truth, so they are not linguistic moral skeptics on my definition.[6] The issue of truth in morality deserves much more careful attention, but I will assume henceforth that moral claims and beliefs can be true or false at least in a minimal way.

Yet another kind of moral skepticism still might be defensible. Error theorists argue that moral claims try to say something about moral properties (such as moral wrongness) of actions, but there are no properties of the kind that is claimed, so all positive moral claims are false.[7] Because ontology is the study of what exists, the view that no moral properties or facts exist can be called *ontological moral skepticism.*

Despite their differences, linguistic moral skeptics and error theorists agree that no moral claim or belief is true. This has direct implications for moral knowledge skepticism. If knowledge implies truth, as is usually assumed, and if moral claims are never true, then there is no knowledge of what is moral or immoral. However, the converse implication fails: even if some moral claims are true, it still might not be possible for anyone to know that a moral claim is true. One reason might be that moral claims cannot be justified, and knowledge requires justification in addition to truth. So, even if linguistic and ontological moral skepticism are false, moral justification skepticism and moral knowledge skepticism still might be true.

Yet another view is often described as moral skepticism. It is common to ask, "Why should I be moral?" Most people admit that there is *sometimes* a reason to be moral, but the controversial claim is that there is *always* a reason to be moral (or to do what is morally required).[8] A denial of this claim is often seen as a kind of moral skepticism. I will call it *practical moral skepticism.*

This view resembles moral justification skepticism in that both skepticisms deny a role to reasons in morality. However, moral justification skepticism is about reasons for *belief,* whereas practical moral skepticism is about reasons for *action.* Moreover, practical moral skepticism denies that there is *always* a reason for moral action, whereas moral justification skepticism denies that there is *ever* an adequate reason for moral belief. Because of these differences, practical moral skepticism does not imply moral justification skepticism. If we are ever justified in believing that an act is immoral, then moral justification skepticism is false. But even if so, and even if there is a reason to act morally in that case, practical moral skepticism still might be true, because there might not be any reason to act morally in other cases.

In sum, then, we need to distinguish the following kinds of moral skepticism:

Linguistic moral skepticism = no moral belief or claim is true or false.
Ontological moral skepticism = no moral facts or properties exist.
Practical moral skepticism = there is not always a reason to be moral.

Moral knowledge skepticism = no moral belief or claim is known to be true.
Moral justification skepticism = no moral belief or claim is justified.

The last view will be the main topic from now on, and I will refer to it simply as moral skepticism.

Philosophers who accept this moral skepticism need not be any less motivated to be moral, nor need they have any less reason to be moral, than their opponents. Moral skeptics can hold moral beliefs just as strongly as nonskeptics. Moral skeptics can even believe that their moral beliefs are true by virtue of corresponding to an independent reality. All that moral skeptics must deny is that their (or anyone's) moral beliefs are justified in the relevant way, but this is enough to make moral skepticism very controversial and important.

Is Moral Skepticism True?

There is an initial presumption against moral skepticism. Most people hold many moral beliefs and think that they are justified. It seems obvious that it is morally wrong to hit your opponent just to get her back for beating you in a game.[9] Furthermore, people often say that they *know* that something is morally wrong. If a father punishes his child by spanking her severely, his neighbors might say, "I know it is wrong for him to spank her, but I don't know what I should do about it." We also often say that people *ought* to know what is immoral. If a stock broker is caught passing inside information but claims that he did not know that this was unethical, many people might respond, "He should have known better," where this does not mean just "He should have known that he would be caught" but rather "He should have known that what he did was unethical." But he could not have known this, according to moral knowledge skeptics; therefore, this moral skepticism conflicts with these common ways of talking and thinking. None of these examples is conclusive, and common beliefs might be wrong on these matters. Yet such considerations create a presumption against moral skepticism. In order to override this presumption, moral skeptics need at least some argument.[10]

Many different kinds of argument have been given for moral skepticism. Some moral skeptics argue that no moral claim or belief can be true (linguistic or ontological moral skepticism), and they infer that no moral claim or belief can be known to be true (moral knowledge skepticism). Others argue that people disagree and make so many mistakes about morality that our moral belief-forming processes are not reliable enough to result in justified beliefs or knowledge. Still others argue that nobody can know what is morally right or wrong unless they are fully informed and impartial, but nobody can be fully informed and impartial about moral issues. And some argue that we cannot know that any claim is true unless the truth of that claim is necessary for the best explanation of some independent fact, but moral truths are never necessary for the best explanation of any nonmoral fact.[11]

Each of these arguments deserves serious consideration, but here I will feature two other arguments for moral skepticism. These two arguments are versions of well-known arguments for general skepticism, which is the view that no claims or beliefs of any kind can be justified or known. I will apply these arguments to morality in particular. Although these arguments can also be used outside morality, they cannot be dismissed just because they are general. If the problems raised by these arguments cannot be solved at least in morality, then we cannot be justified in believing any moral claims, so moral skepticism is true.

The Regress Argument

The first featured argument is a regress argument, which derives from Sextus Empiricus.[12] Its goal is to lay out all of the ways in which a person might be justified in believing something, and then to argue that none of them works.

The regress argument begins by distinguishing two ways to be justified:

> A person S is *inferentially* justified in believing a moral claim that p if and only if what makes S justified is at least in part that S believes something from which S does or could infer p.

Here S's being justified depends on S's ability to infer p from a belief of S, so S would not be justified if S could not draw such an inference. In contrast,

> A person S is *noninferentially* justified in believing a moral claim that p if and only if S is justified but not inferentially justified in believing that p.

Here S's being justified does not depend on any ability of S to infer p from a belief of S. What makes S justified then might be something that is independent of any actual or available belief or inference, such as a nondoxastic perceptual or emotional state; or it might be nothing at all. In this last case, S is *directly* justified.

The first premise of the regress argument then claims that these are the only ways to be justified:

> (1) If any person S is justified in believing any moral claim that p, then S must be justified either inferentially or noninferentially.

The moral skeptic goes on to deny both of these possibilities. First,

> (2) No person S is ever noninferentially justified in believing any moral claim that p.

In other words, S must be able to infer p from some other beliefs of S in order to be justified in believing that p.

Premise (2) is often supported by examples. Thelma believes that it is morally wrong to eat meat; Louise asks "Why?" If Thelma has no reason at all for her moral belief, then she does not seem justified in believing it. Thelma's belief seems to be the kind that needs to be justified by inferring it from some reason. If there is nothing special about this moral belief, then the same point applies to every moral belief. Moral skeptics conclude that noninferential justification never works, as premise (2) claims.

Premise (2) is denied by moral intuitionists, who claim that some moral beliefs are justified independent of any ability to infer them from any other beliefs.[13] What is believed is then sometimes called self-evident or evident by itself. Moral skeptics see this as dogmatism, and dogmatism can be used on both sides of any issue. If Thelma could be noninferentially justified in believing that eating meat *is* wrong, then Louise could also be noninferentially justified in believing that eating meat is *not* wrong, even if neither can infer her belief from any reason.[14] Moreover, Nick could be noninferentially justified in believing that it is morally wrong to eat artichokes or to step on cracks in sidewalks. Moral skeptics claim that there is no way to break such impasses or to avoid such absurdities if any noninferential justification is admitted.

Given (1) and (2), the moral skeptic can draw an intermediate conclusion:

(3) If any person *S* is justified in believing any moral claim that *p*, then *S* must be justified inferentially.

This means that *S* must be able to infer *p* from some other beliefs held by *S*. But which other beliefs? There are two main possibilities:

(4) If any person *S* is inferentially justified in believing any moral claim that *p*, then *S* must be justified either by an inference with some moral premises or by an inference without any moral premises.

Inferences can contain a mixture of moral and nonmoral premises, but the question here is whether *S* can be justified by an inference from nonmoral premises alone without any moral premise at all.

An inference from nonmoral premises might seem to have advantages if nonmoral premises are easier to justify than moral premises. However, even if the nonmoral premises are secure, it is still not clear how nonmoral premises alone could be enough to justify moral conclusions. Some inferences of this kind start from premises that are supposed to be descriptive rather than normative.[15] In a simple example, premises like

(ii) The act has feature F (such as that it breaks a promise);
(iii) The context is of kind C (such as where people depend on each other);

    (iv) People in group G would have reaction R (such as disapproval)[16]

might be used to justify a conclusion like

    (v) The act is morally wrong.

Moral skeptics claim that all such inferences are incomplete because they depend on a bridge principle like

    (i) Any act is morally wrong if it has feature F in context C and causes reaction R in group G.

The point is not only that the argument from (ii)–(iv) to (v) is not formally valid without (i), but also that (i) is needed because (ii)–(iv) would not justify (v) if no bridge principle like (i) were true. Yet bridge principles like (i) seem to be substantive moral claims, so they need to be justified themselves. Moral skeptics conclude that nonnormative premises like (ii)–(iv) are never enough by themselves to justify any moral beliefs.

    Some philosophers have proposed much more complex arguments to justify moral beliefs by inferring them from other kinds of nonnormative premises. These include premises about metaphysics[17] and various sciences, such as sociobiology,[18] developmental psychology,[19] and the psychology of motivation.[20] However, moral skeptics respond that these more complex arguments still depend on bridge principles that are not morally or normatively neutral, and these bridge principles need to be justified themselves. If so, then no moral belief can be justified by inferring it from purely nonnormative premises.

    A related attempt to justify moral beliefs uses premises that are not moral but still are normative in other ways. This approach is taken by many contractarians and others.[21] Contractarians usually start with nonmoral normative premises about who is rational (and sometimes also about who is impartial), argue that these people under certain circumstances would agree to certain moral rules (or norms or standards), and conclude that the corresponding moral beliefs are true (or justified). Even if these premises can be established—which is not easy—such arguments still need another bridge principle to relate the nonmoral premises to the moral conclusion. In one case, the needed bridge principle claims that an act is morally wrong if it violates a rule that would be accepted by all rational, impartial people in appropriate circumstances. This bridge principle might seem innocuous at first, but that is because it has little content until "rational," "impartial," and "appropriate circumstances" are defined. Once these terms are defined, the bridge principle becomes questionable. The problem is that different acts come out morally wrong when this contractarian framework is filled in with different background theories of rationality, impartiality, and appropriate circumstances. This flexibility puts contractarians in a dilemma. If the background theories are *not* detailed enough to yield specific moral beliefs, then the contractarian form of argument will not justify those moral beliefs. On the other hand, if the background theories *are* detailed enough to yield specific moral beliefs, then anyone who wants to deny those moral beliefs can (with equal justification) deny those aspects of the background theories that are needed to yield those moral beliefs. Either way, the contractarian argument will fail to justify the moral belief, according to moral skeptics. There are other arguments from the same or other nonmoral norms, but they seem to run into similar problems.

If nonnormative premises cannot justify moral beliefs, and nonmoral normative premises also cannot justify moral beliefs, then

(5) No person *S* is ever justified in believing any moral claim that *p* by an inference without any moral premises.

When (5) is added to the previous premises (3)–(4), the moral skeptic can draw another intermediate conclusion:

(6) If any person *S* is justified in believing any moral claim that *p*, then *S* must be justified by an inference with some moral premise.

In short, moral beliefs must be justified by moral beliefs.

This creates a problem. Although the justifying beliefs must include some moral beliefs, not just any moral beliefs will do:

(7) No person *S* is ever justified in believing a moral claim that *p* by an inference with a moral premise unless *S* is also justified in believing that moral premise itself.

Premise (7) is denied by some contextualists, who claim that even if a moral belief is not itself justified, if it is shared within a certain social context, then it can be used to justify other moral beliefs.[22] However, the fact that a moral belief happens to be held by everyone in a group is not sufficient to make anyone justified in believing it or in believing anything that follows from it. To see this, suppose that everyone in a small town believes that it is immoral for a black person to marry a white person. They infer that it is immoral for Ray, who is black, to marry Terry, who is white. This conclusion is not justified if the general principle is not justified. Indeed, every belief would be justified if a belief could be justified simply by inferring it from an unjustified belief, since every belief can be validly inferred from itself. The only way to avoid such absurd results, according to moral skeptics, is to accept (7).

But then how can the moral premises be justified? Given (6)–(7), the moral premises must be justified by inferring them from still other moral beliefs that must also be justified by inferring them from still other moral beliefs, and so on. To justify a moral belief thus requires a branching tree or chain of justifying beliefs or premises. This justifying chain can take only two forms, so that

(8) If any person S is justified in believing any moral claim that p, then S must be justified by a chain of inferences that either goes on infinitely or includes p itself as an essential premise.

The latter kind of chain is usually described as circular, although its structure is more complex than a simple circle.

Moral skeptics then deny that either kind of chain can justify any moral belief. First,

(9) No person S is ever justified in believing any moral claim that p by a chain of inferences that includes p as an essential premise.

Any argument that includes its conclusion as a premise will be valid and will remain valid if other premises are added. However, anyone who doubts the conclusion will have just as much reason to doubt the premise. So skeptics claim that nothing is gained when a premise just restates the belief to be justified.

Premise (9) is opposed by moral coherentists. Recent coherentists have emphasized that they are not inferring a belief from itself in a linear way. Instead, a moral belief is supposed to be justified because it coheres in some way with a body of beliefs that is coherent in some way.[23] Still, moral skeptics deny that coherence is enough for justification. One reason is that the internal coherence of a set of beliefs is not evidence of any relation to anything outside the beliefs. Moreover, every belief—no matter how ridiculous—can cohere with some body of beliefs that is internally coherent. If Bill argues that marriage between people with different skin colors is immoral, and Claire points out that the same reasons would show that marriage between people with different hair colors is immoral, then most people would see this as a reason to reject Bill's original belief. Nonetheless, Bill could hold on to his original belief that people with different skin colors should not be married if he also accepts that people with different hair colors also should not be married. He could even derive both beliefs from a general principle against mixing colors. Bill's resulting set of beliefs could be just as coherent internally as it would be if Bill saw neither kind of marriage as immoral. But Bill still does not seem justified in believing that both kinds of marriage are immoral. So coherence does not seem to be enough to make moral beliefs justified.

The final possible form of justification is an infinite chain. Moral skeptics, of course, claim that

(10) No person S is ever justified in believing any moral claim that p by a chain of inferences that goes on infinitely.

Someone who denied this premise could be called a moral infinist, but nobody clearly endorses this approach.[24]

Now the moral skeptic can draw a final conclusion. Premises (8)–(10) imply that

(11) No person is ever justified in believing any moral claim,

which is moral skepticism. This conclusion might seem implausible, but the regress argument is valid, so its conclusion can be escaped only by denying one of its premises.

Of course, every step along the way could be opposed. Moral intuitionists deny premise (2). Moral naturalists and contractarians deny premise (5). Moral contextualists deny premise (7). Moral coherentists deny premise (9). And a moral infinitist would deny premise (10). The regress argument thus provides a useful way of classifying theories in moral epistemology, regardless of whether it succeeds in establishing moral skepticism.

The most important question, however, is whether the regress argument shows that moral skepticism is true. I have tried to say enough to give some initial plausibility to the premises of the regress argument, but each premise deserves much more careful attention. In particular, because they are about how moral beliefs can be justified, these premises and their denials cannot be assessed properly without first determining what it means for a moral belief to be justified. I will address that issue, but first I want to look at the other main argument for moral skepticism. Then I will distinguish different ways for a belief to be justified. Finally, I will use my distinctions to evaluate both arguments for moral skepticism.

Skeptical Hypothesis Arguments

The second featured argument, which derives from Descartes,[25] starts from the common experience of being deceived. For example, yesterday I was driving down a strange road, and I thought I saw a lake in the distance, but my wife said it was just a mirage. Always curious, we turned toward it and found that I was right. We even took a swim. But what if we had not checked it out? Then I would not be justified in believing that what I saw was a lake, because I could not rule out the contrary hypothesis that it was a mirage. My belief would also not be justified if I could not rule out the possibility that it was a river rather than a lake. The general principle seems to be that I am not justified in believing something if I cannot rule out all contrary hypotheses.[26]

Skeptics then introduce hypotheses that cannot ever be ruled out. The famous Cartesian hypothesis is of a demon who deceives me in all of my beliefs about the external world, while also ensuring that my beliefs are completely coherent. If there is such a deceiving demon, then there really is no lake when I think I see one. Nobody claims that such a deceiving demon actually exists, but it is possible.[27] And this possibility cannot be ruled out by any beliefs or sense experiences. Even when I seem to be swimming in a lake, my sensations might all be caused by a deceiving demon. Since there is no way to rule out this skeptical hypothesis, my beliefs about the lake are not justified, according to the above principle. And there is nothing special about my beliefs about the lake. Everything I believe about the external world is incompatible with the deceiving demon hypothesis. Skeptics conclude that no such belief is justified.

This kind of argument can be applied to moral beliefs in several ways. First, another demon might deceive us about morality (either alone or in addition to other topics). Most people believe that it is morally wrong to torture babies just for fun, but we might be deceived in our beliefs that babies feel pain or that they have moral rights. A demon might make us believe that some creatures have moral rights, when really they do not, although other things do; or a demon might make us believe that some creatures have moral rights when really nothing does (just as a demon might deceive us into believing that some women are witches when really none are). Nobody actually claims that a demon distorts our moral beliefs in these ways, but such deception still seems possible. And such a deceiving demon cannot be ruled out by the fact that it seems obvious that babies have moral rights, any more than Descartes's deceiving demon could be ruled out by the fact that it seems obvious to me when I am swimming in a lake.

Moral skeptics do not have to depend on deceiving demons. Different arguments with the same structure can be constructed with skeptical hypotheses that are peculiar to morality. Consider:

Moral Nihilism = Nothing is morally wrong.[28]

Moral nihilism seems consistent in itself as well as logically compatible with all nonmoral facts and with their best explanations.[29] Just as it would beg the question to use common beliefs about the external world to rule out a deceiving demon hypothesis, so it would also beg the question to argue against moral nihilism on the basis of common moral beliefs—no matter how obvious. Thus, neither logic nor nonmoral beliefs nor moral beliefs can rule out moral nihilism. However, moral nihilism implies that it is not morally wrong to torture babies just for fun. So, according to moral skeptics, one must be able to rule out moral nihilism in order to be justified in believing that torturing babies just for fun is morally wrong. Moral skeptics conclude that this moral belief is not justified. More precisely:

(1′) I am not justified in believing that moral nihilism is not true.
(2′) I am justified in believing that "It is morally wrong to torture babies just for fun" (p) entails "Moral nihilism is not true" (q).
(3′) If I am justified in believing that p, and I am justified in believing that p entails q,[30] then I am justified in believing that q.
(4′) Therefore, I am not justified in believing that it is morally wrong to torture babies just for fun.

This moral belief is not especially problematic in any way. Indeed, it seems as obvious as any moral belief. So the argument can be generalized to cover any moral belief. Moral skeptics conclude that no moral belief is justified.[31]

There are two main responses to such skeptical hypothesis arguments. First, some antiskeptics deny (1′) and claim that skeptical hypotheses can be ruled out as meaningless, because the meaning of the phrase "morally wrong" depends on judgments about paradigm cases, such as "It is morally wrong to torture just for fun."[32] However, when a claim really is meaningless, such as "The square root of pine is tree," then its denial is meaningless, too. But the denial of "Torturing for fun is not morally wrong" is "Torturing for fun is morally wrong." The latter claim is not meaningless, so neither is the former. Antiskeptics might reply that "Torturing for fun is morally wrong" is more like "Cows are animals," whose denial is not meaningless but is incoherent, because the meaning of "animal" can be given as "Something like a cow or a fish or. . . ." But then, if there is any question about whether something is an animal, there is just as much question about whether it is a cow. Similarly, if moral wrongness is defined as "Something like torturing just for fun or . . .", then, if there is any question about whether an act is morally wrong, there is just as much question about whether to count it as torturing just for fun in the sense that is supposed to define "morally wrong." Moreover, this account cannot show that any morally wrong act exists. Compare someone who explains what a witch is by saying "Someone like the Wicked Witch of the West or. . . ." This cannot show that any witch exists, so the analogous argument in morality also cannot show that there exists any act that is morally wrong. Finally, even if this conclusion did follow, it would be unclear why moral skeptics or nihilists must accept that moral wrongness can be defined as "Something like torturing just for fun or . . .", or that any claim like "Torturing for fun is morally wrong" is part of the common meaning of "morally wrong." So this approach cannot rule out moral nihilism.

Another common response is to deny premise (3′), which is a principle of *closure*. Since a belief entails the denial of every contrary hypothesis, this closure principle in effect says that I cannot be justified in believing *p* unless I am justified in denying every hypothesis contrary to *p*—that is, unless I can rule out *all* contrary hypotheses. This principle has been denied by relevant alternative theorists, who claim instead that only relevant hypotheses need to be ruled out. On this theory, if skeptical hypotheses are not relevant, then a belief that it is morally wrong to torture babies just for fun can be justified, even if the believer cannot rule out moral nihilism or deceiving demons.

But why would these skeptical hypotheses be irrelevant? They are consistent and contrary to the moral belief to be justified. One might argue that these hypotheses are irrelevant just because they cannot in principle be ruled out, and a moral belief is justified when the believer has done everything he or she can do to check it out. But that just begs the question against skepticism. Besides, hypotheses that cannot be ruled out often prevent beliefs from being justified. Consider Hannah, who is trying to figure out what is inside a wrapped birthday present. She knows that it is not a bike, because it is too small. She knows that it is not clothes, because of how it rattles when shaken. But it still might be either a puzzle or a game. If she believes that it is a game, her belief is not justified unless she can somehow rule out the hypothesis of a puzzle.

Now suppose that the evil donor put the present in an impenetrable box tied with an unbreakable ribbon. Hannah can't do anything else to find out what is in the box, but that does not make her justified in believing that the box contains a game. To the contrary, it keeps her belief from being justified. Similarly, if one cannot rule out the hypotheses of a deceiving demon and of moral nihilism, the fact that one does everything that one can do to determine whether it is morally wrong to torture babies just for fun does not make this moral belief justified, according to moral skeptics.[33]

Where does this leave us? The arguments for moral skepticism seem strong, and yet most people still reject their conclusion. Most people still think that they are justified in believing some moral claims, such as that it is morally wrong to torture babies just for fun. Moreover, such beliefs do seem to have a lot going for them: They seem obvious to many people, and they also connect well with other beliefs. So they seem justified to some extent. Nonetheless, this does not refute or even undermine the arguments for moral skepticism. Arguments cannot be refuted or undermined simply by denying their conclusions. Besides, there seems to be something right in the skeptics' arguments insofar as their premises, such as (1)–(10) and (1')–(3'), rest on general principles that seem plausible in many examples. So both sides seem to contain some truth. To see how this is possible, and to assess the arguments for moral skepticism, we need to look more carefully at what it means to call a moral belief justified.

Kinds of Justification

When someone describes a moral belief and asks whether it is justified, many people often find themselves wanting to say both "Yes" and "No," even when all other facts are settled. This reaction is a signal that separate kinds of justification need to be distinguished.

One initial distinction is between negative or permissive justification and positive or supportive justification. Some people use "justified" in a very weak way. When they say that someone is justified in believing something, all they mean is that the believer does not violate certain standards, so she is epistemically permitted to believe it. This permissive use of "justified" occurs, for instance, when religious believers want to claim only that they are not irresponsible and do not have to give up their religious beliefs. But permissive justification cannot be want moral skeptics and their opponents disagree about. Moral skeptics need not claim that people should stop believing that it is morally wrong to torture babies just for fun. And skeptics' opponents claim more than that there is nothing wrong with moral beliefs. They claim that there is something right about those beliefs—some positive support for those beliefs. So debates about moral justification skepticism are about a more positive kind of justification.[34]

There are, of course, different degrees of positive support. Imagine, for example, that a murder was committed in the library, and the only people in the building were Colonel Mustard, Professor Plum, and Miss Scarlet. A detective finds size thirteen boot prints in the mud outside the library window, and only Colonel Mustard wears size thirteen boots. This is *some* reason to believe that the Colonel committed the murder. Yet if there is no other evidence, the detective is not justified in believing that Colonel Mustard is guilty. The detective ought to withhold belief until stronger evidence is found. So a belief is not justified in the relevant way unless it has *enough* positive support that it ought to be believed.[35]

Thus, the general kind of justification that will be our topic is adequate positive support.[36] Within this general kind, we still need to draw two more distinctions among different kinds of positive support for beliefs. These two distinctions will be central to the rest of this paper.

Instrumental versus *Evidential Justification*

The first distinction is between instrumental justification and evidential justification. It can be illustrated by a simple example.[37] Suppose that a benefactor will give me a million dollars if I believe that there are aardvarks on Mars, and I have a drug that will make me believe this. I am justified in taking the drug, so I am justified in making myself believe that there are aardvarks on Mars, so I am justified in being in this belief state, and my belief seems justified at least derivatively. However, I have no evidence for the content of my belief—that is, for what I believe. In cases like this, I will say that the believer has instrumental justification but not evidential justification.

The crucial difference is that evidential justification is tied to truth in a way that instrumental justification is not. The tie between evidence and truth is not simple, because one can be evidentially justified in believing a falsehood. For example, fresh aardvark droppings on Mars could give you evidence that there are aardvarks on Mars, even if the droppings had been transported from Earth without you knowing it. You also have evidence of aardvarks when you see an animal that looks just like an aardvark, even if it really is a disguised armadillo that fools you. So evidence need not guarantee truth. Nonetheless, evidence for a belief must be such that the content of the belief is more likely to be true given the evidence than without the evidence. So evidential justification is still tied to truth at least probabilistically.[38] In fact, evidential justification could be defined as adequate positive support that is tied to truth.[39]

In contrast, instrumental justification depends only on the beneficial *effects* of the mental *state* of belief.[40] It is being in the state of believing in aardvarks on Mars that gets me the million dollars. The acts of taking drugs that put me in that mental state are also instrumentally justified because those acts also have beneficial effects; but those acts have good effects only because they put me in the belief state; so the instrumental justification attaches to the belief state as well. It is not only the belief state but also its content that matters, because the effects of the belief state depend on its content. I do not get the million dollars unless I have a belief with the right content. Nonetheless, it does *not* matter whether the content of the belief is true. My belief is instrumentally justified whether or not there really are aardvarks on Mars. It doesn't even matter whether this is probable. After all, it is just as easy to imagine that my benefactor will give me a million dollars for believing the opposite, or for believing anything else. In general, instrumental justification depends on the effects of a belief state, and the effects of a belief state do not affect the truth or probability of the belief's content,[41] so instrumental justification is not tied to truth even probabilistically.[42]

This same distinction applies as well to moral beliefs. If a benefactor will give me a million dollars to believe that nuclear deterrence is morally wrong, and if I have a drug that will make me believe this, then I might be instrumentally justified in getting and being in the mental state of believing this. Nonetheless, this instrumental justification still does not show that the content of this belief is true or even likely to be true, any more than in the nonmoral case. So it takes something else for this belief to be evidentially justified. What more it takes remains to be seen, but the million-dollar bribe is enough to show that instrumental justification is different from evidential justification even in ethics.[43]

Everyday versus *Philosophical Justification*

Within each of these kinds, another distinction needs to be drawn between everyday and philosophical justification. This distinction depends on contrast classes, so that is the place to begin. Consider jumbo shrimp. Are jumbo shrimp large? An answer of "yes" or "no" would be too simple. Jumbo shrimp are large for shrimp, but they are not large for seafood. Whether one sees jumbo shrimp as large or not depends on whether one contrasts jumbo shrimp with other shrimp or with other seafood, such as salmon. Speakers need not have any very specific contrast class in mind, but it is silly to argue about whether jumbo shrimp are large if the arguers have in mind very different contrast classes.

Such contrast classes have been useful in many areas of philosophy, but most relevant here is their use in epistemology.[44] If epistemic justification is relative to contrast classes, then a belief can be justified relative to one contrast class even if it is not justified relative to another contrast class. This provides a new perspective on skepticism. Because I cannot rule out Descartes's deceiving demon, I cannot be justified in believing that I am sitting in my office as opposed to being deceived by a demon. But some claim that I can still be justified in believing that I am sitting in my office instead of standing in someone else's office. If so, the problem of general skepticism is reduced somewhat by analyzing justification in terms of contrast classes.

This approach can be extended to moral beliefs. Moral philosophers have produced many moral systems, but students often start with

(A) Act Utilitarianism = an act is morally wrong if and only if it
fails to maximize the good for all,

and

(K) Kantian Absolutism = it is morally wrong to treat any person
as a means only, even if doing so maximizes the good for all.[45]

The professor then describes some counterexample to act utilitarianism, such
as cutting up one healthy innocent person and distributing his organs to save
the lives of five unrelated people. If this act is morally wrong, and if Kantian
absolutism implies that this act is morally wrong, and if act utilitarianism
implies otherwise, then students who are justified in believing these premises
seem to be justified in believing Kantian absolutism as opposed to act utilitarianism. However, even if this argument does accomplish this much, it would
not justify anyone in believing in Kantian absolutism as opposed to some
other system, such as

(R) Rule Utilitarianism = an act is morally wrong if and only if it
violates a general rule such that everyone's obeying or accepting that rule would maximize the good for all,

if this also explains why the act in the example is morally wrong. More
technically, one might be justified in believing moral system K out of the
contrast class {A, K} without being justified in believing moral system K out
of the larger contrast class {A, K, R}. Of course, another argument might
justify one in believing K instead of R, and there are many more theories and
many more arguments. Yet the fact that such arguments provide justification
relative to some but not all alternatives is one reason to think that justification
is relative to a contrast class.

The crucial question is: How far can such arguments go? Can they rule
out *all* alternatives? It seems not. Recall the skeptical hypothesis of

(N) Moral Nihilism = Nothing is morally wrong.

This hypothesis is incompatible with act utilitarianism, rule utilitarianism, and
Kantian absolutism. However, this hypothesis cannot be ruled out by semantics
or by nonmoral facts. It also cannot be ruled out by common moral beliefs
because any argument based on common moral beliefs begs the question
against moral nihilism.

Must one be able to rule out moral nihilism to be justified in believing,
say, rule utilitarianism? That is like asking whether jumbo shrimp are large.
No simple answer is possible. One need not be able to rule out moral nihilism to be justified in believing rule utilitarianism as opposed to act utilitarianism or Kantian absolutism. However, one must be able to rule out moral
nihilism to be justified in believing rule utilitarianism as opposed to moral ni-

hilism. Thus, if one cannot rule out moral nihilism, then one can be justified in believing R out of the contrast class {A, K, R} but not out of the larger contrast class {A, K, R, N}.

This relativization applies not only to general moral theories but also to specific moral beliefs. Suppose that a patient tests HIV +, but his doctor wants to lie to him about the test results, because learning the results would depress the patient. However, the hospital ethics committee discusses the case and concludes that it would be morally wrong for the doctor to lie and not to reveal the test results to the patient. This belief might be justified in contrast with many moral beliefs, such as that lying is usually wrong but not in this case, or that it would be morally wrong to lie in this case but not for the doctor to avoid lying by refusing to tell the patient anything about the test results. Nonetheless, if the ethics committee cannot rule out moral nihilism, then the committee's moral belief is not justified in contrast with moral nihilism. So this moral belief is also justified relative to some contrast classes but not others.

An impatient critic might ask: But is this belief *just plain justified*? That depends, of course, on what "justified" means when it is not qualified. This term might then refer to justification relative to an *unlimited* contrast class that includes all contraries of the belief said to be justified. If so, then anyone who cannot rule out moral nihilism also cannot be justified in holding any moral belief. However, when someone calls a belief justified and does not explicitly specify any contrast class, the speaker usually wants to claim only that this belief is justified out of the *relevant* contrast class. If so, then one cannot determine whether a belief is justified without qualification until one determines which contrast class is relevant.

Which contrast class is *seen* as relevant varies with context and purpose. This variation does not cause trouble, even when no contrast class is specified explicitly, as long as speakers assume contrast classes that are the same or similar enough. However, confusion results when a crucial alternative seems relevant in one context but not in another. Recall the doctor who asks the hospital ethics committee whether it is morally wrong to lie to his or her patient about the unfavorable test results. It would be very unusual for any member of the ethics committee to respond that morality is just an illusion, so nothing is morally wrong. If such nihilism were expressed, it would be dismissed quickly with disdain and without argument. Contrast this with a philosophy course that has studied moral nihilism, egoism, and skepticism all term. Many students have defended these positions in discussion. In the final paper, one student argues that it is morally wrong to lie, but does not even mention moral nihilism, egoism, or skepticism. This student would and should receive a low grade. Confusion arises if someone asks whether the committee's moral belief and the student's moral belief are justified. It seems to many people that the ethics committee is justified in concluding that the doctor should not lie, even though the committee never even considers moral nihilism. But the philosophy student does not seem justified in reaching the same conclusion because that student has no response to the same hypothesis. This is paradoxical: if neither the philosophy student nor the doctor can rule out moral nihilism, how can this inability show that the philosophy student's belief is *not* justified when the committee's belief *is* justified?

The answer is that different contrast classes are assumed to be relevant in the different contexts. Hospital ethics committees usually assume that moral nihilism is not a relevant alternative. That is why they do not consider it. But philosophy classes often assume that moral nihilism is relevant. That is why they discuss it. Consequently, it is fine to say that the hospital ethics committee is justified in reaching its conclusion, but the philosophy student is not justified in reaching the same conclusion, even if neither can rule out moral nihilism. These two statements do not really conflict, because they assume different contrast classes to be relevant.[46] The paradox is thereby resolved. There appears to be a paradox only when different contrast classes are seen as relevant, but these different classes are not specified explicitly. This ability to resolve such paradoxes is another reason to relativize justification to contrast classes.

The point is not that the ethics committee is justified because it has more information or expertise or logical acumen than the philosophy student. Whether one is justified in believing something does depend on one's other beliefs and on one's intellectual abilities. As one gathers evidence and draws inferences, one comes to be justified in more beliefs. However, that kind of variation does not explain why the hospital ethics committee is justified when the philosophy student is not. In my example, the ethics committee and the student hold the same background beliefs and draw the same inferences. But they still differ in what they are justified in believing. So that difference in justification must be due to different contrast classes being seen as relevant.

Since justification can vary even when evidence does not, it is also possible for a single person to be both justified and not justified at the same time in believing the same claim. For example, the hospital ethics committee might be justified in believing that the doctor's lying would be morally wrong out of a contrast class that does not include moral nihilism, but not justified in believing the same claim out of a contrast class that does include moral nihilism. It would be strange and misleading to say simply that the committee is both justified and not justified. However, it would be just as strange and misleading to say that jumbo shrimp are both large and not large. This conjunction can still be true if it means that jumbo shrimp are large for shrimp but not large for seafood. Analogously, the ethics committee can be both justified and not justified, if this means that it is justified out of a smaller contrast class but not justified out of a larger contrast class.

When a belief is justified out of one contrast class but not another, and both contrast classes seem relevant, then there will be disputes about which contrast class *really* is relevant. A philosopher might say that moral nihilism is really relevant even in ethics committees, so the ethics committee is not really justified. But then a practical person might say that nihilism is not really relevant even in philosophy, so the student is really justified. Is there any way to determine which contrast class is really relevant to a particular belief in a particular context? I doubt it. Admittedly, certain contrast classes seem relevant to some contexts.[47] If people form and join hospital ethics committees in order to reduce immoral practices in hospitals, then it is natural for these people to see moral nihilism as irrelevant. However, a single person can have conflicting purposes and can occupy more than one context at once. Moreover, claims about justification can cross contexts: Imagine a philosophy student who claims that the ethics committee is not justified in believing what it does. Is the student's contrast class (with moral nihilism) or the committee's contrast class (without moral nihilism) the one that is relevant to the student's claim about the committee's belief? And what if the ethics committee claims that the student's belief is justified? When contexts cross in this way, we need to distinguish the person with the belief (the believer) from the person who judges whether the belief is justified (the judger). In judging that a belief is justified or not, the context of the believer seems more important if the purpose of the judger is to predict whether the believer will do well on the committee or in the class. In contrast, the context of the judger seems more important if the judger's purpose is to decide whether to endorse the belief or the process that produced it. Since the judger's purpose affects which context and contrast class seem relevant, there is no way to specify which context or contrast class is *really* relevant for judgments of the form "S is justified in believing p" even if one adds "when S is in context C."[48]

Luckily, we don't need to solve this problem here. Regardless of which, if any, contrast class is (really) relevant, we can still talk about justification relative to contrast classes. We can say that the ethics committee is justified relative to a smaller contrast class that does not include moral nihilism, but is not justified relative to a larger contrast class that does include moral nihilism. We can make the same relativized judgments about the philosophy student. And we can understand a speaker who calls a belief justified without qualification because she means that the belief is justified relative to some contrast class that the speaker sees as relevant, regardless of whether that contrast class is really relevant. It can sometimes become important for practical purposes to decide which contrast class is relevant.[49] But judgments about justification relative to a certain contrast class are all we need to describe the epistemological position from the morally neutral standpoint of meta-ethics. Consequently, I will henceforth avoid any talk about what is justified without qualification and any assumptions about which contrast class is relevant. I will talk only about whether a moral belief is justified relative to a specified contrast class.[50]

This approach produces as many levels of justification as there are contrast classes.[51] To be justified relative to {A, K} is different from being justified relative to {A, K, R}, which is different from being justified relative to {A, K, R, N}, and so on. For simplicity, I will focus on two vague contrast classes. As I said, ethics committees usually consider only a limited range of relevant alternatives. The same is true of everyday disputes about important issues, such as abortion or capital punishment. The class that includes all moral positions that would be taken seriously by any ethics committee or any common person will be called *the everyday contrast class,* and I will talk about *everyday justification* when someone is justified relative to the everyday contrast class. I will not try to specify exactly what falls into this contrast class, because it is very large and indeterminate, and most of its members do not matter here. What is crucial here is that the everyday contrast class does *not* include extreme positions, such as moral nihilism. When two people argue about abortion, they usually assume that either it is morally wrong to get an early abortion or it is morally wrong for someone to physically stop a competent adult from getting an early abortion. They take it for granted that *something* is morally wrong, so they assume that moral nihilism is false.

This assumption is *not* made in some moral philosophy classes, such as mine, that take moral nihilism seriously and ask how it could be refuted. The class of moral positions that are taken seriously in such moral philosophy classes will be called the *philosophy contrast class,* and justification relative to this contrast class will be called *philosophical justification.* Roughly, the philosophy contrast class can be seen as including the everyday contrast class plus moral nihilism (and other extreme views). Because of this relation, everyday justification can be explained in terms of philosophical justification. One is everyday justified in believing *p* if and only if one is philosophically justified in believing the conditional: *p* if moral nihilism is false and if our other everyday assumptions are true.[52]

Because everyday justification assumes so much, it might seem that everyday justification cannot depend on evidence or be tied to truth. But it can. To see this, consider an office betting pool where each worker picks one out of the ten horses in a race. Four horses have already been chosen, and the remaining six include a horse named Playboy. Playboy is better in the mud than the five other remaining horses, and rain is forecast for race day. This evidence can make one justified in believing the conditional that Playboy will win if any of the remaining six horses wins. Nonetheless, if one knows nothing about the four previously chosen horses, or if one knows that one of them is an even better mudder than Playboy, then one is not evidentially justified in believing that Playboy will win out of all ten horses.[53] Analogously, one can have evidence that a certain moral claim is true *if* any moral claim in the everyday contrast class is true, even if one has no evidence for that moral claim out of the whole philosophical contrast class. This happens, for example, if the everyday contrast class includes A, K, and R, the philosophical contrast class also includes N, and one's evidence raises the probability that (if A or K or R, then A) without raising the probability that (if A or K or R or N, then A). One can then be everyday evidentially justified without being philosophically evidentially justified.

Thus, the two distinctions together yield four kinds of justification:

Justification	Everyday	Philosophical
Evidential		
Instrumental		

These distinctions can be generalized and applied outside morality, and more and finer distinctions can be drawn, but these four kinds of justification in moral theory will keep us busy enough.

Theories of Justification

Now we can ask which kinds of justification can be achieved. I cannot go through every possible theory about justified moral beliefs, but I will briefly discuss intuitionism, coherentism, and contractarianism, because these are three of the most common theories about how moral beliefs can be justified.

Moral Intuitionism

It seems obvious to me that there is a spot on my pants, because I see one. It also seems obvious that $2 + 3 = 3 + 2$. When such beliefs are formed without inferring them from anything else, they can be called noninferential beliefs. Noninferential beliefs are possible, but are they ever justified? Foundationalists in general epistemology assert that some people can be justified in believing some claims even if they do not or could not infer those claims from anything else that they believe.

Moral intuitionists apply foundationalism to moral claims. In a weak version, moral intuitionism asserts that some people are justified in believing some moral claims even though they *do* not infer those claims from any other beliefs. However, people often do not actually go to the trouble to formulate inferences that they could easily make if they just tried. In at least some of these cases, a person's being justified in believing a moral claim still depends on the believer's ability to draw an inference that she does not actually draw, since the person would not be justified in the belief if she could not draw the inference. But even such an ability to infer is not necessary for some moral believers to be justified, according to a stronger version of moral intuitionism. This stronger version will be our topic here, and I will refer to it simply as moral intuitionism.[54]

Moral intuitionism is then the claim that some people are justified in believing some moral claims in some way that does not depend on the believer inferring or even being able to infer the claim from anything else that the person believes. Some moral intuitionists claim that a believer is justified by some nondoxastic state, such as a perceptual state or an emotion, that could not be a premise in an inference.[55] Other moral intuitionists claim that the believer is justified but not by anything at all. In the latter case, the believer is said to be directly justified, and what is believed is often called self-evident. In both cases, the person is said to be justified noninferentially. My arguments will apply to both versions, so I will ask whether believers can be noninferentially justified.

The moral beliefs that are claimed to be noninferentially justified might be particular moral beliefs, such as

(P) It is morally wrong for this doctor to lie to this patient on this occasion about this HIV + test result,

or more general moral principles, such as

(G) It is always morally wrong to lie without an adequate moral reason (or it is always prima facie morally wrong to lie).

Moral intuitionists need not claim that these beliefs are infallible (that is, cannot be false) or are indubitable (that is, cannot be doubted). Nor need they claim that these beliefs are the object of a special faculty of intuition or that one can become justified in believing (P) or (G) just by staring at them. Instead, moral intuitionists can admit that one must know the facts of the case and must reflect on the concepts in (P) or (G) and on applications to other examples in order to be justified in believing (P) or (G).[56] However, if moral intuitionists require some kind of reflection, such reflection must help only to understand the belief and must not provide premises for inferences to the belief. What moral intuitionists deny is that one must be able to infer (P) or (G) from some conceptual analysis, from the facts of the case, from moral beliefs about other cases, from more general moral principles, or from anything in order to be justified in believing (P) or (G).

A moral nihilist would deny both (P) and (G). What can a moral intuitionist say against such a nihilist? Not much. Moral intuitionists can point out that moral nihilism conflicts with many moral beliefs in which many of us feel great confidence after long reflection. However, to appeal to such a moral belief in an argument against moral nihilism begs the question in much the same way as it would beg the question to appeal to a belief about the external world in an argument against Descartes's deceiving demon hypothesis. Some moral beliefs appear obvious, but that appearance is just what would be predicted by the nihilistic hypothesis that all moral beliefs are illusions, so that appearance provides no evidence at all against moral nihilism. Some moral intuitionists might respond that moral nihilists cannot really understand (G), because (G) is a conceptual truth, so anyone who understands it must accept it. However, there is no independent evidence that all moral nihilists must fail to understand (G), so it again begs the question against moral nihilism to assume that (G) is a conceptual truth. Consequently, moral intuitionism cannot provide philosophical evidential justification for any moral belief. Of course, some moral intuitionists would respond that they do not try to provide philosophical evidential justification, and even that it is a mistake to try to provide that kind of justification, but my point is only that they do not and cannot provide philosophical evidential justification.

What about everyday evidential justification? Suppose that a member of the ethics committee admits that some acts are morally wrong, so he or she is not a moral nihilist, but honestly does not see why lying in this case is morally wrong, as (P) claims, or why lying is always prima facie immoral, as (G) claims. This person can be called a moral deviant, since most people accept (P) and (G). What could a moral intuitionist say in response to this moral deviant? Again, not much. The intuitionist can keep repeating, "Don't you see" or "Reflect some more," but the deviant can honestly try her best and still not agree. The intuitionist might claim that the deviant does not fully understand the disputed claim, but the deviant's understanding is demonstrated by the inferences she draws from her beliefs and by her nondeviant uses of the constituent concepts in other contexts. Then, even if the deviant cannot give any reason against (P) or (G), the deviant still has the same claim to be justified as the intuitionist with the more common beliefs in (P) and (G).

One might think that *both* the deviant and the common moral intuitionist are justified. But consider an analogy. Miss Scarlet and Professor Plum were the only two people in the room when Colonel Mustard was killed. One detective looks at Miss Scarlet and believes that she did it. Another detective looks at Professor Plum and believes that he did it. If neither detective has any evidence, neither seems justified. Both detectives ought to suspend judgment until the opposing hypothesis is ruled out. For the same reason, neither the deviant nor the common moral intuitionist seems justified. Their beliefs might be epistemically permitted, but neither belief has enough positive support to say that anyone ought to believe it instead of the contrary hypothesis.

To get positive support, a moral intuitionist might bring in other beliefs, such as that lying in this case has bad consequences or that other cases of lying are morally wrong. Then some principle of universalizability could be applied. Since a moral deviant accepts some moral judgments, such arguments might give a moral deviant a reason to change her beliefs. However, such arguments also give up moral intuitionism, since a moral belief is not justified *noninferentially* if its justification depends on the ability to infer it from other beliefs.

The only way for moral intuitionists to remain intuitionists is to insist that some moral beliefs are justified without depending on any ability to infer them from any beliefs. But then what *can* make moral beliefs justified? One possibility is that moral beliefs are justified by some mental state that is not and does not imply a belief. Emotions have been said to play this role.[57] But any such mental state could occur in a moral deviant, and the deviant beliefs do not seem justified in the face of the more common contrary beliefs. So such mental states cannot be sufficient by themselves to make a moral belief justified.

A second possibility is that reflection on concepts and examples can make a moral belief justified even if the reflection does not yield anything from which the moral belief can be inferred.[58] However, not just any reflection will do. To make a moral belief justified, reflection must have certain properties: It must be careful and long enough, it must not be distorted by ignorance or self-interest, and so on. Moreover, the moral belief does not seem justified if the believer does not somehow believe that his reflection has these properties.

To see this, imagine someone who says, "I don't think that I reflected long enough, and maybe I didn't reflect on the right kinds of examples, and I might not be impartial or informed, but my reflection still makes me believe that sodomy is immoral." This person does not seem justified in holding this belief. If this belief is not special, then we can generalize to the principle that, if one does *not* believe that one's reflection is adequate or reliable in the circumstances, then one is not justified in trusting the results of the reflection. The problem for intuitionism is then that, if one *does* believe that one's reflection is adequate or reliable in the circumstances, one has all one needs (other than general intelligence) to be able to infer one's moral belief from one's belief about the adequacy or reliability of its source. One might, for example, use an inference like this:

(i') Moral beliefs based on reflection in circumstances like these are reliable;

(ii') My moral belief in (P) is based on reflection in these circumstances;

(iii') Therefore, my moral belief in (P) is reliable (or likely to be true).

A believer need not consciously run through such an inference in order to be justified. Nonetheless, a believer is not justified if she would not see her reflection as adequate or reliable and thus would not accept these premises under appropriate circumstances, so the believer must at least dispositionally believe what is necessary for the inference. Consequently, a moral belief cannot be justified by reflection unless the believer is at least *able* to infer the moral belief from other beliefs. This conclusion is contrary to the central claim of moral intuitionism.[59]

A third possibility is externalism—the view that some beliefs are justified because they have properties that are independent of any other mental state. The most common kind of externalism is reliabilism—the claim that some beliefs are justified because they are reliable (or result from reliable processes). If reliabilism is applied to moral beliefs, then one need not reflect on one's moral beliefs or believe that one's moral beliefs are reliable in order for them to be justified. If one does not believe that one's moral beliefs are reliable, then one cannot *believe* that they are justified, or be *justified* in believing that they are justified, or *show* that they are justified. But one's moral beliefs can still *be* justified as long as they *are* reliable.[60]

This externalist view is consistent, but not convincing. The primary model for reliabilism is vision. However, people usually have evidence that their vision is reliable, since they remember that their visual beliefs in certain circumstances were confirmed in the past by their other senses and by other people. When they saw a cat, they could pet it, and others could see and pet it, too. To test whether reliability *by itself* is sufficient for justification, we need an example in which a believer has no evidence that the belief source is reliable under the circumstances.[61] Imagine that Leslie notices an aura around Joan's head. She hasn't seen anything like this before, and she can't understand why she sees it now, but there seems to be a faint brown tinge where some strange kind of energy seems to be emanating from Joan's head. Leslie considers three hypotheses: either aural energy is emanating, or it is a visual illusion, or there is something wrong with Leslie's eyes. Leslie believes that aural energy is emanating, but is she justified in believing this (instead of the other hypotheses)? It seems not. What if there really are auras, and she is a reliable detector of them? She still does not yet seem justified in believing in auras. One reason is that Leslie need not even believe that she is reliable or justified. If we ask her whether she is any good at detecting auras, she might say, "I have no idea. Maybe; maybe not." That response would make it hard to see her belief as justified. Even if Leslie does believe in her own reliability, she has no evidence for her beliefs or for her reliability or against the other hypotheses. If she continues to see auras and meets other people who see similar auras, and if auras help to explain independent phenomena, then Leslie might become justified in believing in auras. But prior to such evidence, she is not justified in believing in auras.

The reason is *not* that Leslie might be wrong and is not certain. Mistakes are possible even after she gains evidence for her reliability, but her fallibility and uncertainty at that later stage do not keep her from being justified then. The point is also *not* that Leslie has evidence against auras. I assume that auras are compatible with Leslie's beliefs and past experience, and even with science (at least because scientists should initially be open to new forms of energy). And I am *not* saying that Leslie is irrational and should stop believing in auras. Her belief might be permitted epistemically. Nonetheless, Leslie still does not have enough positive support to be justified in believing in auras.

Leslie's aura beliefs are much like noninferentially justified moral beliefs according to reliabilism. If one does not believe and has no reason to believe that one's moral beliefs (or moral belief forming processes) are reliable, then one's moral beliefs are no more justified than Leslie's beliefs about auras, even if one's moral beliefs turn out to be reliable. Of course, most people have experienced agreement with other people's moral beliefs, as well as connections among their moral beliefs and their other beliefs, so their moral beliefs still might be justified on that basis. But in the absence of such other beliefs, moral beliefs seem no more justified than Leslie's aura beliefs, even if both are reliable.

Of course, much more could be said for and against reliabilism, but not here. I hope that I have said enough to suggest why reliability is not sufficient by itself to make moral beliefs justified. I argued earlier that emotions and reflection are also not enough to make moral beliefs justified. There might be other kinds of noninferential justification, but I suspect that they will run into similar problems. So moral intuitionism is wrong about everyday evidential justification for moral beliefs like (P) and (G).

This conclusion assumes that a moral belief like (P) or (G) can be seriously questioned in an everyday context, such as a hospital ethics committee. But what about the belief that it is morally wrong to torture babies just for fun? A view that denied this belief would never be taken seriously in any everyday context. The everyday contrast class was defined to include only those views that would be taken seriously in an everyday context. So, if anything in the everyday contrast class is true, then it is morally wrong to torture babies just for fun. This moral belief is thereby everyday evidentially justified, even if it is not inferred from anything.

However, this is just an artifact of what everyday justification is. To say that a belief is justified at the everyday level is in effect to say that it is justified given our everyday assumptions. It should not be surprising that our everyday assumptions are justified given themselves. That triviality does not even begin to show that such beliefs are true or likely to be true. All it shows is that these beliefs are assumed to be true. Moreover, even this kind of everyday justification will apply only to moral beliefs that are extremely weak. If any normal person would have any serious doubts about a noninferential moral belief, then that belief will lack even this kind of everyday evidential justification.[62] The only ways to avoid all everyday doubts are either to qualify the moral belief so that its application will be in dispute (such as "It is morally wrong to harm for an inadequate reason") or to limit it so much that it does not apply to many, if any, real acts (such as "It is morally wrong to torture babies just for fun"). Consequently, no serious dispute will be resolved by claiming that a moral belief is justified noninferentially.

Moral intuitionism still might provide *instrumental* justification for a wider range of moral beliefs. Whether a belief is justified instrumentally depends on the effects of being in that belief state. If I strongly believe (P) or (G) after careful reflection, then to give up these beliefs might be costly to my self-confidence, my psychological health, and my personal relations, regardless of whether I can justify these beliefs inferentially. If so, the very factors that moral intuitionists cite as justifying some moral beliefs *can* instrumentally justify some moral beliefs. This instrumental justification holds even when moral beliefs cannot be inferred from other beliefs, and even when moral beliefs are contrasted with moral nihilism.[63] So some noninferential moral beliefs are instrumentally justified at both the everyday level and the philosophical level.

There can also be instrumental justification for believing moral intuitionism, that is, for believing that some moral beliefs are justified noninferentially. If one does not believe that one's belief in (P) or (G) is justified noninferentially, then one might think that one needs to infer it from something. But justifying inferences are often hard to find, and their premises are even harder to justify. In fact, one could not form any moral belief if one first had to justify every assumption inferentially. And it does not seem to be worth the trouble to test a moral belief by means of inference in trivial cases where everyone agrees already. So there can be instrumental justification not only for a moral belief but also for the belief that a moral belief is justified noninferentially.

This might explain why many people believe in moral intuitionism, but the point should not be overestimated. Instrumental justification still has no tendency to show that the justified beliefs are true or probably true. Thus, the extent of the justification that is captured by moral intuitionism is very limited. It can be summarized in following diagram:

Justification	Everyday	Philosophical
Evidential	Only trivial cases	None
Instrumental	Some	Some

Moral Coherentism

The next common theory of justification to be considered is coherentism. Coherentists claim that a person *S* is justified in believing *p* to the extent that *p* coheres with a coherent system of beliefs held by *S*. A system of beliefs is coherent to the extent that its beliefs are jointly consistent, comprehensive, and connected by logical, probabilistic, and explanatory relations.[64] And a particular belief coheres with a system of beliefs to the extent that the belief has these relations to the system. When *p* does bear these relations to *S*'s other beliefs, *S* has all it takes (other than general intelligence) to be able to infer *p* from another belief. Thus, coherentists claim that *S* is never justified in believing *p* unless *S* can justify *p* by some inference. Coherentists need not require that *S* explicitly formulate any inference, but what makes *S* justified also makes an inference available. Coherentists also need not require that *S* be able to connect *p* to every other belief in *S*'s system, or that *S* have a completely comprehensive or consistent system of beliefs. This ideal is impossible in practice. Nonetheless, one system of beliefs can still be more coherent than another, and the more coherent *S*'s system of beliefs is, the more justified *S* is in believing what coheres with that system. Coherentists can also hold that some minimal degree of coherence is necessary for a system to provide enough positive support to make *S* justified at all.

The most straightforward application of coherentism to morality occurs when people try to connect disparate moral beliefs about particular cases by inferring them from a general moral principle. This goal is called narrow reflective equilibrium.[65] For a simple example, suppose *S* believes:

(a) It is morally wrong for a student to tell a professor that his dog ate his paper, when this is not true, just to avoid a penalty for late papers;

(b) It is morally wrong for a professor to tell a student that chapter 6 will be on the exam, when it won't, just to make this student study more;

(c) It is morally wrong for a professor to tell a student that chapter 6 will not be on the exam, when it will, just to keep this student from becoming too depressed when he tries to study this difficult chapter.

These beliefs and others might seem to suggest that lying is always wrong, but

(d) It is not morally wrong to lie to prevent a murder.

Beliefs (a)–(d) can all be inferred from a general principle that

(G) It is always morally wrong to lie without an adequate reason,

together with subsidiary beliefs, such as

(c′) Preventing depression is not an adequate reason to lie;
(d′) Preventing murder is an adequate reason to lie.

One can then also infer a particular conclusion in the lying doctor example:

(P) It is morally wrong for this doctor to lie to this patient on this
occasion about this HIV + test result,

because this act comes under (G) and (c′), assuming the doctor's only reason to lie is to prevent the patient's depression. Or course, many more beliefs and principles would have to be added to make this system comprehensive, but then *S* is supposed to be justified in believing (P) because of how (P) coheres with the rest of the system, and *S* is also justified in believing each of the other claims because of how it coheres with the remaining beliefs. This structure is circular, because the justification of (a) refers to (b), and the justification of (b) refers to (a), but this circle is not supposed to ruin the justification if the system is comprehensive enough.

However, this theory runs into several problems. First, it is not clear whether anybody actually has a system of moral beliefs that is comprehensive or connected or even consistent, or that will remain consistent when enough moral beliefs are added to make it comprehensive. If nobody has a coherent enough system of moral beliefs, then no moral beliefs are justified by the standards of coherentism.

Second, even if someone's moral system is coherent, there will always be incompatible systems that are equally coherent. In fact, if one wants to reject any particular conclusion, one can always deny that conclusion and modify one's principles to form another system that is just as consistent, connected, and comprehensive as the original system. For example, if one wants to avoid the conclusion (P), one can keep (a)–(d), (G), and (d′) but replace (c′) with something like

(c″) Preventing depression is not an adequate reason to lie, except
when the depression would ruin the rest of someone's life
before he dies of a deadly disease.

Of course, some people might see (c″) as ad hoc or implausible, but the system with (c″) but not (P) is just as consistent, connected, and comprehensive as the system with (c′) and (P). More particular moral beliefs might be added to argue against (c″), but a defender of (c″) could either deny these moral claims or incorporate them by redefining terms or by adding qualifications or other principles. In the end, there will always be alternative systems of moral beliefs that are equally coherent but conflict in their beliefs about (P).[66]

To solve this problem of underdetermination, Rawls and his followers[67] add that justified moral beliefs must cohere not only with substantive moral principles but also with social science and with ideals of the person and of society. This wide reflective equilibrium might somewhat reduce the indeterminacy of narrow coherence. Nonetheless, uncontroversial findings of social science rarely, if ever, suffice to rule out a competing moral view; and ideals of the person and society are usually just as hard to justify as the beliefs that they are supposed to justify. For these reasons, even wide reflective equilibrium cannot avoid competing, equally coherent systems.

When their coherence is equal, neither system can be justified in contrast with the others on the basis of coherence alone. *S* might already hold the beliefs in one of the systems, or the beliefs in one system might seem more credible to *S*, but that cannot make *S* justified in believing that system in contrast with the other, unless *S*'s prior beliefs or feelings of credibility are somehow justified independently.[68] This justification cannot come from coherence (since the systems are equally coherent) or from moral intuition (because of the arguments in the section on moral intuitionism), so there is as yet no way for *S* to be justified in believing one of the equally coherent systems in contrast with the other.

In addition to underdetermination, coherentism also faces a problem of truth. Coherence provides evidential justification only if a coherent system is more likely to be true, but coherence requires only relations among beliefs inside a system, so how could internal coherence increase the probability of truth?

In response to this problem in general epistemology, many coherentists introduce a new order of evidence.[69] The most common kind of evidence for a first-order belief (such as, that my house is on fire) is another first-order belief (such as, that smoke is pouring out of it). A different kind of evidence cites second-order beliefs about first-order beliefs. In this model, one uses some first-order beliefs to justify second-order beliefs about the circumstances under which certain first-order beliefs are reliable, and then these second-order beliefs are used as evidence for other first-order beliefs. For example, past experience teaches us that we are not reliable at identifying persons by sight when the light is bad, the person is far away, we do not know the person well, and so on; but in the absence of these conditions, visual identifications seem reliable. These beliefs plus my present visual experience then imply that it is probably my wife whom I see next to me. Because such second-order beliefs imply that certain first-order beliefs are reliable or likely to be true, if all of these beliefs form a coherent system, then its coherence might be a reason to believe that the system is likely to be true.

This approach can be extended to moral beliefs.[70] Evidence for beliefs about what is morally right or wrong usually takes the form of other beliefs about what is morally right or wrong. However, one can also cite second-order beliefs about such first-order moral beliefs. For example, one might find that many of one's first-order moral beliefs that were formed when one's self-interest was involved or when one did not fully understand a situation had to be rejected later because they conflicted with many other beliefs. This kind of consideration might give members of an ethics committee reason to discount as unreliable the deviant moral beliefs of a doctor who wants to avoid the unpleasant task of telling a patient that he or she is HIV +. It might also give them a reason to discount the moral beliefs of people who do not understand important aspects of the medical situation.

If one had a complete list of distorting factors, then one might infer that one's moral beliefs are reliable when all of those factors are missing. But many problems arise. First, it would be hard to tell whether one's list of distorting factors is complete. If even one factor is overlooked, it might be the one that distorts one's moral belief. Second, it is not clear whether some factors belong on the list. Is someone's moral view of abortion more reliable or less reliable if they are passionate about the issue? Third, even if we have a complete list of distorting factors, it is often hard to detect these factors in particular moral beliefs. It is usually easy to tell whether my vision is operating in good light, at short distances, and so on, but it is hard to tell whether a moral believer is adequately informed or impartial. Did the hospital ethics committee miss some relevant fact? Is their self-interest involved in some roundabout way (such as that they will want to lie to one of their patients in the future, or will themselves be patients in the future)? Moral beliefs are almost never formed with complete information; they almost always affect one's welfare somehow; and we can't tell when ignorance or partiality is operating; so there is always some reason to doubt their reliability.[71] Finally, even if a moral belief lacks all of the factors that make moral beliefs *un*reliable, this does not prove that the moral belief *is* reliable. Our moral beliefs might not work well even under the best conditions.

Nonetheless, if one finds that, in the absence of a certain range of factors (such as self-interest, ignorance, and irrationality), one's moral beliefs rarely need to be revised, are widely accepted by other people, and support and explain one another, then all of this together is *some* reason to believe in the reliability of moral beliefs formed under such circumstances. One cannot ever be sure that one did not overlook some crucial fact or that one's self-interest is not operating below the surface, but one can still have some reason to believe that a moral belief is not distorted in such ways. In such a situation, one can have some reason to believe that a particular moral belief is true. The belief still *might* be false but that does not remove the reason to believe that it is true, since justification can be fallible.

Does this kind of coherence provide everyday evidential justification? I think that it *can* in some cases. In some cases, all of the alternatives that would be seriously considered in everyday contexts conflict with moral beliefs formed under circumstances that usually lead to moral beliefs that are reliable according to other commonly shared moral beliefs, and there is no support for those alternatives except beliefs that were formed in circumstances that usually distort moral beliefs, again according to commonly shared moral beliefs. This might happen, for example, when all of the members of a hospital ethics committee agree about a case where they do not know any of the parties involved, and do not themselves have to face similar situations, but do take the time to study the case carefully. Even those who disagree, such as the doctor who does not want to tell a patient that he or she is HIV +, might have enough other moral beliefs to require the doctor to admit that his or her own belief in this case is probably distorted. When all of this comes together in the right way, coherence methods can provide everyday evidential justification. This method can work even in some cases where moral beliefs were controversial before being tested by coherence, so it can achieve more than appeals to intuition.

Of course, there will be many other cases where everyday conflicting moral beliefs cannot be dismissed as distorted, and where one does not have adequate reason to believe in the reliability of one's own moral beliefs. Then one's moral beliefs are not everyday evidentially justified. I suspect that most of our moral beliefs fall into this class, because of the problems mentioned above. But the fact that the coherence method fails in most or even almost all cases does not show that coherence cannot yield everyday evidential justification in some other cases.

It is important, however, not to read too much into this claim. Everyday justification just assumes in a way that moral nihilism is false (along with other extreme views); so to have everyday evidential justification that lying is wrong is just to have philosophical evidential justification for believing the conditional that lying is wrong *if* anything is (and if our everyday assumptions are true). Everyday justification can thus be seen as a kind of conditional philosophical justification.

What about *un*conditional *philosophical* evidential justification? To achieve this kind of justification, coherence arguments would have to work against moral nihilism. However, the coherence method needs to use some first-order moral beliefs to justify second-order beliefs about conditions of reliability. Moral nihilists would deny those first-order moral beliefs, along with claims about their reliability. Thus, this coherence method begs the question against moral nihilism.[72] The problem is that the coherence method depends on shared moral beliefs, but moral nihilists do not share any moral beliefs, so the coherence method cannot even get started. This is analogous to the problems in using coherence among empirical beliefs to refute the hypothesis of a deceiving demon. In both areas, coherence can provide at most everyday but not philosophical evidential justification.[73]

What about *instrumental* justification? The main question here is whether coherence with a coherent system of beliefs can make a moral belief state have good effects. It seems so. When a moral belief is connected in certain ways to one's other beliefs, one cannot give up the moral belief and maintain a coherent system without changing many other beliefs. It is sometimes a good thing to shake up one's beliefs, but large changes in one's belief system often have detrimental effects on one's confidence, plans, relations to other people, and so on. When too much change would cause such problems without compensating benefits, one can be instrumentally justified in holding on to a moral belief because of its coherence with one's other beliefs. The same points apply to extreme views. Most people could not accept moral nihilism without radical and disruptive changes in their belief systems, so coherence can make a moral belief instrumentally justified at the philosophical level as well as the everyday level.

There can also be instrumental justification for testing moral beliefs by their coherence with one's other beliefs. Coherence testing takes time, but it can reduce the risk of having to change one's mind later, which can be disruptive in some settings, such as hospital ethics committees. Moreover, people often object when an ethics committee's decisions in different areas appear arbitrary or incompatible, but such objections can be reduced if the committee's various decisions are seen as connected under general principles. For such reasons, the ethics committee and the hospital will tend to run more smoothly if they try to form their moral beliefs into a coherent system. This method can be used improperly, but sometimes it has better effects than not checking for coherence. When this is so, one can be justified instrumentally in checking one's beliefs for coherence.[74]

Nonetheless, this instrumental justification still does not show that coherent moral beliefs are true or even likely to be true. There are reasons to check for coherence and not to give up beliefs that do cohere, but the kinds of justification that are provided by coherence are still limited. They can be diagrammed as follows:

Justification	Everyday	Philosophical
Evidential	Some nontrivial cases	None
Instrumental	Some	Some

Contractarianism

The third common method for justifying moral beliefs is contractarianism. Actually, many different methods go by the name of contractarianism. Often a contractarian framework is used only as a way to display connections among prior moral beliefs, and then coherence is the basic justification.[75] In contrast, other contractarians claim that a moral belief is justified if certain people under certain circumstances would agree to the moral belief, or to a rule or system that yields it, independent of whether the result coheres with prior moral beliefs.[76] It is this latter version of contractarianism that concerns us here, because this version claims that agreement is an independent source of justification.

In contrast with moral intuitionism and coherentism, contractarianism is primarily about when moral beliefs are justified, not about when people are justified in believing them. Most people do not become justified in believing moral claims by arguing or even being able to argue that certain people would agree on any beliefs or rules. Yet if contractarians are right, a person can be justified in holding a moral belief if he or she is justified in believing that the moral belief is justified by some agreement. Moreover, contractarianism need not apply to all areas of morality. Most contractarian theories are mainly about justice and not about benevolence or other virtues. Nonetheless, if any such agreement can make anyone justified in believing any moral claim, this would be enough to refute moral skepticism.

But who must agree in order for a moral belief to be justified? One possibility is that a moral belief or rule is justified because all rational people would accept it. If this kind of argument worked, it would accomplish a lot. Rationality is normative, but it is supposedly not moral, so this argument would justify moral beliefs by reference to nonmoral norms. And if all rational people would accept a certain moral belief or rule, then moral nihilists must be irrational, since they do not accept the moral belief or rule. So this kind of contractarian argument would provide not just everyday but also philosophical justification if it worked.

Of course, this kind of argument will provide justification only to the extent that one is justified in accepting its theory of rationality, instead of one of the many competing theories. Moreover, on any plausible nonmoral theory of rationality,[77] it is hard to see why all rational people must agree on any definite moral belief or rule. The most common examples are moral rules against killing and breaking promises. The basic idea is that, if people in society did not generally accept and follow these rules, then society would break down, which would harm everyone, so every rational person would accept these rules for society. However, this agreement disappears when the rules are defined more precisely. Consider a more limited rule against killing people who are over six feet tall. Shorter people would not accept this rule as the only rule against killing, and they are rational, so not all rational people would accept this limited rule as the only rule against killing. And shorter people might refuse to cooperate with anyone who does not accept a rule that protects them as well. Nonetheless, it still might not be irrational for some people over six feet tall to reject the unlimited rule "Don't kill anyone" in favor of the more limited rule "Don't kill anyone over six feet tall," if these taller people don't have much to fear or to gain from shorter people. If so, neither rule or set of rules must be accepted by all rational people, so neither is justified in this way.

Moral contractarians admit this, so they add other constraints. They claim that a moral belief or rule is justified when it would be accepted by all people who are both rational and impartial. Or they claim that all rational people must agree under certain circumstances (usually tailored to ensure impartiality) or that all rational people need to cooperate with everyone in society. Contractarians often also add constraints on the form of the rules to be chosen.[78]

However, these new constraints create new problems. First, why should a moral skeptic or nihilist accept these constraints? The demand for impartiality and the claim that certain circumstances are appropriate for a social contract themselves need to be justified. It is hard to see how such constraints could be justified without depending on more basic moral beliefs about the nature or content of morality. But that would beg the question against moral nihilism and other extreme views. So such contractarian arguments do not seem to provide philosophical justification.

Even for everyday justification, there is a problem of multiple contracts, similar to the problem of multiple coherent systems. Philosophers have developed many different accounts of rationality, of impartiality, and of the circumstances that are appropriate for the agreement that is supposed to justify moral rules or beliefs. Different accounts of rationality, impartiality, and appropriate circumstances imply that rational impartial persons under appropriate circumstances would agree on different moral beliefs or rules. Thus, one can use the contractarian framework to justify many different moral systems. Simply adjust one's accounts of rationality, impartiality, and appropriate circumstances to fit one's favorite moral system. If the method is flexible enough to accommodate two competing moral systems, then it cannot justify one moral system in contrast with the other. This problem can be solved only by justifying particular theories of rationality, impartiality, and appropriate circumstances that pick out a single moral system. But it is hard to see how this could be done (especially for impartiality and appropriate circumstances) without depending on moral beliefs that beg the question against competing moral systems in the everyday contrast class. So such contractarian arguments do not seem to provide everyday justification for any controversial moral belief.[79]

Even if these problems could be solved, a more basic problem would still arise. There are two kinds of rationality. Sometimes a person is called rational to the extent that she adjusts her beliefs to the evidence. If everyone who is rational in this way would accept a moral belief, then that moral belief would be evidentially justified. However, one could not justify a claim that all people who are rational in this way would accept a certain moral belief if one did not already have separate evidence for that belief. The claim about agreement would not add any new evidence.

In any case, contractarians do not use this evidential kind of rationality. They see people as rational to the extent that they seek good effects and avoid bad effects of some kind. But then, if all rational people accept a belief or rule, this must be because accepting it has good effects or avoids bad effects. And such effects do not show that a moral belief is true or even likely to be true. To see this, suppose that someone will kill anyone who does not believe in Santa Claus, or that anyone without this belief will suffer debilitating depression. Then everyone who is rational in the relevant way would accept the belief in Santa Claus. But none of this provides evidence for Santa Claus.

Similarly, to show that all rational people would accept certain moral beliefs as ways to protect or improve their lives or society does not show that these beliefs are likely to be true or that they are justified evidentially. Instead, contractarian arguments provide only instrumental justification.

Contractarians usually respond that their arguments do not rest on contingent preferences that some people lack and also cannot be used to argue for the opposite moral beliefs. Even if so, this still does not make rational agreement evidence of moral truth. Suppose that a belief in Santa Claus is necessary to prevent everyone from becoming so depressed that they would lose all motivation to do anything, regardless of what they prefer to do. And suppose that no opposite belief could provide any motivation. That still would not be evidence for Santa Claus. In general, the effects of a mental state cannot show that the content of the mental state is likely to be true. So, even if contractarian arguments do not depend on specific preferences and do not work for contrary beliefs, they still provide at most instrumental and not evidential justification.

Another response is that contractarian arguments are about effects of moral rules or standards rather than of beliefs. Rules and standards have the form of imperatives (for example, "Don't kill"), so they have no truth value, and one should not expect them to be evidentially justified. One can still be evidentially justified in believing that killing is morally wrong if this moral claim just means that killing violates a rule or standard that is justified by the effects of accepting it.[80] But is this really what the moral claim means? I doubt it. The claim that an act is morally wrong seems to be about the act and not about the effects of accepting a rule against the act. People can form such moral beliefs without thinking at all about rules or their effects. Moreover, a rule can be beneficial in certain circumstances even though the corresponding moral belief is not true. Suppose that an evil demon will kill everyone who does not accept the rule "Do not dance." Then this rule would be accepted by all rational people, and even by all rational impartial people, so that rule would be justified, according to contractarians. But this is not evidence that it is morally wrong to dance.[81] This example is fanciful, but similar problems arise in common cases. For example, some opponents of abortion admit that society would be better off if people did not accept "Don't kill fetuses" (or at least that not all rational people must accept "Don't kill fetuses"), but they still believe that abortion is morally wrong, because it is unfair to kill fetuses to benefit others. Whether or not they are right, their position is at least consistent. And the same goes for anyone who believes that a harmless act, such as sodomy, is immoral. This shows that "morally wrong" does not mean the same as "violates a rule that is justified by its effects" (or by agreement among everyone who is rational in a way defined by effects). Consequently, moral beliefs are not evidentially justified just because the corresponding moral rules are instrumentally justified.

Contractarians might respond that such noncontractarian beliefs are not really about morality, because the only real morality is defined by rational (impartial) agreement based on the effects of accepting rules. However, that appeal to definition is no better than saying that non-Euclidean geometry is not really about geometry because it does not share Euclidean axioms. Such definitions just change the subject. If all that contractarians mean when they say that abortion or sodomy is not morally wrong is that not all rational (impartial) people would accept rules against these acts, then opponents of abortion can admit that those acts are not wrong on contractarian definitions, or that they are not contractarian-wrong. This does not imply that these acts are not morally wrong in the sense claimed by opponents of abortion and sodomy, and denied by others. Because the original issue was not about rational (impartial) agreement, contractarians cannot resolve that issue by defining moral wrongness in terms of their own theory. Contractarians still might provide evidence for something else, but they do not provide evidence for morality.[82]

Contractarians could, of course, give many more responses, and there are many more kinds of contractarianism. Nonetheless, the basic point remains and can be generalized. Because contractarian arguments show at most that certain moral rules or the corresponding moral beliefs would or should be accepted because of their effects, contractarians do not show that the contents of those moral beliefs are likely to be true. So contractarian arguments do not provide evidential justification. Nonetheless, contractarians still might succeed in showing that certain moral beliefs have better effects in certain circumstances than any everyday alternative, and even than moral nihilism. This would show that some moral beliefs are instrumentally justified at both the philosophical and everyday levels. If this much is granted, then the kinds of justification that contractarians provide can be diagrammed as follows:

Justification	Everyday	Philosophical
Evidential	None	None
Instrumental	Some	Some

Conclusion

All of these theories deserve much more attention than I have been able to give them here. There are also many other theories about justified moral beliefs (including pragmatism, contextualism, derivations of *ought* from *is* or from moral language, and so on) and many other attempts to rule out moral nihilism. I cannot discuss all such theories and attempts here.[83] Nonetheless, I hope that my discussion of the three most common theories has suggested some reasons why these other theories also cannot provide philosophical evidential justification, even if they can provide some everyday justification and some instrumental justification. If so, we can never have philosophical evidential justification, but we can still get some everyday evidential justification for some moral beliefs, as well as instrumental justification at both the everyday and philosophical levels. Thus, some kinds of justification can be obtained, but others cannot.

This conclusion illuminates the arguments for moral skepticism. Skeptical hypothesis arguments assume that we are not justified in our moral beliefs if we cannot rule out skeptical hypotheses, such as moral nihilism. I have argued that this claim is true if it is about philosophical justification. However, we can still be everyday justified in ignoring a skeptical hypothesis, because, if one chooses out of the everyday contrast class, one must choose an alternative that implies the denial of the skeptical hypothesis, since they all do.[84] Thus, the skeptical hypothesis argument shows that our moral beliefs cannot be philosophically evidentially justified, but it does not show that our moral beliefs are never everyday justified.

A similar conclusion can be reached regarding the regress argument for moral skepticism. Premise (2) denied noninferential justification, and premise (7) denied circular justification. But I argued that moral intuitionism and coherentism can supply everyday evidential justification for some moral beliefs. If so, premises (2) and (7) are false if they are about everyday justification. But they are still true of philosophical evidential justification, because moral intuitionism and coherentism do not provide philosophical evidential justification, as I also argued.

I conclude that moral skepticism is right about philosophical evidential justification and wrong about everyday evidential justification and about instrumental justification. I call this conclusion *limited moral skepticism,* because it denies a kind of justification that is important to those of us who want to understand the limits on our human condition. Although everyday evidential justification can be obtained, all this means, as I said, is that we can be philosophically justified in believing that certain acts are morally wrong *if* anything is, since everyday justification simply ignores moral nihilism. Still, some might think that even some everyday evidential justification is enough, so they might see my conclusion as a denial of moral skepticism. I do not care. Whether my view is classified as moral skepticism depends on which contrast class one takes to be relevant and to define moral skepticism. I already said that I will not try to decide which contrast class is most important or relevant. That varies with context and purpose. In the general discussion here, it is enough to determine exactly which contrast classes one can be justified relative to, and how.

Notes

For many very helpful comments, I thank Robert Audi, Malia Brink, Bob Fogelin, Bernie Gert, Mitch Haney, Richard Hare, Stephen Jacobson, Lawrence Kim, John Konkle, Chris Kulp, Paul McNamara, Jim Moor, Peter Railton, Stefan Sencerz, John Skorupski, David Sosa, Bill Throop, Mark Timmons, Jon Tresan, Doug Weber, Nick Zangwill, and audiences at University College Dublin, Trinity College Dublin, Queen's University of Belfast, the Universities of Edinburgh, Glasgow, and St. Andrews, and the Moral Epistemology Conference at Dartmouth College.

1. See Edmund Gettier, "Is Justified True Belief Knowledge?" *Analysis* 23 (1963), 121–3.

2. See William Alston, "Justification and Knowledge," reprinted in *Epistemic Justification* (Ithaca: Cornell University Press, 1989), 172–82.

3. To avoid convoluted phrasing, I will sometimes write about whether a moral belief is justified, but this should be taken as shorthand for whether a believer is justified in believing a moral claim, except where otherwise indicated. In any case, my main points will apply to both notions.

4. "Noncognitivism" is misleading, since etymology suggests that cognitivism is about cognition or knowledge. There are implications for knowledge (see below), but linguistic moral skepticism is directly about truth values.

5. See my "Some Problems for Gibbard's Norm-Expressivism," *Philosophical Studies* 69 (1993), 297–313; and Peter Railton in the volume.

6. See Simon Blackburn in this volume. Some emotivists and prescriptivists who accept only minimal truth in moral claims still might deny moral knowledge if they take knowledge to imply some stronger kind of truth. Then their views still imply moral knowledge skepticism.

7. See J. L. Mackie, *Ethics* (Harmondsworth: Penguin, 1977), 30–42. Error theorists do not see *all* moral claims as false; since, for example, "Abortion is not morally wrong" is true if "Abortion is morally wrong" is false. That is why I restrict the thesis of error theories to positive moral claims.

8. Philosophers also debate whether there is always a distinctively moral (as opposed to self-interested) reason to be moral, and whether there is always enough reason to make it irrational to be immoral or only to make it not irrational to be moral. These debates yield distinct kinds of practical moral skepticism.

9. Throughout, qualifications like "just to . . ." and "just for . . ." are meant to refer not to the agent's motives but only to the absence of any other reason for the act.

10. Here I disagree with David Copp, "Moral Skepticism," *Philosophical Studies* 62 (1991), 203–33.

11. This last argument derives from Gilbert Harman, *The Nature of Morality* (New York: Oxford University Press, 1977), 3–10, although Harman is not a moral skeptic.

12. *Outlines of Pyrrhonism,* book I, chapter 15.

13. See Robert Audi in this volume and my section on moral intuitionism below. The more general claim that some beliefs are noninferentially justified is called "foundationalism." General foundationalists need not embrace moral intuitionism, since they might deny that any moral beliefs are among the noninferentially justified foundations.

14. Thelma and Louise cannot both be noninferentially justified if noninferential justification entails truth or if it entails that anyone who understands the claim believes it. So the skeptical argument would have to be reformulated to apply to such accounts of noninferential justification. The point would then be that neither Thelma nor Louise would have any reason to believe that she is the one who is noninferentially justified.

15. One well-known example is John Searle, "How to Derive 'Ought' from 'Is'," *Philosophical Review* 73 (1964), 43–58, reprinted with responses and related articles in W. D. Hudson, ed., *The Is/Ought Question* (New York: St. Martin's, 1969).

16. For these premises to be descriptive, the relevant F, C, G, and R must be defined without reference to any norms. The relevant group, for example, cannot be the group of mature or normal or rational people.

17. See Alan Gewirth, "The 'Is-Ought' Problem Resolved?" reprinted in *Human Rights* (Chicago: University of Chicago Press, 1982); and *Reason and Morality* (Chicago: University of Chicago Press, 1978).

18. Many sociobiologists are skeptics, but some draw substantive moral conclusions from sociobiology. See Richmond Campbell, "Sociobiology and the Possibility of

Ethical Naturalism" in *Morality, Reason, and Truth,* eds. David Copp and David Zimmerman (Totowa, N.J.: Rowman and Allanheld, 1984), pp. 270–96.

19. See Lawrence Kohlberg, *The Philosophy of Moral Development* (San Francisco: Harper and Row, 1981), chapter 4.

20. See Richard Brandt in this volume, and his *A Theory of the Good and the Right* (Oxford: Clarendon Press, 1979).

21. See Christopher Morris and David Copp in this volume; David Gauthier, *Morals by Agreement* (New York: Oxford University Press, 1986); and Bernard Gert, *Morality* (New York: Oxford University Press, 1988). R. M. Hare in this volume might also be classified in this group, since his justification rests on nonmoral normative claims about rationality and about how we should use moral language.

22. More limited forms of contextualism, such as that developed by Mark Timmons in this volume, might not be subject to the objections in the text, but then it is not clear that they are incompatible with moral skepticism.

23. See Geoffrey Sayre-McCord in this volume; David Brink, *Moral Realism and the Foundations of Ethics* (Cambridge: Cambridge University Press, 1989), chapter 5; and my section on moral coherentism below.

24. See Brink, *Moral Realism and the Foundations of Ethics,* appendix 1.

25. First Meditation, in *Meditations on First Philosophy.*

26. To rule out a hypothesis is to give a good reason not to believe that hypothesis. For example, one can rule out a hypothesis by showing that it is internally inconsistent or that it is incompatible with the facts, although the facts must be established independently so as to avoid begging the question.

In order to be justified, it is *not* necessary to go through any actual *process* of ruling out any hypothesis or to *show* that any hypotheses is false. All that is necessary is that one have the *ability* to rule out certain hypotheses, and that requires only the justified beliefs and intellectual abilities needed to rule out those hypotheses. Consequently, my argument does not conflate the state of being justified with the process of justifying or with showing that one is justified.

27. *Pace* arguments that are sometimes attributed to Hilary Putnam, *Reason, Truth, and History* (New York: Cambridge University Press, 1981), chapter 1.

28. Moral nihilism implies that nothing is morally required, because an act is morally required only if not doing it is morally wrong. A broader moral nihilism would also deny that anything is morally good or bad, morally should or ought to be done, and similarly for all other moral predicates. This more general hypothesis would be needed to argue for skepticism about these other kinds of moral claims, but the arguments would be basically the same, so I will focus on moral wrongness.

Even with this focus, moral nihilism is distinct from (a) the modal claim that nothing *could* be morally wrong and (b) the second-order claim that no first-order claim of the form "*x* is morally wrong" is *true.* Moral nihilism on my definition is (c) the negative existential claim that there does not exist anything that is morally wrong. This quantifier does not range only over acts that have actually been done. Instead, (c) denies any substantive claim that any act or act type is morally wrong. Although (c) is then implied by (a) and (b), (c) still does not imply (a) or (b), because (c) is not about what is possible or about truth values.

29. I just assume these claims here, but I will argue for them in "Skepticism and Nihilism about Moral Obligations" *Utilitas* 7 (1995), 217–36.

30. Some might want to add that it must also be true that *p* entails *q,* or that I am justified in believing the conjunction of *p* and (*p* entails *q*), but these additions would not affect the main points here.

31. Parallel arguments can be constructed with other extreme hypotheses, such as Moral Egoism (nothing is morally wrong unless it is against the agent's interest or, alternatively, nothing is morally wrong if it is in the agent's interest), and Moral Crackism (nothing is morally wrong except stepping on cracks in sidewalks).

32. This kind of response is associated with Wittgenstein and in ethics with Philippa Foot, *Virtues and Vices* (Berkeley: University of California Press, 1978). Compare Simon Blackburn in this volume. Moral constructivism is also sometimes said to make moral nihilism incoherent and thus to rebut moral skepticism, much as phenomenalism rebuts skepticism about the external world. See Brink, *Moral Realism and the Foundations of Ethics,* pp. 19–20 and 31–5. However, if any such theory makes moral nihilism incoherent, that theory will need to be defended.

33. Hannah is also not justified in believing that the box contains a game instead of a puzzle just because either (a) she does not consciously think of the possibility of a puzzle, or (b) she has no positive reason to believe that the box contains a puzzle, or (c) her acts would not be affected if the puzzle hypothesis were true. Thus, not being considered, not being supported by a reason, and not affecting one's acts do not make a hypothesis irrelevant; and this applies to skeptical hypotheses as well.

34. If it is epistemically irresponsible to believe anything without positive support, then a belief might be permissively justified only if it is positively justified. But this antecedent is at least controversial, so permissive and positive justification should be distinguished initially as concepts.

35. How much is enough? That seems to depend on context, which might also affect what counts as support at all. I do not need to resolve these controversial issues here, since my arguments do not depend on requiring any unusual degree of support. In particular, my kind of moral skepticism does not require justified moral beliefs to be certain, as is often claimed by critics of skepticism.

36. Some moral epistemologists ask whether certain factors, such as intuition or coherence, ever provide any positive support that would be adequate if it were neither undermined nor defeated. A moral belief supported to this extent is then said to be *prima facie* justified. However, this weak thesis is compatible with the skeptical view that no moral belief is ever justified adequately, since support for moral beliefs is always undermined or defeated. To address such moral skepticism, I will focus on the question of whether factors, such as intuition or coherence, ever make a belief justified by providing adequate positive support.

37. My distinction derives from David Copp, "Moral Skepticism." Compare also Gregory Kavka, "The Toxin Puzzle," *Analysis* 43 (1983), 33–36.

38. Some philosophers suggest that evidence and evidential justification need only "aim" at truth, but skeptics need not deny that people aim at truth in ways that do not increase their chances of obtaining it, so they need not deny that people can be evidentially justified in the weak sense that requires only aiming at truth.

39. This definition does not require the support to be a belief, so it does not beg the question against moral intuitionists who see some beliefs as justified independently of any other belief.

40. Jon Tresan pointed out that one might call a belief justified because a belief state has value in itself apart from its effects. This kind of justification would not be instrumental, but it also would not provide evidence.

41. There are exceptions, such as that it is more likely that one will be happy if one believes that one will be happy. See William James, "The Will to Believe," *New World* (1896), 327–47. But such special cases do not include moral beliefs, because moral beliefs are not about their own effects.

42. A critic might argue that instrumental justification is not epistemic if it is not tied to truth. Even if so, instrumental justification is still important to moral epistemology, because justifications for moral beliefs are often instrumental. See the section on contractarianism in this chapter.

43. Linguistic moral skeptics and error theorists must deny that moral beliefs can be justified evidentially, because they deny that moral beliefs can be true, but they can still see some moral beliefs as justified instrumentally.

44. On contrast classes in epistemology, see Fred Dretske, "Epistemic Operators," *Journal of Philosophy* 67 (1970), 1007–1023; and Alvin Goldman, "Discrimination and Perceptual Knowledge," *Journal of Philosophy* 73 (1976), 771–91. On contrast classes in explanations, see Lipton and van Fraassen in *Explanation,* ed. D. Ruben (Oxford: Oxford University Press, 1993). I am deeply indebted to these works. The justification of actions is also relative to contrast classes, since I can be justified in paying my debt as opposed to not paying it, even if I am not justified in paying it today instead of yesterday (when it was due) or in paying it with a five dollar bill instead of with five one dollar bills (for which I have no reason). I suspect that all reasons (whether explanatory or justificatory, for acts or beliefs) are relative to contrast classes, but that broader thesis is not essential to my position here.

45. Some scholars deny that Kant was an absolutist, but here I am discussing the absolutist view that is often ascribed (rightly or not) to Kant.

46. Contrast classes do not resolve all disagreements. Ethics committee members can still disagree about whether a belief is justified relative to the same contrast class.

47. Pragmatists and contextualists, such as Mark Timmons in this volume, try to work out the factors that affect which contrast class is (taken to be) relevant; and feminist critiques of authority, such as by Margaret Walker in this volume, ask who gets to say what will be (seen as) relevant. These projects thus complement mine.

48. This suggests that there is no way to settle disputes about whether a believer is justified without qualification, unless judgers happen to share the same purpose. This might lead to another kind of moral skepticism.

49. For example, a government body might have to decide who to follow when protestant hospital ethics committees recommend something that Catholic hospital ethics committees dismiss out of hand. But moral epistemologists need not take sides. We can say that Catholics are justified relative to a Catholic contrast class even if they are not justified relative to a larger Protestant contrast class. This is all we need to say if our goal is to understand the dispute rather than to settle it.

50. Critics might object that these relativized judgments are not normative. However, normative judgments are often relativized, such as when I call certain apples "good for this time of year." See also note 44 on paying bills. Moreover, even if relativized judgments are not essentially normative, they can still be used normatively (that is, for normative speech acts) on particular occasions by people who assume that certain contrast classes are important.

51. I assume that a contrast class must include the belief that is justified (or else one could not believe it *out of* the class) and at least one other belief (or else there would be no contrast) and that all members of the class conflict in some way (to avoid irrelevancies). Actually, the members of a contrast class will be sets of beliefs, but for simplicity I will often speak as if they are single beliefs.

52. I am *not* saying that S is everyday justified in believing p if and only if it is true that: if nihilism and other extreme positions are false, then S is philosophically justified in believing p. This cannot be right, because then one could detach "S is philosophically justified in believing p" when nihilism and other extreme positions are

false and S is everyday justified. My claim is instead that S is everyday justified in believing p if and only if S is philosophically justified in believing the conditional: if nihilism and other extreme positions are false, then p. This allows one to detach "S is philosophically justified in believing p" only when one has the premise "S is philosophically justified in believing that nihilism and other extreme positions are false." I am indebted to John Skorupski for forcing me to clarify this.

My claim is also *not* about justification relative to a contrast class that includes general skeptical hypotheses, such as Descartes's deceiving demon. One might not be justified in believing *any* conditional relative to that unlimited class. But the philosophical contrast class at issue here includes only moral positions that are taken seriously in moral philosophy classes, where general skeptical hypotheses are not considered and many nonmoral beliefs are assumed. The relevant conditional can be justified relative to this moral philosophy contrast class because it is just a claim about evidential relations independent of any substantive moral views. I am indebted to Mark Timmons for pressing me on this point.

53. In a more theoretical analogy, if there are three competing theories of astrology, and two are inconsistent with certain observations, but the third is consistent with those observations, then those observations are evidence that, if any of these theories is true, the third theory is; so one can be evidentially justified in believing the third theory out of this limited contrast class. Judgments like these enable us to make sense out of what astrologers say and do.

54. The main reason to focus on the strong version of moral intuitionism is that skeptical arguments apply if even an ability to infer is required. Notice also that moral coherentists need not deny the weak version of moral intuitionism if they do not require justified believers to formulate the inferences that constitute coherence. There might still be disagreements about when an inference is available and when one is able to infer a belief, but I will not try to pin down these slippery notions here.

55. This claim is sometimes called a moral sense theory and distinguished from moral intuitionism, but I use "moral intuitionism" broadly to include moral sense theories and even moral reliabilism (discussed below).

56. See Robert Audi in this volume.

57. See William Tolhurst, "On the Epistemic Value of Moral Experience," *Southern Journal of Philosophy,* Supplement to Volume 29 (1990), 67–87, and my response, "Moral Experience and Justification," in the same issue.

58. See Robert Audi in this volume.

59. This argument is derived from Lawrence Bonjour, *The Structure of Empirical Knowledge* (Cambridge: Harvard University Press, 1985), section 2.3; and Brink, *Moral Realism and the Foundations of Ethics,* chapter 5, section 5.

60. Some externalists admit that one is not justified in believing (P) if one also believes that this belief is *not* reliable. But all they require is the absence of belief in unreliability. If the person who believes (P) does not have any beliefs about whether or not this belief is reliable, this belief is still supposed to be justified if it *is* reliable.

61. Such examples are given in Bonjour, *The Structure of Empirical Knowledge,* section 3.2, and Keith Lehrer, *Theory of Knowledge* (Boulder, Colo.: Westview Press, 1990), 163.

62. Although the everyday contrast class was defined to include whatever might be seriously considered in any everyday context, the range of views that would be taken seriously in a particular context is often much more limited. More moral beliefs can be noninferentially justified relative to these more limited contrast classes, but this is still only because those beliefs are assumed and not disputed in such contexts.

63. Jon Tresan pointed out that an instrumental justification would beg the question against moral nihilism if it assumed a value that moral nihilism denies, but instrumental justifications can avoid this problem by using nonmoral values.

64. This account of coherence derives from Geoffrey Sayre-McCord, "Coherence and Models for Moral Theorizing," *Pacific Philosophical Quarterly* 66 (1985), 170–90. See also his essay in this volume.

65. By Norman Daniels, "Wide Reflective Equilibrium and Theory Acceptance in Ethics," *Journal of Philosophy* 76 (1979), 256–82.

66. This is an extension of Nelson Goodman's new riddle of induction in *Fact, Fiction, and Forecast* (Indianapolis: Hackett, 1979), 72–83. In terms of contrast classes, Goodman's problem can be partly resolved by saying that past experience justifies us in believing that emeralds are green as opposed to blue but does not justify us in believing that emeralds are green as opposed to grue.

67. See John Rawls, *A Theory of Justice* (Cambridge: Harvard University Press, 1971); and Daniels, "Wide Reflective Equilibrium and Theory Acceptance in Ethics."

68. The problem of credibility is presented forcefully by Stefan Sencerz, "Moral Intuitions and Justification in Ethics," *Philosophical Studies* 50 (1986), 77–95.

69. Especially Bonjour, in *The Structure of Empirical Knowledge,* who builds on the work of Wilfrid Sellars.

70. See Brink, *Moral Realism and the Foundations of Ethics,* chapter 5, sections 7–8.

71. More reasons to doubt reliability in moral beliefs are given by Margaret Walker in this volume when she shows how many moral beliefs depend on dubious relations of power and authority, and by some recent work in cognitive psychology on common mistakes in moral beliefs. See Daniel Kahneman's Tanner lecture, "The Cognitive Psychology of Consequences and Moral Intuition" (forthcoming).

72. The illegitimacy of using nonshared moral beliefs in coherence arguments is admitted by Rawls, "Outline of a Decision Procedure for Ethics," *Philosophical Review* 60 (1951), 183; Brink, *Moral Realism and the Foundations of Ethics,* p. 132; and Daniels, "Wide Reflective Equilibrium and Theory Acceptance in Ethics," p. 259, and "Reflective Equilibrium and Archimedian Points," *Canadian Journal of Philosophy* 10 (1980), 85–89. These coherentists do not, however, see the relevance of this "independence constraint" to moral nihilism.

73. Coherence might provide philosophical evidential justification if one could construct a meta-justification as in Bonjour, *The Structure of Empirical Knowledge,* section 8.3. However, even if this kind of meta-justification works for empirical beliefs, which is controversial, nothing along these lines seems to work for moral beliefs.

74. In addition, if one checks a moral belief against as many other beliefs as possible, one has done as much as one can and as much as can be expected. One cannot then be faulted, and one is permissively justified. Nonetheless, permissive justification does not show that one's moral belief is true or likely to be true. Even if coherence is the best available tool for forming moral beliefs, it still might have no relation to truth, because even the best tools might fail most of the time.

75. See John Rawls, *A Theory of Justice,* p. 21.

76. See David Gauthier, *Morals by Agreement,* p. 269.

77. One could just define "rational" so that a certain moral system would be chosen. For example, one could say that people are rational only if they maximize utility for all, and then all rational people would agree on utilitarianism of some kind. But that just begs the question against alternative moral systems and beliefs.

78. For example, Rawls requires a "veil of ignorance" to ensure impartiality, and

he adds formal constraints, in *A Theory of Justice,* sections 23–24. For criticisms and alternatives, see chapters 5 and 13 of Gert, *Morality.*

79. Some moral beliefs (such as that it is morally wrong to torture babies just for fun) might be justified in any contractarian framework that would be acceptable to any person in any everyday context. Such beliefs would be everyday justified, but this is just because they reflect common everyday assumptions, so this kind of justification would not show that these beliefs are true.

80. See David Copp in this volume.

81. A contractarian might respond that dancing is immoral if it leads the demon to kill someone. However, the demon in my example would not kill anyone for dancing as long as they still accept the rule against dancing, so that they feel bad about dancing. In this situation, accepting the rule is instrumentally justified, but the corresponding moral belief is still not evidentially justified.

82. Contractarian theories might seem to be about morality because their conclusions overlap to some extent with common moral beliefs. I doubt that this is the right way to tell which views are about morality. After all, religious rules often overlap in content with moral rules, but religion is still separate from morality. And moral nihilism is about morality, even though its content does not overlap with common moral beliefs. A better way to determine which views are about morality is to ask which claims are seen as consistent. Moral nihilism is not seen as consistent with moral wrongness, but denials of contractarian-wrongness are seen as consistent with morality. This suggests that moral nihilism is a moral view, but denials of contractarian-wrongness are not moral views.

83. I will discuss some of the other theories in my *Moral Epistemology* (Englewood Cliffs, N.J.: Prentice-Hall, forthcoming).

84. It might also seem that premise (3′), the principle of closure, fails. However, it appears to fail only when its antecedent refers to justification relative to a smaller contrast class than in its consequent. Closure seems to hold as long as the contrast class remains constant, and that is all that should be expected of the principle.

2

Moral Realism:
Prospects and Problems

Peter Railton

The controversy between realists and their opponents has persisted throughout the history of philosophy—but it has not always been the same controversy. Indeed, one might say that the controversy has kept itself alive precisely by changing its character as philosophy itself has changed. Thus we do not find the contemporary philosophical community divided, as it once was, into Realists and Idealists, with Idealists claiming that the world is nothing but Will and Idea and the Realists insisting that some part of reality at least is mind-independent. The Idealists' sweeping thesis is one that few contemporary philosophers would claim clearly to understand, much less to embrace.

But Realism has not really triumphed. Just as Idealism has disappeared, so has its denial. Instead of Realism we find many realisms, each more or less particular to a subject matter: realism about the theoretical entities of science, realism about mathematical objects, realism about mind, moral realism, and so on. Philosophers typically pick and choose. Realists about the theoretical entities of science might be antirealists about morality. And thus we find in recent decades correspondingly many alternatives to realism: skepticism about abstract objects, eliminativism about mind, instrumentalism about scientific theories, irrealism about mathematics, emotivism about morality, and so on. Of course, some philosophers find themselves antirealist over rather a wide swath of these subject matters. Yet even when their views show affinities with the Idealism of old, philosophers tend to avoid this label. Indeed, they often prefer to refer to their views as "realism" of some sort, whether it be "internal realism," "minimal realism," or "quasi-realism."

Here is my plan for this essay: In the first section, I will offer a taxonomy of realism (with a small "r"—realism about a given subject matter). I hope this taxonomy will offer some insight into the relationships among, and motivations for, its various forms. Next, I will develop an inventory of the distinctive

features of one particular subject matter, moral discourse and practice, seeking
to identify those features most relevant to the question of realism about
morality. And finally, I will consider a form of moral realism that will illustrate
how some of the distinctive features of moral discourse and practice might
be captured, and to what degree.

What a prospect! First taxonomy, then inventory, then reckoning degrees
of fit. Sounds about as entertaining as accounting. However, I believe that
the plan is practical and useful, and indeed, much needed. (Like accounting
itself, which some quite charming people have even been known to love.) So
let me see if I can convince you.

Realism

A chief cause of the changing character of the realism dispute over time has
been changes in philosophical approaches to language and meaning. If, like
Plato, one believed that our words and thoughts owe their meaning to their
relationship to independently existing, universal ideas, then the central question for realism about a subject matter would concern the existence of corresponding Platonic ideas. Indeed, the Platonic theory of meaning had an
important influence in philosophy as late as the first half of the twentieth
century, and major contributors to modern ethics, such as G. E. Moore, staked
the fate of realism about morality on the Idea of Good, which he thought we
knew by a special kind of mental intuition. Hence his view has come to be
known as "intuitionism."

But under the influence of Ludwig Wittgenstein, the logical positivists,
and others, twentieth-century philosophy came to reject Platonic theories of
meaning as metaphysically mysterious and incapable of explaining some of
the central phenomena of language—notably language acquisition, linguistic
communication, and the shaping or testing of thought by experience, all of
which draw our attention to the shared and public character of meaning. The
question of what our use of language commits us to became the principal
way of structuring the realism debate: Does shared meaning require abstract
universals? Do scientific theories actually postulate unobservable objects such
as electrons or infinite numbers, or could they be seen as using these terms
merely as useful instruments in arriving at observational predictions? Is moral
discourse really a way of describing some objective reality, or is it essentially
nondescriptive—a vehicle for expressing one's emotions and influencing the
conduct of others, but incapable of truth or falsity? And so on.

To the eye of someone intrigued by the titanic nineteenth-century struggle
between Realists and Idealists, these twentieth-century debates might seem
to trivialize the issue: "They've made it just a question of semantics—all
haggling over words and never getting to the deeper questions." And certainly
there have been moments in twentieth-century philosophy when the charge
of trivialization has been richly earned. Fortunately, the current juncture in
philosophy is not (at any rate, not entirely!) one of those moments: philoso-

phers increasingly are clear that questions about meaning are intimately bound up with questions of metaphysics, epistemology, mind, empirical science, and even rationality and evaluation. Rather than saying that contemporary philosophy sees all of these deep questions from the flattening perspective of language, it would be more accurate to say that contemporary philosophy is suffused with an awareness that any intelligible answer to these profound questions must reflect the potentialities and limitations of language and thought—How is it possible for meaning and reference to accrue to words, activities, or thinking? Issues of language and meaning still provide the principal framework for many debates in contemporary philosophy, but the framework is now seen as possessing many levels and interconnections. Our understanding of realism and its prospects has thereby been deepened, not flattened.

This happy bit of self-congratulation obliges me, however, to mention a resultant difficulty with any brief survey such as the one attempted here. Owing to the multilayered, interconnected character of philosophical issues it is impossible to assess the merits of competing philosophical positions without looking at the whole view in which they are embedded. Moore's intuitionism, for example, might seem plausible as an account of our moral experience until one presses questions about the nature of these Ideas, how we come to know them, how they are supposed to confer meaning upon our words and thoughts, and so on. It is such an expanding network of concerns that has led to the virtual abandonment of intuitionism in ethics. But a relatively brief essay such as this can only gesture at the range of problems and possibilities confronting any philosophical thesis. With that caveat, let us continue.

A Progressive Taxonomy of Realism[1]

General characterizations of realism are frustrated by the fact that some of the dominant images associated with realism about one subject matter do not apply readily, or at all, to realism about others. Those who are concerned with realism in the interpretation of scientific theories sometimes speak of the issue as whether there exists a world with definite properties that is independent of us and our theorizing. Yet this image, even if it could be made less vague, would hardly suit realism about the existence of psychological states, because there the question can hardly be whether there exist beliefs independently of what goes on in our minds. Others who have focused on realism about theoretical science or mathematics have thought of the central question as whether there could be anything to the idea of a theory's being true that would go beyond even the best possible efforts of human inquirers. Could truth be "evidence-transcendent"? Yet an influential tradition in moral philosophy that has come in the wake of Kant, and that certainly in some measure deserves the title "realism," claims that it is constitutive of moral truth that it be accessible to any free, rational agent.

Is there any way to sort these issues out in a systematic manner, seeing commonalities among the various (or the most important) "realisms" that would cut across these various differences in images and subject matters?

Perhaps it is unwise to do so, but let us try. We will begin with more elementary questions and build up a taxonomy of realisms by a succession of "yes" or "no" answers. The result will be a treelike structure, each branch of which represents a position in the realism/antirealism debate. If the job is well done, then the taxonomy should tell us something not only about the relations among various positions—including their relative "strength" or "degree of realism"—but also about the motivations that might drive a philosopher to embrace or reject them.

1. The first and most minimal question facing a philosopher contemplating realism about a subject matter X—theoretical entities in science, other minds, values—is whether discourse about X is *truth-evaluable*.[2] Are seeming statements about X capable of being true or false? Or do judgments in this area of discourse have some quite different function from attributing properties or describing states of affairs, for example, the function of expressing emotions or commitments? It is important to note that the key question is *not* whether seeming statements about X have some *additional* functions beyond stating purported facts. For example, the statement "I'm desperately thirsty" both purports to describe my condition and functions to express how I feel and to encourage hearers to help me obtain a drink. The key question is whether there is a *primary* or *essential* function of X-judgments that is the stating of purported facts. A "yes" answer yields the view of X-language known as *cognitivism,* a "no" answer yields *noncognitivism.*

This is the first branching of our taxonomic tree, but we have not found very good labels for it, since these suggest that only cognitivists believe our "cognitive faculties"—thinking, reasoning, inference, and so on—are used in X discourse and that noncognitivists would deny this, treating X discourse as nonrational or emotive only. Perhaps some noncognitivists are like this. There is a view about ethics known familiarly as "Ray-Booism," according to which saying "A progressive income tax is unjust" is simply saying "Boo to the progressive income tax!" Someone who disagrees and insists that, on the contrary, the tax is just, is simply saying "Hooray for the progressive income tax!" This interpretation of moral discourse yields the untoward result that these two disputants are merely sounding off and not making any claims to have justification or reason on their side. If this were right, it would be hard to distinguish a moral dispute from a soccer match—opposite sides do not contradict one another, they just root for different outcomes and fight to see who will win. It would be easy to argue against this crude noncognitivism. However rarely people engaged in moral arguments actually succeed in engaging one another in a process of citing reasons, it would be a manifestly inaccurate description of moral practice to say that they do not even *mean* to be doing this.

In other words, it is important to attempt, insofar as possible, to separate the question "What do our words mean when we speak of such-and-such?" from the question "What is really going on when people think or talk about

such-and-such?" The first concerns (among other things) what people standardly intend to say or think when discoursing about such-and-such. The
second is a matter of (among other things) what might they actually *achieve*
thereby—or what might be left of such discussion were all rhetoric or illusions
stripped away. Ordinary speakers of English use the term "mean" for both
kinds of question. For example, we ask both "What does 'family values'
mean?" and "What does all this talk of 'family values' really mean?" These
are two proper but different questions. The first might be answered by giving
a synonymous word or phrase, an etymology, or, if the questioner is a foreigner,
a translation; the second by a sociological or political explanation, say, that
it represents a reaction to the changing roles of women. In discussing realism,
we are interested in both kinds of question. But noncognitivism about X
discourse is, strictly speaking, an answer to the first. Some philosophers might
be tempted to noncognitivism about X discourse as a way of debunking X
talk or X practices, the way that Ray-Booism seems to debunk morality.
But few noncognitivists about morality embrace Ray-Booism, a view more
frequently mentioned by noncognitivism's critics than its defenders. Nothing
prevents a noncognitivist from claiming that X discourse is vital, well-founded,
and backed by rational considerations of the first importance.

For this reason among others, alternate labels have been proposed for the
first branch-point. One such pair of labels is *factualism/nonfactualism.* The
person who denies that discourse about X is truth-evaluable thinks that seeming statements involving X do not really function to state facts, so there
are no "X facts" at stake in the discourse. This avoids the suggestion that
"noncognitivist" philosophers are all saying that we engage in X discourse with
our upper brains in neutral. But "nonfactualism" carries another unwanted
suggestion: that nonfactualists believe "There is nothing to this X discourse—no real facts, just a lot of hot air." But of course a discourse can
function other than to state purported facts without thereby being hot air.
Consider orders or commands. These are not assertions of fact as such. If I
order that the floodgate be shut, the fact that no one stirs to close the floodgate
does not make my command *false,* only ineffectual. But orders are not all hot
air. An order to close a floodgate might be wise, well justified, and disastrous
to ignore. Moreover, statements that *do* describe facts (or that purport to do
so) can be hot air. Jones's latest list of personal accomplishments, sent to his
chairman in hopes of a raise, might be mere puffery.

Thus taking X discourse to be a serious, rational enterprise is distinct from
being a realist about it, since the realist, at a minimum, rejects noncognitivism
(or nonfactualism—but we'll stick to the more familiar label, or speak of
"truth-evaluability" from here on) and claims instead that X discourse is truth-
evaluable.[3] We must be brief, so let us not pause for further explanation but
climb instead to the next branch-point in our taxonomy.

2. The realist embraces cognitivism about X discourse, yet this is a claim
only about what X discourse purports to do—to state truths, to describe

facts—not about whether it actually succeeds in referring to anything real. The classic atheist, for example, gives a cognitive interpretation of religious discourse. He sees statements like "God created the universe" as attempts to describe actual states of affairs, but as getting things wrong. Though a cognitivist about religious discourse, such an atheist certainly is not a theistic *realist.* So we reach our second branch-point.

The realist about X discourse believes that at least some of the central, affirmative statements characteristic of X discourse are true (even if we cannot now be certain which). Here the opposite number to the realist is not the noncognitivist, but the *error theorist,* who claims that X discourse, though cognitive, systematically fails to refer or otherwise is pervasively in error. An atheist is an error theorist about religious discourse. By contrast, a theist espouses a kind of realism about religious discourse, which can be understood as involving denial of an error theory.

The distinction between the first and second branch-points—that is, between cognitivism and the denial of an error theory—can be made clearer by noting that a noncognitivist need not think that X discourse itself is systematically in some sort of error. Suppose I believe that moral judgments function not to describe facts but to express attitudes toward them. Of course, I then could not see such judgments as systematically in error *in the strict sense,* because they do not make genuine assertions that could be false. But there are many ways of being off-base besides falsehood. Consider an example of an utterance that expresses an attitude rather than describing a state of affairs: "Shame on you for lying!" This utterance could be appropriate or inappropriate, sensible or foolish. The possibility of a noncognitivist version of an error theory arises from the fact that one might view an entire area of discourse as *systematically* inappropriate and unreasonable. Perhaps, for example, one thinks that shame is never appropriate, since it is an emotion that is tied to ideals of personal honor or privacy that in the end strike one as incoherent or otherwise indefensible. Thus there is room within noncognitivism for debates that mimic a number of the features of the error-theorist/non-error-theorist dispute among cognitivists.

What is the connection between this dispute and the issue of *skepticism,* so prominent in epistemology? It should be clear that cognitivism does not preclude the possibility of skepticism. Indeed, formulations of skeptical theses typically presuppose that the discourse in question is truth-evaluable (e.g., we are invited to entertain the thought that our beliefs are systematically wrong). Even those who reject an error theory of a given domain need not think that skepticism is out of the question—they can hold their nonerror-theoretic view in a fallibilist spirit.[4]

It should also be clear that noncognitivists need not be skeptics. Noncognitivism is a view about the best semantic interpretation of a discourse X; whether someone holding this view *also* believes that there is something systematically off-base about X discourse is an open question. Many leading advocates of noncognitivism about X have advertised its value in helping to *avoid* skepticism, since noncognitivism holds out the promise of enabling us to see how

X discourse—moral, modal, mathematical—could be in perfectly good order and capable of its proper sort of objectivity without controversial metaphysical or epistemological assumptions. At the same time, we have seen that it is open to a noncognitivist about *X* discourse to embrace a kind of skepticism about it, perhaps because he sees it as plagued with unjustifiable assumptions or untenable attitudes.

In any event, the second realist branch-point is cognitivism *plus* the denial of error theory. Such a position involves both interpreting the domain of discourse as purporting to describe facts and holding that at least some of its central, affirmative claims succeed (or at least very possibly could do so[5]).

3. Does the combination of these two positions make for a robust realism? Not terribly. Here is an example: One sort of phenomenalist holds the view that ordinary talk of physical objects is problematic because it purports to describe an "external world" of things-in-themselves, which lie behind our experiences. The phenomenalist believes that because these things-in-themselves would "transcend" actual experience—they could exist, for example, independently even of whether they could *ever* be experienced—thinking in terms of such notions is a recipe for skepticism about physical objects. So we should sanitize our discourse about physical objects by interpreting claims about the external world solely in terms of actual and possible experiences. According to such a view, the claim "There is a ripe tomato before me" should be interpreted as "I am currently experiencing consistent red, c..cular sensations in the middle of my visual field" or something like that. This sort of phenomenalist offers a cognitivist interpretation of physical-object discourse—statements about sensations can be seen as descriptions of states of affairs. And he typically does not adopt an error theory. Indeed, his whole point is to reduce the risk of systematic error in our physical object discourse by purging it of problematic metaphysical commitments.

But even if cognitivist and non-error-theoretic, this sort of phenomenalism does not look much like realism about physical objects. Indeed, it is frequently said that phenomenalism would rob us of the ability to talk about physical objects, *literally understood.* And that is one way of formulating the third branch-point. For we expect a full-blooded realist about *X* to claim that statements involving *X* terminology are at least sometimes true (or capable of being true) when literally understood as referring to *X*'s. The phenomenalist translation of talk of physical objects into sensation statements arguably is *nonliteral,* failing to preserve the ordinary meanings of our words.[6] (Some evidence of this is furnished by the incredulity one characteristically encounters when introducing philosophy classes to "analytic phenomenalism," a view according to which the sensation statements afford an accurate account of what we have meant all along when we have spoken of tables and chairs, trees and tomatoes.)

But when is an interpretation literal? It seems plausible to say that the phenomenalist reduction of physical-thing language to the language of sensation does not capture our pretheoretic meanings. Similarly, it seems plausible to say that an operationalist reduction of scientific discourse about electrons, DNA, and so on, to a discourse of observation reports—meter readings, color changes in litmus paper, traces on photographic film—is not a literal interpretation. Thus, for example, a practicing scientist is more likely to call these reports *evidence for* theoretical claims than to call them the very subject matter of his or her research.

But not all forms of reduction are, or lead to, nonliteral semantic reductions. After all, chemists reduce the ordinary-language substance table salt to NaCl, yet this does not seem to tell against our ordinary understanding of the term "table salt," or to carry any suggestion that there really is no such stuff. On the contrary, we think of the ordinary-language term "table salt" as one that has been vindicated rather than explained away by modern chemistry. Compare its fate with that of "witch" or "vital spirit" or "bodily humor," for which science found no corresponding substantial reduction.

Moreover, not all attempts at reduction are scientific. Some twentieth-century theologians have urged that we interpret statements like "God exists" as being without supernatural import, and equivalent instead to (something like) "I am committed to a positive outlook on the human prospect." Such an interpretation would indeed make belief in the existence of God less metaphysically weighty, but for that very reason it seems not to capture the literal significance of ordinary talk about God.

This is not the place to enter into the complexities of characterizing a literalist construal of language in general or moral language in particular. We have some pretty clear examples before us: table salt, literally understood, is NaCl; physical objects, literally understood, are not sensations; God, literally understood, is a supernatural being rather than an optimistic attitude. So let us assume that we have some intuitive idea of whether a given proposed interpretation is or is not literal in the relevant sense. We thus have reached third branch-point. A realist about X discourse holds at least the following: X discourse can be given a cognitivist interpretation, and at least some statements involving X are (or quite possibly could be) true, when literally construed.

4. But realism is also associated with another set of issues, having to do with the images we discussed at the outset of facts that are in some sense *independent* of our opinion of them. The intuition here is a very strong, even primal one: there is a world that existed well before humankind appeared, and of which humankind is now but a small part; humans use language and thought to form notions of this world, and act with varying degrees of success on these notions, but their language, thought, and cognitive capacity are not unlimited in power and scope, and the opinions they form might fail to correspond to the world in various ways. That, the realist typically believes, is how things sit.

Sometimes this is called belief in an *objective,* as opposed to merely subjective, reality, and with it comes the possibility of characterizing "objective knowledge" as belief that owes its truth to the nature of, and to inquiry into, this independent reality. We have here an image of an "order of explanation," to adapt a phrase made popular by Mark Johnston and Crispin Wright: Can we explain our belief that P as owing to the fact that P? Or does the fact that P somehow depend upon our belief that P? The former suggests a kind of independence—lest the explanation fall flat—congenial to the realist.[7]

These images of objectivity and explanatory order are not without difficulty. The idea of an order of explanation depends upon fixing upon an uncontroversial sense of "explanation" and of "direction," shared by realist and antirealist alike. Yet the antirealist will typically claim to be able to say (in his own way to be sure) that my belief that my desk is made of wood can be explained by the fact that my desk is indeed made of wood. And the primal image of objectivity mentioned above might even be incoherent, since it supposes that we can use language to describe and refer to a situation that goes beyond the limits of language.

Moreover, both images also seem to fit ill with forms of realism that touch upon the part of reality that *is* partly constituted by the human psyche—beliefs, meaning, social norms, and so on. No realist need demand that the truth about our very own beliefs is strictly independent of what we believe—that would be absurd. It is one thing to say, "Whether or not electrons exist is independent of whether anyone *believes* they do," but quite another to say, "Whether or not humans have beliefs is independent of whether we *believe* that we do." If we believe anything, then the matter of the existence of beliefs is settled. This is especially relevant to our concerns here, since we should expect *moral* truths, if there be such, to be deeply involved with human psychology. So it seems unlikely that we will be able to characterize moral realism in terms of an independent moral reality in this sense.

We therefore must formulate our idea of the third branch-point a bit more carefully. Let us begin by noting that whether or not a person P has a belief that Q does seem to be independent of whether he *believes that he believes* that Q. Surely a person's opinion about what he believes is not authoritative—we all have seen enough of human psychology's deviousness and indirection to know that. We thus can reinstate an "opinion independence" of the kind the realist is after, a picture of humans trying to puzzle out a world that is not merely constituted by their opinion of it—even that part of the world that is their own mind.[8]

Let us then understand objectivity as a kind of independence of a domain of our opinions of it. This yields a fourth branch-point. The realist about X gives an account of X discourse that is cognitive, non-error-theoretic, literal, and opinion-independent (objective, in our sense). Each of these categories poses unresolved problems of interpretation, which cannot be addressed here.

**Branching Taxonomy of Realism
about a Domain of Discourse and Practice *X****

Are statements of *X* truth-evaluable?

	Yes
No	Cognitivism
Noncognitivism	

Are at least some central, affirmative claims in *X* true
(or very probably so)?

	Yes
No	Non–error theory
Error theory	

Are the terms in *X* being given a literal interpretation?

	Yes
No	Literalism
Eliminative Reductionism	Moderate Revisionism
Strong Revisionism	

Are *X* discourse and practice objective ("opinion-independent")?

	Yes
No	Realism (thus far!—
Nonrealism	there are further issues
	not discussed herein)

Moral Discourse and Practice

Realism nowadays, we noted earlier, typically is adopted as a position toward
a specific area of discourse and practice—realism about *X*—rather than as a
global worldview. For example, whereas many philosophers are happy to call
themselves realists about actual, midsize physical objects, there has been
sharp disagreement regarding the tenability of realism about possible objects,
unobservable objects, numbers, universals, causal powers, and so on. For a
large number of philosophers, the "default position" is one that admits only

---

*With special thanks to Gideon Rosen, who first drew this sort of chart for me. He
is not responsible, however, for any errors that might have crept into the present version.

the objects of ordinary experience and explains away the rest. What about morality? There might be some reason to view nonrealism about morality as the default position. After all, it is not wonderfully clear what it would mean to say that there are "moral facts" in the world. And epistemic considerations—What would it be like to encounter, or come to know, a moral fact? Does it not seem that we lack any method for testing claims to know moral facts?—have been seen as raising significant difficulties for moral realism.

Thanks to the taxonomic work in the section on "Realism," we now have a quick way of formulating the moral realist's thesis: The "objective world" (as characterized at branch-point (4)) contains whatever must be presupposed if we are to give a cognitive (1), non-error-theoretic (2), literal (3) interpretation of moral discourse and practice. Moreover, the moral realist will have some answer to the epistemic challenges to be faced if this presence of moral phenomena in the "objective world" can be shown to be the sort of thing capable of exerting an appropriate shaping force on the evolution our moral beliefs.

To develop and defend such a moral realism would obviously be quite a piece of work. Instead, I propose in the present section to take the measure of this task a bit more fully, and then in the final section to indicate a possible way of actually carrying it out. Therefore, in the rest of this section we will survey briefly some of the features of moral discourse and practice that any satisfactory interpretation must either accommodate or explain away. These features must be fairly uncontroversial, because they serve to fix the subject matter—to convince us that it is *moral* discourse we are dealing with, not something else. In the third section, with this list of features in hand, we will ask about the prospects of a form of moral theory that might both accommodate these features and deserve the name "moral realism."

An Inventory of Moral Discourse

(a) Whether or not the noncognitivist is right about the underlying character of moral discourse, it is universally recognized that moral discourse is (what might be called) *surface cognitive*—on its face it bears all the marks of cognitive discourse.[9] We make and deny moral assertions, attribute to ourselves and others moral beliefs, draw inferences using moral language, intermix moral and nonmoral terms freely, and so on. In short, nothing on the face of moral language suggests that it is in any way separate from ordinary descriptive, truth-evaluable discourse. If there is a "fact/value" distinction, it is not evident in grammar or logic.

Consider this example: The following argument is deductively valid (valid arguments need not have true premises or conclusions, but only be correct in their logical form).

(i) Anyone who sincerely believes "I am in pain" really is in pain.
(ii) John sincerely believes "I am in pain."

(iii) John really is in pain.

But this is not a valid argument:

> (i) Anyone who sincerely believes "I am in pain" really is in pain.
> (ii′) "Ouch!" [uttered sincerely by John].
> _____
> (iii) John really is in pain.

The second sequence cannot be a valid argument because it is not an *argument* at all. Line (ii′) is not a statement, but rather an ejaculation that expresses John's feelings. It cannot be combined with a statement like (i) to logically imply the statement (iii).

Now the following sequence seems just as much a valid argument as the first:

> (i″) If stealing is wrong, then encouraging others to steal is also wrong.
> (ii″) Stealing is wrong.
> _____
> (iii″) Encouraging others to steal is wrong.

Yet if the noncognitivist is right, (i″)–(iii″) is not a valid argument. Indeed, it does not contain even one line of argument, since each line (i″)–(iii″) contains a phrase—"stealing [or: to steal] is wrong"—that is more like an ejaculation such as (ii′) than a statement capable or truth or falsity, such as (i) or (iii).

Noncognitivists have recognized that there is something odd about denying (i″)–(iii″) the status of a valid argument. So they have developed various ways of trying to explain (what one might call) the "argument-flavor" of this third sequence in terms of nondeductive notions of validity that are intended to have a surface appearance just like deductive validity.

(b) A related set of issues arises concerning practices of moral disagreement. Moral disagreements seem to involve conflicting moral assertions. Thus, when I say the end justifies the means and you disagree, we seem to be making contradictory remarks. We cannot both be right—that much seems truistic. This sort of disagreement can be contrasted with two other ways in which you and I might not be of the same opinion.

Suppose that you and I are traveling together by car. You say "I'm famished," and I say "Well, I'm not." A difference exists between us—we are not "of one mind." And conflict might result if, say, we are deciding whether to break our journey for a meal. However, this sort of difference between us is not one that requires one or the other of us to be wrong. Both can be perfectly right in reporting their hungriness, or lack of it.

Moral disagreement is not like that. When I say "The end justifies the means" and you say "The end does not always justify the means" our two remarks are meant to compete, to have a shared subject matter. We cannot both be right.

Consider a second example: We are watching Boston play New York, and you cheer "Go Red Sox!" while I cheer "Go Yankees!" We decidedly are in a certain kind of conflict—we again are "not of one mind." Unlike the previous case, we seem to have a common subject matter—the ball game. But we are not making contradictory *assertions* about it. We have simply expressed different hopes and loyalties. We need not think: "Well, one of us must be wrong." For it is unclear in what sense an expression of loyalty could be right or wrong. It could be ill-considered, or ingratiating, or uncongenial. But your rooting and mine compete in ways other than for truth or correctness.

Moral disagreement is not like this, either. When you say, "The end does not always justify the means," you might in part be declaring your loyalty, but you are also doing something else. You are expressing a judgment that is contrary to the one I expressed when I said that the end does justify the means. There is more to moral disagreement, then, than a difference in the attitudes or loyalties expressed.

We might see this as just another example of the surface cognitivism of moral discourse—the fact that moral judgments behave like ordinary assertions. But in the hunger example you and I are both making ordinary assertions. Moral judgments appear on the surface to be assertions about a *common* subject matter, one *not linguistically relativized* to the speaker. To be sure, some philosophers have argued that, at bottom, moral judgments can only achieve a kind of relative validity—as sincere expressions of the speaker's convictions, say. The point here is that this relativistic philosophical position is a *revision* of our ordinary understanding of moral debate, a challenge to our preconceptions. If we fully accepted it, we would probably comport ourselves differently in moral debate. Once two moral disputants had determined their sincere convictions, there would be nothing left to discuss. (This would be more like the case of determining whether one really is or is not hungry.)

Let us formulate this further feature of moral discourse in the following way: statements of moral principles, and therefore the stances taken in disagreements over such principles, are on their face nonrelativistic, or *surface universal.* Sometimes we do restrict our moral statements—"This is OK for you, given your convictions, but it would be out of the question for me"—but we need not do so. Such restrictions are optional, not built-in features of moral language.

(c) Moral judgments typically are linked to motivation in various ways. We would not challenge the sincerity of someone who tells us, "The Christian Democrats swept the election" by saying, "But *you* have always voted Liberal!" Yet if someone says, "You *ought* to vote Christian Democratic—they would be best for the country," and you suspect him of being covertly pro-Liberal, you will see his remark as insincere. "He does not *really* think you should vote Christian Democratic," you will say to yourself, "He must be saying this for some other reason." Of course, he might set a context for his remark: "I come from a Liberal family, and just can't bring myself to vote

Christian Democratic. But I really do think they would be best for Sylvania and urge anyone who can to vote for them." Or: "The Christian Democrats would introduce a property tax, and that would ruin a bunch of my best investments. So I'll vote Liberal. But I don't kid myself that this would be best for Sylvania as a whole." Both of these contexts suggest that he does, after all, have some pro–Christian Democratic sentiment or motivation, and feels in some sense apologetic or even somewhat guilty about not voting for them. In these contexts, his original recommendation no longer seems insincere or otherwise inappropriate.

It is difficult to give a wholly uncontroversial description of this linkage between moral judgment and motivation. One widely accepted view is *judgment internalism*: a moral judgment *J* can sincerely be made or asserted only by someone who is (or who believes himself to be) motivated to some extent either to act in accord with *J* or to feel guilty for failing to do so.[10] Judgment internalism, however, is not a thesis about the surface of moral discourse but about the nature of moral belief. What moral discourse shows on its surface is what we will call *surface judgment internalism:* typically (at least) those who make sincere moral assertions will be found to have corresponding motivations. Whether this connection is exceptionless or a necessary truth is more controversial, and not really a surface matter of the kind for which we are searching.

(d) Motivation figures in other ways in moral judgment as well. Although we might question the sincerity of someone making a moral recommendation who feels in no way in favor of seeing it followed, we typically do not see the absence of motivation as an excusing condition in morality. If George is a white-water river guide who tells us that he "can't be bothered" to keep his gear looking neat, we might be inclined to say, "Well, suit yourself." But if George also says he "can't be bothered" to provide life vests for his passengers, we have a different response, "Who cares whether you find it a bother?—If you can't bestir yourself to provide proper safety equipment you should get out of the business." We might be unhappy about the way George's gear looks, and think he should be, too. But we do not think he should be punished, or feel remorse, for failing to keep it Bristol-fashion. If, on the other hand, one of his passengers were to drown because he "couldn't be bothered" to provide life vests, we would feel that punishment and remorse were appropriate.

Moral philosophers sometimes call this the "categorical" aspect of moral judgment—ordinary lack of motivation or willpower on the part of the person subject to the judgment is not an excusing condition but rather a fault, liable to sanction. Some philosophers question how deeply or pervasively this aspect runs. Let us simply say that moral attribution is *surface categorical.*

(e) Why do we think we have any business imposing moral judgments on those who are not motivated to comply? Why don't we just mind our own affairs? Typically, I suppose, we do not think our moral judgments are—or should be—arbitrary, personal preferences. They instead purport to be based on good, nonarbitrary reasons for action. Indeed, they are based on reasons of certain kinds rather than others.

What would we say to George, after all, to convince him to provide life vests for his passengers? We might make a legalistic or prudential appeal: "The law requires commercial guides to provide adequate life vests, so you're risking your license" or "If someone drowns on your trip and you have not provided a life vest, you could be sued into oblivion." These are certainly good reasons, but they do not have a moral ring. Indeed, in the case of some regulations or threats of lawsuits, we think there is nothing *morally* wrong with the response, "I'll take my chances." ("I know the law requires that we get a permit for our neighborhood Fourth of July parade, but I also know that it would take hours of work and weeks of waiting to go through the process. No one is going to volunteer to take *that* on. But everyone in the neighborhood enjoys the parade, and a lot of people would be disappointed if it didn't happen. And if the police get upset? We'll cross that bridge if we come to it.")

We move onto moral turf, or at least closer to it, if we say to George, "Look, your passengers are dependent upon you—they're often inexperienced and unequipped. They come expecting some risk, but they also expect that you've met basic safety standards. You know just how dangerous these rapids are, and providing life vests wouldn't be either crushingly expensive or burdensome. All the other operators manage to do it. So whether or not you care, and even if the law didn't require it, you should provide them adequate safety equipment."

The range of reasons thus presented is really quite large: considerations of the welfare of others, of reasonable expectations, of relations of dependency and implicit promise. These are all, on the surface at least, coin of the moral realm. No easy summary is possible, but these features can readily be distinguished: the reasons are in some sense positively concerned with welfare, they are not partial (that is, they take into account the well-being of all affected, not just some one individual or privileged group), and they are linked to mutual expectations or, more generally, to the conditions for mutual cooperation. Other features might be added, or these might be qualified, but let us say for now that moral discourse is *surface justified by reasons of well-being, nonpartiality, and cooperation.*[11] This feature helps explain the previous one, surface categoricalness, since reasons of this kind are not exclusively constituted by the agent's own preferences, so moral judgments need not be tailored to his preferences and can be thought to stand even in spite of them.

Are these "good" reasons? Again, we must keep in mind that in this section we are considering only the surface of moral discourse. It suffices for now to say that they are ordinarily taken to be good and important reasons. That is readily understandable. Each of us is concerned with his or her own well-being, and the well-being of those whom we care about. We therefore are concerned with whether others will cooperate with us or attend to our well-being (or that of our kith and kin).

Are these overriding reasons? That is more controversial, even in ordinary moral practice, because we sometimes seem to act as if we thought that considerations of prudence, of special personal relationships, of artistic integrity, or of religious conviction can legitimately outweigh moral considerations.

(f) In my experience, a peculiar mixture of confidence and uneasiness attends moral discourse and practice in contemporary society. We often are reluctant to moralize about a fellow adult in his or her presence, yet we spend countless hours moralizing aloud about others in general or moralizing in private about particular individuals who do not have the benefit of hearing what we say.[12] We care whether our moral opinions are accepted by others in word or deed, but also typically worry that, if pressed, we could not offer a definitive defense of our moral opinions or demonstrate that our own lives are lived fully in accord with them. We recognize that, historically, there have been moral pioneers, individuals who opposed virtually the whole weight of common opinion but who seem in retrospect to have been vindicated. We think that moral debate is often pointless, and perhaps not the chief vehicle of whatever moral progress we have witnessed. And we are unsure about "moral progress' itself. Surely, after the atrocities committed in this century, any talk of moral progress is bound to produce a grimly ironic response. Yet we also think that moral opinion has undergone notable, important, and positive evolution since epochs in which slavery, the subjugation of women, blood feuds, and the open piracy of nation upon nation were commended in theory and practice.

Although we often speak as if moral concern were on the wane, we relentlessly moralize almost every aspect of life, from health and diet to sexual conduct and business activities to our relations with nature. A candidate for college president who claimed not to have definite religious commitments might be a hard sell to the Regents; and one who claimed not to have strong political commitments might be seen as too wishy-washy; but one who claimed to lack firm *moral* commitments would speedily be dropped.

All of this suggests a complex attitude toward morality. We certainly act as if moral knowledge were possible, and as if we possessed at least our share. Yet we do not treat moral knowledge like scientific or mathematical knowledge. There is no comparable recognized body of experts and no comparable confidence that disagreements and uncertainties can be resolved or at least systematically reduced by rigorous pursuit of well-developed methods. Yet at the same time, someone who denies certain moral principles—for example, the wrongness of torturing unwilling, innocent individuals for pleasure or the injustice of hereditary slavery—will be seen in contemporary society as woefully uninformed at best, and disqualifying himself as a candidate for our allegiance.

Perhaps it would be fair to say that moral knowledge is treated as both *possible* and to some degree *actual,* but also as *epistemically problematic.* We are very confident of certain moral claims, but less confident that we know how they might be defended. We are quite sure that we have gained moral knowledge from experience—both as individuals and as a society—but not so sure we can explain exactly how. A word or phrase is needed for this complex attitude toward moral epistemology, but "possible," "actual," and "problematic" yield only the unfortunate acronym *pap*. And whereas some do indeed view morality as pap, I have been at pains to suggest that this is hardly the dominant view. So let us simply stipulate that the meaning "possible, actual, and problematic" will be assigned to the phrase "epistemically viable." Morality is (at least) *surface epistemically viable*. Like a viable newborn, it is alive and kicking, the outcome of a process we all experience but only dimly understand, and worthy of our attention—indeed, crying for it—but not guaranteed to grow into a sober and responsible citizen.

(g) The final distinctive surface feature of moral discourse and practice that I would like to emphasize has an established name in the philosophical literature, though its significance is far from clear: supervenience.

We can put the matter somewhat colorfully by drawing a contrast between morality and magic. Though moral skeptics sometimes describe moral thought as magical, our moral practice belies this. Magical properties, if such there be, are not supervenient. A pair of identical twins could be just alike in every nonmagical aspect, but one could be "hexed" by a magic spell while the other is "blessed." From then on, things would go inexplicably badly for one and miraculously well for the other. That is, magical properties could be *added* to other properties at will, and would have their own special supernatural contribution to make to explaining the world's events, above and beyond any natural causes or forces. Moral properties, if they exist, are not like that. Twins who were genuinely identical in their psychological, physiological, and circumstantial condition (if that were possible) would also be identical in their moral character, and we could not alter this without altering one or the other of them in some nonmoral way—making one more attentive to the interests of others, say, or bolder in defense of his principles. This is the idea that moral properties are not "self-standing," they are *supervenient* on nonmoral properties.

The supposition that morality, unlike magic, is supervenient makes itself felt in ordinary moral life a familiar strategy of moral argument. Once someone has said that an act of type A in circumstances of type C is morally right, then he arguably is committed to viewing all other acts of the same type in essentially similar circumstances as also morally right. "If you think it's OK for you to keep the wallet you've found, then you must think it would be equally OK for someone to keep your wallet if they found it." We treat this as a demand for moral consistency, but really it is more than that. For it demands a very particular kind of consistency: one must give the same moral evaluation of any two phenomena alike in all of their nonmoral characteristics.

To be sure, no two phenomena (like no two twins) are perfectly alike. In practice we implicitly treat certain dimensions of similarity as morally relevant or irrelevant. Mere difference in *who* is involved we deem irrelevant, though certain psychological or historical differences among individuals (e.g., in their capacity to make or be guided by moral judgments, in their family histories, etc.) might be relevant. This carries us back to feature (e): moral judgments are thought to be justified by certain kinds of considerations rather than others. We now can add: such considerations do not include "bare" moral differences—differences that are not based upon any nonmoral differences.

Supervenience also constrains what we say about "moral explanations." Unlike hexes and blessings, moral properties play a role in explanation that is itself supervenient. Whenever we point to a moral difference to give an explanation—"Jean never even considered denying her involvement because she's too honest"—there will also be nonmoral properties that underlie such explanations; for example, Jean has a certain psychology. The "moral explanations" might be simpler and more familiar in some cases than their "supervenience base." For example, there appear to be quite varied underlying "depth" psychologies that yield honest personalities. So moral explanations sometimes afford us insights into commonalities across situations and persons that the nonmoral explanations might not afford. But they always are linked to nonmoral explanations.

But are there really moral properties? Do they really supervene on nonmoral properties? Is this a metaphysical or conceptual matter? These are not our concerns in the present section (unlike the next), because here we are only concerned with surface features of moral discourse and practice. And we have already indicated that moral evaluation is *surface supervenient* on nonmoral assessment. Whether or not there *are* moral properties, we talk and act as if there were, and as if they supervened on the nonmoral.

Moral Realism

We now have before us two agendas, so to speak, which might or might not overlap. Can we give an account of moral discourse and practice that satisfactorily accommodates features (a)–(g) while also attaining any or all of the elements of realism, (1)–(4)? If so, then we would have shown moral realism to be a possible position, though a closer examination of its costs and benefits would be necessary in order to judge whether it is a postion we should adopt. And why should any of this matter? Is it merely a question of theoretical interest—whereas ethics is above all a matter of practice? This seems to me a false dichotomy, as I hope the following discussion will suggest.

Subjectivism and Its Contrasts

A general answer to the question about satisfying agendas (1)–(4) and (a)–(g) is beyond our ambition here. It will have to suffice to try out a possibility or two and see what this might reveal. The particular possibilities I would like to consider belong to a family of views usually called "subjectivist," though it will quickly emerge that this family comprises some very different characters.

Actualist subjectivism. The simplest subjectivism is what might be called "first-person (singular) actualist subjectivism," a view that probably occurs to most of us at some point in our intellectual development as a way of explaining the disappointing character of much moral debate. When someone says "*X* is wrong," according to this view, they are really only saying "I disapprove of *X* and want you to do so, too." This view occurs to us when we are in a debunking mood. Depressed by the lack of moral agreement, and aware of the strong correlation between a person's moral positions and his or her own interests, we conclude: *Despite the fanfare about moral impartiality and objectivity, morality really is just a way for people to dress up their subjective preferences to bolster their own egos and browbeat others.*

This view is not without predictive value. One can be pretty confident which side individuals will take regarding the issue of taxing fossil fuels, for example, once one knows whether they are ardent backpackers or RV-owners. And one can be equally sure that these individuals will "dress up" their opinions in oral garb whenever they face each other in public debate.

Moreover, first-person actualist subjectivism would satisfy a number of items on both of our agendas: it would interpret moral discourse as (1) truth-evaluable (moral judgments would be straightforward statements of preference) and (2) non-error-theoretic (people do have heartfelt preferences they want others to share); and it would accommodate (a) surface cognitivism, (c) surface judgment internalism (if I sincerely approve of something and want others to do so as well, then I am to some degree motivated to pursue and advocate it), and (f) surface epistemic viability (we know a lot about our preferences, but also know on the basis of experience that it often is hard to form definite preferences, that our real preferences can escape our own awareness, and that preference is changeable in ways that are not well understood).

But notice how conspicuously first-person actualist subjectivism would fail in other respects. It is unclear how it could capture the surface characteristics of moral disagreement, as reflected in (b), the surface universality of moral claims. If saying "*X* is wrong" were *only* saying "I disapprove of *X* and want you to do so, too," then when the ardent backpacker says, "We ought to increase taxes on gasoline" and the owner of an RV says, "Increasing taxes on gasoline would be unfair," they would not be contradicting each other but describing (presumably accurately) different personal reactions. Moreover, this sort of subjectivism would not fit well with (e), the surface justification of moral judgments by reasons of well-being and cooperation considered without partiality. For although one's personal preferences might be free of partiality, this is hardly typical.

Indeed, we might have realized right away that first-person actualist subjectivism was defective as an account of moral discourse as soon as we introduced the idea that moral terms are used to "dress up" personal preferences. If moral terms simply *meant* "I approve/disapprove of *X*," there would be no dressing up involved.

This suggests that first-person actualist subjectivism does not give a *literal* interpretation of our moral terms. G. E. Moore long ago proposed an "open-question" test that has been widely used in ethics to distinguish literal from

nonliteral interpretations.[13] If "*X* is wrong" simply meant "I disapprove of
X," then for a competent speaker of English the following sort of question
should make little sense: "Yes, I know that I disapprove of *X*, but is *X* really
wrong?" The question would be about as pointless as "Yes, I know that Smith
is an unmarried adult male, but is he really a bachelor?" We would hardly
know what to say—other than, "Consult a dictionary"—to someone who
claimed to be fully familiar with the term "bachelor" but persisted in pressing
this question. But no such puzzlement would attend someone who asked,
"Yes, I know that I disapprove of wearing religious symbols in public schools,
but is it really wrong?"

Moore's test is not surefire. Language is complex, and individual competent
speakers need not have full and clear understanding of the significance of the
terms they use. We can, for example, have perfectly intelligible conversations
about bacteria and viruses, but how many of us could give satisfactory definitions of these terms? Yet Moore's test does give us a start on the question of
literal significance. And it strongly suggests that "I disapprove of *X* and want
you to do so, too" is *not* a literal interpretation of "*X* is wrong," even if in
our more cynical moments we think it might not be entirely off as an account
of what usually "lies behind" someone saying "*X* is wrong." So, by criterion
(3), a first-person actualist subjectivism, even though truth-evaluable and non-
error-theoretic, would not be a form of "moral realism." This accords with
our intuitive sense that accepting first-person actualist subjectivism would be
"debunking" moral discourse. Morality would be given a revisionist rather
than literal interpretation, taking it down a peg or two from its lofty purport
of universality, nonpartiality, and objectivity.

Idealized subjectivism. But subjectivism has other forms. We can, I think,
move forward on both of our agendas—simultaneously capturing more of the
surface characteristics of moral discourse and exhibiting further the possibility
of moral realism—by modifying first-person actualist subjectivism in three
ways.

The first modification is to move from first-person *singular* to first-person
plural subjectivism—from "I" to "we."[14] If the ardent backpacker and the
RV-owner were claiming not a personal approval or disapproval of taxation
of fossil fuels but rather to report what everyone thinks, then they would be
contradicting each other after all. However, they would also both evidently
be in error: there is no uniform attitude on this question across the whole
society. They would be closer to stating something true if the "we" were
restricted to "me and my ilk"—to backpackers in one case, to RV-owners in
the other. But even this would not make them fully correct, because backpackers and RV-owners are not so monolithic in their opinions. And this restriction
would cost the advantage of second-person subjectivism just touted; because
unless the populations of backpackers and RV-owners overlap, there would
be no real contradiction in their surface moral disagreement.

Are we barking up the wrong tree? Neither side in the debate over taxation
of fossil fuels seems interested in making a psychological or sociological statement about attitudes, personal or social. Each side recognizes that existing

opinion is divided on the subject, and each is staking out his own view while also trying to convince others to adopt it. Each believes he has the force of argument on his side, not necessarily the majority of current public opinion. This suggests a further modification of subjectivism. Moral judgments do not purport to reflect current thinking, but rather what *would* be thought if we knew what we were about and could set aside all partiality.

In other words, subjectivism should be put in an *idealized* rather than actual form. And this is done by our second and third modifications of subjectivism. Recall that the first modification took us from an exclusive "I" to an inclusive "we." The second takes us from what people *do think* about a question to what they *would come to think*—from actual to hypothetical opinion. And the third concerns the nature of the hypothetical: what our opinions would be if we were well-informed and free of partiality or prejudice. Thus, for example, in the nineteenth century people in general approved of lashing disobedient children because they shared the conviction "Spare the rod, spoil the child." But as opinion changed about the salutariness of whipping and as the point of view of the children themselves came to be taken more seriously, this sort of punishment became less and less widely approved of. We take this later opinion to be an important *correction* of the earlier opinion—and not just a change in fashion—because we believe ourselves to be better informed about the actual consequences of whipping and more attuned to the welfare of children. This reflects item (e) in our inventory of moral discourse and practice: moral judgments are (at least on the surface) justified in certain ways rather than others.

We therefore arrive at a more credible subjectivism by following the epistemology of moral justification. Ask which considerations count for us as justificatory in moral deliberation and discourse, and then idealize these considerations. If the result of this process of improvement is a stable, consensual opinion, then we will say that this is what it is for a moral judgment to be correct. That is, "*X* is wrong" means "We the people (i.e., people in general, including the speaker) would disapprove of allowing *X* as part of our basic scheme of social cooperation were we to consider the question with full information from a standpoint that considers the well-being of all affected without partiality."[15] This would be a form of first-person-plural idealized subjectivism.

Obviously the effort to make subjectivism more plausible also makes it more wordy! And it would be still more wordy by the time we finished spelling out the various clauses that this proposal now leaves vague: What is well-being? Who are "people in general"?[16] What is "full information"? And so on.

But wordiness is the least of our problems in formulating such a view. After all, we would expect any real clarification of our moral discourse and practice to be a complex matter. The more serious concern is that our idealized subjectivism is either false or circular—not an attractive choice. How does this dilemma arise?

Take one component, such as "consider[ing] the well-being of all affected without partiality." Almost any social policy or course of action is likely to affect the well-being of some more positively than that of others, and there will be alternative policies or acts that would alter this distribution of benefits and burdens. How are we to balance gains and losses to assess such alternatives? The short answer, and the one that has the greatest chance of making our idealized subjectivism correct, is to say "the morally appropriate way." But now we have introduced the notion of moral appropriateness into our very explanation of that notion, making the subjectivism circular. We could avoid circularity by specifying some particular way of weighing competing interests—the most usual is "equal weight," though that certainly would need spelling out. Yet any particular choice runs the risk of making our subjectivism false. To the extent that people have disagreements over whether—or in what sense, or at what level—morality involves equal weighing of interests, a theory of moral language that settles this question in advance would fail to explain how this could be a genuine debate. It would force us to see the disputants not as raising substantive moral questions, but as simply needing to learn better the meaning of moral terms. And that seems wrong.

A more promising response is to attempt to avoid this dilemma by leaving the subjectivist view deliberately open-ended on the question of how the balancing of interests is to be effected. This need not be just a fudge, because a good rationale can be given for it. The justification of principles of rightness or wrongness in ordinary moral discourse *does* presuppose that moral considerations involve nonpartial weighing of competing interests. Even defenses of the special moral obligations of parents to children are given in terms that are not partial to any particular individual child or parent.[17] But ordinary moral discourse does seem to leave open for debate exactly how this nonpartial weighing is to be understood. So our ordinary moral terms are to that extent vague, and an account of their meaning or use should be vague in similar ways.

Perhaps this is disappointing, because one might have hoped that a better understanding of moral discourse and practice would remove vagueness. But theories of this kind should illuminate rather than preempt normative practice. Perhaps in the course of our evolving moral debates we will develop a more definite, shared understanding about appropriate balancing. To the extent that this understanding becomes uncontroversial, the idealized subjectivist account could itself be made correspondingly more definite. A philosophical account of an area of discourse and practice must tread a fine line between providing useful clarification and insight, on the one hand, and following closely the contours of actual use and understanding, on the other. This leads us to the next question,

Is it adequate to moral discourse and practice? How well would such an idealized subjectivism (which, despite its need for refinement, we will simply take as fixed from here on) fulfill the second agenda, (a)–(g)?

It yields (a), surface cognitivism, because it treats moral judgments as complex questions about how people would view things and, barring some nontrivial problems about idealized counterfactuals, answers to these questions would be capable of truth or falsity.[18] It approximates (b), surface universality, because although it is a first-person view—and therefore makes special reference to the speaker in particular—it is a first-person plural, reaching out to "people in general" rather than any specific group of persons. Given our formulation, idealized subjectivism by definition accommodates (e), surface justification by reasons of well-being, nonpartiality, and cooperation. This brings with it (d), surface categoricalness, because the applicability or scope of a moral judgment does not vary with merely personal changes in opinion or goals, but depends instead on the "objectifying" process of idealized endorsement.[19] Moreover, it brings with it (g) as well, surface supervenience, because it makes moral judgment depend upon nonmoral considerations of well-being, cooperation, and so on, but not upon mere differences in who is judging or when.

What of (f), surface epistemic viability? If the idealized subjectivist is right, then there should be a correspondence between those areas of ordinary moral thought where we have the greatest confidence and those areas where we think we have the best grasp of the facts and of what a view of the situation free of partiality and alive to the requisites of social cooperation would look like. I suspect that most of us are confident in our moral disapproval of chattel slavery, of rape and other forms of assault, and of theft; and confident, too, that we have good and adequate information about how these activities would look if impartially viewed. I suspect that we are less confident on the whole about policies on natural resources, cultural autonomy, redressing poverty and discrimination, and abortion. In these latter areas, I think, we are much less confident of our facts, of our ability to identify what partiality consists in, and of our ability to overcome partiality in practice. There is, then, reasonable prospect of capturing surface epistemic viability with idealized subjectivism.

This leaves only (c), surface judgment internalism. Surely this is the most difficult-to-accommodate aspect of moral discourse and practice for an idealized subjectivism of this kind. Recall that judgment internalism is the idea that making or accepting moral judgments involves a motivational element, such that there is something untoward when someone claims sincerely to believe that breaking a promise is wrong and yet neither feels motivated not to break a promise whenever it suits him nor has any feeling of guilt or regret about this lack of motivation. Such a person seems to be misleading us—or deceiving himself—about his real beliefs.

Actualist first-person subjectivism promised to meet condition (c), since it linked moral judgment to the actual approvals of the agent, and to genuinely approve something does involves some sort of positive, motivating attitude toward it.[20] Now idealized subjectivism is also linked to approval, but not necessarily the actual approvals of the person making the judgment. Rather, it is tied to the hypothetical approvals of "We, the people" when we are well-informed, nonpartial, and so on. Does this distance between the actual and the hypothetical preclude meeting (c)? Perhaps not. Consider three kinds of case:

In the first case, you now approve of laws permitting smoking in public spaces and think of those bent on banning smoking as busybodies without a moral leg to stand on. Yet you might also think: "If I were to learn that secondhand tobacco smoke is seriously harmful to the lungs, then I would no longer approve of such permissive laws." This statement of conditional approval (what you would approve if . . .) might or might not be correct. Perhaps your approval would not change as you predict. But very likely you are right, and, more important for our purposes, your remark reveals something significant about moral motivation. We all recognize that our approvals and disapprovals are based upon what we believe as well as what we feel. When we defend our approvals as a basis for collective conduct, including moral conduct, we typically claim that they are based upon adequate information. Therefore, we are disposed to say that the approval would be withdrawn if serious error could be found to underlie it. In this sense, then, although our hypothetical approvals under full information are not our *actual* approvals, there is a kind of "internal" motivational linkage between judgment and hypothetical approvals. Even as we actually are, we find that it matters to us whether our approvals are based upon fact or error. This can be put by saying that our hypothetical approvals under full information have a kind of *motivational force* or *authority* for us even as we now are. That seems an appropriate way of meeting (c),[21] since we would not want an account of surface judgment internalism that treated our actual approvals—even when badly misinformed—as authoritative for us.

Yet the conditions on hypothetical approval are much stronger than "full information." They include a *nonpartial* concern with well-being and social cooperation. How is this compatible with surface judgment internalism? Most of us are quite partial.

Consider a second case: A friend rushes up to me in the corridor. "Did you hear? We got the grant!" "Fantastic!" I say with untold relief after months of working, organizing, grant-writing, and waiting. Needless to say, I heartily approve of the grant committee's choice. But would I say—am I trying to say—that the committee made the *morally* best choice? Not necessarily. I might be well aware of other, equally worthy applicants, some of whom might be working on projects of much greater social importance and be in much more desperate need of funding. Our project is a fine one, perhaps, but it concerns an esoteric area of knowledge and is currently funded at a level that would at least sustain it.

Suppose, then, on the other hand, that my friend had come up to me and said, "Bad news, the grant went to Bredvold's project on ethnic rivalries." I might respond: "Oh, hell! Well, not completely bad news. Hers is a first-rate group, and it is probably the most urgent project in the whole bunch. At least the committee didn't fall for Ross's project on high-speed blimp transport."

When I purport to assess the *moral* significance or status of an action, I implicitly take a different stance from any personal assessment. I attempt to speak, not from self-interest or even group-interest, but from a standpoint that is less partial, more beneficent, more concerned with the requisites for social cooperation. And just as I have various tendencies to approve or disapprove actions from my personal standpoint or that of my group, I also have tendencies to approve or disapprove when I attempt to occupy this "more objective" standpoint. It seems consonant with actual moral discourse to say that it is these latter tendencies, not the personally or group-oriented tendencies, that we take to be most relevant to moral assessment. Someone who missed this point—who could only see his own interest or that of his group when making what he took to be moral judgments—would soon lose credibility. We would not go to him for moral advice or consultation, and we would cease to "hear" his judgments as moral judgments. We would factor them into our thinking in some other way: "Don't let Congressman Barrell's criticisms get to you—he always talks about justice but he's really only thinking that it would be bad for his constituents back in Omaha."

Finally, our idealized subjectivism refers to an inclusive "we"—to "people in general." But this seems quite opposed to judgment internalism, which claims a link between an agent's judgments and *her* motivations. Mightn't she consider herself not to be part of "people in general"? Couldn't she still have moral opinions?

Consider a third case, which might involve a bit of science fiction. People have been known to lose their sense of smell, or their memory, or even their capacity to feel pain as the result of various injuries. Suppose someone lost his sense of taste. Still, he will find that he needs to make judgments about whether food is good-tasting, well cooked, and so on, whenever he has guests for dinner. Using his sense of smell and various other cues of appearance, texture, and so on, he might become quite acute as a judge of what tastes good. When he pronounces his soup delicious and ready to serve, he is not claiming that it tastes good to him—he can't really taste it in the familiar sense—but simply that it tastes good and that people with discriminating palates would agree.

Now—and this could be the science fiction part—suppose you had, as a result of an unfortunate croquet accident, lost your sense of sympathy for others. Still, moral judgment is important in your life; for example, the freak accident does not convince you that you should be any less concerned whether your next croquet club president is morally decent. And a fellow club member might come to you for advice: "Do you think Kyle really is a decent person—or is he just an opportunist?" Your fellow member wants your opinion on this particular question. How would you reply? You would not simply ask yourself what most people think of Kyle, because they might not be well informed, or might be very partial in their sympathies. Anyhow, that's not the question you were asked. Nor would you ask yourself how *you* feel about the prospect of Kyle as president, since you know you are no longer sympathetically attuned. Instead, you might ask how you would feel about the question if you were a beneficent, nonpartial, well-informed person with no extraordinary disabilities or motives. Using various cues and other information, you would try to piece together an answer: "Let's see, I don't want to ignore how his past behavior has affected other people in the club, even if I can't say that I myself feel any particular sympathy for them." In the end, you might reach an opinion you think to be well-founded, and convey it to your friend. You might not yourself find this opinion immediately engaging motivationally—after all, you lack sympathy. Yet you think it a more nearly correct answer to the question "Is Kyle morally decent?" than an answer more attuned to your particular motives.

On this view, judgment internalism as a *typical* feature of the surface of moral discourse is compatible with speaking of "people in general" because people in general are overwhelmingly like "people in general"—by and large we share some range of feelings, sympathies, capacities for engagement, and so on. In the rare—perhaps fictional—case of someone who began life with the typical sympathies of "people in general" but then lost them, it would seem that his most earnest attempts at moral judgment would be more closely linked to the sympathies he had lost than the sympathies he now has. (Some psychologists believe that sociopaths are individuals who never possessed the normal range of sympathies, and that their incapacity to develop normal moral ideas or scruples, or even to work out sustainable relations with others, stems from this.) A person with this rare disability who nonetheless was concerned to make genuinely moral judgments would perhaps try to situate himself like "people in general" in order to compensate for his peculiar incapacity.

All three cases bring us to the same point, at bottom. When, in normal discourse, we invoke specifically moral terms to characterize our opinions, we attempt to speak not with a voice that is confined to our own interests, particularities, idiosyncrasies, and incomplete information. Rather, we attempt to speak on behalf of a perspective that is "more objective." For most of us, this perspective is a natural extension of many of our subjective motives. But it *is* an extension, and we do not always welcome the view it affords. The "distance" between the hypothetical approvals of idealized subjectivism and our actual approvals is meant to capture just this feature of moral discourse. It might thus be seen as an asset, not a liability, of idealized subjectivism.

Is it realism? What, then, of our other agenda? Could idealized subjectivism as characterized here be a view that deserves the name "moral realism"?

In the first section we considered four branch-points on the road to realism, so let us consider these in turn.

1. *Truth-evaluability.* Idealized subjectivism interprets moral judgments in a way that makes them potentially true or false, depending upon whether the object of judgment would be approved by people in general under conditions of full information, and so on.[22] There is considerable vagueness and indeterminacy in this specification, and so it could be the case that a given course of action that comes out as morally right under one method resolving vagueness and indeterminacy would come out wrong under another. This is less threatening than it sounds to truth-evaluability, since essentially the same thing is true of many of our predicates. How long is the shoreline of Newfoundland? (Do we follow every indentation along the shore, or "smooth" some out? How far do we follow rivers upstream?) Is there any milk in the fridge? (Does the old spill on the shelf count?) And so on.

2. *Non-error-theoretic.* Would moral judgments turn out to be systematically false (or otherwise awry) if the idealized subjectivist were right? The

possibility cannot be fully closed, because we do not know just what would become of people's approvals as they became perfectly informed, nonpartial and so on.[23] We do know a fair amount about this, for we have ample experience of how changes in information, in sympathies, and so on, can shape a person's approvals. Perhaps the most sensible thing is therefore to expect more of the same if this process were carried further. Yet it might be seen as an advantage of idealized subjectivism that does not rule out error theory in advance of inquiry, a priori. The possibility of error theory, or skepticism, certainly seems an intelligible one, and this suggests that our account of the significance of moral terms should make room for this possibility even if it is not made to seem very probable.

3. *Literal interpretation.* This is a hard one. Given its complex history—partly religious, partly secular, tied to variable folk cultures and changing conceptions of value and rationality—moral discourse cannot be expected to submit to a univocal, clear interpretation. So any philosophical account that seeks to provide unifying insight into moral discourse is bound to differ from some people's "ordinary understanding" in some ways. Perhaps the real question is whether a given account captures *enough* of the central features of the discourse, and thus enables us to say *enough* of what we want to say, so that we find it compelling relative to competing accounts, including the account that dismisses moral discourse as involving irreconcilable elements.[24] Our discussion of features (a)–(g) of moral discourse was meant to show this for idealized subjectivism at the *surface* level of moral discourse. To assess whether idealized subjectivism succeeds at deeper levels—by enabling us not only to mimic the surface of moral discourse but also to give expression to our strongest moral concerns and questions—would require considerable reflection. (Recall here the example of phenomenalism—do we wish to say on reflection that it clarifies our notion of a physical object, or eliminates it?) My sense is that idealized subjectivism has sufficient prospect of capturing our concerns to make it a promising candidate. After all, it explicitly links moral judgment to the concerns people in general would have—if informed, nonpartial, benevolent, and so on—about how to establish and regulate their mutual cooperation.[25]

4. *Objectivism.* Of course, idealized subjectivism is, after all, a form of subjectivism. This might seem to disqualify it from the start as a candidate for the fuller sort of objectivity found at the fourth branch-point of realism. Yet we can see it as a highly *objectified* subjectivism—the conditions of idealization remove crucial elements of subjectivity from moral judgment (idiosyncratic beliefs, partiality, indifference to others) and leave only the central idea that morality has to do with what could, in principle, elicit the approval of human beings who are able to see, without fear or favor, what they are about.

No sensible realism about a domain X would demand more objectivity than the domain X itself. A psychologist who wishes to be a realist about belief, as we noted at the very beginning, should not insist that beliefs be "objective" in the sense of existing no matter what any human thinks. And arguably moral discourse and practice need not aspire to a higher level of objectivity than psychology. Indeed, morality shares with humanistic or socio-psychological inquiries a subject matter that fundamentally involves subjectivi-ties—perspectives, points of view, significance, well-being.

Nonetheless, we can ask whether idealized first-person-plural subjectivism is objective enough to qualify as a form of full-blooded realism. Consider a seemingly parallel view about belief. According to this view, to say that a person *P* believes that *Q* is to say that we (people in general) would stably agree on an interpretation of *P* that attributes to him *Q,* given the fullest possible information about his nonmental properties (behavior, neural organi-zation). This view would be an objectified form of *attributionalism,* to be sure, but it would still be an attributionalism. Why equate the claim that *P* believes that *Q* with even the best possible evidence for that claim? Doesn't that confuse epistemic questions about "How we know" with semantic or metaphysical questions about "What we purport to know"?

Of course, someone might find in this sort of challenge to attributionalism nothing but confusion. Perhaps it is incoherent to regard belief as an underlying state of a person, itself not publicly observable, which nonetheless accounts for his observable behavior. But this claim sounds like an argument for *aban-doning* realism about belief.

If "idealized attributionalism" does not seem to be a kind of realism about belief, perhaps "idealized subjectivism" should not be thought of as a realism about morality. If so, then we should ask—if only briefly—whether there is a more realistic view of morality that has some hope of being a compelling interpretation of moral discourse and practice.

Consider a view like the following: Suppose we could, without using moral notions, identify for each person what his or her own good or well-being consists in. Many have suggested that happiness, seen as a psychological state, is the most plausible candidate for this role. This view has its difficulties, but it is plausible enough to serve present purposes. Suppose, too, that we could measure happiness at least well enough to make comparisons across individuals and to form comparative *sums* for a number of individuals ("There is consider-ably greater happiness in the student body now than before the reforms"). Now consider a familiar form of moral theory, utilitarianism. A utilitarian like John Stuart Mill identifies a wrong act as one that would be subject to sanction—either by negative opinion or by outright punishment—in a social code that most promotes happiness overall.[26]

Such a view would make moral properties as objective as psychological properties, and would enable us to distinguish even ideal evidence for moral properties (say, the settled opinion of impartial, well-informed individuals) from the properties themselves. It thus would afford an example of a more full-blooded moral realism. And it would not seem to presuppose a bizarre epistemology. Measuring and comparing psychological well-being is no easy empirical enterprise. But if it can be carried out at all, then this sort of moral realism would require no special epistemology. It would be of a piece with empirical inquiry in general.

Such a view might succeed better than idealized subjectivism at passing branch-point (4) in our account of realism. But would it be literal enough? How well would such a view capture features (a)–(g)? This is a large question, which must be left for other occasions. It is not, however, a novel sort of question. It can be tackled using whatever philosophical techniques we employ in general to decide whether a given account of an area of discourse and practice is adequate—indeed, the very techniques exemplified in our discussion of idealized subjectivism's adequacy to moral practice.

What does it matter? After we have come thus far, this is a potentially embarrassing question. We have seen an example of an interpretation of moral discourse that holds out some promise of being both adequate to practice and realist—idealized subjectivism. And we have briefly mentioned a perhaps more realist alternative. If at all convincing, this discussion should enlarge our sense of what is possible. In particular, the discussion should help dispel the idea that the prospects of moral realism are tied to the possibility of a peculiar "moral epistemology." On both accounts, moral epistemology turns out to be continuous with epistemology in general. But is this relevant to anyone beyond those who suffer philosophical preoccupations?

I am not inclined to disparage philosophical preoccupations. Many of them strike me as growing organically from concerns that first arise in the theory and practice of ordinary life and in the attempt of thoughtful people who are not paid philosophers to reconcile their various conceptions of the world. We were led to idealized subjectivism by following the thread of moral epistemology—asking how people assess, dispute, and defend moral opinions. Whenever there is such a practice of assessment and argument, it will occur to us to wonder whether there is anywhere we might be going with it: are we learning something and, if so, what? Given the many controversies that surround or enter into moral discourse, and given the conflicting interests often at stake, these worries arise chronically in moral thought.

Idealized subjectivism affords one way of understanding what we are up to in moral thought and practice that helps address, without altogether removing, these worries. It enables us to see, without recourse to myth or mystery, how we might be using moral terms with shared meanings and getting at something important. Other accounts of moral discourse could do so as well, some more realist and some less. Some of the nonrealist accounts might seem more "economical" because they eschew moral facts. But, as we noted earlier, the economies of philosophical accounts must be reckoned holistically. The most widely espoused nonrealist accounts involve very serious costs as well as economies. Noncognitivism involves wholesale semantic revisionism. Error theories involve wholesale epistemic revisionism.[27] If idealized subjectivism has reasonably high plausibility, then the fact that it avoids such drastic revisions and also allows us to see moral claims and moral knowledge as of a piece with other claims and knowledge surely commends it as a way of responding to a question we all encounter at some point: Can moral discourse and practice stand the light of full reflective scrutiny?

Notes

Many individuals have helped me to improve this text. I am particularly indebted to Walter Sinnott-Armstrong both for his many thoughtful comments and for his work, along with Mark Timmons, in organizing the conference on moral epistemology at Dartmouth for which this paper was written. I learned a great deal from my co-participants at that conference, and I would like to record my debt to them. Special thanks for Malia Brink, an undergraduate at Dartmouth, who helped me to see how this text might be made more accessible to students.

1. This taxonomy draws heavily on an entry, "Realism," which Gideon Rosen and I wrote for the *Blackwell Companion to Metaphysics.* J. Kim and E. Sosa (eds.), *A Companion to Metaphysics* (Oxford: Blackwell, 1995).

2. Here and elsewhere, unless otherwise indicated, I intend that terms like "discourse," "judgment," "statement," etc. include thought as well as speech.

3. Some philosophers who have been habitually identified as noncognitivists would insist that their view should not be so categorized. R. M. Hare, for example, advocates the view that moral judgments should be interpreted as prescriptions rather than descriptions, but denies that this prevents us from speaking of such judgments as true or false in the ordinary sense. Similarly Simon Blackburn, in his contribution to this volume, argues that his quasi-realism carries no suggestion of noncognitivism since it employs a minimalist or pleonastic theory of truth. Suppose that we accept these self-characterizations. Thus we pass over some delicate questions about the stability of a mixture of quasi-realism and minimalism (e.g., What remains to be *quasi*-about if *all* the truth platitudes apply to a discourse?). Then we should see the antirealism of Hare and Blackburn as emerging at a later branch-point in our taxonomy, specifically, in the region of the tree where we characterize types and sources of objectivity.

4. Many realists, who by our taxonomic definition reject an error theory, see it as an advantage of their position that it makes skepticism an intelligible possibility. Skepticism is intelligible, according to such realists, precisely because the purport of statements—namely, to describe a reality independent of our opinions of it—leaves room for the possibility they might go systematically wrong. Critics of realism as a *general* thesis often argue that global skepticism is not genuinely coherent, however intelligible it might seem to be on the surface.

5. Realists vary on this score. Some take it to be central to realism that one believe our going theories of the world are actually (mostly) true. Others think this commitment is inessential to realism and emphasize that the realist in particular should be alive to the possibility that we could be quite wrong, even systematically wrong. Realists of this second kind place greatest weight not on the (near) truth of current theories, but on the independence of the world from even our best epistemic achievement (see branch-point (4), below). Typically, however, they also emphasize the idea that we can appeal to an independent reality to give an account of experience and experiment as a kind of feedback through causal interaction. Their attitude toward our going theories is modeled on the fallibilist attitude common among working scientists: previous theories have often been found to be quite wrong in many respects, so we should expect current theories to continue to undergo modification as inquiry proceeds; yet at the same time we seemed to have learned a great deal along the way from our increasingly extensive and ambitious interaction with the world, and we can expect much of this learning to be vindicated in some form by subsequent developments.

6. *Literal* here is contrasted not with *figurative* or *metaphorical*, but with *nonliteral* in the sense of *revisionist*. The revision in question is with respect to the ordinary meanings of our words. Sometimes philosophers label their views as explicitly revisionist. Thus, for example, Richard Brandt gives an account of the meaning of "rational" through a "reforming definition." He commends this definition to us as a replacement for our ordinary, confused sense of the term. See his *A Theory of the Good and the Right* (Oxford: Oxford University Press, 1979).

7. For some discussion see the contributions of Mark Johnston and Crispin Wright to the volume *Reality, Representation, and Projection,* eds. J. Haldane and C. Wright (Oxford: Oxford University Press, 1993).

8. This strategy will not, however, work for any beliefs that are "self-evidencing" (beliefs that, if held, must be true). Some philosophers hold that a person's beliefs about sensation or meaning are self-evidencing: for example, if someone believes she is in pain, then, necessarily, she is. Because there is considerable doubt about the existence of such "self-evidencing" beliefs, I will not discuss their relation to the realism debate here.

9. Others have attempted such an inventory. Usually, however, they have had the aim of identifying one or two decisive characteristics of moral discourse. Although I have greatly benefited from their work—I am especially indebted to C. L. Stevenson, R. B. Brandt, R. M. Hare, and W. K. Frankena—I believe there is something to be gained by seeking a somewhat more inclusive list. One then can ask of any proposed interpretation "How competently does it capture a *range* of elements?" without insisting that all viable interpretations must capture them all. Because there may be no comprehensive interpretation, it is important to know how close we can come.

10. The phrase "judgment internalism" is attributable to Stephen Darwall. See his book *Impartial Reason* (Ithaca: Cornell University Press, 1983).

11. I do not here assume that moral reasons must give *equal weight* to the welfare of all potentially affected, although some have thought that moral impartiality does imply this. I also do not assume any particular theory of welfare. Are there moral judgments that are unrelated to anyone's welfare? It is claimed that there is moral opposition to certain sexual practices, regardless of their effects on welfare. However, I do not find this sort of example convincing: for example, it seems to be that in practice opposition to sodomy, to the extent that it portrays itself as *moral* and not religious, is always tied to some or other conception of human flourishing.

12. Who is "we" here (and in the remarks that follow)? Lots of people, I am supposing. But I am recording my impressions of the contemporary scene, not summarizing the results of any serious research. Research might show my breezy generalities to be just that. And we know in advance that such generalities will smooth over a great deal of cultural and personal variability and social contestation.

13. *Principia Ethica* (Cambridge: Cambridge University Press, 1903), chapter 1. My way of framing the question differs form his.

14. Such a shift is suggested in the writings of Charles L. Stevenson, for example, in "The Emotive Meaning of Ethical Terms," *Mind* 46 (1937), 14–31.

15. This form of subjectivism reflects the work of a number of philosophers, most notably Roderick Firth, "Ethical Absolutism and the Ideal Observer," *Philosophy and Phenomenological Research* 12 (1952), 317–45; and Richard B. Brandt, *A Theory of the Good and the Right.*

16. And what real role is being played by "we"? A moral theory might emphasize the question of whether the norms of approval and disapproval are ones that could

be *collectively* agreed upon and enforced. Some contractualist theories of justice could be seen as idealized subjectivisms of roughly this sort. (I am indebted here to a comment of Margaret Gilbert's.)

17. Consider also *moral egoism,* the view that each person should consult only his own interests in deciding how to act. Such a view is not in itself partial to any particular individual, and its defenders argue for it on the ground that it would advance not *their* well-being in particular, but well-being in general. (If they claimed only that it would benefit *them,* this would hardly strike us as a moral consideration.) We are told, for example, that if each individual minds his own business and leaves it to others to mind theirs, we will be better off on the whole.

18. Counterfactuals are sentences of the form "If———were the case [as in fact it is not], then———would be the case." In the recent past there was a lively philosophical debate about whether statements of this form can have truth values in the ordinary sense. The predominant view at present is that they can. For some discussion, see the essays in Ernest Sosa, ed., *Causation and Counterfactuals* (New York: Oxford University Press, 1972).

19. I should emphasize that this is only one aspect of categoricalness. According to the Kantian tradition in moral philosophy, categoricalness is a matter of affording reasons for action that would necessarily motivate any rational being, regardless of its empirical psychology. No such notion of categoricalness is in play here.

20. What is *approval?* According to the simplest forms of subjectivism, approval is a straightforward *preference.* More complex forms treat approval as a "higher-order" preference—a preference about what to prefer. Still other forms of subjectivism treat approval as a kind of *judgment.* Of course, this last sort of subjectivism would be circular as an account of moral discourse if the sort of judgment involved were characterized as *moral* judgment. Now some subjectivists do not see this as a defect. Instead, they have emphasized that circularity is no barrier to truth and that circular accounts can enlighten by showing interconnections among our concepts. Thus, for example, dictionaries are enlightening, yet many dictionary definitions are circular after only one or two steps. Part of a typical definition of "red" is "the color of blood," yet if we look up "blood" we find that it is defined as "a red liquid flowing in the veins and arteries of living animals." For a defense of circular subjectivism, see David Wiggins, "A Sensible Subjectivism?" in his *Needs, Values, and Truth* (Oxford: Basil Blackwell, 1987).

21. Recall that element (c) is *surface* judgment internalism—the presence on the surface of moral discourse and practice of a strong association between judgment and motivation. No particular philosophical theory of the nature of this association (e.g., as conceptually necessary rather than nomological, say) is presupposed.

22. As noted earlier, there are some philosophical issues about whether counterfactual statements might systematically fail to have truth conditions.

23. This worry is not the general problem about counterfactuals, noted earlier. Rather, it is a specific worry about counterfactuals that involve indefinitely specified or never-realized idealization conditions such as "full information." One might not be skeptical at all about whether "If Jack were to learn he had missed the exam, he would be upset" has a definite truth value. But one could be quite dubious about whether there is any definite truth value to "If Jack were to be perfectly informed, he would still want to take the exam." How Jack might change in response to perfect information, and how such uncontrolled factors as the order or vividness or familiarity of the information might affect him, could be sufficiently indeterminate to leave us quite unsure as to the answer.

24. See Brandt's discussion of "reforming definitions" in his *A Theory of the Good and the Right.*

25. We will consider some limitations of idealized subjectivism as a literal interpretation of moral discourse at the end of the next subsection.

26. The *locus classicus* of this view is his 1863 essay *Utilitarianism.* For a contemporary view with some of the same features, and that might be thought of as realistic in a similar sense, see Peter Railton, "Moral Realism," *Philosophical Review* 95 (1986), 163–207.

27. Moreover, the distinctions here are less than perfectly strict. Any "reforming definition" involves an element of error theory; and any "reconstructionist" error theory involves an element of vindication of some aspects of moral thought. Any plausible "noncognitivism" or "nondescriptivism" must allow moral language to have some important descriptive content; and any plausible cognitivism must recognize that the practice of moral assertion has expressive or commending force as well as descriptive content.

3

Securing the Nots: Moral Epistemology for the Quasi-Realist

Simon Blackburn

Not Noncognitivism

It is possible to doubt whether there is such a subject as moral epistemology, and I am conscious of some misgivings over both words. Perhaps "moral" is not quite right, for one might be concerned with the larger sphere of values in general. And perhaps "epistemology" is not quite right either. Epistemology is traditionally the investigation of whether we know *that* various things are the case. Ethics, in my view, is more to do with knowing *how*: how to live and feel and act. It is a familiar thought that goodness can be inarticulate: one can imagine the tongue-tied good person, just as one can imagine artists who cannot put into words what they do well. You cannot in the same way imagine an inarticulate expert on physics or history: their knowledge is essentially capable of articulation, and if someone literally cannot tell (at least to themselves, for they might be paralyzed) the content of such a theory or the events in such-and-such a war, then they do not know them. Such knowledge is essentially propositional; ethics and the creation of art are not. Nevertheless, I also think that my position on ethics ought to have implications for whatever it is that moral epistemology at its most respectable turns out to be. At any rate, one of the motivations for the package that I promote is that it makes the business of ethical confidence less fraught than it is on other approaches; part of this is purely negative (at least I avoid intuitions, and a doubtful moral sense analogous to other senses), but to convert this to a real advantage, something more positive must be offered.

People may be surprised that anything more positive is indeed on offer. People often label positions of my kind "noncognitivism," suggesting that they think such views and knowledge simply do not mix. At the very least I want to establish that this is a mistake. Although readers of my work may

82

guess the kind of positive story I am likely to sketch, it is good to have an opportunity to fill it in a little. I do, after all, think we have bits and pieces of moral knowledge: we know that happiness is better than misery, and that malicious lying is a bad thing; we know that many of our acquaintances are decent people, and that others are too much one thing or another. Of course, the exact form of many such claims, and the place of prima facies, pro tantos, and ceteris paribuses can be debated, but I am not ready to deny that somewhere in these areas there is something we know, however difficult it is to state it accurately. I return to the issue of accurate statement in due course.

First, a brief explanation of the position I defend. I think we should not theorize about morality and ethics as if they are in the business of describing aspects of the world—the moral and ethical aspects of the world. I think we should see their function differently. To enter a moral or ethical claim is to perform an action with some function like this: it is, amongst other things, to set oneself for or against something, to invite others to share this orientation, to prescribe courses of action, to lay down boundaries and give warning against trespass, or to smile encouragingly on conformity. It is to take up an attitude or stance, and centrally it involves making an emotional response to contemplated events and states of affairs. It may license or forbid various movements of the mind, from facts to attitudes, for example. A person's morality is shown in their way of being in the world; the things they do with pleasure, as opposed to those they do with difficulty, or will not do at all. And it is shown too in endless delicate accordances and discords, as they sympathize with the emotions and attitudes of others around them. Moral and ethical vocabulary is there primarily to articulate this network of attitude and emotion. It enables us to share our stances with others, to shape our sensibilities in light of the opinions of others, and to hear and voice assent and dissent. This is the core of the expressivist or projectivist position in ethics. The *essence* of ethics lies in its practical function. Ethical language is not there to describe further facts—the ethical facts—or to give a peculiar description of more ordinary natural facts, but to voice the responses we are to make to affairs.

It seems so obvious to me that this is the place to start that I have difficulty hearing much of what passes for contemporary moral theory, and that appears to start somewhere else, for instance, with an unanalyzed, captial-letter concept of Reason, or with perceived moral facts. But many contemporary philosophers have felt, with John Mackie, that ethics purports to be "something more."[1] We think of ethical facts, they say, as independent, objective, demanding, and none of this is explicable by expressivism. Or, they say, we discuss ethics in terms of propositions that are supposed to be true or false, and this too is something the expressivist cannot explain. To show that such objections are misguided, I invented the persona I call the "quasi-realist," who attempts to remove these obstacles from the expressivist position. Quasi-realism seeks to explain, and justify, the forms of thought we practice as we think about what to do and how to behave. Technically, in the philosophy of language, it tries mainly to justify what I call the "propositional surface" of ethics, or the fact that we voice our reactions in very much the way in which we describe facts. It is this surface similarity that misleads theorists into think-ing that we *are* fundamentally describing facts, and anyone like myself, who thinks that this is not the best way of seeing what we are doing, needs to address the issue of why the appearance is deceptive. In a wider emotional setting, the quasi-realist tries to make people comfortable with the disen-chanted, value-free world in which it begins by setting us. The comfort it provides is that of restoring a due dignity and weight to moralizing (at its best) as an essential and respectable activity, preventing it from being seen as simply "sounding off," or worse, imposing one's own prescriptions on others by means of a kind of cheat.

In the philosophy of language the obstacle to overcome is associated with Frege. We can put it as a simple objection to the idea that there can be anything to know on the expressivist picture. We know things, the objector says, that are capable of truth value. But for the expressivist there is no such object of knowledge to hand. There is only the subject and his or her attitudes. Truth does not enter into it; hence neither does knowledge. The ways this crisp objection may be filled out are well known. For the purpose of this paper I shall only sketch the kind of answer that I think it deserves.[2] It is true that in some sense there is only we, the subjects, and our attitudes. But there is also the need to communicate, revise, and adjust attitude; to rehearse moral scenarios together and to coordinate our responses; to encourage some atti-tudes and to discourage others. All this explains and justifies the propositional surface of our commitments: needing something better than an impoverished "boo-hooray!" language, we move to talking of moral properties and their application. Just as we seamlessly move from "yummy!" to "that's nice" without thinking of ourselves as crossing a perilous Fregean abyss, so we move to thinking and talking of values, rights, duties, and the rest as a way of together configuring the pressures on action and motivation that we desire to encourage. There is no error here, at least in principle (there might be moral error if some of the attitudes encouraged and represented by certain kinds of vocabulary would have been better suppressed: this may often be so with talk of rights, for example).

A famous case of the apparent split between the propositional surface and anything the expressivist can offer is the conditional form. Opponents have charged that the expressivist can make no sense of "if Alaric saves Bertha, he will be behaving well" or "if Alaric behaves well, he will be rewarded" where no attitude to Alaric's behavior is actually expressed. The response on behalf of expressivism is to look at the overall function of these conditionals. Like other conditionals, they can be seen as a device for reflecting upon and endorsing a movement of thought. They stand close to the movement ex-pressed by "Alaric saved Bertha, *so* he behaved well, or "Alaric behaved well, *so* he will be rewarded" (as Ryle put it, the primary point of *learning* the conditional form is to acquire the ability and readiness to infer from *p* to *q,* and to acquiesce in the corresponding inferences of others).[3] A conditional is the way we express our commitment: either not-*p* or *q*. We want to discuss being tied to these alternatives, and we focus on the conditional when we do so. But this function is necessary when we are in the domain of moving from belief to attitude, or amongst attitudes, or from attitude to belief. Being tied to combinations of belief and attitude needs just as much discussion as being tied to combinations of belief and belief. So it should not seem surprising that we have a conditional form in these areas as well. But once we have this need, then we also need to express our moral commitments in the indicative, sentential form, or we get grammatical nonsense ("if hooray for Alaric, then Alaric will be rewarded"). This is the kind of story the quasi-realist tells in order to explain (and justify) such things as the use of the indicative form. It is this that gives us the propositional surface of ethics.

It must be stressed that whereas pursuing these themes gives an explanation of the propositional surface, it remains true that the real essence of ethics lies not so much in the networks of propositions that it has people asserting, but in the underlying contours of their sensibility: the contours of attitude and emotion that drive them in their actions and their relations to others. This is as it should be. There are studies that show decisively that some kinds of brain-impaired patients have the propositions of moral and social life perfectly under control, but, because they cannot respond emotionally to the scenes they contemplate, are unable to live normal lives.[4] Their decision making and their responses to their own needs or those of others are destroyed, but their purely propositional capacities are not. I return to this later, in connection with the Wittgensteinian sense that the essence of ethics may even be inexpressible, lying beyond capture by ethical language. But what is perfectly clear, surely, is that were we *normally* like these unfortunates, there would be no ethics. When acceptance lacks its emotive and practical force, there is nothing left of value in contemplating the bare propositions.

It may be useful here to enter a warning about the popular contemporary debate about moral "internalism," or the issue of whether a moral commitment is in and of itself motivating, or whether there might be psychologies that take up an entirely external attitude to moral facts, registering them, but feeling no impulse to act upon them. It is often supposed that the projectivist must be an internalist, claiming that to assent to an ethical proposition necessarily carries an affect or motivation toward or against its subject. I do not think that is quite right. We might want to say that one of these brain-damaged people believes, for instance, that prudence is important, because he says as much, and in thinking in a cool hour about practical decisions he recognizes that prudence is often the way to go but feels no inclination to be prudent. What is more clear is that the concept of importance simply could not play its ordinary role if we were all like that. Similarly, someone may love someone yet the attitude or emotion may fail to motivate them on an occasion, because of listlessness or despair. But love is essentially practical, for all that. So I distinguish between the right way to theorize about such a mental state, which is surely to explore its normal affective nature, and claiming that it has that very affect on each and every occasion. The latter claim ignores the holism of the mental, or the changes in the effects of mental states that can be induced by surrounding attitude and belief.

Once the propositional surface of a discourse is in place, the truth-predicate comes in its train. We want to report that Angus said three true things and one false one whether Angus was talking about ethics, mathematics, or empirical fact. Anyone thinking that there is more to truth, or only strict and literal truth, in one such area, and that there is none in others then needs to identify what this extra content is, and the history of such attempts is not at all encouraging. At any rate, for the purpose of this essay I shall adopt a minimalist attitude to truth, and allow my expressivist to say that ethical commitments are strictly and literally true. The expressivism came not in denying this, but in explaining how it comes to be so given that we are in the realm of attitude. And then, once the truth-predicate is in place, there is no principled difficulty about supposing that we know some ethical truths, but may, for instance, be uncertain about others.

Some people may already find this confusing, and many ways of drawing up debates in this area encourage the confusion. For example, the map drawn by Peter Railton in his chapter in this volume contains no place for this kind of expressivist to stand—or at least, it only allows him to stand in positions labeled realist. This is because this kind of expressivist will say that there are ethical truths, and even that they are independent of us and our desires.[5] But it is confusing to call the position realist, precisely because at no point does it regard our behavior in this area as explained by any kind of awareness of an area of reality, or a real feature or property of things. It is here that the "quasi" comes in: we *end up* saying things that sound superficially distinctive of realism, but *the explanation* of what we are doing in saying them and of how we get to say them is different.

Someone may (grudgingly, as it were) suppose that the quasi-realist can get this far, but still deny that he can properly talk of knowledge. I imagine someone recognizing that the quasi-realist will turn the Fregean objection by giving a story about the way in which evaluations come to be apt for truth; this is the story about the way the propositional surface of our commitments is best explained. But, according to this next kind of opponent, whom I shall call the reliabilist objector, such devices only give us at best a thin conception of the truth of an evaluation. In particular they give us no thick, robust conception of an ethical *fact,* and therefore no conception of ourselves as more or less reliably responding to such facts. But, according to the objection, this reliable responsiveness to fact is the essence of knowledge. Hence, once more, the expressivist fails to justify or earn talk of knowledge.

In modern terms, the objection to which I have already sketched an answer denies that evaluative commitments are truth-apt; the current objection allows that technically they may be, but insists that the kind of truth for which they are apt falls short of the kind that can enter into reliable connection with our verdicts. We therefore cannot, in ethics, regard ourselves as reliable indicators of the truth, and that means that we cannot regard ourselves as knowing anything, if the expressivist is right about the fundamental explanation of the discourse.

I now want to show that this second objection cannot be sustained. If evaluative discourse is minimally truth-apt, as the quasi-realist purports to show, then only a very crude reliabilism will prevent the truths we hit upon from being properly connected, in a way that justifies talk of knowledge, to our success in hitting upon them. I do not regard reliabilism as anything like an analysis of knowledge, and for reasons I have sketched elsewhere I am doubtful about the entire enterprise of analyzing the concept by attempting to identify ever more sophisticated natural links as just the ones that sustain claims to knowledge.[6] Nevertheless, reliability is surely part of our standards for regarding ourselves and others as knowing things; unless a believer is functioning properly, on an occasion, he or she does not know what she believes, and proper functioning demands using faculties—perception, memory, testimony, reason—that make us reliable detectors of the truth. That much, I believe, is uncontroversial. Then suppose that someone testifies to a fact, *p*. To be said to know what they reported, they must then be in a kind of situation, such as having received some perception or other evidence, which makes them reliable at whether facts of the kind *p* obtain.

This may be a necessary condition of knowing *p,* but I do not think it is sufficient. The attribution of knowledge to ourselves and others is governed by norms determining its correctness, and I think that one of these norms is that no improvement in the subject's acquaintance with the facts would properly undermine the belief that *p*. That is, in the familiar cases where people are behaving perfectly rationally, but are wrong-footed by misleading pieces of evidence, we deny that they know what they believe, even when what they believe is true, because we see that a better acquaintance with the situation could undermine or destroy the belief they have acquired. Notice that this norm itself uses evaluative terms: to apply it we must judge what counts as an improvement in an epistemic situation, and what counts as properly undermining a belief. I do not think this can be avoided. If we tried to substitute some description of what would normally count as an improvement, such as further acquisition of evidence or further thought, we would run foul of cases where the acquisition or the thinking obfuscates the issue and is really no improvement at all. It is when we accept that someone is reliably placed with respect to the fact whether *p* and also accept that no further useful investigation or thought ought to undermine the belief, that we allow the attribution. This element of the concept of knowledge is capable of different kinds of expression. We might wonder whether it is enough that no improvement *would* undermine the belief, or whether there must be no *chance* that an improvement would undermine the belief, or whether, at the strongest, there must not even be a bare *possibility* that this should happen. Roughly, if we only require that no improvement would undermine the belief, we seem likely to let in more cases; cases in which, for instance, someone is luckily possessed of evidence that points, like all the other evidence, in just the one way, but has no real reason to suppose this. On the other hand, if we think that the bare possibility of error destroys a claim to knowledge, we seem hostage to scepticism, for as Descartes showed, bare possibilities are extremely cheap. For these reasons I favor something in the "no chance" area of the spectrum: we know something when we have exercised reliable judgment, and there is no chance of an improvement overturning our verdict.

So the question for the expressivist is whether sometimes our situation in making evaluations is one in which we are reliably situated, and in which there is no chance that an improvement in our position would undermine the evaluation. And the answer to this question is that surely we sometimes are in such a position. Consider firstly a middle-size, clear-cut judgment: regardless of danger, at some cost, but successfully, alone among the spectators, Alaric jumped in to save the drowning Bertha; and I commend his action, judging that he behaved well. Let us allow that I know that the action was as specified (it is no part of the position I am rebutting that there is no knowledge of this kind). My favorable attitude to this kind of action gains expression when I say that Alaric behaved well. Am I reliable? If Alaric had not behaved well I should not be going around thinking that he did. The close possible worlds in which he did not behave well are ones, presumably, in which Bertha was not in the water, or in which she was but he averted his eyes or slunk away, and if these things had happened I would not be thinking that he behaved well. Furthermore, there may be no chance that further acquaintance with the situation reverses my verdict: there are not hidden wrinkles waiting to turn up, proving that the whole thing was a publicity stunt or whatever. So I know that Alaric behaved well.

The objector will urge that this is not the point: the question is whether the fact-value link is reliably judged, and what can the expressivist say about that? Well, I can start to wonder about at least two kinds of thing. I can wonder whether there are possibilities in which actions as specified do not deserve commendation. I might decide that there are, but that they are remote: possibilities in which there are additional wrinkles, such as Bertha having so behaved that she really ought to drown, or Alaric having a yet more urgent and virtuous act to perform. But this is not how it was on this occasion, and judging that these are mere idle possibilities, I see no threat to the solid reliability of my verdict from them. Or, more interestingly, I might start to wonder about my own propensity to admire saviors of Alaric's stamp. Am I perhaps too quick to hero-worship? Do I sentimentalize victims, or underestimate the Darwinian fitness of a world in which incompetents like Bertha are swept away? Perhaps. While I have such thoughts, I will retreat from any claim to knowledge, precisely because I am contemplating *as improvements* changes in my moral sensibilities that would undermine the verdict. But I can return from such thoughts not undermined but braced. I am not hero-worshiping Alaric, or sentimentalizing Bertha, and fiddlesticks to the Darwinian struggle: Alaric behaved well. I know that he did, and perhaps we all do.

Not Relativism

There are several moves the hostile reliabilist might make to this robust reaffirmation of our values. The first is the most important. It is the complaint that this is all the reply really amounts to: it is only a reaffirmation of the very values whose detection the reliabilist queries. Reliability has not been underpinned from without, but reasserted from within. But if this is all that can be done, the objector demands that you should see yourself as one amongst many putative shoppers in the marketplace of values. You pick or have foisted upon you a basket of values, and you then affirm and reaffirm them, even handing yourself the dignities of knowledge and certainty. But you must recognize that others, carrying different baskets, will be doing the same, and in none of this is there more than the contingent consilience or clash of attitude. There is no independent criterion of right or wrong or good or bad, and therefore no certification that you are reliable as an indicator of them. In short, the pit of relativism looms in front of us.

The right response to this relativistic threat is to think about the standpoint that the objector occupies. The objector asks us to occupy an external standpoint, the standpoint of the exile from all values, and to see our sensibilities entirely from without. But it is only by using our sensibilities that we judge value. So it is as if we are asked to judge colors with a blindfold on, and the inevitable result is that values are lost, and our sense of ourselves as reliable indicators of them is lost along with them. But why does this matter? Consider, as a parallel, how it would work with secondary qualities. Suppose I protect my claim to know that grass is green in a similar way to that I gave above: I am careful and reliable, and there is no real chance of any improvement in my position reversing the verdict. But now the scientifically minded reliabilist insists that we think of a neutral, colorless world (the scientific world, perhaps) and a distribution of color sensitivities, with some creatures responsive to some lights, and others to different ones, but each of them able to use color vision to discriminate surfaces and get around the world efficiently. In none of this is there truth or error—there is no sense to saying that one particular color sensitivity gets the world *right,* so how can I regard myself and others like me as reliable about colors? The answer is that if this is the playing field, I cannot; but this playing field is not level to the point of being a precipice. My confidence about colors is simply not beholden to this kind of challenge.

In the theory of value the situation is slightly more complex, because in the secondary quality case it is not difficult to imagine simply shrugging aside the possible or actual existence of creatures with radically different sensitivities. We simply ignore them as we make our own discriminations and award ourselves our own titles to knowledge (this is the germ of truth explored but I think exaggerated in dispositional or "response-dependent" analyses of color terms).[7] In the case of values a radically different sensibility seems to pose more of a challenge. This challenge is, however, not posed by the mere actual or possible existence of a different way of taking things. It is of no interest that there might be someone who thinks that Alaric's behavior was indifferent or even shocking. By itself such a personality poses no threat to my values: it merely itself invites some kind of regret or condemnation. What would be of interest would be a sensibility that cannot be dismissed as inferior, and which issues in this attitude. But in assessing the chances of there being such a thing, we are back working from within. We are no longer playing the fake externalist game of trying to certify values without using values. Instead we are reimmersed in the kinds of judgment already mentioned: we find ourselves asking whether this sensibility stresses the Darwinian struggle inappropriately or is romantically Nietzschean in some other defective way. Is it really a challenge, or is it visibly worse than our own in ways that command our confidence? And the answer, once more, is that we may indeed return from contemplating such a rival with our confidence diminished, and a respect for different ways of looking at the situation that does undermine a breezy confidence that we alone are right. But on the other hand we may also return braced and reinvigorated, more secure in our own tested judgment. The essential point is that in either case we are deploying values in order to sort out the putative conflict, and there is no escaping doing so.

This response to this particular form of the reliabilist challenge is not unique to expressivism: the same insistence that we only "work from within" is common to other philosophies looking for an anthropocentric or response-dependent account of valuation, but it is not my brief here to detail the issues between expressivism and these other neighbors.

Does this dispose of relativism? Such a hardy perennial has many roots, and it is unlikely that they can all be dug up in one scoop. But what it does do is make it extremely hard to see how relativism is going to be stated. There is the platitude that different actual or possible sensibilities exist, and issue in different and sometimes conflicting attitudes. But relativism tries to go beyond the platitude and derive from it something significant for the concept of ethical truth. But what can it derive? It aims at something such as this: in some cases *it is equally true* that p and that $-p$ (one is true for us, and the other for them, for instance). But if p is one of my commitments, I have no business allowing that it is true that $-p$. Doing so induces incoherence in my set of attitudes. Of course, I can allow the solecism "it is true for them that $-p$" when this just means that they hold $-p$, since that gets us nowhere beyond the platitude.

Perhaps the idea is that I should not have a commitment to p, once I recognize the other sensibility. But why not? As I said above, it is only if the other sensibility commands some respect that my own commitment is even prima facie threatened, and then in balancing the respect, the threat, and the depth of my commitment I am back working from within my own framework of values, as of course I must do. There is no telling in advance whether it is the respect for the other sensibility, or the depth of my own commitment that is likely to lose in this process.

Although I think this is a satisfactory answer to relativism, in many areas it can be strengthened. In the twentieth century we have all been impressed by the diversities of human nature and human culture, but it is worth remembering some of the constancies that impressed earlier thinkers. We are social animals, with certain biological needs. We have to coordinate our efforts; we have to establish systems of property and promise-keeping and sometimes even government. We can then take comfort in reflecting that there are not so many admirable, coherent, mature, livable ethical systems on offer; indeed rather than being faced with a whole shopping basket of such things, our usual problem is to find as much as one that survives critical reflection. All I can do is struggle to make mine possess these and perhaps other virtues, and accept what help I can from people further up the mountain. Persons on different mountains need not perturb me, except, as it were politically, unless they can show that they are where I ought to be. But to show that they must do some ethics, and I in turn will be using my values as I respond to theirs. The upshot is that nothing intrinsically relativistic ever gets said or thought.

Not (Entirely) Epiphenomenal

An epiphenomenal property is one that is itself inert. It lies on top of the phenomena, but plays no part in making things happen. It cannot be cited as part of any causal mechanism. So a second, different way in which the reliabilist might pursue the attack is by invoking concepts such as causation and explanation. Baffled at trying to prevent the expressivist from claiming quite adequate reliability over Alaric's good behavior, someone may still insist that, according to the expressivist, the virtue of that behavior is not part of the cause of the verdict, and plays no role in explaining the verdict. But, the claim goes, only facts that cause or explain verdicts confer the title of knowledge. It is only when my belief that Bertha was in the river is caused or explained by Bertha's being in the river that I know she was. But expressivism must surely deny that my verdicts are ever caused or explained by moral facts, for this is not only a major motivation for expressivist theories, but even perhaps constitutive of them. An essential negative claim of expressivism should surely be that values are not part of the explanatory and causal order.

My response to this is once more to distinguish where we start, as we attempt to give a theory of ethics, and where we end up. I fully acknowledge the need to explain valuing without invoking values to which we respond. I cannot conceive of an axiarchic system—one in which rules and norms really do things—that remotely makes sense of the natural world and what we know about ourselves within it. This is indeed a main motivation toward expressivism. But once we have placed valuing within the natural order, and once we have become happy with the kinds of expression that we give to our commitments, does it follow that we must go on denying ourselves the right to explanatory, or even causal, claims that invoke values, rights, duties, and the rest? I do not (quite) think so. Perhaps Alaric is being feted by the rotary club because he behaved so well. His outstanding virtue explains his success. If Alaric had not behaved well he would not be being so honored. How can I say that? Obviously, I assess the explanation by considering the near possible worlds in which Alaric did not behave well. I conceive him as having acted in ways that do not command my admiration: for instance, Bertha never fell in, so nothing eventful took place; or she did, but he averted his eyes or ran away. In none of those worlds is Alaric being distinguished by the rotary club! Once more, the key is the expressivist ability to appropriate and evaluate counterfactuals. Once that is in place, true and false explanations invoking values can routinely be offered and appraised.

Explanation and causation may not be the same thing, but I see no principled difficulty in making the same moves with respect to causation: Alaric's behaving well set in train or brought about—caused, in other words—the rotary club's celebration. Any issues that remain puzzling about this are really problems of understanding different levels of causation, or causation by supervening properties. My own attitude is catholic: I see nothing unscientific or Pickwickian in allowing genuine causal power to supervening properties. For instance, Bertha's swallowing some river water may supervene on Bertha's swallowing a particular liter of river water; but it may be Bertha's swallowing some river water that makes her ill. Perhaps doing that always causes illness. Certainly it was also Bertha's swallowing *that* liter of river water that made her ill, but it is not as if there is any kind of mysterious causal overdetermination. There is no competition here, and it is not as if swallowing some river water is a mere epiphenomenon. It may actually be misleading to mention the particular contours of the event if it is the more general features that enter into the causal laws, as may be so in this case.

In ethics, I think that this is hardly ever so.[8] I do not think that the actions that it is right to admire, for instance, form a causally natural kind. It would be very difficult to think of a kind of cause that always produces them, or a kind of effect they always have. This being so, *better* explanations are found by looking downward to the subvening basis. Although it is true that Alaric's behaving well made him a social success, it is nearly always more illuminating to mention the underlying features: the promptness, the disregard for personal safety, and so on. After all, the rotary club would still be feting him for acting promptly and in disregard of personal safety even if, for some bizarre reason unknown to them, he was not in fact acting well (he suffered a temporary sequence of hallucinations that led him to go perfectly through the motions of acting well, and left no trace); and they would not be feting him had he acted well but in some quite different way (praying for Bertha, perhaps).[9] In this respect moral metaphysics is unlike that of other areas in which we have variable realization of a supervening level at the subvening level, but in which it may be causally illuminating and indeed scientifically essential to frame laws at the level of the supervening properties (temperature, for example, is a perfectly good explanatory concept in physics, although the temperatures of things are due to all kinds of different underlying sources of energy).[10]

Does this suggest that moral properties are epiphenomenal? One is talking of moral properties only in a minimalist spirit, of course: the propositional surface of the discourse means that we have moral predicates, and where we have predicates we ascend to properties. But do these properties have sufficient life to actually make things happen? I do not think my preference for subvening levels of explanation means that there is a principled obstacle to *casual* use of moral categories in explanation. We can talk of people revolting because they were treated unjustly, or thriving because they were treated well. I think we should accept these folk-causal stories as they are intended. Although it may be better for some purposes to descend to the subvening level, enough purposes may be served by indicating the moral features of the situation and relying on peoples' awareness that when a situation is one to which it is appropriate to react by talking of rights being transgressed or justice denied, then various consequences are likely to ensue.

We should note here that in the context of opposition to moral knowledge, it ill behooves a reliabilist to take the other tack, of disallowing genuine causal efficacy at the supervening level. If, prompted perhaps by a prejudice in favor of the microphysical, someone reserves causal efficacy to some favored level of atomic interaction, then they cannot possibly combine this with the view that we only know about features that have causal potency, or they will disallow most or even all of what we normally know about the world. For very few, if any, of us know of properties that have much chance of featuring in the lowest-level, final, basic, physical story, if indeed there could be such a story (I express skepticism about this in the paper cited in note 10). Hence, they will have to disengage knowledge from privileged, real, causal efficacy, and hence there will be no argument against moral knowledge deriving from the alleged causal inefficacy of the values that are its object.

Not Skepticism

We live in troubled times. Opinions conflict. The people need a sign. They check into the moral maze, but, like the cockroaches in the legendary motel, they do not check out. History gives us some understanding of our plight: Judaic ethics, classical ethics, Christian and Enlightenment values, are all tributaries of the present stream, but the waters do not mix and the currents are turbid. Perhaps we are irreversibly corrupted, no longer adapted for moral knowledge. Some even claim that we are only able to look with nostalgia on a dim golden age when it all was easy.[11]

Can an expressivist make sense of this range of thought? I think as much sense as can be made of it, for it does not really represent a coherent range of thought, so much as the expression of a mood of disenchantment or hopelessness. Certainly I hold that we can make sense of *particular* occasions of skepticism: times when we are apt to proffer an opinion, but are uneasily aware that we might be wrong. We contemplate, I say, a potential improvement in our sensibility, manufactured by the bringing to bear of facts and standards in ways that we would approve (that is, we would regard the processes leading to change with approval) and resulting in a shift of attitude. This is the ordinary process of education or correction of attitude, parallel to the correction of everyday empirical belief by the onset of further evidence or the realignment of defective theory. It is what goes on in everyday moral discussion, and first-order ethics makes its brave attempts to lubricate its progress.

The iteration of local improvements might eventually mean a revision of *each* attitude and commitment seriatim, as we spiral away from whatever defects mar our present sensibilities. In this sense we can even contemplate the possibility that we are everywhere in error. We might get to a place from which we can see our present attitudes as all infected with error (consider, for an example of how this might happen, doubts about whether it is appropriate to work in terms of concepts like "rights," or "obligation").

What is not guaranteed by this kind of thought is the intelligibility of a different, radical kind of global error: the possibility that the truth may be nowhere that we can get to from here. Just as Cartesian skepticism is not guaranteed to be coherent by reflection on everyday processes of belief revision, so the idea that moral truth may be entirely and totally hidden from even our best efforts at improvement is not guaranteed to be coherent by reflection on those efforts and their structure. Nevertheless, possibilities are things that we allow or disallow, and the policy of allowing a possibility may in principle have benefits that outweigh the impossibility of verifying whether it is realized. Wittgenstein seems to have embraced this pragmatic attitude, but he did not fully see what it would really require to work:

> We must not forget: even our more refined, more philosophical doubts have a foundation in instinct. E.g. that expressed in "We can never know. . . ." Continuing accessibility to further arguments. We should find people to whom we could not teach this mentally inferior. *Still* incapable of forming a certain concept.[12]

His conception is one of global skepticism playing a regulative role. It is not that the possibilities that a Cartesian skeptic cites have to be thought of philosophically as genuine possibilities, but rather that there is something right about the state (attitude) of *regarding* them as possibilities. Regarding them as real, open possibilities is a part of mental hygiene, and being unable to do so would be a mark of mental inferiority. Wittgenstein however only sketches the alleged benefit: the "continuing accessibility to further argument." The trouble is that this is really no defence of a friendly attitude to radical Cartesian skepticism: first, continued accessibility to further argument is already justified by the fallibilist attitudes that allow that we may be wrong on any particular occasion, without allowing that the truth may be nowhere that we can get to; and second, Cartesian skepticism is not actually an apt way of expressing continued accessibility to argument. By raising the possibility that the truth is nowhere that we might get to from here, it only stifles and stultifies the rationale for argument. What is the point in doing our best if our fallen natures are such that our best may have nothing to do with the real truth?[13] If anything, the pragmatics of the matter speak firmly against allowing this kind of radical global skepticism as a possibility, for its effect can be nothing but paralysis.

So let us disallow radical global moral skepticism. At least we can never be shown wrong to do this, because nobody can sketch the kind of awakening that might await us. Of course, one might be poleaxed into some total change, along the lines of being born again. But the work of representing such a change as an *awakening* would already guarantee that it is somewhere we might get to from here. And after all, is not this the sensible attitude? We can beat the breast for lost moral knowledge in the study perhaps, but paraphrasing a rather happier move of Wittgenstein's, just try in a real case to doubt that some situation is not as good as it could be, that someone's benevolence is not a virtue, and so on. Or try to think that maybe goodness and virtue really lie somewhere quite different from where we imagine them—in pointlessly counting pebbles on the beach or doing handstands, for example. It does not work, and the reason is that our attitudes of approval, admiration, shame, and guilt are adapted for certain kinds of ends—ones of social coordination and human flourishing—and have no object when those ends are missing. It might be asked pointedly whether such an explanation is available to anyone other than an expressivist, but I am not here concerned with polemics of this kind.

Not Just Coherence

When talking about knowledge I urged that the notion of what counts as an improvement in an epistemic position sits firmly in the center of the picture and resists analysis or displacement by any less overtly evaluative notion. Similarly, when we make sense of the idea that we may be wrong in one of our values, we contemplate the possibility of improvement that may make us change our minds. What kinds of improvement might be in view? Contemporary moral epistemology offers a number of pointers, but none of them, in my view, comes near to exhausting the field.

Suppose first that someone suggests that moral epistemology is entirely *coherentist,* so that the content of our worry is in effect that our current system is not coherent. Well, is it likely that becoming more coherent is the *only* kind of improvement in may own sensibility that I can contemplate? No increases of imagination, sensitivity, or empathy? No cultivation of hidden joys or unlocking of virgin springs of contentment, no larger views or wider sympathies? This sounds like nonsense. And similarly the like view that the method must be entirely one of improving reflective equilibrium. Such suggestions appear to take the current *stock* of attitudes as the datum, with the problem only that of making them rub along properly with each other; whereas often real improvement must require an expansion and change of the stock. We struggle not only for something coherent, but also for something sufficiently large and comprehensive to do justice to the complexities of human living. For all I can see a morality firmly centered on the decalogue may be coherent, and its adherents may pride themselves on their equilibrium, but I could hardly regard it as adequate because of that. Sensibilities are defective often not through being incoherent, in the sense that they issue in conflicting attitudes, but through being immature, inadequate, oversimplified, or out of key in other ways.

There are, however, complexities here. Let me call the kind of coherence just identified and contrasted with wider imaginative expansion, a *close-minded* coherence. Then we can imagine someone proposing that a more generous, open-minded attitude to the possibility of expansion nevertheless is a kind of ideal of coherence. We saw in the last section that we can only deal with the idea of improvement in terms of places that we can get to from where we are. In other words, if a blossoming of the imagination presents itself as an improvement, then there must be something in our present attitudes that commends it. This being so, our present attitudes contain some kind of incoherence, so long as the blossoming has not taken place. We realize that we are apt to be forming inadequate judgments, even while we cannot yet see how to improve them. Seen this way, ideals of comprehensiveness in attitude can seem to be part of the idea of total coherence.[14] I am not, however, convinced that much hangs on this. The point remains that we can generate examples of irrational and underexamined sensibilities whose defects are not most naturally described as defects of coherence, but in other terms. The fact that when we fear that we are like that we have only our own conceptions of what would count as improvement to work with should not disguise that central truth.

Maturity, then, is an ideal just as much as equilibrium. But is the latter an ideal at all? Let us say that in a strong sense a sensibility is in reflective equilibrium if it never issues in conflicting attitudes to any actual or possible situation. Its possessor is never tugged equally toward condemning and allowing the same course of action, or both commending and disapproving of a single character. Is strong reflective equilibrium then an ideal? The answer is not obvious. Certainly, a lot of first-order ethics consists in illustrating places where our attitudes conflict, and encouraging processes of resolution. It seems, as we indulge in such exercises, that we have as an ideal a sensibility that just knows the one answer and that while giving due weight to conflicting claims nevertheless identifies which answer it is. On the other hand, being susceptible to conflicting tugs does not seem to be a vice; on the contrary, someone who does not feel the conflict in difficult cases is often myopic or ideologically close-minded, and it is this very single-mindedness that often needs rectification. One might then be inclined to substitute a different ideal, one of weak reflective equilibrium, thought of as a state at which one knows that one has done one's best. The ship can be repaired no further, at least not by me, or not without external awakening. But this best may be insufficient to remove dilemmas and perplexities. That this is always so is the characteristic claim of ancient skepticism, which contemplates cheerfully the inevitability of *isosthenia,* or the equal strength of opposing arguments, and of course counsels the eventual suspension of judgment and resulting *ataraxia* or tranquility. I do not for a moment believe that this is always so, but it may sometimes be so, and the possibility that it is so more often than we like to think certainly puts a question mark in front of much of the practice of first-order ethical theory.

Not Abstract Principles, Not Situations

In the final sections I will sketch some thoughts that are not strictly consequences of a quasi-realist construction of the practice of ethics, but seem to be supported by it, and seem perhaps to offer it support in return. What I have in mind is a phenomenon, or perhaps a range of phenomena, that we can call the human scale of ethics. By this I mean that ethical truth is not found either at the glacially abstract level of simplistic deontology or at the teeming, multiplicitous level of total situations. It occupies a middle ground.

What does this mean? Consider first the suggestion that in ethics we respond only to "total situations." The analogy is with aesthetics. In aesthetics it is often impossible to abstract out features of a successful work of art and imagine them as transferable—apt to confer the same success on any work that possesses them. For example, the success of the painting may have something to do with the contrast between the yellow and the blue, but in another painting the contrast might be neutral, and in another it might jar. The rapt expression on the face of a saint that is so ravishing in a Bellini could only be embarrassing or kitsch in a Warhol. Aesthetics resists abstraction, and the particularist suggestion is that ethics does likewise. The suggestion fits well, of course, with a predominantly perceptual theory of moral discrimination, which emphasizes the similarity between seeing the virtue or value of a subject matter with seeing its beauty, or seeing any other property that supervenes upon only the whole complex of other perceptual features.

Such a position is attractive as a particularist antidote both to simplistic deontology and simplistic consequentialism. But it is important to realize that it cannot possibly be right as it stands, because a great deal of ethical thought, and indeed the cutting edge of ethics, concerns how to act. But such thought is essentially a matter of selecting and weighing features that recur from one situation to another. In trying to discover what to do, we imagine different actions, and register their good and bad features. It is essential to this process that these features are reliably extracted from any contexts or total situations in which we have come across them, and carry some moral import when transplanted into the new hypothetical situation. We need to be able to think the action *a* would involve disappointing the children, but *b* would mean breaking a promise to Grandma, and *c* would be difficult to justify to Uncle, and so on. If these features lost their moral import just as soon as they were abstracted from other cases, in which they had been marinaded with others to give some holistic moral gestalt, then this process would be totally unjustified.

The artist, too, can wonder what to do, and it may be objected that a situation ethics can suppose that our thought processes mimic those of the creative artist. But this is not the way it is. The artist may deploy his or her powers of imagination, trying as hard as may be to visualize how this painting would be with such-and-such a feature, or how this symphony would sound with such-and-such an addition. It is not usually antecedently given that the feature will bear a positive or negative charge on the particular occasion. It has to be tried out, either in imagination or, frequently, on the canvas or keyboard. Whereas in ethics we usually know in advance that it is going to count as an objection to a course of action that it disappoints the children or means breaking a promise to Grandma. Certainly, the extent to which such values must give way to others will hinge on which other features the situation displays. But that they have a weight, and point in one direction or the other, is given antecedently to any more concrete engagement with the details of the case. Otherwise it would be a creative act even to know which features to think of. It might just not occur that promise-breaking is even relevant, just as it does not occur to the artist to put a saintly Bellini face into the middle of his landscape. The point can actually be made without introducing time: if we want to recount a past feat of heroism or villainy, we know which aspects of the situation must be told. And it is significant that we can do this without aspiring to a kind of action replay of the total event, whereas in aesthetics a description of a painting is no basis at all for a genuine judgment of its merit. Conversely, we can know in advance that whatever the decision-making situation, certain features, even quite substantial, obvious empirical features, are going to be morally irrelevant, whereas it is doubtful that you could ever know in advance that whatever the painting, some substantial empirical feature will be irrelevant to its aesthetic value.

It is harder to prove that it is an error to reverse direction entirely, and to hope for abstract principles of consequentialism or deontology that are simple to express and absolute in bearing in the same way and with the same weight on each and every case. The continued existence of systems that embrace just such principles suggests that the purposes of ethics might be served in such a way. But I take it that they do not stand up well under scrutiny: absolute duties of allegiance, or respect for property, or truth-telling, promise-keeping, and the rest seldom appeal to the theoretically innocent when tyrants, axe-men, emergencies, and the other nightmares of ethics are introduced.

As its wisest practitioners have always known, ethics should therefore present a human scale, neither totally resistant to discursive abstraction nor wedded to it to the exclusion of mitigating detail.[15] This is exactly what we should expect if we think of ethics created as a system of pressures on thought and action, adapted to human needs and serving human purposes. Obviously, if what I said above was correct, a totally particularist ethics would not enable us to think about hypothetical situations in the way we can (and the dismal history of casuistry gives an actual example of the degeneration that ensues). On the other hand, we do not need to fly abstract principles outside the human atmosphere; we do not need that it is always absolutely wrong to tell a lie provided we reliably feel the pressure against doing so, regret situations where it becomes necessary, and so on. The human scale means that we can fruitfully argue about moderately new situations, deploy comparisons and look for analogies without fearing that all such thought is irrelevant, as a pure particularist supposes, or at best a holding operation until the final big principle arrives, as the other extreme requires.

For the expressivist, the explanation of the human scale is easy. We are attempting to adjust attitudes in order to meet needs and further purposes, and these needs and purposes are themselves on a human scale. For other theories, the explanation may not be so smooth. Might moral truth not be as the particularist supposes: irredeemably particular, and never capable of abstraction? Or might it not be as the absolutist supposes, absurdly simple and highly abstract? A realist, as I see it, should address such questions by thinking about the contours of the moral truth to which we are able to respond, but then it is hard to see any a priori reason why that truth should be on a human scale. There is even the unpleasant possibility that the real truth is on one end of the extremes, even though we are condemned to operate in the middle. Once more, then, expressivism has a distinct explanatory advantage over at least some other kinds of approach.

Not (Basically) Propositions

There is a final explanation in this area that also deserves consideration. Why is it so difficult to frame interesting candidates for moral knowledge? Why is it easier to believe that there is knowledge of some kind in an area (lies are bad, happiness is good) than it is to fill out the propositions we might be supposed to know? I started by mentioning the inarticulate good person; the Tolstoyan saint whose knowledge of life and feeling remains essentially practical. He or she just knows how to sympathize, when to be firm, when to act, and when to withdraw. The expressivist diagnosis is that to serve their function, attitudes do not need to be reflected in a fully determinate propositional content, ascribing each act a determinate merit in any possible context. For most living it is enough to feel the everyday pressures: we are for benevolence and humanity, against ingratitude and lying. We do not normally have to confront the puzzle cases philosophers develop, in which we are forced to rank these attachments, or to choose one against another. Vague benevolence, and vague sympathy with the public interest and the rules that protect it is usually enough. We are not trained for every kind of dilemma, stress, crisis, or emergency, and there is no reason to expect the network of attitudes that serves us in normal life effortlessly to cover new cases. We may hope there is one right answer, and may struggle to find which answer best accommodates all our concerns. And for good reason we may be reluctant to give up this struggle and shrug our shoulders. But there may be a time when in spite of that we are creatively extending old ways of feeling, or even creating new ways of feeling, rather than automatically extending old ones. Extending the moral circle by taking the disadvantaged, or future generations, or animals into the moral community may be salient contemporary examples.

The view that there is sometimes this residue of creativity may be a melancholy for any practitioners of first-order ethics who dedicate themselves to resolving new problems in the light of old and relatively settled ideas. All I can say is that I personally find the flexibility it substitutes quite liberating, and even a small cause for cheer.

Notes

1. John Mackie, *Ethics, Inventing Right and Wrong* (New York: Penguin, 1977).
2. Probably my most accessible discussion is in *Spreading the Word* (Oxford: Oxford University Press, 1984), chapter 5.

3. Gilbert Ryle, " 'If,' 'So,' and 'Because' " in *Collected Papers,* volume 2 (London: Hutchison, 1971).

4. See Antonio Damasio, *Descartes' Error* (New York: Putnam, 1994), especially chapter 3.

5. The way I come to say this is best explained in *Spreading the Word,* chapter 5.

6. See my "Knowledge, Truth, and Reliability" in *Essays in Quasi-Realism* (New York: Oxford University Press, 1993).

7. So I argue in "Circles, Finks, Smells, and Biconditionals," *Philosophical Perspectives,* volume 7, ed. James Tomberlin (Atascadero, Cal.: Ridgeview Publishing Co., 1993).

8. Here I am almost completely in agreement with Jeremy Waldron, as in his review of Alan Gilbert's *Democratic Individuality* in the *California Law Review* 80 (1992), 1361–1441.

9. An apposite and amusing application of the same point is Jeremy Waldron's discussion of the Donner tragedy, instanced by Michael Moore, who claimed (in "Moral Reality Revisited," *Michigan Law Review* 90 [1992], 2492–93) that it was because Passed Midshipman Woodward was "simply no damn good" that the party perished. Waldron correctly points out that it was because his no-damn-goodness was realized in rather specific ways that the party perished; had Midshipman Woodward been no damn good in various other ways, all might have been well. See also my "Just Causes" in *Essays in Quasi-Realism.*

10. A complicated discussion of the issues here is given in my "Physics, Identity, and Folk Burglar Prevention" in *Essays in Quasi-Reaslism.*

11. Alisdair MacIntyre, *After Virtue* (London: Duckworth, 1981).

12. Ludwig Wittgenstein, *Culture and Value* (Oxford: Basil Blackwell, 1980), 73.

13. It is interesting in this connection that a real problem for Puritan divines and philosophers was always to locate the bit of us (accessibility to revelation, or reason) that was not quite as fallen as the rest. I am indebted here to remarks by Michael Gill.

14. Michael DePaul (in "Two conceptions of Coherence Methods in Ethics," *Mind* 96 [1987]) makes the distinction between conservative and radical coherence methods, where radical methods involve changes that are not made by following through the implications of extant judgments. DePaul calls this a coherence method, although I do not think he directly defends the description.

15. I have in mind Aristotle and Hume, who seem to me to be at one on this.

4

Intuitionism, Pluralism, and the Foundations of Ethics

Robert Audi

Ethical intuitionism is historically important, widely referred to, and generally considered a major position in the foundations of ethics. But it is not widely discussed in depth. This is in part because, although it is held by some leading philosophers, its resources are often underestimated. It is certainly conceived divergently among ethical theorists, and those who find its central elements compelling may often think it easier and better simply to argue for their position under another name than to indicate what kind of intuitionism they hold and defend their position under that rubric. My aim here is to clarify intuitionism, to bring out some of its strengths and weaknesses, and to reassess the case for giving it a more significant place in contemporary ethical theory.

The timeliness of an explication and appraisal of intuitionism can be seen through examining the apparent tension between the almost unquestioned relevance of *intuitions* to philosophical method and the apparently easy rejection, by many who appeal to them, of intuitionism.[1] The appeal to intuitions is a pervasive and approved strategy in contemporary philosophical discourse. A good philosophical theory is widely taken to be one that gives an adequate account of our intuitions about the subject matter of the theory. A good ethical theory, for instance, should largely explain our intuitions about when we are or are not being unfair, when we must go out of our way to help others, and when we may or may not break a promise. But only a few of the many philosophers who appeal to intuitions as support for their ethical theories (or, similarly, to "considered judgments," to what "seems plausible," or the like) would maintain ethical intuitionism. This calls for explanation. One would think that in virtually any form, intuitionism in ethics is above all an approach which justifies generalizations in ethics by appeal to intuitions, as one might support the generalization, "We should not interfere with the liberty of others," by considering judgments about cases, including cases in which one's own liberty is restricted. It might be said, e.g., that our intuitions go against the view that those who can increase the sum total of happiness in the world by having children are obligated to do so whether they want to or not.

Many who oppose intuitionism make such appeals to intuitions in establishing a basis for their ethical views. Why, then, do so many ethical theorists strongly resist combining their appeal to intuitions with maintaining some form of intuitionism? Given the degree of evidential cogency commonly ascribed to intuitions, one would think that intuitionism might at worst be guilty, not of building castles in the sky, but of resting too much on intuitive foundations that cannot sustain the weight they are meant to bear.

To assess ethical intuitionism and the role of intuitions in supporting it, we need a clearer conception of what it is, an account of its relation to ethical intuitions, and a theory of how both are related to the distinction between rationalism and empiricism in moral epistemology. If this task of explication succeeds, it will yield more than a deeper understanding of intuitionism. It will provide the raw materials of a framework for moral theory that overcomes many of the difficulties confronting intuitionism, accounts for the role of intuitions in moral reasoning, and provides the outline of a moral epistemology. In the light of the conception of intuitionism that emerges from the first three parts of this essay, I will briefly develop this framework. The concluding parts will appraise intuitionism as a restricted version of this wider framework.

Traditional Ethical Intuitionism

There are currently two main uses of the term "intuitionism." On one use, intuitionism is conceived as an overall kind of ethical theory; on the other, it is a moral epistemology held to be characteristic of such theories. My aim is in part to determine whether either of these common conceptions is adequate to the best intuitionist theories available.

In the former, overall conception, intuitionism has three main characteristics. (1) It is an ethical *pluralism,* a position affirming an irreducible plurality of basic moral principles. (2) Each principle centers on a different kind of ground, in the sense of a factor implying a prima facie moral duty, such as making a promise or noticing a person who will bleed to death without one's help. (3) Each principle is taken to be in some sense intuitively known. (1) and (2) are structural and conceptual; they affirm a plurality of basic principles affecting different kinds of conduct, and they thus deny, against both Kantian and utilitarian theories, that there is just one basic moral principle. (3) is epistemological; it locates the basic principles with respect to knowledge.

In the second, epistemological conception of intuitionism, the view is roughly the thesis that basic moral judgments and basic moral principles are justified by the noninferential deliverances of a rational, intuitive faculty, a mental capacity that contrasts with sense perception, clairvoyance, and other possible routes to justification. A number of writers, particularly critics of intuitionism, conceive intuitionism as implying the stronger thesis that the intuitive faculty yields indefeasible knowledge of self-evident moral truths. One concern of this chapter is whether this stronger conception is justified.

The position of W. D. Ross is widely regarded as a version of intuitionism in both the overall and epistemological senses: as pluralist and as implying that we have intuitive moral knowledge.[2] My chief concern is intuitionist moral epistemology. This epistemology is, however, fundamental in intuitionism as an overall ethical view, and an examination of the epistemology will ultimately lead us to a discussion of the pluralism of the view.[3] We can best clarify this epistemology and appraise the adequacy of the formulation of it just given, if we explore a representative intuitionism. Ross is at once an important moral philosopher and an excellent example of an intuitionist. We can learn much by examining the basic elements of his ethical theory. In the light of that examination, and building in part on a reconstructed Rossian theory, I will outline a general (though not a complete) account of justification in ethics. Intuitionism in various forms can then be seen as largely a restricted version of that account.

In what is probably his most important ethical work, *The Right and the Good* (1930), Ross proposed, as fundamental both to philosophical ethics and to everyday life, a now famous list of prima facie duties: duties of fidelity (promise-keeping, including honesty) and reparation, of justice and gratitude, of beneficence and self-improvement, and of noninjury.[4] In calling these duties prima facie, Ross meant to indicate that even when we acquire one, say by making a promise, the act in question need not be our final duty, since a competing duty, for instance to attend a sick child, might override the original duty.[5] This does not imply that a prima facie duty ever lacks *moral weight;* one should, e.g., regret having to break a promise, and perhaps must make reparations for it, even when one did right in breaking it. The point is simply that a prima facie duty is not necessarily final, and to recognize such a duty as applicable to oneself is not sufficient for knowing what, all things considered, one should *do.*

A word of further explication is in order. Because it is only under certain conditions that a prima facie duty indicates a final duty—roughly, a duty "all things considered"—prima facie duties are sometimes called *conditional duties.*[6] This misleadingly suggests that we have prima facie duties only when they prevail (i.e., express one's duty all things considered). Worse yet, it may suggest that the *content* of prima facie duties is conditional, as where you promise to pay a bill *if* your friend does not have enough money. Here there is a condition for your *having* the duty to pay, at all: your conditional duty becomes "operative" only if your friend does not pay. But whether, if you do have this duty, it is just prima facie rather than final, is left open. Prima facie duties, far from being possessed only conditionally, are necessarily possessed when their grounds are present, and they are often not conditional in content. To illustrate both points, if you promise to pay the bill (period), then you thereby have a prima facie duty to do so; and you still have this duty even if a conflicting duty, say to save a life, overrides your prima facie duty to keep the promise. This is why one needs an excuse for not keeping the promise and may owe an explanation to the disappointed promisee. Without a satisfactory excuse, one is to some degree morally deficient.

The central idea underlying the Rossian notion of a prima facie duty, I suggest, is that of a duty which is—given the presence of its ground—*ineradicable but overridable*. The presence of its ground (a notion Ross does not explicate) is crucial. If, e.g., others could not benefit from our help, there would be no prima facie duty of beneficence, since our ground for the duty would be absent. A prima facie duty that is ineradicable given the presence of its ground, is nonetheless *cancelable* by removal of that ground. Consider the duty to keep a promise. Where the promisee releases one from a promise or where the fulfillment of the duty becomes impossible, say because the person one had a duty to help has died, there is no longer any such duty. But overriding conditions do not cancel the duty they override. A duty's being overridden by conflicting prima facie duties implies that its ground is outweighed, but not that it is removed. A superior counterforce blocks, but does not eliminate, the force it overpowers.

Ross stressed a number of features of his position, and at least some of these have become part of the common conception (so far as there is one) of intuitionism. First, he insisted on its irreducible pluralism; he argued that there is no one thing, such as enhancing goodness in the world, that is our only direct, overall duty.[7] Second, he emphasized the self-evidence of the propositions expressing our prima facie duties. Here is the central passage:

> That an act *qua* fulfilling a promise, or *qua* effecting a just distribution of good . . . is *prima facie* right, is self-evident; not in the sense that it is evident from the beginning of our lives, or as soon as we attend to the proposition for the first time, but in the sense that when we have reached sufficient mental maturity and have given sufficient attention to the proposition it is evident without any need of proof, or of evidence beyond itself. It is evident just as a mathematical axiom, or the validity of a form of inference, is evident. . . . In our confidence that these propositions are true there is involved the same confidence in our reason that is involved in our confidence in mathematics. . . . In both cases we are dealing with propositions that cannot be proved, but that just as certainly need no proof.[8]

Third, Ross apparently intended this claim of self-evidence to hold for certain kinds of act, not particular deeds. He says, e.g., "we are never certain that any particular possible act is . . . right," and, clarifying this, that "we apprehend *prima facie* rightness to belong to the nature of any fulfillment of a promise. From this we come by reflection to apprehend the self-evident *prima facie* rightness of an individual act of a particular type. . . . But no act is ever, in virtue of falling under some general description, necessarily actually right; its rightness depends on its whole nature and not any element in it."[9] His positive point, applied to promising, is in part that when one thinks clearly about what it *is* to promise a particular friend to do something, one can see that doing the deed is called for and would be right barring special circumstances, such as a medical emergency. His negative point, in the Rossian terminology just introduced, is something like this: from a general description of the grounds that yield a prima facie duty, e.g. from the description of an act of mine as a promise, it does not follow that the duty (here the duty to keep the promise) is not overriden, nor is it self-evident that it is not overridden, however clear that may be in many cases. It is not self-evident, for instance, that no medical emergency will intervene and override my duty to keep the promise.

The fourth and final point here is that in explaining how we apprehend the moral truths in question, Ross appealed to something like what we commonly call intuitions. He said that if someone challenges

> our view that there is a special obligatoriness attaching to the keeping of promises because it is self-evident that the only duty is to produce as much good as possible, we have to ask ourselves whether we really, when we reflect, *are* convinced that [as he takes G. E. Moore to hold] this is self-evident . . . it seems self-evident that a promise simply as such, is something that *prima facie* ought to be kept . . . the moral convictions of thoughtful and well-educated people are the data of ethics, just as sense-perceptions are the data of a natural science. Just as some of the latter have to be rejected as illusory, so have some of the former; but as the latter are rejected only when they conflict with other more accurate sense-perceptions, the former are rejected only when they conflict with convictions which stand better the test of reflection.[10]

Ross does not make clear whether the imagined conflicts are ever resolvable by appeal to generalizations, such as one to the effect that promises to meet with students have priority over promises to campaign for political candidates. Suppose I discover that keeping a promise to comment on a long manuscript will take vastly more time than anyone could foresee. Something rather general may then occur to me (if I follow Ross): that I have prima facie duties of other sorts, arising, for instance, from duties of beneficence as well as from other promises, such as promises to my family or friends. As I think, in this light, about my overall duties, my sense that I must prepare the comments may conflict with my sense that I should fulfill other duties. Ross countenances this kind of conflict; but because he treats "the verdicts of the moral consciousness of the best people as the foundation on which we must build" and is thinking of judgments about concrete moral options, he seems to hold the view that ethical generalizations do not *independently* carry evidential weight in such conflicts. One should not, e.g., appeal to a second-order generalization that duties of justice are stronger than duties of fidelity. Rather, one should focus on the specific facts and, in that light, determine what one's actual duty is.

The task of conflict resolution here is very much like that of using Aristotelian practical wisdom in dealing with a moral problem. It is possible, for Ross as for Aristotle, that a rule emerges *on the basis of the resolution* one reaches; but there is not necessarily any rule *antecedently* governing each particular case one may encounter. I may, through my reflection on such a conflict of duties, frame a rule for similar future cases; but I do not bring to every case a ready-made rule that, irrespective of my intuitive judgments about that case, will tell me what to do.

In this rejection of the view that there are always second-order generalizations available to resolve conflicts of prima facie duties, Ross seems to be, as regards judgments of overall obligation, a *particularist* rather than a generalist:

he holds that we must attend to particular cases in order to determine what generalizations hold, even if it is repeatable features of those cases, such as their being acts of promising, that reveal the general truths we reach through reflection on the cases.[11] This is not a point about what *can* be known, but about the order of knowing: our basic moral knowledge—even of prima facie duties—comes from reflection on particular cases, especially those calling for moral decision, where those cases are properly conceived in terms of their repeatable features. Our basic moral knowledge does not come from reflection on abstract, universal moral propositions. We do not, for instance, grasp the Kantian categorical imperative a priori, and then apply it to the issue at hand with a view to formulating, on the basis of it, a "theorem" that resolves our problem. That abstract, monistic approach is also precluded by Ross's pluralism. But pluralism is not his only demand: he would also reject even a set of mutually irreducible rules if they were abstractions imposed on particular cases in the way the categorical imperative or utilitarianism might be, rather than derived from reflection on particular cases.

An example of commitment to such a set of rules would be an a priori *hierarchism,* a view on which some of the prima facie duties automatically outweigh one or more others. Ross would reject this because, for him, as for intuitionists in general, there is neither a *complete* ordering of duties in terms of moral weights—a ranking of duties from strongest to least strong—nor even any *pairwise ordering*—a ranking of some pair of the prima facie duties, as where the duty of nonmaleficence (say, to avoid killing) is always said to outweigh that of beneficence (e.g., to save life).[12] These points do not entail that *no* comparisons between strengths of (prima facie) duties can be proper objects of intuition. Given a typical pattern of facts concerning a babysitter annoyed by a cranky infant, one might have an intuition that the babysitter's duty not to flog the child to death is stronger than the duty not to give it a heavy but nonfatal dose of vodka.

We can now compare Ross's view with the common conception of intuitionism (in moral epistemology) noted above. He fits that conception in holding that the basic moral truths—which he takes to be constituted by his principles of prima facie duty—are self-evident. But he does not posit a special rational faculty. He is not committed to the existence of a "part" of the mind, or even "capacity of reason," required only for moral thought. He talks, to be sure, of moral consciousness and of "apprehension" (roughly, understanding) of those self-evident truths (by "apprehension" he often means a species of what is commonly meant by "intuition," which will be explicated in the next section. But in presenting his moral epistemology he emphasizes that the prima facie moral duties are recognized in the same way as the truth of mathematical axioms and logical truths.

Ross also speaks (e.g., in the same passage) of our apprehending the self-evidence of the relevant moral and mathematical propositions. He does not always distinguish apprehending the truth of a proposition that *is* self-evident from apprehending *its self-evidence.*[13] This is an important point, since (if there are self-evident propositions) it should be easy to apprehend the truth of at least some of them, whereas the epistemic *status* of propositions (e.g. their justification or self-evidence or apriority) is a paradigm source of disagreement. It should be noted, however, that even apprehension of the self-evidence of propositions does not require having a special faculty. But suppose it did: Does Ross's overall position commit him to our having noninferential knowledge of the self-evidence, as opposed to the truth, of the relevant principles? I think not, and if I am correct then one apparently common view of intuitionism can be set aside as a misconception. Let me explain.

We might know that a moral principle is self-evident only on a limited basis, say from knowing the conceptual as opposed to empirical (e.g., observational) character of the grounds on which we know that principle to be true. We would know its truth *on* these grounds; we would know its self-evidence through knowledge *about* the grounds. For instance, if we take ourselves to know a moral proposition, say that there is a prima facie (moral) duty to keep promises, (a) on the basis of understanding the concepts involved in this proposition and (b) noninferentially (roughly, without dependence on one or more premises as evidence), we may plausibly think it follows, from our having this kind of knowledge of the moral proposition, that it has the status of self-evidence. This way of knowing the status of a Rossian proposition expressing a basic prima facie duty requires having concepts of self-evidence, of noninferentiality, and, in effect, of a priori knowledge. But *none* of these concepts is required simply to know that there is a prima facie duty to keep promises. It is, however, that first-order proposition, the principle that promise-keeping is a duty, and not the second-order thesis that this principle is self-evident, which is the fundamental thing we must be able to know intuitively if a Rossian intuitionism is to succeed. As moral agents we need intuitive knowledge of our duties; we do not need intuitive (or even other) knowledge of the status of the principles of duty.

This brings us to the last key point in the most common conception of intuitionism: the idea that it posits *indefeasible justification*—roughly, justification that cannot be undermined or overriden—for any cognition grounded in a genuine intuition. Ross is not committed to this general idea, even if he might have regarded some moral beliefs as indefeasibly justified. Once it is seen that the primary role of intuition is to give us direct, (i.e., noninferential) knowledge or justified belief of the *truth,* rather than of the self-evidence, of moral propositions (especially certain moral principles), there is less reason to think that moral beliefs resting on an intuitive grasp of principles must be considered indefeasibly justified.

Indeed, even if self-evidence were the main element that is intuitively apprehended, Ross would be entitled to hold—and in fact stresses—that there can be conflicts of moral "convictions" in which some are given up "just as" in scientific inquiry some perceptions are given up as illusory (see the quotation above from *The Right and the Good,* pp. 39–40). If intuitions are sometimes properly given up in this way—and the convictions in question are apparently a species of what are commonly called intuitions—the justification possessed by intuitions is plainly defeasible (subject to being undermined or overridden);

and so, at least with respect to moral judgments of particular deeds, defeasibility is to be expected.

This brings us to something that does not seem to have been generally noticed by critics of intuitionism and is at least not emphasized by Ross. The view that the justification of moral intuitions is defeasible, even when grounded in the careful reflection Ross thought appropriate to them, is quite consistent with his claim that the self-evident truths in question do not admit of proof. That a proposition does not admit of proof is an epistemic fact about *it* and leaves open that a person might have only poor or overridden grounds for *believing* it. This logical and epistemic fact does not entail that one cannot lose one's justification for believing it, or even fail to become justified in believing it upon considering it, or fail to find it intuitive.

It must be granted, however, that by putting us in mind of the simplest logical and mathematical truths, Ross's unprovability claim easily creates the mistaken impression that genuine intuitions are either infallible or justificationally indefeasible, or both. Nonetheless, there is nothing in Ross's theory as set out in *The Right and the Good* which is inconsistent with the rather striking disclaimer made by his great intuitionist predecessor, G. E. Moore, following his sketch of what, in his view, constitutes an intuition.[14] Moore says that in calling propositions intuitions he means

> *merely* to assert that they are incapable of proof; I imply nothing whatever as to the manner or origin of our cognition of them. Still less do I imply (as most Intuitionists have done) that any proposition whatever is true, *because* we cognise it in a particular way or by the exercise of any particular faculty: I hold, on the contrary, that in every way in which it is possible to cognise a true proposition it is also possible to cognise a false one.[15]

Apparently, for Moore as for Ross, even if the truth or self-evidence of a proposition can be apprehended by reflection, there need be no special faculty yielding the apprehensions; and whatever the basis of those apprehensions, it is of a kind that can produce mistaken beliefs, including some that one would naturally take to be apprehensions of self-evident truths.[16] Anyone who is aware that mistaken beliefs can arise from apprehensions or intuitions (or in any other way one can "cognise" a proposition) should be willing to regard intuitions as capable of being unjustified or even false.

Intuitions, Intuitionism, and Reflection

We have seen that if Ross's view is a paradigm of intuitionism, then a widely held conception of intuitionism is inadequate. Above all, he is (by his major views) committed neither to the existence of a special faculty of intuition—such as a capacity peculiar to ethical subject matter—nor to the epistemic indefeasibility of the "self-evident" judgments that reflection yields. The same seems true of Moore, for reasons I have suggested, but I cannot pursue Moore's views separately here. This section will clarify further what an intuitionist like

Ross *is* committed to. I begin with a sketch of the notion of an intuition. I mean, of course, "intuition" in the *cognitive sense,* a psychological state like (and perhaps a kind of) belief. We have not been discussing, and need not explicitly discuss, intuitions in the *propositional sense,* that is, propositions of the kind Moore (as quoted above) took to be unprovable, a kind supposed to be fitting objects of intuitions in the cognitive sense.

To summarize my negative points about intuitions, I have contended that they need not be infallible or indefeasibly justified deliverances of a special faculty that is distinct from our general rational capacity as manifested in grasping logical and (pure) mathematical truths, and presumably other kinds of truths, ethical and nonethical, as well. What, then, is distinctive of an intuition? I shall suggest four main characteristics.[17]

First, an intuition must be noninferential, in the sense that the intuited proposition in question is not—at the time it is intuitively held—held on the basis of a premise. Call this the *noninferentiality (or directness) requirement.* Some intuitionists have emphasized this, and it is at least implicit in Ross and Moore.[18] If we do not grant it, we cannot explain why Ross and Moore should hold the stronger view that what we know intuitively is not provable; for if they took intuition to be potentially inferential and thus potentially based on premises, they would surely have addressed the question whether, for at least some intuitively known propositions, there might be premises to serve as a ground or a proof of those propositions and thereby as an inferential basis of the intuitions in question. I should add that despite appearances the *ungroundability thesis,* as we might call it—the view that what is intuitively known cannot be (evidentially) grounded in premises—does *not* imply that a proposition intuitively known is a priori or necessary. Ross apparently believed, however, that the universal moral propositions in question (notably his principles of prima facie duty) are both a priori and necessary; but it is doubtful that he regarded as a priori one's apparently primitive sense that one has a prima facie duty to keep *this* promise. If he held some such aprioristic, rationalist view regarding particular cases, it would presumably have been qualified so as to avoid empirical assumptions, as does the position that one apprehends the truth of a concrete generalization like "*If* one sees someone fall off a bicycle and can easily help with what appears to be a broken arm, one has a prima facie obligation to do so." Consider, by contrast, the unconditional proposition that I actually have this obligation; this presupposes both my existence and that of the injured person(s) and hence is plainly neither a priori nor a necessary truth. The conditional generalization, on the other hand, even if one grasps it in application to an individual case, is simply not about any actual case. I emphasize this because, while Ross was doubtless a rationalist in his epistemology, his intuitionism—taken simply as a pluralist view committed to intuitive moral knowledge, at least—does not entail moral rationalism.

Second, an intuition must be a moderately firm cognition—call this the *firmness requirement.* One must come down on the matter at hand; if one is up in the air, the jury is still out. In the contexts that concern us, intuitions will typically be beliefs, including cases of knowing. But the term "intuitions" may include (sincere) judgments or other mental events implying belief. A mere inclination to believe is not an intuition; an intuition tends to be a "conviction" (a term Ross sometimes used for an intuition) and to be relinquished only through such weighty considerations as a felt conflict with a firmly held theory or with another intuition. Granted, a proposition one is only inclined to believe may be or seem intuitive; but one does not have an intuition with that proposition as its content until one believes the proposition. We might speak here of intuitive inclinations as opposed to intuitions, and the former need not be denied some degree of evidential weight, though it would be less than that of intuitions proper: the data, we might say, would be less clear, just as a view of an unexpected island in the fog is less clear than it would be in sunlight and provides less reason to alter one's map. The concepts of intuition and of the intuitive are not sharp, but nothing in what follows will turn on their vagueness.

Third, intuitions must be formed in the light of an adequate understanding of their propositional objects—call this the *comprehension requirement*. That they are formed in this light is doubtless one reason for their firmness, as is their being based on that understanding rather than on, say, inference from premises. As to the required adequacy of this understanding, Ross, like Moore, insists that, before one can apprehend even a self-evident moral truth, one must get precisely that true proposition before one's mind. In many passages (including one quoted above) Ross indicates that reflection is required to see the truth of the proposition in question. The more complicated the proposition, or the richer the concepts figuring in it—like the concept of a promise—the more is required for an adequate understanding of that proposition.[19] Intuitions are sometimes regarded as arising quickly upon considering the proposition in question; they need not so arise and in some cases probably should not so arise.

The fourth requirement I suggest is that intuitions are pretheoretical: roughly, they are neither evidentially dependent on theories nor themselves theoretical hypotheses. If this *pretheoreticality requirement* entailed their being *preconceptual* or, more broadly, uninformed, it would undermine the comprehension requirement: without at least a minimal understanding of the concepts figuring in a proposition, one is not even in a position to find it intuitive. But clearly Ross and other intuitionists intend our "convictions" (intuitions), including those of other people, to be used as data for moral generalization somewhat in the way sense perceptions are data for scientific theorizing. Given his understanding of this idea, not only will an intuition not be an inference from a theory, it will also not be epistemically dependent on a theory even in the general sense that the theory provides one's justificatory ground (even a noninferential ground) for the intuition. This point does *not* entail that intuition has a complete independence of theory: an intuition may be defeated and abandoned in the light of theoretical results incompatible with its truth, especially when these results are supported by other intuitions. This is a kind of negative epistemic dependence of intuition on theory: the justification of the intuition does not derive from the impossibility of such untoward, hypothetical results, but it can be destroyed by them if they occur. Such defeasibility on the part of intuition is not a positive justificatory dependence on any actual theory: it is a negative dependence on—in the sense of a vulnerability to—disconfirmation by theories, whether actual or possible.[20]

In some ways, the perceptual analogy can mislead. For one thing, an intuition is more like a belief based on a careful observation than like an impression formed from a glimpse, though that impression is nonetheless perceptual and can produce belief. One could, however, speak of sensory intuitions in reference to cognitions that rest on observational sense experience in the way perceptual beliefs commonly do when they are formed under favorable conditions. Consider, for instance visual beliefs, acquired in good light, about an island seen before one. From this point of view, my four conditions are probably too broad; but to build in, say, that intuitions are nonobservational cognitions of a conceptual or at least classificatory kind, would probably make the conditions too narrow, and the breadth of the characterization is appropriate to our purposes.

The perceptual analogy is also misleading because intuitions need not be about observables: rights are not observable, yet we have intuitions about them. We may see them in the sense of recognizing them, as where one sees a right to refuse feeding tubes, but they are not seen visually. If what is both nonobservable and significantly complex is thereby theoretical, then we certainly have intuitions about theoretical entities; but such "theoretical" intuitions need not be epistemically dependent on any theory.

It is of course controversial whether, in either intuitive or perceptual cases, there *is* anything pretheoretical to appeal to. But if not—if, for instance, to have concepts sufficient for judging a theory one must be biased by either that theory or another one relevant to judging the theory—then it is not only Ross who has a problem. One would hope that even if every judge has some biases, there are some judges who at least have no biases that vitiate their decisions on the cases they must resolve.

Even if no cognition is entirely pretheoretical, perhaps some may be pretheoretical *with respect to* a moral generalization needing appraisal. Granted, this would rule out only theoretical biases. Intuitionists apparently hope that no others are ineliminable, but absence of *all* bias is apparently not part of the concept of an intuition; the effects of biases may indeed help to explain how an intuition can be mistaken. Nor is it necessary, for purposes of working out a satisfactory intuitionism, that biases always be unavoidable; it is enough if, as Ross apparently thought, they are always correctable by further reflection. Such reflection may include comparison with the intuitions of others, just as in scientific inquiry one might compare one's observations with those of coinvestigators.

There are two points that may significantly clarify the sense in which intuitions might be pretheoretical. One point (implicit in what has been said) is that an intuition's being pretheoretical does not imply that it is indefeasible—not even indefeasible by judgments based on the theory we build from a set of intuitions including the one in question. Recall the case in which I see that keeping a promise is not my final duty because, reflecting on my general duties, I realize that other duties override my duty to keep the promise. Here, the basis of the other moral considerations is the same sort as that of the first duty. The second point is that an intuition that is pretheoretical at one time can evolve into a judgment grounded in a theory. A Rossian view is committed to the existence, at any time when our convictions provide the data for ethics, of pretheoretical intuitions; but it is not committed to denying that yesterday's intuitions can be today's theory-laden assumptions—or that they can be given up because they are undermined by the reflection of "thoughtful, well-educated people."

Let us suppose for the sake of argument that either there are no pretheoretical intuitions or, more likely, *some* of the intuitions needed for confirmation of basic moral principles are in some way theoretical. We can still distinguish between theories that bias the appraisal of a moral principle and theories that do not. If, for instance, a theory of the psychology of persons is needed for the capacity to have certain moral intuitions (e.g., the intuition that flogging an infant to death is prima facie wrong), this need not vitiate the appraisal. The intuition may depend on a theoretical (psychological) understanding of the pains caused by flogging and of (biological) death, but neither the kind nor the level of the relevant theory undermines the justifiability of the intuition. We might, then, distinguish between what is *relatively* and what is *absolutely* pretheoretical: the former is simply pretheoretical relative to the issue in question, say the moral status of the act-type, flogging an infant to death. Perhaps a relative notion of the pretheoretical is all that intuitionism needs in order to meet the objection that theoretical dependence vitiates the justificatory role it claims for intuitions.

If intuitions are noninferential and pretheoretical, one might wonder to what extent they represent rationality, as opposed to mere belief or even prejudice. Here it is crucial to recall Ross's requirements of adequate maturity and "sufficient attention." I propose to go further: There is a sense in which an intuition *can* be a conclusion formed though rational inquiry. Consider listening to someone complain about a task done by a coworker, where one has been asked to determine whether the work was adequate. In a way that is impersonal and ably documented, Timothy criticizes the work of Abby. One might judge, from his credible statements of deficiencies in her work, that it was shoddy. This is a response to evidential propositions. Now imagine being asked a different question: whether there might be some bias in the critique. One might now recall his narration in one's mind's eye and ear, and from a global, intuitive sense of Timothy's intonations, word choices, selection of deficiencies, and omission of certain merits, judge that he is jealous of her. This is a response to an overall impression. Let us call the first judgment—that the work is shoddy—a *conclusion of inference:* it is premised on propositions one has noted as evidence. Call the second judgment a *conclusion of reflection:* it emerges from thinking about the overall pattern of Timothy's critique in the context of his relation to Abby as a coworker, but not from one or more evidential premises. It is more like a response to viewing a painting or seeing an expressive face than to propositionally represented information. One responds to a pattern: one notices an emotional tone in the otherwise factual listing of deficiencies; one hears him compare her work to some that he once did; and so forth. The conclusion of reflection is a wrapping up of the question, similar to concluding a practical matter with a decision. One has not added up the evidences and formulated their implication; one has obtained a view of the whole and characterized it overall.

It might be objected here that one is really inferring, from the tone of Timothy's complaint and of his comparison of Abby's work with a job he once did, that he is jealous; this is not something just "seen" on the basis of a careful, overall look. To say that the case must be so described is to confuse the grounds of one's judgment with beliefs expressing those grounds. Granted, if I *articulate* my noninferential grounds, they will then be available to me as premises. If, for instance, I say to myself that his tone was quite emotional given the factual character of the deficiencies he listed, I now have a premise for the conclusion that he was jealous of her. But if this point implied that my belief that he is jealous of her is inferential *prior* to my articulating my ground and "basing" my conclusion on it, the same would hold for perceptual beliefs based on visual impressions whose evidential force can be articulated. We would have to say that since the statement that I have a visual impression of gold-lettered buckram before me is a premise for believing there is a book before me, I concluded that there is a book before me, on the basis of this premise, even when I merely *had* the impression, had not articulated my having it, and from it spontaneously formed the belief that there is a book before me. But surely my having a ground that is *expressible* in a premise does not imply that I must *use* that ground *in* a premise in order to form a belief on the basis of the ground.[21] I suggest, then, that this kind of conclusion can be an intuition in the sense just sketched. Not all intuitions are of this sort, but it is essential to see that particularly when a case, real or hypothetical, is complicated, an intuition may not emerge until reflection proceeds for some time. Such an intuition can be a conclusion of reflection, temporally as well as epistemically; and it may be either empirical or a priori.

This example and other paradigms of intuition might suggest that intuitions are always about *cases* as opposed to generalizations. They typically are, and arguably a generalization can be only *intuitive*—roughly, highly plausible considered in itself—as opposed to being the object of *an* intuition. The intuitive status of a proposition is consistent with its being inferentially believed, or with its being the object of an infirm cognition, or with both. But this restriction of intuitions to cases as opposed to generalizations is neither entailed by the four general conditions I have proposed as roughly necessary and sufficient for an intuition nor implicit in the history of the notion.[22]

A generalization can be intuitive in much the way a singular proposition about an example can be; and just as some intuitions can be better grounded and firmer than others, some generalizations can be more intuitive than others. It is true that an intuitive generalization can be supported by intuitions about examples, but it does not follow that its only way of being intuitive is through such support. Kant might have found the generalization that one ought to keep one's promises more intuitive than the singular proposition that I ought to keep my promise (to my sister) to educate her daughter; Ross might find the latter more intuitive (and would reject the generalization unless it is understood to refer to prima facie duty).[23]

Self-Evidence and the Systematization of Intuitions

In order to appreciate the sense in which Ross's basic moral truths might be plausibly considered self-evident, it seems to me absolutely essential that we distinguish his actual case for them from his analogy to mathematics and logic. He knew full well that it takes more reflection and maturity to see the truth of the proposition that promises generate prima facie duties than to see the validity of a logical principle like the syllogistic "If all As are Bs and all Bs are Cs, then all As are Cs." On this score, the disanalogy between the moral case and that of logic and other domains of self-evidence both undermines the plausibility of Ross's view and gives ethical intuitionism a burden it need not carry. Logic can (let us assume) be axiomatized given a few self-evident propositions (e.g., that if (a) either p or q and (b) not-q, then p). Their substitution instances (e.g., the proposition that if either Jim is in his office or he is home, and he is not in this office, then he is home) have a similar axiomatic self-evidence. Moral principles, by contrast, seem to many reasonable people neither self-evident nor comparably simple. Ross might have pointed out that self-evidence, at least of the kind in question, should not be expected in substantially vague generalizations. He might also have done more to distinguish different kinds of self-evidence; for it seems to me that only one of them need be claimed by intuitionists as possessed by some moral truths.

Two kinds of self-evidence are especially relevant here. Let me first establish a general conception of self-evidence, and in that light we can distinguish them. I shall assume that the basic notion of self-evidence is this: A self-evident proposition is (roughly) a truth such that understanding it will meet two conditions: that understanding is (a) sufficient for one's being justified in believing it (i.e., for having justification for believing it, whether one in fact believes it or not)—this is why such a truth is evident *in itself*—and (b) sufficient for knowing the proposition provided one believes it on the *basis* of understanding it.[24] Two clarifications are needed immediately.

First, as reflected in (a), the self-evidence of a proposition does not entail that if one understands (and considers) the proposition, then one believes it. This non-belief-entailing conception of self-evidence is plausible because one can fail initially to "see" a self-evident truth and, later, grasp it in just the way one grasps the truth of a paradigmatically self-evident proposition: one that is obvious in itself the moment one considers it. Take for example a self-evident proposition that is perhaps not immediately obvious: If there never have been any siblings then there never have been any first cousins.[25] A delay in seeing something, such as the truth of this, need not change the character of what one sees. What is self-evident can indeed be justifiedly believed on its "intrinsic" merits; but they need not leap out at one immediately. In some cases one can see *what* a self-evident proposition says—and thus understand it—before seeing *that,* or how, it is true.

Second, the understanding in question must be adequate, as opposed to mistaken or partial or clouded, understanding. Adequate understanding of a proposition is more than simply getting the general sense of a sentence expressing it, as where one can parse the sentence grammatically, partially explain what it means, and perhaps translate it into another language one knows well. Adequacy here implies not only seeing what the proposition says, but also being able to apply it to some appropriate cases, being able to see some of its logical implications, and comprehending its elements and some of their relations. If inadequate understanding is allowed, it will not be true that understanding a self-evident proposition provides a justification for believing it, nor that beliefs of the proposition based on understanding it constitute knowledge.

Given these points about (a) and (b), we may distinguish those self-evident propositions that are readily understood by normal adults (or by people of some relevant description, e.g. mature moral agents) and those understood by them only through reflection on the sorts of case they concern. Call the first *immediately self-evident* and the second *mediately self-evident,* since their truth can be grasped only through the mediation of reflection.[26] The reflection may involve drawing inferences, but their role is limited largely to clarifying what the proposition in question says: as self-evidence is normally understood, a self-evident proposition is knowable without inferential grounds. One may require time to get it in clear focus, but need not climb up to it on the shoulders of one or more premises.

Immediately self-evident propositions are *obvious;* roughly, their truth is apparent as soon as one considers them with understanding, which is usually as soon as one is presented with them in a natural formulation in a language in which one is competent. The obvious need not be self-evident, however. It is obvious that there exists at least one person, but this is not self-evident: the proposition is not evident in itself; but if we consider a natural formulation of it in a language we understand, we have ample ground *in that situation* for seeing its truth (at least if we know we are persons). Moreover, there are *degrees* (as well as kinds) of obviousness, but there are *kinds* rather than degrees of self-evidence.

Granted, some self-evident propositions are more readily seen to be true than others, but this is a different point. Even immediately self-evident propositions can differ in obviousness, whether for everyone or for some people or for one or more people at different times. Consider the proposition that if all As are Bs and all Bs are Cs, then all As are Cs. This is "very intuitive" and very obviously true, or at least that holds for its ordinary substitution instances, such as "If all cats are furry creatures and all furry creatures are animals, then all cats are animals." It is also, for many people, more readily seen to be true, even if perhaps not in the end more intuitive than, the proposition that if no *A*s are *B*s and all *C*s are *B*s, then no *C*s are *A*s, or the proposition if there never have been any siblings then there never have been any first cousins. As these examples suggest, mediately self-evident propositions need not be (psychologically) *compelling:* they need not produce belief the moment they are understood, nor, even after reflection on them, in everyone who understands them.[27]

Once we distinguish between the immediately and the mediately self-evident, and appreciate that a self-evident proposition need not be obvious or even compelling, we can see clearly that an intuitionist, indeed, even a rationalist one like Ross, may be a fallibilist about the sense of self-evidence. He can thus make room for error even in thoughtful judgments to the effect that a proposition is, or is not, self-evident. He might grant, then, that a non-self-evident (or even false) proposition may seem to someone to be self-evident. Moreover, not every self-evident proposition need be "intuitive," just as not every proposition believed on the basis of intuition need be self-evident. If there are self-evident moral truths, the sense that one has grasped such a truth can be illusory, and at least the majority can be expected to be in the mediate category.[28]

Two further points may help here. The first is that particularly when a proposition is questioned, if only by a skeptic or by someone who wants a derivation of it in order to understand it better, then where the proposition is not obvious or immediately self-evident we may think that it is not self-evident at all, even if it is. Yet surely we can know a proposition to be true even if we cannot show it to be true, or even defend it by argument, as opposed to illustrating or explaining it.[29] This is how it is for most people with respect to the proposition that if all *A*s are *B*s, and all *B*s are *C*s, then all *A*s are *C*s. They can explain it by example but can find no prior premises for it and may not even be able to defend it by (non-question-begging) argument if confronted by skillful objections. The second point is that as I have characterized intuitions, they are not only justificationally defeasible, but need not even be prima facie justified. Still, insofar as they are like certain perceptual beliefs (e.g., in being noninferential, "natural," and pretheoretical)—and perhaps more important—insofar as they are based on an understanding of their propositional object, there is reason to consider them prima facie justified (in part because in such cases one tends to find it at best difficult to see how the proposition might be false). This may be as much as a moderate intuitionism needs to claim, and it does not entail that an intuition, as such, is prima facie justified. It leaves open that, say because one has an inadequate understanding of a proposition or believes it on a basis other than one's understanding of it, it could become the object of an intuition for one yet, at the time, that intuition might fail to be prima facie justified.

In closing this section, I want to bring out the importance of the distinction between the immediately and the mediately self-evident and to introduce a special case of the former. By comparing his candidate basic moral truths to the (elementary) truths of logic and mathematics, Ross wrongly implied that the former are of the first kind. Indeed, when he went on to say that proving them is impossible, he created the impression that he would place them in a yet narrower category: that of propositions which are *strongly axiomatic,* in a sense implying not only immediate self-evidence, which is often taken to be roughly equivalent to simple axiomatic status, but also the further property of unprovability from anything epistemically *prior.* Such unprovability is, roughly, the impossibility of being proved from one or more premises that can be known or justifiedly believed without already knowing or justifiedly believing the proposition in question.[30]

A different way to express the difference between self-evidence and strong axiomaticity is this: A self-evident proposition can function as an epistemic *unmoved* mover—it can be known, and can provide support for other propositions, without itself being seen to have (and perhaps without there even existing) a basis in something constituting evidence for it. But, unlike a strongly axiomatic proposition, it need not be an *unmovable* mover, one such that there cannot be further evidence for it, since the existence of that evidence would move it upward from the lowest possible foundational level.[31]

These points about self-evidence have far-reaching implications for intuitionism. I believe that Ross said nothing implying that there cannot be good arguments for certain self-evident propositions, even the immediate ones. What is evident "in itself," even if immediately self-evident, need not be such that it cannot also be evident in some other way. If need not be known through premises; but this does not entail that it cannot be so known. Let us explore this point in relation to a further problem concerning his view.

What is it that makes all of Ross's principles moral, and might their truth be known in terms of the same account that explains why they are moral? Ross probably thought that even if there is an answer to the first question it provides no answer to the second.[32] If there is just one fundamental obligation, and hence the property of being obligatory is (even if not by definition) equivalent to, say, that of optimizing happiness, then all moral principles can be seen as endorsements of behaviors that optimize—or condemnations of those that do the opposite. Ross rejected this view. Consider, by contrast, a Kantian unification of moral principles, including Ross's principles of duty. The intrinsic end formulation of Kant's categorical imperative is suggestive. Above all, it stresses respect for persons: it says they are to be treated as ends and never merely as means. Is it not plausible to hold that in lying, breaking promises, subjugating, torturing, and the like one is using people merely as a means? And in keeping faith with people, acting benevolently toward them, and extending them justice, is one not treating them as ends, roughly in the sense of beings with intrinsic value (or whose experiences can have intrinsic value)?[33] The point is not that Ross's principles can be deduced from the categorical imperative (though we need not rule out the possibility of an interpretation of it that permits such a deduction); rather, the intrinsic end formulation of the imperative expresses an ideal that renders the principles of duty intelligible or even expectable.

Ross apparently thought that the existence of a theoretical account of the prima facie duties is inconsistent with their self-evidence, at least if they are deducible from some more general principle. He may well have taken it to be also inconsistent with their plurality. But, to take the second point first, the existence of such an account would not entail that there really is just one duty, only that one moral principle can be a unifying ground for others. Unification of a set of principles in relation to a single one, say one that entails or explains them or both, does not imply that there is really only one principle. Nor does exhibiting several duties as serving a larger one entail that there is just one duty (as opposed to one basic duty). Regarding the first point—that unification of the Rossian principles of duty is not inconsistent with their self-evidence—the truth of a theoretical unification of the kind imagined would, to be sure, be inconsistent with the strong axiomatic self-evidence of these other principles. That, however, is not the kind of self-evidence to which Ross is committed by his account of how we know the moral principles corresponding to his prima facie duties.

If, then, we take that account, rather than Ross's analogy to logic and mathematics, as primary in understanding his intuitionism, we arrive at the surprising conclusion that a Rossian intuitionist—even construed as also a moral rationalist—can allow for *epistemically overdetermined moral knowledge*. There can be a moral theory that both explains and provides inferential grounds for moral propositions which, given sufficient reflection, can also be seen, noninferentially, to be true. What is, at one time, only a conclusion of reflection—and in that way a candidate to be an intuition—can become a conclusion of inference. It can still derive support simultaneously from both the newly found premises for it and any remaining intuitive sense of its truth. An appropriately noninferential, pretheoretical sense of its truth may survive one's inferring it from premises. Seeing a thing in a new light need not prevent one's still seeing it in its own light.[34]

To be sure, the categorical imperative is not immediately self-evident.[35] Indeed, it may not be self-evident at all, but knowable (assuming it is true) only on the basis of a derivation from nonmoral principles—or, as Ross might argue, as a generalization from more restricted, intuitively justified principles such as his own. That is not the issue here. What unifies moral principles need not be self-evident; presumably it need not even be a set of moral principles, but might come from a general theory of practical reason.[36] The point is that once we appreciate that the kind of self-evidence to which intuitionism is committed is only mediate, we can allow that intuitive moral principles, even if they are self-evident, are knowable through premises as well as by reflection on their content. We can also see that these moral principles can be supported by their providing an account of our intuitions, and not just through a direct intuition of their truth or self-evidence.

Reflection as a Basis for Moral Judgments

If anything has emerged from this study as common to all the ways of knowing that deserve to be called intuitive, it is reflection, above all reflection on the concepts figuring in, and on the necessary implications of, the moral or other propositions whose status is supposed to be knowable through intuition. The reflection may be as brief as simply focusing clearly on the proposition, or it may require many sittings, possibly spread over many years. It turns out, however, that what is knowable in this reflective way—or can be at least justifiedly believed in this way—need not be strongly axiomatic, in a sense implying that there cannot be epistemically independent grounds for it. What can be justifiedly believed "in its own terms" is not thereby precluded from being justified by premises.

I have already shown how, from a broad moral principle such as the categorical imperative taken as expressing respect for persons, one might try to derive the Rossian duties. Call this *justification from below* (from something plausibly held to be "deeper"). I now want to argue that intuitionism—or at least the method of inquiry that seems to be the core of it—can allow *justification from above,* in part by appeal to what philosophers commonly call intuitions. We can then begin to articulate the overall framework for moral theory that is a major concern of this essay.

In deriving intuitive moral principles from below, one does not presuppose them, even for the sake of argument, but builds them from one or another kind of supporting ground. By contrast, their justification from above proceeds by provisionally presupposing them and exploring the consequences one infers from them. Above all, we do two sorts of things. First, we deduce from them what kinds of decisions we would make, and what kinds of lives we would lead, if we took the principles to be true and regularly acted on them. Second, we reflect on (or with), as Ross would put it, what we really think about these possibilities (i.e., on our intuitions about them). We might, for instance, contemplate a life in which we recognize duties of beneficence versus one in which we do not, and consider whether, in the light of what we really think about those lives and about the beneficent social practices they would imply, the relevant duties still seem to be prima facie duties, as opposed to, say, mere charities or even meddling with others. If we are satisfied by what we find, we regard the principles as confirmed, as we do scientific hypotheses borne out by predictions derived from them. Granted, we may *now* form an argument that seems to proceed from below: namely, that since the assumption of these principles has these "intuitively appealing" consequences (or best explains them), we may take the principles as likely to be true and to that extent as justified. But this mode of argument is not a route to discovery of its conclusion, as argument from below may be; and it need not proceed, like the latter, from epistemically independent premises, since some of the judgments we make about cases may be partly based on the principle we are testing.

Argument from above can also result in revising, rather than confirming, the principles we began with. We may find that if, for example, we restrict the cases in which promising yields a prima facie duty—say, to situations in which it is fully voluntary—we get a better principle. A Rossian view can surely countenance such a procedure, and using it may result in enhancing our justification as well as in our revising our initial view, whether that was justified or not.

We are now in a position to see something else. The use of reflection made by Ross is quite consistent with—and indeed seems to anticipate—the procedure of reflective equilibrium as described by (among others) John Rawls.[37] One can compare one's intuitions with each other, with those of people one respects, with the results of applying plausible generalizations to the situations that the moral intuitions are about; and one can strive to get all these items—revising them if necessary—into a stable, coherent whole: this is the equilibrium resulting from one's comparative reflections. The intuitionist might, to be sure, use the procedure more to refine moral principles already accepted than to discover moral principles; but this is a contingent matter that depends on what principles are accepted at the start of the process and on how many new principles or refinements of old ones it produces.

How wide the appropriate equilibrium should be is also contingent, and is quite variable: whether, for example, nonmoral considerations such as psychological facts should be in equilibrium with a body of plausible moral principles is left open. Some styles of reflection might proceed from principle to consequence and back again; others, such as Ross's, from case to principle first. One might think about individual promises and thereby frame standards for promise-keeping, or instead posit initially plausible principles governing this activity and refine them by looking at cases.

In a moral theorist whose basic method is reflection of a kind we find both in Ross and Rawls and others, the order of discovery can diverge, as it does in science, from the order of justification. For example, we might first discover a principle on the basis of serendipity, by simply guessing at the truth about the subject we are investigating, and might later get justification, and pass from conjecture to belief, by doing confirmatory experiments. Or we might both justify and discover a principle by deducing a new generalization from more comprehensive ones already established. But regardless of the kind of procedure by which we discover or justify moral principles, intuitions about cases should cohere with intuitions about the principles that apply to those cases. Inferential justification, moreover, can support intuitive justification regarding either cases or principles.

It is no accident that I have been trying to exhibit common ground between intuitionism and some of its critics. It seems to me that when one looks closely at the best intuitionists, such as Ross, one finds something that transcends their own characterization of what they are doing. It is the *method of ethical reflection:* roughly, judiciously bringing to bear on moral questions, especially general ones such as what our duties are, careful reflection on what these questions involve. To take the case of promising as a source of moral duty, one reflects on what a promise is, on what a duty to keep it is, on what duties can conflict with that one, on what counts as a reason for action or—arguably equivalent to this—as an intrinsically good or bad thing, and on what human life would be like if we took certain kinds of acts to be duties and regarded certain conflicts of duties as properly resolved in some particular way. Facts, then, come into the process. Such reflection is what, more than any other method, seems to yield reliable intuitions (roughly, intuitions likely to be true), or at least intuitions we can rationally hope will remain credible as we continue to reflect on them. Reliable intuitions may or may not be conclusions of reflection.[38]

Inference of any kind, whether from below or above, can figure in the reflection that generates or tests intuitions. But the primary case of such reflection is that in which one arrives at conclusions of reflection or at (temporally) immediate intuitions, not at inferential judgments. If no such primacy of noninferential reflection were recognized, then we would have to ask what else might serve to ground one's premises for inference.[39] Factual assumptions can figure in such reflections—and must if the reflections concern what specific action to take under various future contingencies. But in the most basic cases, we consider what ought to be done *given* certain factual assumptions (e.g., the assumption that we have made a promise which the promisee expects us to keep, or that we can help someone and we have no conflicting demands on us). For purposes of justifying general moral standards, the most important epistemic element is our intuitions regarding cases with factual assumptions built in, not those assumptions themselves. We may need to make observations to determine whether keeping a specific promise, say to return a set of car keys, will actually harm the promisee; but on the assumption that no harm will be produced, it will be intuitive that one has a prima facie duty to keep the promise.[40]

The framework for ethical theorizing I have introduced here might be called *ethical reflectionism*. Its major thesis is that the method of reflection is and deserves to be our basic method for justifying ethical judgments, especially general moral principles or general judgments of what has intrinsic value, and among our basic methods for discovering such judgments. Discovery is, as in scientific inquiry, less constrained than justification. If tea leaves help us think up hypotheses, we may use them; but we may accept the hypotheses we thus arrive at only if they pass certain rigorous tests. By attacking the most common conception of intuitionism—the infallibilist, immoderately rationalist, special faculty view—I have tried to make intuitionism more plausible, with reflection as its chief method.

It is not only intuitionism, however, that uses the method of reflection; the method seems implicit in any appeal to intuitions as a way of justifying, refining, or discovering general moral principles. Using it does not commit one to intuitionism. A nonintuitionist empiricist, for example, might hold that our intuitions reflect a sense, perhaps a quasi-perceptual one, of moral properties. There might, after all, be evolutionary reasons why injustice should be grasped directly, say by the application of conscience, conceived as an empirical moral faculty, even if injustice is a natural phenomenon and can also be inferentially known to exist. We respond noninferentially and almost instinctively to the difference between happy and angry faces, yet this does not preclude their being characterized theoretically and known inferentially. In responding to Katherine's smile I do not and probably could not single out the lines and movements that produce my pleasure, but the psychology of perception could in principle describe the causal connections in detail. Ethical reflectionism allows for a similarly complex relation between morally sensitive observers and various moral phenomena. We can feel indignation over one person's slighting of another even if we cannot put our finger on what it was in the demeanor of the first that offended the second.

In taking reflection seriously as a ground of justified noninferential judgment, then, one need not commit oneself to any particular account of why it succeeds. For similar reasons, one can combine it with various kinds of ethical theory. Ross may have thought, as is natural for a rationalist, that one grasps necessary relations between propositions or concepts, but one could also hold, as an empiricist might, that we simply regard deeds like lying and killing as causing pain—a contingent (causal) feature of those actions—and hence as prima facie wrong. This sense could precede, rather than derive from, hedonistic utilitarianism, just as the sense of duty to keep a promise of a certain kind one is reflecting on can—and Ross seemed to think does—precede, rather than derive from, the conviction that in general one has a duty to keep promises. He apparently was (as suggested earlier), a particularistic intuitionist, rather than a generalist: he took us to apprehend moral facts more basically in, or at least in the context of reflecting on, particular instances, whether actual or hypothetical, than in the abstract and universal propositions we know through (but not by ordinary inductive inference from) these instances. By contrast, there are places in which John Stuart Mill talks as if what is primary is the grasp of pleasure and pain as intrinsically good and bad, and from this, inferentially or otherwise, we see individual phenomena as good or bad, and right or wrong.[41] Use of the method of reflection does not commit one to either the particularist or the generalist view.

Similar considerations show that the method is neutral with respect to the controversy between naturalism—by which I mean roughly the view that nature is all there is and the truths of nature are the only basic truths—and nonnaturalism. There may be a sense in which ethical reflectionism is *methodologically a priori,* because its major demand is that we think adequately about moral questions, using, above all, the concepts essential in their formulation. It does not imply that moral concepts are analyzable in any particular way; and, epistemically, it is compatible with various accounts of the grounds of the justification that, in its nonskeptical forms, it takes reflection to yield. This justification can derive from an a priori grasp of conceptual relations or from an empirical sense of what sorts of acts have morally relevant properties, such as causing pain. Either approach is consistent with various forms of naturalism as well as with nonnaturalism.

Different theorists may put differing constraints on the appropriate kind of reflection. At the extreme rationalist end of the reflectionist spectrum, where some forms of intuitionism may lie, we may need only to think of what rational beings are in order to see by reflection what general moral principles apply to them. At the empiricist end, it may be held that since only pleasure and pain are intrinsically good, only reflection that reveals plausible assumptions about how action affects them can yield general moral principles. Any plausible theory, of course, will require our making factual assumptions in *applying* moral principles to daily conduct, and so in reflecting on what concrete action is a duty or is otherwise morally appropriate. I cannot, from a sense of obligation to keep a promise, know that I should actually do the deed unless I have adequate grounds to believe that I in fact promised to do it; and I cannot know that I should, all things considered, do it, unless I can have adequate grounds to believe that it will not violate stronger duties I have.[42]

The method of reflection is also neutral with respect to ethical noncognitivism, which we may construe as roughly the view that in making moral judgments we do not perform the cognitive act of stating facts (or falsehoods) but express attitudes, typically of (moral) approval or disapproval. We are, in this way, being "prescriptive" (or evaluative), not "descriptive." Noncognitivism takes the objects of reflection to be in crucial cases nonpropositional, but it allows for moral justification of the attitudes that one expresses in making moral judgments. We must often reflect on whether certain pro or con attitudes are appropriate, but we may bring facts and logic to bear in appraising them: inconsistency and factual error make an attitude objectionable, even though not false. This justification is potentially grounded in reflection, and presumably in intuitions of some kind, in a way analogous to the grounding that other theorists take to justify moral judgments construed as true or false. What cognitivists may take to show that I should keep a promise, noncognitivists may take to show that it is reasonable to have the positive attitude I express in saying I ought to keep that promise.[43]

One might wonder whether any substantive view is ruled out by ethical reflectionism. Given its methodological character, it is not meant to rule out any particular ethical position. But an ethical view might be partly methodological and thereby ruled out. Ethical reflectionism seems inconsistent with a crude divine command view (perhaps never seriously held) for which an act-type's being commanded, or forbidden, by God (e.g., as indicated in Scriptures) are by definition its only morally relevant properties: moral properties are grounded wholly, directly, and indefeasibly, in divine will. For here reflection with contrary results would be irrelevant; discovery of properties independently relevant to moral judgment is precluded. Reflectionism is not inconsistent with the theory that moral truths are ultimately (nondefinitionally) grounded in divine will and knowable jointly through natural theology and Scripture—a view can be argued to be supported by reflection of an appropriate kind. A second view ruled out by reflectionism would be an instinctual theory that grounds moral knowledge and justified moral beliefs—by definition—in a moral instinct, one that makes the kinds of brute deliverances sometimes thought to be characteristic of a faculty of intuition.[44] For here there would be no need for reflection and perhaps even no role for it: certain judgmental tendencies are simply built into us, whether by evolutionary factors, divine artifice, or some other power. It is quite otherwise with certain moral sense theories, or their contemporary successors that claim we have moral perceptions arising in moral experience and capable of conferring moral justification in a way similar to the generation of perceptual justification from vision and hearing.[45] For the relevant kind of perception grounded in moral experience is not only conceptual but requires the sort of sensitive understanding needed even to "intuit" a truth straightaway. Such intuition is the minimal case of reflection as I construe it.

Modified Ethical Intuitionism

I hope by now to have shown that there is good reason to think that ethical reflectionism is a framework of moral inquiry that is far more common than it may appear. Let me reiterate why it may seem otherwise and, in response to objections to the framework, cite some of its advantages. We can then consider intuitionism as a restricted case of reflectionism.

Because what is known through reflection is commonly taken to be a priori, moral empiricists, and even nonempiricists who stress moral experience, may reject ethical reflectionism. Because reflection (often) yields noninferential judgments, which may seem indefeasible, fallibilists may also reject the view. Because, in its paradigmatic, cognitive uses, reflection appears to yield justification or knowledge regarding moral propositions, noncognitivists may reject the view. Because, in being neutral with respect to naturalism in ethics, it leaves open whether moral properties may be natural, nonnaturalists, including the historically prominent intuitionists, may reject it.[46] And because the view allows that what is known noninferentially and intuitively at one time may also be known, at another time, by inference from above or below, and in that sense "proved," traditional intuitionists in moral epistemology may reject it. But none of these theorists need reject ethical reflectionism. It is neutral with respect to rationalism and empiricism; it is, in its most plausible forms, not only fallibilistic, but easily combined with the procedure of reflective equilibrium; it is consistent with noncognitivism and with naturalism; and it can be combined with an overarching moral theory that unifies the disparate moral judgments which intuitionists have commonly thought to be incapable of justification by appeal to premises, yet it allows that those judgments can be self-evident and thereby noninferentially knowable.

Ethical reflectionism is not as such a form of ethical intuitionism, but its truth provides the best explanation of what the most credible forms of ethical intuitionism are committed to. In these forms, I suggest, ethical intuitionism is, in outline, the view that we can have, in the light of appropriate reflection on the content of moral judgments and moral principles, intuitive (hence noninferential) justification for holding them. Most of the plausible versions of intuitionism also endorse a plurality of moral principles (though Moore is notable for holding an overarching, ideal utilitarian principle of right action), and most versions are also rationalist, holding that there are a priori moral principles. But an intuitionist could be an empiricist, taking intuition to be capable of providing an experiential ground for moral judgments or principles. Intuitionists typically hold that moral knowledge as well as moral justification can be intuitive, but the major ones are not committed to the view that this justification or knowledge is indefeasible, and they tend to deny that it is.

If the arguments of this paper indicate how intuitionism as just broadly characterized can be plausible, they also show how an overall rationalistic intuitionist theory like Ross's can be strengthened. Moreover, if what is said above in support of reflectionism indicates how an intuitionist view in moral epistemology is compatible with empiricism—even if it also brings out why it is natural for intuitionists to be rationalists—it also shows how a rationalist moral epistemology can be freed of the apparent dogmatism and associated arbitrariness, the implausible philosophy of mind, and the immoderate epistemic principles often attributed to it. Let me comment on each of these points and in that light proceed to some conclusions by way of overall appraisal of intuitionism conceived, as it should be given the overall views of Ross and its other major prominent proponents, as a rationalist view.

I will stress the rationalism of the reconstructed Rossian intuitionism developed above—construed as the view that we have intuitive justification both for some of our particular moral judgments and for a plurality of mediately self-evident moral principles—because the controversy between empiricism and rationalism as epistemological perspectives is apparently very much with us in ethical theory, despite how few ethical theorists are openly committed to either perspective. I believe, moreover, that most of the plausible objections to a broadly Rossian intuitionism are either motivated by empiricism or are best seen as objections, not to its appeal to intuitions, but to the underlying rationalism of the view: roughly, to its taking reason, as opposed to observation, to be capable of supplying justification for substantive truths, such as (if they are indeed true) Ross's moral principles of prima facie duty.

Is intuitionism dogmatic, as some have held?[47] It might well be dogmatic to claim both that we have intuitive, certain knowledge of what our prima facie duties are *and* that we cannot ground that knowledge on any kind of evidence. But I have argued that Ross, at least, is not committed to our having "certain knowledge" here—where the certainty in question implies having indefeasible justification for moral propositions. Far from it. Despite his in some ways unfortunate analogy between moral principles and, on the other side, elementary logical and mathematical ones, he provides a place for reflective equilibrium to enhance—or override—our justification for an "intuitive" moral judgment. Nor does anything he must hold, *qua* intuitionist, preclude his allowing a systematization of the moral principles he suggests in terms of something more general. If such systematization is achieved, then contrary to what the dogmatism charge would lead one to expect, that systematization might provide reasons for the principles and a possible source of correctives for certain intuitions or apparently intuitive moral judgments.

From these points about the issue of dogmatism, it should be evident that intuitionism also need not be arbitrary, in the sense that it permits simply positing, as reasonable moral standards, any that one finds "intuitive" and then claiming to know them. Intuitionism requires that before one can be intuitively justified in accepting a moral standard, one must have an adequate understanding of the proposition in question; this often requires reflection. What reflection yields as intuitive is not arbitrary; and although products of prejudice or whim may masquerade as intuitive, this does not imply that they cannot be discovered to be deceptive. Reflection can correct its own initial results or even its repeated results. In sophisticated forms, intuitionism may also require an appeal to reflective equilibrium as a condition of justified adherence to a set of basic principles. This procedure often provides justifying reasons for, or for that matter indicates a need for revision or withdrawal of, the posited principle.

Moreover (and this is something not noted above), given how intuitions are understood—as deriving from the exercise of reason and as having evidential weight—it is incumbent on conscientious intuitionists to factor into their reflective equilibrium the apparent intuitions of *others*.[48] Ross appealed repeatedly to "what we really think" and drew attention to the analogy between intuitions in ethics and perceptions in science. Intuitions, then, are not properly conceived as arbitrary. They normally have a history in human society and a genesis in reflection. Moreover, anything arbitrarily posited would be hard-pressed to survive the kind of reflection to which conscientious intuitionists will subject their basic moral standards. Thus, even if an intuition might arise as an arbitrary cognition, it would not necessarily have prima facie justification and could easily be defeated by other intuitions or those together with further elements in the reflective equilibrium a reasonable intuitionist would seek.

One might protest, in response to some of what I have said in arguing that intuitionism is not dogmatic or arbitrary, that if Moore and Ross claim strong axiomatic status for their candidate basic moral principles one should take that claim an essential to intuitionism, at least insofar as they are paradigmatic intuitionists. I reject this principle of interpretation on the ground that the best theoretical classification of a philosopher's view comes not from simply putting together all its proffered theses, but from considering its overall purposes and thrust. If, moreover, a view takes its name from a major phenomenon—such as intuition—and if, in addition, the relevant notion is pivotal throughout the development of the theory, there is some reason to take the overall operation of that notion in the theory as more important in characterizing the theory than relatively isolated theses which proponents of the theory advance about the notion. This certainly applies to what I have developed here in connection with Ross's view: a reconstruction of the theory intended to be among its most plausible versions, even if that means only strong continuity with its historical embodiments rather than a descriptive articulation thereof.

We can perhaps be briefer on the associated philosophy of mind, if only because the chief issue we encounter here applies to philosophy in general. Is there any reason to think that a rationalist epistemology, in ethics or elsewhere, entails an implausible philosophy of mind? Does the view presuppose either a mysterious mental faculty or a scientifically unlikely mode of access to entities that cannot causally affect the brain? It *may* be that there can be a priori knowledge or a priori justification only if we in some sense grasp abstract entities, such as the concept of a promise, where this grasp is conceived as something more than a having a set of behavioral tendencies, including linguistic ones, and requires some kind of apprehension of abstract entities that do not figure in causal relations. But if this is so, it is not obvious that the comprehension in question is either obscure or in any event not required for a grasp of arithmetic truths and other apparently a priori propositions essential for both everyday reasoning and scientific inquiry.

It is true that we will have a simpler philosophy of mind, at least ontologically, if we can avoid positing any "nonempirical" objects, such as numbers or propositions or concepts. But if properties are abstract entities, as many philosophers hold, then it is not clear that even empirical knowledge of generalizations about the physical world can be known apart from a grasp of abstract entities. I believe it is fair to say that there is at present no clearly adequate, thoroughly empiricist account of justification in general, applicable to logic and mathematics as well as to epistemic principles.

I turn now to the matter of epistemic principles: roughly, principles indicating the bases or nature of knowledge and justification—say that if, on the basis of a clear visual impression of faces, I believe there are faces before me, then I am justified in so believing. There is no conclusive reason to think that Ross or other intuitionists are committed—by their intuitionism, at least—to implausible epistemic principles. I have already suggested that they need not, as intuitionists, hold the principle that if a proposition is self-evident, then it cannot be evidenced by anything else. I now want to suggest that Ross's basic principles of duty are at least candidates for a priori justification in the way they should be if they are mediately self-evident. Keeping in mind what constitutes a prima facie duty, consider how we would regard some native speaker of English who denied that there is (say) a prima facie duty not to injure other people and—to get the right connection with what Ross meant by "duty"—meant by this something implying that doing it would not be even prima facie wrong. Our first thought is that there is a misunderstanding of some key term, such as "prima facie." Indeed, I doubt that anyone not in the grip of a competing theory would deny the proposition.

Imagine, however, a steadfast instrumentalist about practical rationality: someone who holds that one has a reason to do something only in virtue of its advancing one's basic desires, and then insists that doing something can be wrong only if there is reason for one not to do it. Such a person would say that there *need* not be in anyone a basic desire advanced by not injuring others, so Ross's principle of nonmaleficence is at best contingent.

Sophisticated versions of instrumentalism are quite powerful, and they are especially plausible in the current climate because they appear to be consistent both with empiricism and with naturalism, yet instrumentalists need not claim to reduce normative properties to nonnormative ones.[49] This is no place to explore instrumentalism in detail.[50] But we should notice an implication of it: either there is nothing intrinsically good or bad, including pleasure and pain or, if there is, the existence of things having intrinsic value, even things within our grasp, provides, apart from what we or someone else actually wants, no reason for action. This will seem to go against many intuitions, in the standard sense of "intuition" that is neutral with respect to intuitionism. Is there not a reason why I should not burn a friend with a red-hot iron (and is this not an evil of some kind), even if at the moment, perhaps because my brain has been tampered with, I have no desires bearing on the matter? And even if I have lost all motivation in life, is there not reason, and indeed reason for me, not to burn myself? If the answer is, as it seems to be, affirmative, then there can be noninstrumental reasons favoring my action.[51]

I have granted for the sake of argument something intuitionists would generally (and I think plausibly) deny: that one could justifiedly hold that there are things of intrinsic value, yet deny that they provide, independently of actual desires, even prima facie reasons for action. Imagine that an opponent of intuitionism takes this route. What would justify holding that there *is* anything of such value? It is not obvious that one could have an empirical justification of this thesis. To be sure, there are things people *value intrinsically* (e.g., toward which they take a positive attitude directly rather than on the basis of believing these things to be a means to something further). But this psychological fact about human *valuation* does not entail the normative conclusion that the things in question actually *have* intrinsic *value.*[52] I believe reflection will show that it is at least far from clear that justification for believing there is anything of intrinsic value—including intrinsic moral value—does not have to rest at least in part on a priori considerations of the kind Ross describes. But I put this forward only as a challenge. The issue is highly debatable.

What is perhaps less controversial is that if we do not ascribe to reason the minimal power required in order for a moderate intuitionism of the kind I have described to be a plausible theory, then we face serious problems that must be solved before any instrumentalist or empiricist ethical theory is plausible.[53] For one thing, instrumentalists must account for their fundamental principle that if, on my beliefs, an action serves a basic (roughly, noninstrumental) desire of mine, then there is a reason for me to perform the action. This principle appears to be a better candidate for mediate self-evidence than for empirical confirmation.[54] This is not to say that a moderate intuitionism is true. The point is that unless reason has sufficient power to make that principle a plausible candidate for truth, then it is not clear that instrumentalist theories are plausible candidates either.

If I have been roughly correct in this defense of a reconstructed Rossian view, then intuitionism in moral epistemology, and in the foundations of ethics, should be a more serious contender for contemporary allegiance than it is. For many of the same reasons, there is more room for a rationalist moral epistemology than is generally realized. Once it is seen how reflection of an at least methodologically a priori kind is central in ethical theorizing, some of the major obstacles in the way of a rationalist account of the foundations of ethics are eliminated. There is much to commend in a fallibilist, intuitionistic moral rationalism that uses reflection as a justificatory method in the ways described here, encompassing both intuitions as prima facie justified inputs to ethical theorizing and reflective equilibrium as a means of extending and systematizing those inputs. Whatever our verdicts on intuitionism and rationalism, however, when they are rightly understood they can be seen to carry less baggage than is often attributed to them and to provide, in their best embodiments, a method of ethical inquiry that may be reasonably used in approaching any basic moral problem.

Notes

Earlier versions of this chapter (which draws heavily on my previous work) were presented at Santa Clara University, Texas A and M University, the University of Memphis, the University of Texas at Austin, and at the 1994 Moral Epistemology Conference at Dartmouth College. I benefited much from the discussions on those occasions (particularly at the Conference), as well as from comments by Malia Brink, Bernard Gert, Christopher Kulp, Hugh McCann, Stephen Sencerz, William Throop, Mark Timmons, Douglas Weber, Patrick Yarnell, Nick Zangwill, and, especially, Walter Sinnott-Armstrong.

1. John Rawls comes to mind here, especially *A Theory of Justice* (Cambridge: Harvard University Press, 1971), 34. The following passage from a review of Rawls's *Political Liberalism* (New York: Columbia University Press, 1993) and Thomas K. Seung's *Intuition and Construction* (New Haven: Yale University Press, 1993), typifies contemporary attitudes toward intuitionism: "Intuitionism makes metaphysical claims and epistemological demands that run counter to modern thought . . . when science emphasizes observation and verification, can we still believe in a 'brooding omnipresence in the sky?' " See William Powers, Jr., "Constructing Liberal Political Theory," *Texas Law Review* 72, no. 2 (1993), 456. (Seung himself defends a Platonic intuitionism; this passage is presumably meant to represent what Powell takes Seung to consider wrong with intuitionism of the kind found in Ross, to be examined below.) For further critical discussion of intuitionism (and a good example of a theorist who often appeals to intuitions but rejects Rossian intuitionism), see Jonathan Dancy, *Moral Reasons* (Oxford: Basil Blackwell, 1993), esp. chapters 4–6.

2. See W. D. Ross, *The Right and the Good* (Oxford: Oxford University Press, 1930; reprinted by Hackett, Indianapolis, 1988), especially chapter 2, 16–39. Rawls finds the pluralism so important that he considers it the basic feature of ethical intuitionism, though he grants that intuitionism is usually taken to have other important properties. See *A Theory of Justice*, pp. 34–35. According to Bernard Williams, in the 1950s and 1960s "it was taken for granted that intuitionism in ethics was an epistemological doctrine . . . the kind of view held, for instance, by W. D. Ross and H. A. Prichard." See "What Does Intuitionism Imply?," in R. Dancy, J. Moravcsik, and C. Taylor, eds., *Human Agency* (Stanford: Stanford University Press, 1988), 198. Williams credits Rawls with changing "our understanding of the term" so as to "restore an earlier state of affairs" (ibid.). For William K. Frankena, "An intuitionist must believe in simple indefinable properties, properties that are of a peculiar non-natural or normative sort, a priori or nonempirical concepts, and self-evident or synthetic necessary propositions." See *Ethics*, 2d ed. (Englewood Cliffs: Prentice-Hall, 1973), 103.

3. I am not alone in so conceiving the matter; see Walter Sinnott-Armstrong's valuable account of intuitionism in *The Encyclopedia of Ethics* (New York and London: Garland, 1992), 628–30.

4. See Ross, *The Right and the Good,* p. 21.

5. Ross often used "actual duty" where I use "final duty" but this is misleading: as explained below, even an overridden duty is actually possessed. For discussion of the actuality of Rossian duties see Scott Landers, "A Defense of Ross's Distinction between *Prima Facie* Duty and Duty *Sans Phrase,* All Things Considered," presented to the Central Division of the American Philosophical Association in 1994.

6. Ross himself spoke this way: "I suggest '*prima facie* duty' or 'conditional duty' as a brief way of referring to this characteristic . . . which an act has, in virtue of being of a certain kind (e.g., the keeping of a promise), of being an act which would be a duty proper if it were not at the same time of another kind which is morally significant" (*The Right and the Good,* p. 19).

7. He contrasts his view with that of "Professor Moore and Dr. Rashdall, that there is only the duty of producing good, and that all 'conflicts of duties' should be resolved by asking 'by which action will most good be produced?' ", ibid., pp. 18–19.

8. *The Right and the Good,* pp. 29–30. Cf. H. A. Prichard, "Does Moral Philosophy Rest on a Mistake?" (1912), in his *Moral Obligation* (Oxford: Oxford University Press, 1949). The mistake is "supposing the possibility of proving what can only be apprehended directly by an act of moral thinking" (p. 16).

9. Ibid., pp. 31 and 33. Ross's examples show that he is thinking of the possibility that an act has some properties in virtue of which it is prima facie right and some in virtue of which it is prima facie wrong, and in such cases "we come to believe something not self-evident at all, but an object of probable opinion, namely that this particular act is (not *prima facie* right but) actually right" (p. 33). The note on page 33 admits his overstating the no-general-description claim; his point could be taken to be a version of the thesis that no factual description entails an *actual* obligation, but might also be considered epistemic: no set of facts makes it self-evident, even if it does entail, that a specific act is one's actual duty. The crucial point is that Rossian intuitionism does not claim that intuition yields knowledge of what to do in conflict cases. For Ross it would be a mistake to say, "intuitionism is so called because it says intuition is what tells us what duty prevails," as remarked by Joel Feinberg in *Reason and Responsibility* (Belmont, Calif.: Wadsworth, 1993), p. 445. Regarding what to do given conflicts of duty Ross cites Aristotle's dictum that "the decision rests with perception," which he did not identify with apprehension or anything else plausibly taken as a kind of intuition (*The Right and the Good,* pp. 41–42).

10. *The Right and the Good,* pp. 39–41.

11. The quotation is from page 41; for the primacy of reflection on specific cases see, for example, pp. 41–42. In *The Foundations of Ethics* (Oxford: Oxford University Press, 1939), he says, of "insight into the basic principles of morality," that it is not based on "a fairly elaborate consideration of the probable consequences" of certain types of acts; "When we consider a particular act as a lie, or as the breaking of a promise . . . we do not need to, and do not, fall back on a remembered general principle; we see the individual act to be by its very nature wrong" (pp. 172–73). Speaking approvingly of Aristotle, Ross said of right acts that, while first "done without any thought of their rightness," when "a certain degree of mental maturity" was reached, "their rightness was not deduced from any general principle; rather the general principle was later recognized by intuitive induction as being implied in the general judgments already passed on particular acts" (p. 170). The reference to induction is not meant

to imply that the knowledge of "basic principles of morality" is inferential. As the later intuitionist A. C. Ewing put it in referring to intuitive induction, it "is not reasoning at all but intuition or immediate insight helped by examples." See "Reason and Intuition," *Proceedings of the British Academy* 27 (1941), reprinted in his *Non-Linguistic Philosophy* (London: George Allen and Unwin, 1968), 38, note 1.

12. This is relevant to problems of euthanasia. I would stress that the absence of any a priori hierarchy does not prevent Ross's countenancing either prima facie generalizations to the effect that one duty is stronger than another or generalizations to the effect that under certain conditions a type of act, such as unplugging a respirator, is preferable to another, say a fatal injection. He says, for example, "normally promise-keeping comes before benevolence" and then *roughly* specifies the conditions under which it does (*The Right and the Good*, p. 19).

13. This may be in part what leads R. B. Brandt (among others) to consider intuitionism as such committed to the possibility of intuitively grasping self-evidence, as opposed to truth. See *Ethical Theory* (Englewood Cliffs, N.J.: Prentice-Hall, 1959), chapter 8. Cf. Jonathan Harrison: "According to this view [intuitionism], a person who can grasp the truth of ethical generalizations does not acquire them as a result of a process of ratiocination; he just sees without argument that they are and must be true, and true of all possible worlds." See "Ethical Objectivism," *The Encyclopedia of Philosophy* (New York: Macmillan, 1967).

14. I do not think that this point is contradicted by Ross's *Foundations of Ethics,* cited in note 11.

15. G. E. Moore, *Principia Ethica* (London: Cambridge University Press, 1903), *x*. See also page 145. Cf. Henry Sidgwick, *The Methods of Ethics* (London: Macmillan, 1874) citing "an ambiguity in the use of the term 'intuition,' " he says, "by calling any affirmation as to the rightness or wrongness of actions 'intuitive,' I do not mean to prejudice the question as to its ultimate validity ... I only mean that its truth is apparently known immediately ... any such 'intuition' may turn out to have an element of error, which subsequent reflection and comparison may enable us to correct" (p. 211). For detailed explication of Moore and an ethical theory in the Moorean tradition, see Panayot Butchvarov, *Skepticism in Ethics* (Bloomington: Indiana University Press, 1989). For further pertinent discussion and a number of helpful references, see Caroline J. Simon, "The Intuitionist Argument," *Southern Journal of Philosophy* XXVIII (1990).

16. Such fallibility is not strictly entailed by the defeasibility of the justification of the intuition in question. An intuition of a logical truth could be defeasible—as where one finds what looks on careful reflection like a disproof—without being fallible; one could thus lose justification for the proposition even though, objectively, one's intuition, being of a logical truth, could not have been in error.

17. I restrict discussion to *propositional intuitions—intuitions that,* intuitions of some proposition as true, as opposed to *property intuitions—intuitions of,* roughly, apprehensions of some property. Suppose, however, that the former must be based on the latter (e.g., an intuition that a triangle has three sides might have to be based on an intuitive grasp of the nature of a triangle or, perhaps better, of the concept of a triangle). The points to follow concerning propositional intuitions will hold whether or not there is such an epistemic dependency.

18. A. C. Ewing is explicit on the point, at least for basic intuitions. See, for example, *Ethics* (London: English Universities Press, 1953), 136, where he says that "propositions, particularly in ethics but also in other fields of thought, sometimes present themselves to a person in such a way that he ... knows or rationally believes them to be true without having reasons or at least seems to himself to do so ... some

ethical propositions must be known immediately if any are to be known at all." Cf.
his *The Fundamental Questions of Philosophy* (London: Routledge and Kegan Paul,
1951), 48–49.

19. Ross even comments on the difficulty of determining exactly what a promise
is (*The Right and the Good*, p. 35).

20. An intuition may also be caused by commitment to a theory, as where reflection
on the theory leads one to explore a topic and one thereby forms intuitions about it.
But this causal dependence of the intuition on the theory has no necessary bearing
on the justificatory status of the former.

21. To some readers this will need argument or further explanation; both are
given in some detail in my *The Structure of Justification* (Cambridge and New York:,
Cambridge University Press, 1993), esp. chapter 4, "The Foundationalism-Coherentism
Controversy: Hardened Stereotypes and Overlapping Theories."

22. Sidgwick, for example, speaks of our discerning "certain general rules with
really clear and finally valid intuition," *The Methods of Ethics*, pp. 100–104.

23. Kant might not find the singular proposition intuitive *at all*, at least prior to
one's grasp of the moral generalization applying to it. He stresses that it is a disservice
to morality to derive it from examples—*Foundations of the Metaphysics of Morals*, p.
408; this, however, apparently indicates a rejection of particularlism and a view about
the relative *priority* of intuitions about examples versus generalizations, rather than a
commitment to the view that we cannot have intuitions about examples.

24. Two qualifications will help. First, if the belief is based on anything *other* than
understanding the proposition, that understanding must still be a sufficient basis (in
a sense I cannot explicate now). Second, there may be a non-truth-entailing use of
'self-evident,' which would allow for false and hence unknowable self-evident propositions; but I assume that any such use is at best nonstandard. What is more controversial
about my characterization is that—apparently—only a priori propositions satisfy it.
Note, however, that the analysandum is self-evidence simpliciter, not self-evidence *for*
S. There is some plausibility in saying that it is self-evident, for me, that I exist. I leave
open whether such cases illustrate a kind of self-evidence, but the relevant proposition
asserting my existence is surely not self-evident.

25. Someone might argue that this is not evident in itself, because it is knowable
only through knowledge that (1) first cousins are children of siblings and (2) if there
never have been any siblings then there never have been any children of siblings. But
(1) is a definitional truth, in a sense implying that (2) simply *is* the proposition in
question—that if there never have been any siblings, then there never have been any
first cousins—formulated with "children of siblings" in place of "first cousins." Seeing
its truth requires understanding what it says, but not separately believing a definition
and inferring the proposition from that as a premise. Cf. the more complicated proposition that first cousins have at least one pair of grandparents in common.

26. Two clarifications: (1) Assuming one cannot reflect in the relevant way on the
concepts in question without *some* kind of understanding of them, I take it that there
is a level of understanding of mediately self-evident propositions, or at least of parts
of them, not by itself sufficient for justification but capable of leading to that as the
understanding develops by reflection. (2) The term *normal adults* is vague, but that
begs no questions here; the problem is largely eliminable by relativizing, making
the basic notion mediately self-evident *for S*, or for adults with a certain level of
conceptual sophistication.

27. The suggested characterization of an immediately self-evident proposition does
not entail that such a proposition is compelling; but it would at least be true that for

normal persons in normal circumstances it would be compelling. None of this rules out there being a notion of self-evidence *for a person;* but the concept we need is that of a self-evident proposition, and that is my focus. That concept has implicit *reference* to persons, or at least minds; but this does not make it *relative* to persons, in the sense that we cannot call a proposition self-evident except *to* some particular set of persons.

28. This paragraph and the remainder of this section draw on my "Moral Epistemology and the Supervenience of Ethical Concepts," *Southern Journal of Philosophy* XXIX Supplement (1990).

29. This is a broadly foundationalist assumption. I defend it in *The Structure of Justification,* cited in note 21. For further defenses and relevant references see W. P. Alston, *Epistemic Justification* (Ithaca and London: Cornell University Press, 1989) and Paul K. Moser, *Knowledge and Evidence* (Cambridge and New York: Cambridge University Press, 1989). For a contrasting view applied to moral judgments, see David Copp, "Considered Judgments and Moral Justification: Conservatism in Moral Theory," in David Copp and David Zimmerman, eds., *Morality, Reason and Truth* (Totowa, N.J.: Rowman and Allanheld, 1985).

30. Two comments are in order. First, while priority may suggest the Aristotelian notion of being "more easily known," that elusive notion is not the one characterized in the text. Second, I am taking the provability relation to be, unlike mere logical derivability, asymmetrical, so that the relevant premise is *not* provable from the proposition it can be used prove, and is in that way prior to the latter. Third, some might require strong axiomatic status as a condition for being an axiom at all, but notice that a proposition can systematize a body of theorems even if derivable from some prior proposition, and even without being immediately self-evident. That it might itself be a theorem relative to something else does not change this, though it does suggest that an *elegant* system would put in place of the proposition a prior, strongly axiomatic one.

31. In *Posterior Analytics* 72b, where Aristotle introduced his famous epistemic regress argument, he seems to imply that the appropriate foundations for knowledge must be strongly axiomatic. But even what cannot be moved higher in the epistemic hierarchy of a person might perhaps be moved *out* of it: indefeasibility (the impossibility of one's justification's being overridden) is perhaps not entailed even by strong axiomaticity.

32. For a somewhat Rossian case against there being a correct answer to the second question by appeal to a derivation of moral principles from some overarching moral principle, see Bernard Gert, *Morality: A New Justification of the Moral Rules* (Oxford and New York: Oxford University Press, 1988).

33. Cf. Christine Swanton's point (noted after the above was written), in a rigorous defense of intuitionism, that "there is no reason why an intuitionist could not appeal to such a conception in grounding both the first-order principles of the system and the second-order principles for resolving conflict. Such a conception may be a conception of human flourishing founded on an Aristotelian system of human virtue. . . . Alternatively, the underlying moral conception could be contractualist, involving an understanding of the point of morality as a system which renders possible co-operation amidst conflict of interest." See "The Rationality of Ethical Intuitionism," *Australasian Journal of Philosophy* 65 (1987), p. 175. This line is not developed in relation to any account of self-evidence nor shown to be an option for Ross in particular. Moreover the grounding is not said to be potentially deductive, though that is allowed and perhaps intended by the text. See also Sinnott-Armstrong, *The Encyclopedia of Ethics,* for a formulation of the consistency of intuitionism with a kind of derivability.

34. Perhaps in part because of the way Moore and Ross (among other intuitionists in moral epistemology) put their views, many philosophers have taken the intuitionist moral epistemology itself, as a positive account of how general moral truths can be known noninferentially, to imply that these propositions cannot be justified inferentially. Speaking of Prichard, J. O. Urmson says, "Moral philosophy, regarded as the attempt to provide a basis and justification for common morality, was a mistaken enterprise because the essentials of common morality were immediately apprehended. . . . One can apprehend that to lie or break a promise is as such wrong, *so that any attempt to show that it is wrong . . . must be wrongheaded"* (italics added). See "Prichard and Knowledge," in Dancy, Moravcsik, and Taylor, eds., *Human Agency,* p. 14. I maintain that the inference attributed to Prichard is invalid. Cf. Frankena, *Ethics,* p. 103.

35. Here and elsewhere I speak as if there were just one categorical imperative. Even if that is not so, the point here probably applies to all the formulations.

36. This possibility is explored by many writers. Plato and Aristotle surely explore it, as do Hume and Kant. Rawls's theory of justice explores it from a restricted, largely instrumentalist conception of rationality—only largely because, for one thing, he assumes that a rational person does not suffer from envy (*A Theory of Justice,* p. 143). Another approach, and relevant references, are provided in my "Moral Epistemology," cited above. An examination of Rawls's assumption in relation to instrumentalism is given in my "Autonomy, Reason, and Desire," *Pacific Philosophical Quarterly* 72 (1992).

37. See *A Theory of Justice,* for example, pp. 46–52. It is true that Rawls suggests that reflective equilibrium is a coherentist procedure, whereas Ross is a foundationalist; but Rawls is probably taking foundationalism to posit indefeasible starting points, as Ross need not do. A. C. Ewing is even more emphatically defeasibilist and fallibilist than Ross; see, for example, "Reason and Intuition," pp. 58–63, and *Ethics,* chapter 8 (both cited above). If I am correct about intuitionism, then even if Rawls is right in saying that it is "not constructive" (p. 52), this limitation would be extrinsic. For discussion of Rawls's general strategy of ethical justification and of reflective equilibrium in particular (with an indication why it need not be viewed as a coherentist procedure), see R. B. Brandt, *A Theory of the Good and the Right* (Oxford: Oxford University Press, 1979) and Roger Ebertz, "Is Reflective Equilibrium a Coherence Method?," *Canadian Journal of Philosophy,* (1993). Another valuable study of Rawlsian reflective equilibrium, with special attention to its use of intuitions, is Stefan Sencerz, "Moral Intuitions and Justification in Ethics," *Philosophical Studies* 50 (1986).

38. At least if we are realists, we will count intuitions reliable only if we believe we may also hope they are true. For nonrealists, reliability may be more a matter of, say, coherence over time. On either view, reliable intuitions may or may not be conclusions of reflection.

39. This point suggests that *some* kind of foundationalist assumptions underlie the method (as is certainly plain in Ross). That a moderate foundationalist approach is reasonable in general is defended in detail in *The Structure of Justification* (cited in note 21). There is no implication, of course, that noninferentially justified elements are indefeasible; and the method is fully compatible with the use of reflective equilibrium as a corrective and confirmational technique.

40. The notion of harm may not be purely "factual," but the factual components in it will serve our illustrative purposes. There may be other factors: perhaps if the promisee would, reflectively, no longer *want* us to keep the promise this would remove the very ground of our obligation; it would certainly weaken the prima facie obligation.

41. See especially *Utilitarianism,* chapter 1.

42. This is a good place to note the relation of ethical reflectionism to R. B. Brandt's "qualified attitude" method for appraising moral judgments. We are to arrive at attitudes that are impartial, informed by an awareness of "relevant facts," not the result of an abnormal state of mind, and consistent and general." See *Ethical Theory* (cited above), especially pp. 244–52. This method appears to be a (good) theoretical extension of the method of reflection, perhaps something like an application of it, and less basic. Would it not be by reflection that we determine (e.g.) what sorts of facts are relevant, what partiality is, and that partiality can vitiate moral judgment? It is arguable that reflection is not specifically moral if it does not take account of such factors as Brandt describes; but even if that is so, I want to leave open that the basic moral principles or standards might derive from the more general point of view of practical reason.

43. This higher-order proposition may be given either a cognitivist account as, say, a claim in meta-ethics, or a noncognitivist account as an evaluation, and what some cognitivists call self-evident propositions some noncognitivists might reconstrue as expressions of self-evidently rational attitudes. (I bypass problems about how 'self-evidently rational' might be characterized on such a view.)

44. Compare a reliabilism that says moral knowledge and justified moral beliefs can be produced by reliable processes to which we may have no access by reflection. This would not be ruled out by reflectionism so long as the results of the relevant processes can be validated by reflection (as is not the case for a crude divine command view), in which case we would have inductive evidence that moral beliefs of a certain kind, say those delivered by a moral sense, are true. Even if knowledge can arise in the former way, however, justification seems to require accessible grounds, as I have argued in *The Structure of Justification,* cited above. I am not aware of any ethical theorist's holding such a reliabilism about moral justification, but the position is a good foil for reflectionism.

45. For a specimen view of this sort see William Tolhurst, "On the Epistemic Value of Moral Experience," *Southern Journal of Philosophy* XXIX, Supplement (1990). Cf. Michael DePaul, "The Highest Moral Knowledge and the Truth Behind Internalism," and Adrian M. S. Piper, "Seeing Things," both in that issue.

46. I do not see the emphasis on nonnatural properties that is so prominent in Moore as required by the core of Ross's view, and I therefore do not make nonnaturalism a commitment of intuitionism in general.

47. See, for example, Stephen C. Pepper, *Ethics* (New York: Appleton-Century-Crofts, 1960), 237.

48. On the importance of this in ethics see Margaret Urban Walker's "Feminist Skepticism, Authority, and Transparency," in this volume.

49. There is a temptation on the part of many instrumentalists to do this, as may be noted in places in Richard A. Fumerton's *Reason and Morality* (Ithaca and London: Cornell University Press, 1990); for an indication of relevant passages see my review of this book in *Philosophical Review* 101 (1992).

50. Thomas Nagel's *The View from Nowhere* and Bernard Gert's *Morality* are far-reaching critiques of instrumentalism; I have explored it in, for example, *Practical Reasoning* (London and New York: Routledge, 1989) and "The Architecture of Reason," in *The Structure of Justification.* I offer an account and critique of ethical naturalism in "Ethical Naturalism and the Explanatory Power of Moral Concepts," in Steven J. Wagner and Richard Warner, eds., *Naturalism: A Critical Appraisal* (Notre Dame, Ind.: University of Notre Dame Press, 1993).

51. One might, as Walter Sinnott-Armstrong has pointed out to me, posit future desires as sources of reasons here, for example, my future desire not to be a person who has burned a friend. But unless I now have—what I may lack—a second-order desire to give some weight to future desires, this move in effect gives us a significantly changed instrumentalism, as would the related move of giving weight to present desires I *would* have under various conditions, such as reflection on my options. Why should a real instrumentalist be interested in future or hypothetical desires? It is not as if, for example, rational persons must give equal weight to all stages of their lives. That would be appropriate to an *overall* desire-satisfaction theory of reasons for action, but that is a different theory—and, I suspect, not plausible unless there is something intrinsically good about desire satisfaction. For detailed critical appraisal of instrumentalism, see Gert, *Morality: A New Justification.*

52. A point missed, I think, by John Stuart Mill in his attempted proof of the principle of utility in chapter 4 of *Utilitariansism.*

53. I neglect noncognitivism here; I believe that it encounters serious problems of its own, but it is a significant contender. See, for example, Allan Gibbard, *Wise Choices, Apt Feelings* (Cambridge: Harvard University Press, 1990). For criticism of Gibbard's position, see Walter Sinnott-Armstrong's "Some Problems for Gibbard's Norm-Expressivism," *Philosophical Studies* 69 (1993). I also neglect R. B. Brandt's modified instrumentalism; see his *A Theory of the Good and the Right* (Oxford: Clarendon Press, 1979). I have appraised Brandt's overall view of rationality in "An Epistemic Conception of Rationality," in *The Structure of Justification,* cited above.

54. Some empiricists might claim that it is analytic, say because to have a reason for action just *is* to have such a basic desire and set of beliefs. But this is at best highly controversial, in part because it simply begs the question against intuitionism and other prominent views.

5

Coherentist Epistemology
and Moral Theory

Geoffrey Sayre-McCord

Moral knowledge, to the extent anyone has it, is as much a matter of knowing *how*—how to act, react, feel and reflect appropriately—as it is a matter of knowing *that*—that injustice is wrong, courage is valuable, and care is due. Such knowledge is embodied in a range of capacities, abilities, and skills that are not acquired simply by learning that certain things are morally required or forbidden or that certain abilities and skills are important.[1] To lose sight of this fact, to focus exclusively on questions concerning what is commonly called *propositional knowledge,* is to lose one's grip on (at least one crucial aspect of) the intimate connection between morality and action. At the same time, insofar as it suggests that moral capacities can be exhaustively accounted for by appeal to peoples' cognitive states, to focus on propositional knowledge is to invite an overintellectualized picture of those capacities. No account of moral knowledge will be adequate unless it does justice to the ways in which knowing right from wrong, and good from bad, is not simply a matter of forming the correct beliefs but is a matter of acquiring certain abilities to act, react, feel, and reflect appropriately in the situations in which one finds oneself. And this means a satisfying treatment of moral epistemology must give due attention to what's involved in knowing how to be moral.

I mention this now, at the beginning of my paper, as a partial corrective to what follows. For in the rest of this paper I will not be giving due attention to what's involved in knowing *how* to be moral. I won't even give much attention to what's involved in *knowing that* something is moral (or not). I will be concentrating instead almost exclusively on questions concerning the *justification* of moral belief, and will then be focusing—even more narrowly—on questions of epistemic, rather than moral, justification, giving only indirect attention to issues relating to moral justification.[2] I will be asking:

Under what conditions are a person's moral beliefs epistemically justified? And so: Under what conditions are *our* moral beliefs epistemically justified?

What I hope to offer here is an account of epistemic justification that can do justice to the epistemic challenges our moral beliefs face, while leaving room for some of those beliefs, sometimes, to count as justified in precisely the same way our more mundane nonmoral beliefs, sometimes, do. I don't mean to suggest, and I certainly won't argue, that our moral beliefs are actually as justified as many of our other beliefs are. I think many of them are not; the challenges they face properly induce epistemic humility. But I do think that some of our moral beliefs are justified and justified in the same sense (if not always to the same degree) as are many of our other beliefs.

As a result, what I'll be doing is primarily defending in general—and without special regard for morality—a theory of the epistemic justification of belief that applies across the board to all our beliefs. Despite my being especially concerned with the status of our moral beliefs, then, a great deal of the discussion that follows will be put in terms that self-consciously and intentionally don't speak directly to morality. So far as I can see, the epistemic evaluation of our moral beliefs is of a piece with that of all our other beliefs; there is no distinctive epistemology of moral belief.

Nonetheless, our moral beliefs do have distinctive features that render them epistemologically suspect. Most notably, our moral beliefs are disturbingly hard to justify in the face of disagreement. All too often we are reduced to invoking convictions that seem more obviously right than any justification we might offer for them, even as we recognize that others find incompatible views (that they are no better able to defend) equally obvious. Even if we are confident that we can explain away what we take to be their mistaken views by appeal to their particular situation, experience, and especially training, it takes no leap of the imagination to see that similar explanations of our views are available to them. Worse, those explanations are available to us; when we turn our attention to the explanation of our own views, just the same sorts of explanations seem to go through—explanations that appeal to physical, psychological, and social facts, but not to moral facts, as the determinants of our beliefs. We seem ourselves to be able to explain all our own moral views without having to suppose that any of them are actually true.

The difficulties merely compound when we wonder what it would take for those beliefs actually to be true, even given our inclination to think some of them are. On reflection, it is not at all clear, for instance, how moral properties (assuming there are some) might fit into and relate to the world as we know it. Unlike everyday nonmoral properties of normal-sized objects, moral properties seem to make a claim on us regardless of our tastes, preferences, and affective attitudes. They seem to have a distinctive normative authority that allows them legitimately to command the allegiance of everyone. That some course of action is right, that some thing is good, that some character admirable, apparently necessarily gives us reason to act or respond in some way or another, whereas that some act is legal, or some thing blue, or some character uncommon, seem in themselves to provide no particular reason to act or respond at all. Yet it is a mystery how moral properties might come by this authority. Moreover, as different from others as these putatively authoritative facts seem to be, they do not float free of the more mundane physical, psychological, and social properties of people, actions, or institutions. In fact, people, actions, and institutions apparently have the moral properties they do always thanks to their nonmoral properties, even as their being right or wrong, virtuous or vicious, just or unjust, looks to be something over and above their exhibiting whatever nonmoral properties they do.

At the same time, for us to be able to discover moral properties (if we ever do), it looks as if we would have to rely on some means other than those we normally use to learn about the world. We don't seem to see, taste, hear, smell, or touch moral properties, nor do we seem to rely on common methods of empirical investigation and confirmation to discover them. Although we speak of *feeling* that something is wrong, or right, the suggestion that these feelings are extra or suprasensory perceptions, the product of some special moral faculty, is hardly plausible. Despite the apparent dependence of moral properties on nonmoral properties, the results of empirical investigation appears to be altogether irrelevant to the justification of our moral views (although not to their application). Our moral beliefs have, at best, it seems, only a tenuous connection to experience, a connection evidently established more by the moral convictions we bring to bear on that experience than by the untainted input of experience.

All told, then, what these moral properties might actually be and how we might manage to learn about them is, at least, mysterious. Their very mysteriousness naturally raises doubts about what grounds we might actually have for our moral beliefs.

These concerns are not at all easily or confidently put to rest. They work together not simply to undermine confidence in our particular convictions, but also to suggest that our moral views as a whole might best be seen as an explicable illusion.[3] Some would even say that these problems offer good grounds for embracing noncognitivism—for thinking our moral attitudes are best viewed not as beliefs at all but rather as expressions of preference, or a projection of our sentiments, or a reflection of norms we (just happen to) embrace. When it comes to our moral attitudes, they say, epistemic evaluations are out of place because the attitudes in question are not the sorts of things that can be true or false.[4]

I am not myself inclined to noncognitivism. And, in another context, I would argue that when the reasons adduced to justify some action or attitude succeed, they simultaneously provide grounds for one's thinking, of certain moral judgments concerning the actions or attitudes, that they are true.[5] But that argument is not so important here, since the main questions I need to address—concerning the justification of belief (whether moral or not)—can and should be raised about the epistemic credentials of the noncognitivism I am inclined to reject.[6] Consequently, in the rest of the paper, I will simply assume (contentiously) that people do sometimes have moral beliefs and that we can reasonably wonder about them whether they are epistemically justified in believing as they do.

In what follows, I will defend a coherence theory of epistemic justification according to which our beliefs, moral and otherwise, are justified only if, and then to the extent that, they cohere well with the other things we believe. On this view, whether a person's beliefs are justified is a matter of how well they hang together. One person, then, may be justified in holding some belief that another would be justified in rejecting, and how justified the first person would be is not a matter of her belief actually being true, nor a matter of it satisfying some epistemic standard wholly independent of the other things she believes, but rather a function precisely of what else she believes.

In the end, and perhaps not surprisingly, what recommends this view is that it coheres well—better than its competitors—with what we already believe concerning justification. Most especially, I will be trying to accommodate two features of justification. The first is that a person may be justified in holding a view we recognize to be false, and massively so. This is the force and implication of dramatic examples well known in epistemology that appeal to evil demons and brains in vats. But the same recognition crops up in everyday situations in which we recognize someone as justifiably holding the views they do despite their being unfortunately ill-informed or understandably misled by the partial information they have available. The second feature is that holding justified beliefs represents an accomplishment that is bound up with actually having some reason to think what one believes is true. So although one might justifiably believe what (as it happens) is false, one must, even in those situations, have reason to think it true.

Of course, the fit between the coherence theory and our initial convictions concerning justification will at points be less than perfect, and later in the paper I will be at pains to explain away, rather than accommodate, some of the views that make other accounts of justification seem attractive. Nonetheless, the coherence theory does an extremely good job of explaining, and in other ways making sense of, the variety of views people have concerning the nature of epistemic justification. At the same time, I'll suggest, it has the significant advantage of making good sense of our actually being, at least to some extent and concerning some things, epistemically justified in holding our moral beliefs.

Before spelling out the coherence theory of epistemic justification and defending it, I want first to back into the discussion by describing (what might be called) the coherence *method* for moral theorizing. This foray into method is appropriate for two reasons. First, I will, in effect, be applying the method to questions of epistemology, relying on the approach the method recommends in an attempt to identify and defend an acceptable theory of epistemic justification. Second, the coherence theory's recent appeal, especially in moral theory, can be traced directly to the attractiveness of this method. In fact, many have thought that the coherence method is the only approach to moral theorizing that promises any hope of progress, and more than a few have seen the method as being intimately intertwined with the coherence theory. I should emphasize right off, though, what will become clear: that someone might value the method without thinking that the justification of our resulting views is a matter of their relative coherence. Although anyone attracted by the coherence theory will be inclined to endorse the methodology, adoption of the method is compatible with rejection of the coherence theory of justification.[7]

Coherence and the Method of Reflective Equilibrium

The coherence method, or at least evidence of its use, shows up throughout the history of moral theorizing. Yet the coherence method has risen to recognized prominence in moral theory only recently thanks to John Rawls' *A Theory of Justice*.[8] Referring to it there as the method of reflective equilibrium, Rawls characterizes the process of developing an acceptable moral theory as a matter of shifting back and forth among the various moral judgments one is initially inclined to make and the more or less abstract theoretical principles one is examining and attempting to develop, altering the collection of principles to fit better the judgments and adjusting the judgments so as to bring them, as best one can, in line with plausible principles.

The method is anything but static; it is meant to be deployed continually as one's set of convictions shifts thanks to expanding experience and in light of reflecting on the grounds one might have for those convictions. All along, as the method would have it, one should increase the coherence of one's beliefs by eliminating inconsistencies, articulating principles that are already implicit in one's judgments, and seeking out further grounds that would justify and unify these judgments and principles, always being willing to shift one's view in light of the developments. As things progress, some of the initial judgments will have to be put aside as ill-informed, misguided, or otherwise suspect (perhaps because there seems to be no plausible way to defend them), and new commitments will come on board thanks sometimes just to expanding experience, and other times to seeing what is implicit in, or required by, what else one believes.

The underlying idea is that, while we inevitably start with whatever attitudes, convictions, and beliefs we have, and properly rely on them in adjusting our opinions, we should not rest content with things as they stand, but should instead subject our evaluative attitudes to the pressures of reflection—doing what we can to render systematic, by providing general principles for, the hodgepodge of convictions with which we begin. Starting with our initial convictions we are to forge, as best we can, a consistent, unified, set of beliefs that inter-relate in ways that allow our more particular convictions to find support from more general principles, which themselves find support from their ability to account for the more particular judgments.

The process is at least analogous to the one we rely on in developing our scientific theories, where we start with various observations, hypotheses, and hunches and then work to bring these together within a coherent system. All the while, we are adjusting the theoretical principles so as to fit the relevant observations, articulate the general hypotheses, and follow our hunches, even as we are refining our observations, altering our hypotheses, and reevaluating our hunches, to bring them in line with our best theories.

There are dangers, of course, in over-extending the analogy between scientific and moral methodology, dangers that come, for instance, from thinking that the initial moral judgments must, like some perceptual observations, be due to the operation of a special faculty, or from thinking that moral principles must, like scientific laws, explain our making the judgments we do, or from thinking that moral theories, like scientific theories, tell us how things are but not how they should be. In many striking ways scientific inquiry differs substantially from moral inquiry.

Yet there are dangers as well in ignoring the methodological analogy, dangers that come, most especially, from ignoring the extent to which moral judgments are sensitive to reflection and argument, and from thinking that experience has no role to play in expanding and confirming our moral views. Regardless, so far as the method is concerned, our aim should be to bring our various views, no matter what they concern (physics, ethics, epistemology, or mathematics), into a reflective equilibrium.

Two sorts of equilibria might be sought in moral theorizing: a narrow equilibrium that is reached if one settles on a set of moral principles that cohere well with the moral judgments that, on reflection, one is willing to embrace; and a wider equilibrium that requires more, as it brings into the mix not just particular moral judgments and general moral principles but also judgments and principles concerning whatever psychological, social, physical, or metaphysical matters might prove relevant—including judgments and principles about the relevance of these other areas. Either would count as a *reflective* equilibrium as long as the various elements have been, and can continue to be, embraced in light of the pressures of reflection; yet their scope will vary according to what sorts of considerations are brought to bear. The actual equilibria that we establish, such as they are, are I suspect always, at best, only more or less wide. So while the method itself may forever encourage attempts to broaden the scope and deepen the understanding provided by one's theories, actually achieving a comprehensive reflective equilibrium will almost surely remain always at most an ideal.[9]

Recommending the method right off is the fact that it seems, in some sense, simply to work. By trying to articulate principles that would underwrite, elaborate, or refine the various judgments we're already inclined to make we often uncover (what we take to be) reasons for thinking the initial judgments were insufficiently subtle, or excessively parochial, or distressingly unsupportable. And we often find as well that various judgments we remain confident of, and can now support by appeal to more general principles, have implications we hadn't recognized and wouldn't have taken account of but for the attempt to understand what reason we might have for accepting them. Engaging in the attempt to establish a reflective equilibrium often leads us not just to change our initial judgments but to change them, as we think, *for the better.*

The question naturally arises: In what sense are our judgments better? One answer is that they are not better, at least not in any important sense. After all, the thought might go, any method that simply starts with the beliefs one happens to have and then works to generate a set of principles consistent, so far as possible, with those beliefs, is at best a recipe for a set of coherent principles that have no claim to our interest. Admittedly, if we had some independent reason for thinking our initial views accurately reflected the nature of morality, or that the coherence of a set of beliefs was reason to think them true, then we might have some reason to use the method. But we have no reason to think these things.[10]

Against this answer, I will eventually defend the method and its results on epistemic grounds, arguing that as one approaches a (wide) reflective equilibrium one thereby increases the extent to which the beliefs one holds are epistemically justified. On this view, what recommends the method is that using it is one and the same with trying to proportion one's beliefs to the available evidence. And this means that the method, successfully used, results in beliefs that are better because better justified. Since actually achieving wide reflective equilibrium is a matter of embracing a fully coherent—and so, in light of the coherence theory, well justified—set of beliefs, the method has conspicuous attractions for anyone who thinks, as I do, that the coherence theory of justification can be defended. Furthermore, I will argue, the attractions remain even though what reason we have for thinking our initial moral views accurate is not independent of the moral views they end up supporting in reflective equilibrium and even though we should not think that the mere coherence of our views gives us reason to think that they are true.

While adopting the method makes obvious sense for anyone who accepts a coherence theory of epistemic justification, many have found the method attractive on other grounds. Some have recommended the coherence method as a useful way of discovering justified beliefs, despite their holding that the justification of those beliefs turns on something other than their cohering well with the variety of considerations the method brings to bear.[11] This heuristic account of the value of the method of reflective equilibrium retains the view that the method's use results in a collection of beliefs that might be epistemically justified. What it rejects is the coherence theory's account of their justification as being mutually dependent and turning on their relative coherence.

Others who have found the method attractive trace its appeal not to the epistemic value of the resulting beliefs but to the moral importance of acting on principles one can, on reflection, consistently embrace. The underlying idea here is that one counts as having acted on principle at all only if the principle in question is such that one is willing to endorse its implications for cases other than those at hand. And one does that only when, in effect, the principle stands in reflective equilibrium both with one's other principles and with one's other judgments about particular cases, actual and possible, beyond those one happens to face. To claim to be acting on some principle, only to disown its implications for other cases, is to belie one's allegiance to the principle and to forfeit the backing it would otherwise offer for one's action.

While views of this sort offer a reason to value the coherence method, the reason offered is squarely moral; and while we might be tempted to ask why we should believe true the claim that we have such a reason, the claim itself is not an epistemic one. If people do have a moral reason to act only on a set of principles that stand in reflective equilibrium, then using the method, and restricting one's actions to those endorsed by the resulting set of convictions, would make good sense even as it leaves aside completely questions of whether the beliefs are epistemically justified.

Yet another way to defend the method, again without appealing to its epistemic value, is to argue that its use has significant practical advantages. Just as all sorts of advantages are secured by requiring that judges make explicit the rationale behind their decisions, so too, we might think, practical considerations require something similar of ordinary people. After all, moral thought and reflection obviously play a crucially important role in social life; to the extent this role might best be served by people being able to articulate and defend the principles on which they act, using and recommending the method of reflective equilibrium would seem eminently reasonably. Not least of the advantages is that successful deployment of the method puts one in a good position to offer (either to oneself or to others) a coherent set of principles that might be open to scrutiny and evaluation. Widespread use of the method of reflective equilibrium, individually, or perhaps collectively, might even give us hope of our developing a coherent public morality—the advantages of which may have nothing to do with truth.

The practical value of the method is reflected in the fact that most effective forms of moral argumentation appear to work by revealing to people that their own views need shoring up or changing if those views are to cohere with others they are unwilling to jettison. Threats and promises might get people to change what they say, but when it comes to getting people actually to change their minds little works so well as showing them that, on balance, the views they already accept recommend the position one is defending. Of course, we should not exaggerate the effectiveness of this approach or its relative importance as a way of getting people to change their views. Clearly, its effectiveness is significantly constrained by peoples' willingness either to refuse to see the consequences of what they accept or, when they do, to accept those consequences no matter how implausible they are. And its relative importance needs to be measured with a steady eye on the frequency with which people change their views as a result of experience and exposure, imagination and empathy, rather than reflection and argumentation. Nevertheless, when we do work to change someone's view or to see whether our own might be improved, the considerations we bring to bear regularly play precisely the role the coherence method would recommend.

Just how good these moral and practical defences of the method are, I'm not sure. I doubt that we have anything like a moral responsibility always to act on principle, let alone on a set of fully articulated principles of the sort the method would encourage us to seek. Too often, and in too many contexts, it looks as if people are morally justified in acting as they do despite their inability to identify anything remotely like a clear set of principles. Responsible moral behavior doesn't seem to require reflective access to such principles. I doubt too that our various practical and social aims are well advanced by the more rarified and arcane results a full deployment of the method is likely to produce. Almost surely a point of diminishing practical returns will be reached well before the method's requirements have been satisfied.

Even if these doubts are borne out, however, I think they wouldn't fully undermine an appeal to moral and practical considerations as relevant to a defence of the method. Actually, because I believe the method results in epistemically justified beliefs, and believe as well that we have a moral obligation of sorts to see that the moral convictions we act on are epistemically justified, I am committed to our having moral, and not just epistemic, reasons for using the method of reflective equilibrium. Still, I believe that the value of the method is not exhausted when a person satisfies this moral responsibility, such as it is. For part of what is valuable about the method is simply that it helps us to secure epistemically justified moral beliefs.

In fact, one of the key advantages of the coherence theory of justification is that it can explain well what reason we have to use the method even after our moral responsibilities have been satisfied and our practical aims met. At least so I think. This suggestion will be plausible, however, only if good sense can be made out of the coherence theory of justification, and it is to that task that I now turn. So the rest of this paper can reasonably be seen as an extended defense of the peculiarly epistemic value of the coherence method.

Epistemic Justification

What does it take for a person to be justified in holding some belief?[12] Different, and often incompatible, answers will be plausible depending on the sort of justification that is at issue. I'll mention three obvious possibilities.

First, we might be concerned with whether a person is *morally justified* in holding the belief, in whether her holding of the belief satisfies the relevant moral standards. If so, we'll be interested, say, in whether she is within her rights to believe it, or in whether her believing it is (or is expected to be) conducive to the greatest happiness, or in whether her believing it is compatible with her other obligations. Which, if any, of these considerations should be invoked depends on what the right standards of moral justification actually are. (I've here only mentioned some leading candidates.)

Second, we might be concerned with whether a person is in some other way *pragmatically justified* in holding the belief, in whether her holding of the belief satisfies the relevant pragmatic standards. If so, we'll be interested, say, in whether her believing it advances her interests, or in whether her believing it is (subjectively or objectively) likely to contribute to the satisfaction of her preferences, or in whether her believing it will lead to a fulfilling life. Which, if any, of these considerations should be invoked depends on what the right standards of pragmatic justification actually are. (Here too I've only mentioned some leading candidates.)

Or third, we might be concerned with whether a person is *epistemically justified* in holding the belief, in whether her holding of the belief satisfies the relevant epistemic standards. If so, we'll be interested, say, in whether her believing it is appropriately sensitive to her evidence, or in whether her believing it means it is (subjectively or objectively) likely to be true, or in whether her believing it is the result of a reliable belief-forming process.[13] This time, which, if any, of these considerations should be invoked will depend on what the right standards of epistemic justification actually are. (And, again, I've only mentioned some leading candidates.)

With these three sorts of justification in mind, we need to distinguish between justifying what is believ*ed*—the content of the belief—and justifying the state or act of believ*ing*. As I've described moral, pragmatic, and epistemic justification, the concern was with the latter, with whether a person was justified *in holding* a particular belief, not with whether the belief was justified.

Sometimes, though, when we describe someone's moral belief as morally justified, we are interested in what she believes—in the content of her belief. And what we have in mind is that what she believes can be justified by appeal, say, to some more general moral principle. So we might say that a person's belief that she ought to support a local soup kitchen is morally justified and not mean that she is morally or epistemically or pragmatically justified in believing it, but instead that what she believes is both true and, say, justified by the more general duty we have to help others. We may even count what she believes as justified in light of moral principles we accept without thinking she either recognizes those principles or would endorse them if she did. In these cases we are not concentrating on *her* moral or epistemic or pragmatic justification for believing as she does, nor on what justification she might have for the belief, but rather on what grounds there might be (even if she doesn't have them) for the belief she holds—on what reason there might be for thinking it true.

And in general, in our epistemic evaluations of peoples' beliefs, we standardly focus on what is believ*ed* rather than on the state or act of believ*ing*. Even when we are concerned with whether someone is epistemically justified in holding a belief, we are usually interested not primarily in her holding of the belief but in, for example, whether the belief she holds is supported by the evidence available to her, or in whether the belief is either self-evident or appropriately grounded in her experience. In these cases, we are interested in what justification she might have for the belief. In fact, the temptation is to maintain that whether a person is epistemically justified in holding the belief turns on whether the belief she is holding is itself justified, and that *that* turns on there being some suitable connection between what is believed and the evidence available to her. I will, in what follows, acquiesce to this temptation.[14]

When it comes to epistemic justification, if we distinguish, in the way I've been suggesting, between when a person's *belief* is justified and when *she* is justified in holding it, we can capture the dependence of the latter on the former by saying: the person, if she is to be justified in holding some belief, must be holding it *because* it is justified—that the belief is justified must be part of the explanation of why she is holding it. If instead a person holds a belief because of wishful thinking or fear or carelessness, or in some other way without regard to the evidence she actually has, then her believing it is unjustified even if what is believed happens to be supported by the available evidence. On this view, no matter how strong the evidence for the belief might be, and regardless of whether the belief is true, the person is not justified in holding the belief, if her holding it is insensitive to the evidence.[15] This *basing requirement* demands that a person's beliefs be based in an appropriate way on her evidence, if the beliefs are to count as justifiably held.[16]

The distinction between a belief being justified and a person being justified in holding the belief is in some ways reminiscent of Kant's distinction between merely acting in accordance with duty and acting *because* it is one's duty.[17] On Kant's view, a person is morally justified in acting only if both: (i) the action satisfies the Categorical Imperative; and (ii) that fact matters to whether the act would be performed. Pushing the analogy, we might identify an Epistemic Imperative to the effect that one should *Believe only as the preponderance of one's evidence would allow*. We can then say that a person is epistemically justified in holding some belief only if both: (i) the belief satisfies the Epistemic Imperative; and (ii) that fact matters to whether the belief would be held.[18] And just as Kant's *Act only on that maxim through which you can at the same time will that it should become a universal law* doesn't require one to act on all such maxims, so too the epistemic imperative should be read not as requiring one to believe everything one's evidence would allow, but as requiring that one believe *only* as one's evidence would allow.[19]

I think the Epistemic Imperative together with the basing requirement articulate one crucial dimension of the epistemic evaluation, and I will take them as capturing, albeit in quite general terms, the core of our notion of *epistemically justified believing*. But obviously there are other dimensions of epistemic evaluation. We evaluate people as more or less knowledgeable, in light of the extent to which what they (justifiably) believe is actually true; as more or less perceptive, in light of how sensitive they are to the world around them; as more or less sophisticated, in light of their ability to identify and deploy reasons for the beliefs they hold; and as more or less responsible, in light of their efforts to gather and reflect on evidence. Each of these evaluations invokes standards that seem either to go beyond or to be completely independent of the considerations that matter to justification. Often they impose a kind of epistemic strict liability (inappropriate to questions of justification) according to which how one fares epistemically does not turn on what one had reason to do or believe. Even though I set these other epistemic evaluations aside in what follows, keeping them in mind is important when it comes to sorting out the various ways a person who is justified in believing as she does might suffer significant shortcomings, epistemic and otherwise.

In particular, recognizing that a person is epistemically justified in holding her beliefs may still leave us thinking the beliefs not just false but—as will often enough be the case with peoples' moral views—repugnant. A person might be epistemically justified in holding her beliefs, and yet be holding beliefs that are morally abhorrent, just as with more mundane matters a person might justifiably believe what turns out to be false.[20] Needless to say, a person who holds abhorrent beliefs will, in an important sense, not be holding the beliefs she should. Worse, she might, on the basis of those beliefs, act in deeply objectionable ways. But the grounds we have for thinking her actions immoral and her views horribly mistaken might (sadly) be unavailable to her; and if they are unavailable to her, and we recognize this, we may have to grant that she is epistemically justified in holding her position.

Whether she is depends crucially on what evidence is available to her. I suspect that, in many cases, those who hold abhorrent views actually have volumes of evidence, to which they are insensitive, that stand against their convictions. To the extent they hold their views because of prejudice, or fear, or self-interest, or insecurity, they are not appropriately basing their beliefs on the available evidence and so are not justifiably holding their views (no matter how coherent their epistemically insensitive system of beliefs is). At least in principle, though, some people might be raised in an environment so distorted that the evidence they have, such as it is, actually supports their repugnant views. We will of course have reason to try to change their views and their behavior to the extent we can, and we certainly needn't think their beliefs are ones we might reasonably accept. Still, if their beliefs are supported by the evidence actually available to them, I think they are epistemically justified in holding them, even though they are morally the worse for their views.[21]

Foundationalism and Coherentism

Against this background, let's return to the question, now made more specific: What does it take for a person to be *epistemically* (as opposed to morally or pragmatically) justified in holding the belief she does? Under what conditions, for instance, would she be justified in accepting utilitarianism or in rejecting Naziism, or in thinking courage virtuous, or pleasure good?

When concerned with belief in general, with no special focus on moral beliefs, answers have traditionally divided into two camps, one foundationalist, the other coherentist. Both approaches normally accept the basing require-ment—the view that when the belief is justified a person is justified in believing as she does only if, in addition, she believes as she does because her belief is justified. Where the contrast between foundationalism and coherentism shows up is in their respective accounts of what it takes for a belief to be epistemi-cally justified.

The foundationalist's account involves appealing to some class of *epistemically privileged* beliefs (that enjoy their privilege independently of their inferential/evidential connections) and then holding that a belief, moral or otherwise, is justified if and only if either: (i) it is member of that privileged class; or (ii) it bears an appropriate evidential/inferential relation to a belief that is a member of the class.[22]

Different versions of foundationalism emerge as different classes of belief are singled out as foundational and as different evidential/inferential relations are countenanced as appropriate. Just to mention a few of the familiar suggestions, beliefs might count as foundational in virtue of being certain, or incorrigible, or formed under the appropriate circumstances, while an inferential relation might count as appropriate if it is deductive, or inductive, or abductive, or explanatory. Precisely how the details are filled in will make a huge difference to both the stringency of the requirements imposed and the plausibility of the theory that results. What all the versions share, though, is the view that there is an epistemically privileged class of beliefs that are justified independently of the evidential/inferential relations they might bear to other beliefs and that all other beliefs are justified, when they are, in virtue of the support they receive from foundational beliefs.

In characterizing foundationalism this way, I'm steering clear of attributing to foundationalism a number of more extreme views it often travels with—for instance, the view that all justification must flow unidirectionally from the foundational beliefs to the others, and the view that the foundational beliefs are infallible,[23] and the view that a fully developed system of justified beliefs will take the shape either of a pyramid with all the foundational beliefs eventually supporting a single ultimate principle or of an inverted pyramid with a single foundational belief supporting the whole superstructure.[24] While a foundationalist might ultimately be forced into one or another of these views by her own arguments, she might not be. What matters to her foundationalism, as I see it, is that she thinks there is a privileged class of noninferentially justified beliefs without which no other beliefs would be justified at all.

Suppose, then, that some of our moral views are justified. Suppose that we are justified in thinking that cruelty is wrong, Naziism is evil, racism repugnant, kindness required, promises binding, or whatever. How would our justified moral beliefs (assuming there are some) fit into the foundationalist's picture of justification? Foundationalists who hold that some moral beliefs *are* justified must hold either that some moral beliefs are epistemically privileged or that, although none are, some moral beliefs are nonetheless justified inferentially by appeal ultimately to some nonmoral beliefs that are.

The vast majority of foundationalists working in moral theory have gone the first route and embraced a *moral foundation,* holding that some of our moral beliefs qualify as epistemically privileged. Influenced by Hume's observation that one cannot legitimately infer an "ought" from an "is," they've held that our nonmoral beliefs, taken alone, can provide no evidence whatsoever for our moral convictions.[25] There is, they think, an inferentially unbridgeable gap between nonmoral and moral beliefs (or at least between nonevaluative and evaluative beliefs).

Whether Hume himself thought the problems plaguing such an inference were insuperable is controversial. But his responsibility for making those problems felt is beyond question. In any case, as Hume saw the issue, the problems center on the transition from claims about what is the case (e.g., that God commands something, or that a course of action will produce happiness, or that the majority of people approve of some trait) to claims concerning what ought to be done or what should be approved. Take whichever nonevaluative premises you like concerning how things are, were, or will be, and it seems (Hume suggested) that no conclusion follows concerning how they ought to be, absent the aid of an evaluative premise. Suppose, for instance, that some course of action would promote happiness. From that it doesn't follow that people should so act—unless we appeal to an additional evaluative premise, e.g., that people should act so as to promote happiness. Of course, it might be that an appropriate additional premise is true. The point is that apparently some moral premise or other is needed to secure a moral conclusion from nonmoral premises. If this is right, it means that, on a foundationalist's view of justification, the only way any of our moral beliefs could be justified is if some of them are epistemically privileged—otherwise they are all ultimately unjustifiable. The central problem facing such a position is to make plausible the suggestion that at least some moral beliefs are properly viewed as epistemically privileged. And this is no small problem since all the concerns that raise general epistemic worries about our moral views devolve onto any particular proposal one might make to the effect that some subset of those views is epistemically privileged.

In any case, among those who think some moral beliefs are foundational, many have treated the privileged moral beliefs as roughly on a par with perceptual judgments and suggested that the justification of our various moral principles parallels the kind of justification our scientific principles receive from perception.[26] Others have thought that our privileged moral beliefs concern, instead, the most general and abstract principles of morality, and that these in turn serve to justify (or not) our other beliefs deductively. The crucial difference between these views is found primarily in the kind of inferential support each believes the foundational beliefs provide for the others. I think the difference is more or less fairly captured by saying the first group treats the justification of our nonfoundational beliefs as involving inductive, abductive, and explanatory considerations, whereas the other treats the justification of nonfoundational beliefs as a matter of showing that they follow deductively, with the help of nonmoral assumptions, from the foundational beliefs. Either way, at least some moral beliefs—the foundational ones—are held to be justified independently of whatever inferential/evidential relations they might bear to other beliefs.

Coherentists, in contrast, reject precisely this view, maintaining that whatever justification our moral beliefs enjoy is due to the relations they bear to other things we believe. Those who think the gap between nonmoral and moral beliefs (or at least between nonevaluative and evaluative beliefs) is forever unbridgeable, maintain that all our moral beliefs receive what justification they have only from other moral (or at least evaluative) beliefs. Others, though, hold that, whatever the nature of the "is"/"ought" gap, it does not work to insulate completely our moral judgments from nonmoral (and nonevaluative) considerations. On their view, metaphysical, epistemological, social, and psychological considerations might all be relevant to the justification of our moral views. Significantly, defenders of this version of moral coherentism needn't hold that nonmoral beliefs *alone* either entail or in some other way inferentially support moral conclusions; they may well hold that our moral views themselves establish the epistemic relevance of nonmoral considerations. This means that a coherentist can accept all the standard arguments for the "is"/"ought" gap without being committed to holding that all the evidence we have for our moral views come from moral considerations. In fact, given just how implausible it is to see any of our moral views as epistemically privileged, a great attraction of coherentism is its ability to make sense of our moral views being (to a greater or lesser extent) justified even in the face of the "is"/"ought" gap.

It's worth mentioning that an epistemological coherentist might well end up holding a kind of (nonepistemic) foundationalism with respect to morality. Here I have in mind a view that defends, on coherentist grounds, the idea that there is some single criterion for, or some fundamental principle of, morality. Someone might argue that an action is right if and only if it would be approved by the agent on full and informed reflection and then rely on considerations of what an agent would approve under those conditions to defend certain moral principles. Or someone might similarly rely on the view that an action is right if and only if it would be rational for the agent to perform it; or if and only if it is licensed by rules people could rationally agree to; or if and only if it satisfies the Categorical Imperative; or if and only if it maximizes overall utility; or if and only if it accords with God's will. In a perfectly reasonable sense, each of these views proposes a "foundation" for morality. Yet the arguments standardly offered in their defense regularly appeal, in just the way coherentism would predict, to a wide variety of other considerations (concerning what people value, how they reason, the effect their attitudes have on their actions, the authority they accord to their moral views) as evidence for the fundamental principle in question. For all coherentism says, any one of these proposals might be true. Moreover, any one of them might be justifiably believed by a coherentist. What coherentism is committed to is the claim that, if any one of these views is justifiably believed by a person, it will, and must, be in light of what else she believes. None of these views, and no other view, is justified except in this way (according to the coherentist).

The heart of the difference between foundationalism and coherentism, as the distinction applies generally, is found in coherentism's rejection of the view that there is an epistemically privileged subset of beliefs (moral or not), and its rejection of the view that all other beliefs are justified only in virtue of the relations they bear to such privileged beliefs. This difference turns on what foundationalism asserts and coherentism denies.[27] Yet coherentism goes beyond the denial and offers a positive account of what it takes for a person's belief to be epistemically justified.[28]

The coherentist's positive account involves articulating a conception of what it is for one belief to cohere with others, and then arguing that a person's belief is epistemically justified only if, and then to the extent that, the belief in question coheres well with her other beliefs. There is, on the coherentist's view, no subset of beliefs that counts as epistemically privileged (at least none whose privilege is independent of the inferential connections its members bear to other beliefs). Instead, beliefs, moral and otherwise, enjoy whatever epistemic credentials they have thanks to the evidential/inferential relations they bear to other beliefs. The more and better the relations, the greater the degree of coherence enjoyed by the set and the stronger the justification. Predictably, different versions of coherentism emerge as different evidential/inferential relations are countenanced as appropriate.[29] Also predictably, precisely how the details are filled in will make a huge difference to both the stringency of the requirements imposed and the plausibility of the theory that results. What all the versions share, though, is the view that the extent to which a belief is justified turns simply on the evidential/inferential relations it bears to other beliefs.

In characterizing coherentism in this way, I am steering clear (as I did with foundationalism) of attributing to it some of the more extreme views it often travels with—for instance, the view that all justification is global and nonlinear, and the view that to be justified in believing anything a person must believe of her beliefs that they form a coherent system, and the view that coherence itself provides evidence that a system of belief is likely to be true. While a coherentist might ultimately be forced into one or another of these views by her own arguments, she might not be. What matters to her coherentism, as I see it, is that she thinks (negatively) that there is no epistemically privileged class of beliefs and (positively) that beliefs are justified only if, and then to the extent that, they cohere well with the other beliefs one holds.

To forestall a natural confusion, I should emphasize that coherentism, no less than foundationalism, can admit that not all of our beliefs, not even all of our justified beliefs, are actually inferred from others. We often believe things thanks to the promptings of experience, for example, even though we do not infer what we believe from anything else we already believe. Such beliefs are, in an important sense, cognitively spontaneous. Yet the fact that they are caused in the way they are doesn't preclude them from standing in various inferential/evidential relations to the other things we believe.[30] And it is how they stand, *vis á vis* these other beliefs, that on the coherentist's account determines whether they are justified.[31]

I am going to put off, for a time, offering a positive account of coherence and its relation to justification, turning first to one argument, *the regress argument,* that is commonly thought to show that no version of coherentism has a chance of being right regardless of the specific account of coherence it offers. I will, in the next two sections, argue that a coherentist can consistently recognize the force of the regress argument and yet satisfyingly stop the regress without having her position collapse into a version of foundationalism. With that argument made, I will then offer a positive account of coherence as a backdrop for replying to several other objections to coherentism many have found persuasive.

The Regress Argument

The regress argument is by far the most influential argument against both coherentism in general and coherentism as applied to our moral beliefs. As this argument would have it, if any beliefs are justified at all, some must be justified independently of the relations they bear to other beliefs. In other words, coherentism has got to be false.

The argument, which goes back at least to Aristotle,[32] begins with the assumption that one belief provides justification for another only if it is, itself, justified. For any given belief, then, the question arises: what sort of justification does it enjoy? If it is justified by other beliefs from which it is inferable, then the beliefs on which its justification depends must themselves be justified and we can raise the same question about them, and then again about whatever beliefs justify those. If we are to avoid an infinite regress, there are only two possibilities (compatible with holding that the initial belief is justified). Either:

(i) The path of justification from one belief to those from which it is inferable, to those from which they are inferable, leads back to the initial belief, in which case the justification comes objectionably full circle; or

(ii) There are some justified beliefs that are justified independently of the support they might receive from others (say, because they are self-justifying or because they are justified by something other than a belief, perhaps an experience), in which case the regress can be satisfyingly stopped.

Foundationalists have taken comfort from this argument thinking, first, that coherentism is saddled with defending some version of the apparently indefensible (i) and, second, that the kind of beliefs their theories identify as epistemically privileged would play just the role that (ii) makes clear needs to be filled.

Skeptical and nonskeptical foundationalists alike have relied on the regress argument to attack coherentism. According to nonskeptical foundationalists, there are in fact beliefs that can stop the regress, and they serve as the foundation on which the justification of all other beliefs depends. According to skeptical foundationalists, there are no such beliefs (concerning the domain in question), so although foundationalism provides the correct account of what it would take for beliefs to be justified, no relevant belief is in fact justified—regardless of what other beliefs one holds.[33]

Against both skeptical and nonskeptical foundationalists, coherentists hold (at least) one of three things: that the way in which one's justification for a belief might come full circle is not, after all, objectionable; or that a coherentist might, despite appearances, acknowledge that there are some justified beliefs that are justified independently of the support they might receive from others; or that there's some third option. Although I am tempted by the first option, in the course of what follows I shall defend the second as available to a coherentist. To that end, I'll argue that on one interpretation the initial assumption of the regress argument (that one belief can justify another only if it is, itself, justified) makes the argument too strong even for a foundationalist to resist, while on another interpretation a coherentist can, consistent with coherentism, stop the regress in the same way a foundationalist can—by appeal to beliefs that are justifiably held despite their having no inferential support. Either way, the regress argument won't work to support foundationalism as over against coherentism.

Now nonskeptical foundationalism has commonly been thought to face at least three significant difficulties. First, there seem to be no uncontroversial candidates for the role of foundational belief. Second, even if there were some plausible candidates, the foundation they would provide would, as many think, be too paltry to support anything like the number and kind of beliefs we take to be justified. And third, once we distinguish between a belief being justified and a person being justified in holding a belief, it looks as if even putatively foundational beliefs won't stop the regress, because people won't justifiably hold them in the absence of evidence, and that evidence, in turn, must be such that they are justified in accepting it—and that simply re-invites the regress.

All three difficulties have been taken, at various times, by various people, to pose insuperable difficulties for anyone hoping to establish the nonskeptical view that our beliefs are sometimes justified. While I will briefly discuss each of the worries, the third is, I will suggest, eventually the most telling (although not in the form it usually takes). And the right response to the difficulty, I will argue, is not to embrace a skeptical foundationalism but to reject the view that justified belief requires the sort of privileged beliefs foundationalism champions. Let me go through the difficulties in order.

First, as I've said, many have thought that there are no beliefs that might plausibly be treated as foundational. This problem has seemed especially pressing since, traditionally, foundational beliefs have been credited with all sorts of wonderful properties, with being, for instance, infallible, or indubitable, or incorrigible, or certain. The more exalted the claims made on their behalf, the less plausible it is that any belief lives up to the claims. Yet foundational beliefs needn't have any especially dramatic properties to stop the regress. They needn't be infallible, nor indubitable, nor incorrigible, nor certain. All they need to be is: justified not on account of the inferential relations they bear to other beliefs. They can even work to stop the regress if what justification they do have is both over-ridable (in the face of the inferential implications of other beliefs) and underminable (in certain contexts where their presumptive justification disappears). As long as there are some beliefs that are justified independently of any support they may receive from other beliefs, the regress can be brought to a halt. That there might be such beliefs is at least plausible, one might grant.

It could be that our beliefs to the effect that we feel pain, or see red, or seem to be thinking, or (to move to beliefs with a moral content) that cruelty is wrong, or courage honorable, or pleasure good, are each justifiably believed, independently of the support they might receive from other beliefs, as long as they are neither over-ridden by contrary evidence nor undermined by the circumstances. Each of these, one might think, could serve as suitable stopping places in an otherwise infinite regress of justification.

But then, second, to the extent these beliefs, or some others, are plausible candidates for stopping the regress, people have thought such beliefs would be so few in number or so narrow in scope or so devoid of implications that only a very small percentage of the beliefs we're inclined to think are justified actually are. So even if wholesale skepticism goes too far, the few beliefs that (let us grant) are justified independently of the inferential relations they bear to others, and the few beliefs they might adequately support, apparently constitute an embarrassingly small collection of relatively little interest. We may then be justified in believing a few things, the worry goes, but we are likely to have on this view no justification for our beliefs about the external world, about other minds, about the future, or about substantive moral issues. A reasonable response to this worry, though, is not to think that such beliefs are unjustified, but rather to think the worry arises only if one over-constricts one's view either of which beliefs count as foundational or of what those beliefs might serve to support. The nonskeptical foundationalist can, with more than a little plausibility, maintain that any theory that purports to articulate our notion of justification has got to be wrong if it has as an implication that virtually none of our everyday beliefs are ever justified.

Finally, third, it has seemed to many that we shouldn't in any case grant what I've been allowing for the sake of the argument: that there might be beliefs that could be justifiably held in any way independent of the relations they bear to other beliefs. For it looks as if, whatever beliefs a foundationalist settles on as appropriate regress stoppers, a person will be justified in holding the belief only if she has some evidence for it, some reason to think it true. This thought introduces a collection of arguments many have thought decisively undermine stopping the regress in the way the foundationalist proposes. Not all of the arguments in the collection are, I think, compelling. Working through the dialectic they introduce, however, is a useful way of showing, I'll suggest, that the best defense available to a foundationalist provides as well the resources a coherentist needs to resist the regress argument.

The first member of the collection of arguments appeals to the basing requirement and interprets it as demanding (what might be called) *doxastic ascent.* As this argument would have it, a person holds a belief because it is justified, and so satisfies the basing requirement, only if she both believes of *it* (the belief in question), that it has some epistemic credential, and holds the belief on those grounds.[34] So, for someone to satisfy the basing requirement when believing that there is something red before her, she must believe of her belief that, say, she formed it under the appropriate circumstances (e.g., in good light, and thanks to her visual apparatus working properly); and for her to satisfy the basing requirement when believing that some law is just she must believe of her belief, say, that she formed it under the appropriate circumstances as well (e.g., when free of the influence of self-interest, and thanks to her appreciating the law's real effects on all).[35]

Interpreted in this way, the basing requirement is met only if a person has beliefs concerning her beliefs to the effect that they are justified or have some property in virtue of which they are justified. But that is to allege that her justifiably holding the first belief (whatever its content, regardless of her circumstances) requires that she have another, distinct, belief that serves to justify her holding it. Acknowledging that requirement is just to abandon the claim that the belief in question is appropriately foundational—even if it is infallible, or indubitable, or incorrigible, or certain, or whatever. Moreover, if the second order belief is to justify holding the "foundational" belief, it too must be justifiably held, and that requires yet another belief, this time concerning it . . . and we're off on a new regress, but now with no hope of stopping it by appeal to beliefs that are justifiably held not in virtue of the inferential support they receive from other beliefs. Many coherentists have thought this argument establishes that foundationalists no less than coherentists must find a way out of the regress other than that provided by appealing to some privileged class of beliefs.

Against this argument, a foundationalist might well, and I think would rightly, resist the proposed interpretation of the basing requirement. A foundationalist can and should deny that to be justified in believing something we must believe of the belief that it is justified. What the requirement properly understood demands, the foundationalist should say, is that, if a person's holding of a belief is to count as justified, the belief must in fact be held because it is justified, but she needn't have any beliefs to the effect that her belief is justified. What matters is that she believes as she does because of her evidence rather than, say, because of wishful thinking or dogmatic faith. She needn't even be aware that her beliefs are regulated by her evidence, as long as they are. Thus a person may have a set of well-justified beliefs even if she is unaware of herself as a believer—as long as her beliefs are, in fact, themselves appropriately sensitive to the evidence she has.[36] If this is right, a system of justified beliefs needn't have anywhere in it a belief to the effect that "My belief that _____ is _____." Obviously, a person who lacks beliefs about her beliefs will not be in a position to offer a direct justification of her *holding* the beliefs she does, since she is (by hypothesis) unaware of herself as holding beliefs. Yet she would still be able to justify her particular beliefs; she would be able to offer reasons for believing as she does, by appealing to the available evidence (such as she believes it to be).

Of course, once a person does acquire beliefs about her beliefs, all sorts of worries may emerge about her own reliability that can well and truly shake up her justification. And, as it happens, we are all aware of ourselves and aware as well that we often form false beliefs. This fact about us means that the thought "I might in this case be mistaken" needs to be taken into account in evaluating the support our beliefs provide for one another. What self-awareness as epistemic agents introduces into the mix is an ever-relevant concern with the possibility that we might be mistaken. Still, the thought that we might be mistaken, if we have no particular reason to think we actually are, presumably doesn't provide much reason in itself for thinking our view false, just as the thought that all the particles in a room might rush to one corner of it, doesn't provide much reason in itself for thinking they will.

In any case, I think the foundationalist would be right to resist the demand for doxastic ascent as a condition on justifiable belief. But there is a variation on the first argument that captures its spirit without insisting on doxastic ascent. It picks up on the regress argument's initial assumption and turns it against foundationalism by insisting that a belief is not justifiably held at all unless one has at least some evidence for it—some reason to think it true (although the reason need not involve any claim about one's beliefs). A belief held without reason, the argument would have it, is not justifiably held. I'll call this the *epistemic ascent* argument since, in demanding that each justified belief be backed by some reasons that support it, it suggests we should always be able to ascend from one belief to the reasons that back it. The upshot of this assumption seems immediately devastating to the foundationalist: a belief unsupported by other beliefs—the content of which constitute the available evidence—will be one believed for no reason and so will be unjustified. And this means it can't serve to stop the regress. The very immediacy of this upshot makes it plausible for the foundationalist to claim the argument in effect begs the question by assuming all justified beliefs are inferentially justified. In fact, the very point the foundationalist tries to make with the regress argument is that some beliefs must be justified independently of the support they receive from others.

Two different moves are available to foundationalists here. Foundationalists might accept the argument's assumption that every belief justifiably held must be supported by reasons and yet maintain that some beliefs are justified by reasons that are not the contents of a belief.[37] Or they might reject the assumption and maintain that some beliefs are justified in the absence of any positive reason to believe them.

Against the first option, I would press a version of what is often called *internalism*.[38] This view starts with the observation that, when it comes to people being justified in believing as they do, the reasons *they have* for believing one way or another must be available to them. Then it contends that the reasons become appropriately available only when the considerations that count *as reasons* become the content of those people's beliefs (or the content of something so like a belief, for instance, "an awareness that . . .", as not to be worth distinguishing from belief in this context).[39] On this view, the considerations a person has for a belief come into her cognitive economy appropriately, and so become available to her, only thanks to being the content of some cognitive state.[40]

An externalist who, for example, treats a person's beliefs as justified by the fact that they are appropriately caused (e.g., directly by experience or by a reliable belief-forming mechanism) will have to hold either that a person has no reason to believe as she nonetheless justifiably does, or that what reason she has might be unavailable to her despite its serving to justify her belief. The first is no help if we let stand the present argument's assumption that a belief is justified only if the person has some reason to hold it. The second commits one to saying implausibly that considerations unavailable to a person can count as reasons *that person has* for believing one way rather than another.

Rejecting externalism is compatible, clearly, with acknowledging that when *we* recognize that someone's beliefs are appropriately caused, that fact might well provide *us* with reason to accept what she believes; just as, when we know someone's beliefs are not appropriately caused, we might have reason to reject what she believes even as we recognize her as justified in holding her (false) beliefs. Nevertheless, as long as she remains unaware of the causal pedigree of her belief, it seems strange, to say the least, to think that the pedigree provides *her* with any reasons whatsoever. It is that strange claim the externalist being considered here has to hold.

Someone might suggest, though, that both coherence and the basing relation are, by my own account, reasons people have for believing as they do even when they have no beliefs concerning either of them. After all, I am committed to treating both as conditions on justified believing, and yet I admit, even insisted on behalf of the foundationalist, that a person might justifiably hold her beliefs without having beliefs about them, and so without believing of her beliefs either that they are coherent or that they satisfy the basing requirement. But this suggestion involves a crucial misunderstanding. Neither coherence nor the basing relation are offered as *reasons* for the person in question to believe anything (unless she comes to have beliefs concerning them). Of course, according to coherentism, what matters to the justification of her belief is the extent to which the belief being evaluated (as justified or not) coheres with her other beliefs, and what matters to her being justified in believing as she does is that her belief is appropriately based on her evidence. Yet what counts as a person's evidence for a belief is not its relative coherence with her other beliefs, nor her sensitivity to the evidence, but rather the content of those beliefs of hers that provide deductive, inductive, and explanatory support for the content of the belief in question. Relative coherence is a reflection of the extent of that support, not an extra bit of support.

Foundationalists, however, might accept these points and admit that what count as reasons an agent has for believing must be the content of some belief or some suitably similar cognitive state. They still can and should take the second option and maintain that the epistemic ascent argument simply begs the question by assuming that all justified beliefs are justified by something that provides a person with reason to believe as she does. The force of the argument dissolves, they might say, once we distinguish between permissive and positive justification. A belief is permissively justified, the suggestion goes, when a person does not have, on balance, reason to reject it,[41] whereas a belief is positively justified when a person has, on balance, positive reason to hold it. With this distinction in hand, the foundationalist can grant that, when we're talking about positive justification, no belief is justified unless a person has some evidence for it, and yet insist that, when it comes to stopping the regress, all that's needed are some permissively justified beliefs.

Whether the regress can actually be stopped this way depends on how the assumption that starts the regress is interpreted. As originally put, that assumption was: one belief provides justification for another only if it is, itself, justified. With the distinction between permissive and positive justification on hand, though, we can distinguish two relevant readings of this assumption. On one reading, the assumption is: One belief provides *positive* justification for another only if it is, itself, *positively* justified. On the other, it is: One belief provides *positive* justification for another only if it is, itself, *permissively* justified.[42] Read in the first way, the assumption makes an appeal to permissively justified beliefs irrelevant, for on that interpretation beliefs that are merely permissively justified provide no positive justification. But this strong reading of the assumption isn't available to the foundationalist once she has accepted the internalist's claim that all positive support is provided by (the contents of) beliefs. On her own view, the privileged class of beliefs that are supposed to stop the regress (whatever they are) are themselves, at least initially, not justified by others—and that means they are not positively justified.[43] Fortunately, though, the second reading of the assumption is both strong enough to get the regress going and weak enough to allow the regress to come to an end in beliefs that require no others for their justification. Thus, by relying on the second reading of the assumption, the foundationalist is able to put the regress in motion without falling victim to its momentum.

This distinction between permissive and positive justification, and the resulting appeal to permissively justified beliefs, has at least three advantages. First, it can explain how the regress might be stopped; it comes to an end if and when we arrive at beliefs that are permissively justified. Second, it leaves room for regress-stoppers that, despite their "regress-stopping" role, might be both over-ridable and underminable; permissively justified beliefs will lose their status when, for instance, new evidence is acquired that tells against them. Third, it avoids saying that among a person's reasons for believing as she does are reasons constituted by considerations that are unavailable to her; whether a belief counts as permissively justified turns only on whether the other things she believes provide, on balance, evidence against the belief.[44]

The foundationalist is thus well placed to argue that all we need, to stop the regress, are some permissively justified beliefs; the regress comes to an end when we appeal to the contents of beliefs we actually hold that we have (on balance) no reason to reject. There is no need for the foundationalist to attribute to them any special properties, and there may well be enough of them to support an extensive and plausibly rich set of inferentially justified beliefs. This means an appeal to permissively justified beliefs as appropriate regress-stoppers serves the foundationalist well when it comes to avoiding the three difficulties, mentioned earlier, that regularly haunt foundationalism. It is, in any case, the only plausible position available to those who grant that what reasons a person has are always found in the contents of her beliefs.

Strikingly, though, coherentists can admit permissively justified beliefs, and rely on them to stop the regress in just the way the foundationalist is proposing, *without abandoning coherentism.* Such a coherentist will still deny that there is an *epistemically privileged set* of beliefs that enjoy their privilege independently of their inferential connections—since which beliefs count as permissively justified depends upon the evidential/inferential relations they bear to others. Moreover, such a coherentist can continue to hold that what positive reason we have for any belief will still always depend solely on what other beliefs a person has. This sort of coherentism, then, grants the regress argument's initial assumption: that a belief can provide (positive) justification for another belief only if it is itself (permissively) justified. It grants as well that, to the extent an unacceptable regress threatens, it can be brought to a stop with the recognition that beliefs can be justified in either of two senses. What it denies is foundationalism's characteristic—and defining—claim that some beliefs (the regress stoppers) are epistemically privileged independently of the inferential/evidential relations they bear to other beliefs. It insists instead that whether a belief can serve to stop the regress, whether it counts as permissively justified or not, is fully determined by the evidential relations it bears to other beliefs, and that when it does so count it itself enjoys no positive justification, even as it is available to provide positive support for other beliefs.

The coherentist won't hold that the permissively justified beliefs that bring the regress to a stop have anything else to recommend them independently of how they relate to other beliefs; their primary role is to provide the epistemic input—the initial bits of evidence—one justifiably relies upon in seeking out views that are positively justified.

Nor will the coherentist say that every belief spontaneously formed will count as permissively justified. Even if one forms a belief noninferentially, say as a direct result of some experience, whether it counts as permissively justified will depend on what else one believes. If I turn my head and come to think there's a dog at my feet, the proven past reliability of beliefs of this kind gives me reason to trust this belief as well, and it will count as one I am positively (and not just permissively) justified in believing, even though it is cognitively spontaneous. Whereas, if I find myself yet again confident that this time, finally, I will win the lottery, I have ample reason to distrust the belief, and if I believe it any way, it will count as unjustified (and not permissively justified at all). In the great majority of cases, we might expect, people will have various background beliefs that serve either to support or to undermine the new beliefs they just happen to find themselves with.

And, standardly, any belief's status as merely permissively justified will be comparatively unstable, in that it is likely either to emerge as positively justified as it becomes intertwined with, and in various ways supported by, other beliefs or to become unjustified as one discovers reasons not to trust it. Looked at over time, one's initially merely permissively justified beliefs will regularly get swept up by others so as to become positively justified (as we find reason to think them true) or get sifted out as unjustified (as we find reason to think them suspect).

Permissively Justified Beliefs and Positive Support

As long as beliefs that are merely permissively justified can provide positive justification for other beliefs, foundationalists and coherentists alike can successfully stop the regress, and the regress argument will tell not at all against coherentism. However, if permissively justified beliefs cannot provide positive justification, an appeal to permissively justified beliefs won't help either the coherentist or the foundationalist, when it comes to stopping the regress.

So we need to ask: Can beliefs we have no reason to accept really provide positive support? The temptation is to think not. Even if some permissively justified beliefs (say, the visually prompted belief that there's something red in front of me) can serve to justify others (say, that there's something colored in front of me), it looks as if not all permissively justified beliefs can play this role. In fact, people often seem to hold beliefs that are apparently permissively justified (since they seem to have on balance no reason to reject them) that pretty clearly couldn't serve to justify any other belief. Wild hunches, weird forebodings, and spurious superstitions are, after all, commonplace; and permissively justified though they may be, such beliefs seem not at all able to justify those beliefs that are based on them.

Now a foundationalist might step in at this point hoping to re-establish a role for epistemically privileged beliefs. Unlike coherentists, she is able to distinguish those permissively justified beliefs that can justify others from those that can't, by treating some as epistemically privileged and others not. She might hold that the difference is found in whether the person is being epistemically responsible in holding the belief or in whether the belief is properly caused by experience, or in whether it is suitably concerned with one's private experience. It is open to the foundationalist to hold that epistemic responsibility, or proper etiology, or appropriate content, might mark the difference between those permissively justified beliefs that can, and those that can't, provide positive justification for other beliefs. A coherentist, in contrast, has to say that all permissively justified beliefs can serve to justify other beliefs, if she is to avoid a surreptitious appeal to privileged beliefs.

Problems arise for the foundationalist, however, as soon as one turns to the question: Why do the specific features identified (whatever they are) make a difference to one's justification? Any attempt to distinguish between permissively justified beliefs that will and those that won't provide positive evidence seems inevitably to face a dilemma.

In every case, the proposed grounds for drawing the distinction will either involve considerations that are potentially unavailable to the person in question or not. If they do, then the account will involve, I'll argue, an implausible kind of externalism; if they don't, then by adducing considerations that are available to that person, the view will in the end not be able to mark a difference among permissively justified beliefs in a way that counts only some as capable of providing positive support for other beliefs.

Suppose the foundationalist embraces externalism and (for instance) takes the etiology of the particular belief to be crucial to its ability to justify other beliefs. In a particular case, a person might then hold a belief that lacks the proper history and yet be unaware of that fact. And so far as her evidence is concerned, the belief will be no different from other beliefs of hers that enjoy the proper history. When it comes to the evidence she has, her merely permissively justified beliefs are indistinguishable. That the difference would nonetheless make a difference to her being able justifiably to rely on her belief to justify others seems quite implausible.

It's easy to imagine situations in which two people have the very same beliefs, rely on them identically in reaching various other beliefs, and so are *apparently* equally justified in what they believe, even though they differ (unbeknownst to them) in what originally caused their permissively justified beliefs. One of the two might be in the hands of an evil demon or entranced by a virtual reality machine while the other is not, or one might be experiencing a drug-induced hallucination while the other is really living the life the first imagines, or one might be undergoing an optical illusion indistinguishable ("from the inside") from the accurate visual experiences the other is having.[45] In each of these cases, if we were to assume that only those beliefs with the proper etiology will serve to justify other beliefs, we would be committed to holding that those who have no reason whatsoever to think they are victims of deception, manipulation, drugs, or illusion, though they are, differ substantially, in the justification they have for believing as they do, from those others who are not victims but who have exactly the same grounds available to them for believing as they do. No doubt they are not equally well-placed epistemically. No doubt too we have reason to distinguish between them. Yet when it comes to the justification each has for her own view, they appear to be identically situated. Similar concerns plague any other externalist proposal a foundationalist might offer as grounds for distinguishing among permissively justified beliefs when it comes to their ability to contribute positively to the justification of other beliefs.

Alternatively, and for good reason, the foundationalist might avoid externalism and suggest marking the distinction between permissively justified beliefs that can, and those that can't, provide positive support, by appealing to considerations the person in question has available. But then the considerations adduced will either tell against certain putatively permissively justified beliefs, and so establish the beliefs as not permissively justified at all, or tell in favor of certain beliefs, and so establish them as positively justified. If the first, if the person herself has reason not to hold the belief in question, then coherentist and foundationalist alike will rightly resist seeing the beliefs that are at issue as capable of establishing positive justification, since the beliefs are not even permissively justified. If the second, if the person has reason to rely on the belief, then the belief is positively justified and we simply shift the issue back to the status of the considerations the foundationalist identifies and ask of them whether they can provide positive support. At some point, if an infinite regress is to be avoided, we will inevitably appeal to some permissively justified belief as providing positive support for others, but at this point with no grounds for saying that only some such permissively justified beliefs can play this role.

Plainly, the objection I've pressed against the externalist proposal is not irresistible. One might want to insist that people who are identically situated *so far as they can tell* still differ when it comes to how justified they are in holding the view they share. And insisting on this would not be unmotivated, since otherwise one is committed to the still apparently counter-intuitive idea that beliefs one has no reason to hold might nonetheless provide grounds for holding other beliefs. Thus an important part of the coherentist's position turns on being able to defuse this concern. So let me turn to that.

I suspect that resistance to the idea that permissively justified beliefs might provide positive support for other beliefs is bolstered substantially by the cases of wild bunches, weird forebodings, spurious superstitions, etc., that I have already mentioned. These seem to be cases where a person's permissively justified beliefs pretty clearly couldn't serve to justify others. Yet the appearance is misleading, not usually because the beliefs can serve to justify others but because (when the cases are compelling) the beliefs are not actually permissively justified. A great many of the supposedly permissively justified beliefs we reject as unable to support others are beliefs we think the person herself has reason to suspect (even if she doesn't in fact suspect them). In fact, cases of wild hunches, weird forebodings, and spurious superstitions, count as *wild, weird,* and *spurious,* precisely because we think of the beliefs in question as ones the person has reason to reject.

The same general point holds for cases that don't involve wild, weird, or spurious beliefs but instead appeal, say, to beliefs that a person recognizes to be unsupported in situations where (we think) they have reason to think support is needed (as when they should realize that the belief is, in the absence of positive evidence, unlikely to be true). All the time, our expectations concerning which background beliefs a person will naturally hold regularly influence our particular judgments concerning whether they are justified in relying on some putatively permissively justified belief to justify others. As the coherentist sees things, though, what matters to the person's justification is that she actually have those background beliefs, and if she doesn't, then they will neither tell against nor support her beliefs. As coherentism would predict, even beliefs we consider to be wild, weird, or spurious are beliefs we simultaneously recognize to be such that people, in another time or culture, would be justified in accepting. We are not, of course, thereby expressing an endorsement of what they believe, but we are acknowledging them as justifiably believing as they do given the evidence available to them. If we narrow our view to those beliefs that really are permissively justified—those the person in question actually has no reason, on balance, to reject—the plausibility of seeing these beliefs as all capable of providing some positive support for others increases dramatically.

Still, one might be inclined to think that any belief one has, on balance, no reason to hold can't possibly serve to justify anything else. This will seem reasonable, even unavoidable, as long as we think of evidential relations roughly on the model of logical relations as simply justification preserving in the way logical relations are truth preserving. If evidential relations among beliefs serve merely as conduits of justification, one belief will receive positive support from others only to the extent those others themselves have some positive support to convey. On this view, some belief may, thanks to the support it receives from several other beliefs, itself enjoy more positive justification than any of the others, yet the total positive justification it can enjoy is limited nonetheless by the positive justification those other beliefs collectively have to offer. Underwriting this view of evidential relations is the intuition that one belief can be seen as epistemically valuable in light of the relation it bears to others only if the others are themselves epistemically valuable. Just as one action will count as good because of its consequences only if its consequences are good, so too some belief will count as positively justified by other beliefs only if those others are positively justified. Clearly, if this view is right, then beliefs that are merely permissively justified will be useless when it comes to providing positive support for others and an appeal to them won't serve to stop the regress on behalf of either foundationalists or coherentists.

What the coherentist must say (and the foundationalist will have reason to say as well) is that the intuition, and the view of justification it underwrites, are mistaken. Fortunately, in ethics and in epistemology, there's an alternative view that has its own appeal: that the value of an action or a belief depends upon both what it is related to and, more importantly for our purposes, how it is related to them. The intuition here is that the value of the whole may not be a function of the value of its parts considered independently of how they are related.[46] Just as things that are valueless considered in isolation may come to be related in such a way as to constitute something of significant value, so too beliefs that enjoy no positive justification considered in isolation may come to be evidentially related in such a way as to constitute a set of positively justified beliefs.[47]

The appeal of this alternative view depends upon our ability to see the evidential relations themselves as making a difference to the justifactory status of the beliefs they relate. They might be seen as making a difference in either of two ways: The relations themselves might work to enhance and not merely preserve justificatory value; or they might serve as a condition of the justifactory value of the beliefs they relate. The first suggestion, which is the more straightforward (but I think in the end less attractive) one, would enable us to appeal to the justifactory value of the evidential relations when it comes to explaining how it is that a belief supported by another that is merely permissively justified may in light of the relation they bear to one another count as positively justified.[48] The second suggestion would pick up on the fact that the common distinction between things that are good in themselves and things that are good for their consequences can be supplemented with a distinction between things that are only conditionally good and those that are unconditionally good.[49] The idea, then, would be that our beliefs, to the extent they are justified, are only conditionally justified—the condition being set by their being appropriately related to other beliefs the person has. Significantly, this latter view needn't be accompanied by any commitment to there being beliefs (or evidential relations) that are unconditionally justified; it would be enough if some beliefs might be conditionally justified. In any case, either account would serve to explain how it is that a belief's being properly related to another that is only permissively justified might render it positively justified.[50]

A full story following up either suggestion would involve explaining the distinctive epistemic contribution the evidential relations are supposed to play. However the details go, the epistemic role of such relations—their status as *evidential* relations—will presumably be bound up with their having a systematic if indirect connection to truth. Of course, evidential relations won't be such that, when they hold among beliefs, the beliefs are thereby sure to be, or even likely to be, true. Rather, I suspect, the relations that are in fact evidential will be those determined by canons of reasoning that are truth conducive (and not just truth preserving) in that systematically respecting them would have the tendency of shifting views towards the truth in the long haul, given accurate information.[51] Obviously, a person might respect the relevant canons of reasoning over time and so hold beliefs that are evidentially related (on this view) and yet, because of lack of evidence, or misleading evidence, actually consistently have evidence for false views. But in these cases, as well as happier ones, if the beliefs are in fact supported by the weight of the evidence available to the person, they count as justified, at least according to the coherentist.[52] In any case, while coherentism is committed to there being a fact of the matter as to whether, and to what extent, two beliefs are evidentially related, it is not wedded to any particular account of those evidential relations.

As should be clear, coherentism, at least the kind I'm advancing, grants that there are conditions on justifiable believing that may hold (or not) independently of what a person has reason to think. In particular, to the extent coherentism defines the relative coherence of a set of beliefs in terms of relations among those beliefs (that a person might have no beliefs concerning), the coherentist must accept a kind of externalism about justification.[53] Whether a person's beliefs are actually appropriately related turns on considerations that might be unavailable to her. The appropriate evidential relations might hold when she has no beliefs concerning them, or in cases where she thinks they don't, or they might fail to hold even in cases where she thinks they do hold. What matters is that her beliefs are appropriately related, not that she thinks they are; and if she does think they are, whether that belief is itself justified will turn on whether it is appropriately related to her other beliefs, not on whether she thinks it is.

Importantly, though, the externalism here concerns not what counts as a person's reasons for believing as she does but rather what counts as a justified belief. Nor does it allow that people identically situated, when it comes to the evidence available to them, might differ in the justification they have for holding their beliefs. This sort of externalism is virtually unavoidable if we hope to get any purchase on there being a difference between some belief being justified and a person thinking of it as justified. Even if we were to end up advancing criteria of justification that are sensitive to the criteria the person in question accepts, we would need to distinguish between a belief satisfying those criteria and a person thinking it does.

The Nature and Role of Coherence

To address several of the concerns one might have about the coherence theory of justification, I need now to say something more specific about the connection between the relative coherence of a set of beliefs and the evidential/inferential relations that hold among the beliefs. According to coherentism, I've said, a belief is justified only if, and then to the extent that, it coheres well with the other things the person believes.[54] Along the way, though, I've also attributed to the coherentist the view that a belief is (i) permissively justified if and only if the weight of the evidence available to the person does not, on balance, tell against the belief; and (ii) positively justified if and only if the weight of the evidence, again on balance, tells in favor of the belief (just how positively justified it is will be a matter of how strong the evidence, on balance, is). Seeing how these characterizations of justification relate to one another is crucial to seeing the sort of coherence theory I am advancing.

How then does the relative coherence of a set of beliefs reflect the evidential relations that hold among those beliefs? And how does the relative coherence of one's beliefs relate to their being justified? I will take these questions in order.

The relative coherence of a set of beliefs is a matter of whether, and to what degree, the set exhibits (what I will call) *evidential consistency, connectedness,* and *comprehensiveness.*[55] The first, evidential consistency, sets a necessary and sufficient condition for (minimal) coherence, while the second and third, connectedness and comprehensiveness, serve, when present, to increase the relative coherence of a set that is minimally coherent. Each, though, is a property of a set of beliefs, if it is at all, only in virtue of the evidential relations that hold among the contents of the beliefs in the set.

Thus, a set of beliefs counts as (minimally) coherent if and only if the set is evidentially consistent—that is, if and only if the weight of the evidence provided by the various beliefs in the set don't tell, on balance, against any of the others.[56] Given an evidentially consistent, and so at least minimally coherent, set, just how coherent the set is will be a matter of the connectedness and comprehensiveness it exhibits.

Clearly, a set of beliefs can count as minimally coherent even if none of the beliefs in the set are evidentially supported by any of the others. However, an evidentially consistent (and so coherent) set might contain some beliefs that are, to a greater or lesser extent, evidentially related to others in the set in a way that means they, on balance, receive support from the others, or provide support for them, or both. In these cases, the evidential relations among the beliefs induce in the set some degree of what I've called connectedness. The stronger and more extensive the support, the more connected, and more coherent, the set. Thus, a set will be more or less coherent, assuming it is evidentially consistent, to the extent the beliefs in it enjoy positive support from others in the set. At the same time, for any given set that is at least minimally coherent, its relative coherence, because comprehensiveness, will increase when other beliefs are added to the set, assuming it remains evidentially consistent. The more comprehensive the set, other things equal, the more coherent it will be.[57]

It goes without saying that virtually no one's total set of beliefs will count as even minimally coherent, although subsets of those beliefs will presumably count as more than minimally coherent. Similarly, virtually no one holds beliefs all of which are justified, although subsets of most peoples' beliefs will presumably count as positively and not just permissively justified.

When it comes to relating the relative coherence of a person's beliefs to their status as justified beliefs, the coherentist's suggestion is, first, that those beliefs of hers that are justified are all and only those that belong to the subset of her beliefs that is maximally coherent and, second, that a belief will belong or not to that subset in virtue of the evidential relations it bears to everything else she believes. A subset of a person's beliefs will count as maximally coherent only if it is evidentially consistent and then if, when compared to all the subsets of her total belief set that are evidentially consistent, it exhibits a greater degree of coherence over-all (thanks to its connectedness and comprehensiveness) than do the others.[58]

If a person has a belief that is evidentially related to no others, it will belong to the maximally coherent subset of her beliefs (because any subset not containing it would be less comprehensive and so less coherent than one that differed from that set only by including it) and will count as permissively justified. If she has, as she presumably will, a belief that is evidentially related to others, whether it will count as justified merely permissively, or positively, or not at all, will turn on whether it and the beliefs to which it is related are members of the maximally coherent subset of her beliefs. It may be that the belief, but not those that are evidentially related to it, will be a member of that set, in which case it will count as permissively but not positively justified. It may be, though, that it along with at least some of the others that support it are members of that maximally coherent subset, in which case it will count as positively justified in virtue of the positive support it receives from them (whether or not those others are themselves positively justified). Or it may be that it, and the beliefs that support it, are (even taken together) such that the weight of the evidence provided by other things the person believes tells against them, in which case, though a person has some evidence for the belief neither it, nor the beliefs that provide the evidence she has for it, count as justified.

One consequence of this view is that even beliefs one is unjustified in holding will, when held, nonetheless count as providing evidence for believing other things. That they provide evidence for believing other things, though, doesn't mean that they are permissively justified, since the person herself has reason not to accept them. Nor does it mean that the beliefs they provide evidence for will count as positively justified, since the considerations that tell against the original beliefs undercut the support they provide to others.

If, for instance, I have an unjustified belief that there will be a draught in Guatemala (unjustified because the evidence actually available to me tells against it), that belief, along with some others, will provide me with some reason to think coffee prices will rise. If I then do believe that coffee prices will rise, I will have some reason. Yet that new belief, like the (by hypothesis) unjustified one on which it depends, is presumably unjustified in light of the other things I believe. Not every belief a person has some reason to hold counts as a justified belief. Still, and perhaps at first disturbingly, if in time I acquired a quite formidable subset of beliefs built originally in light of some unjustified beliefs, there could in principle come a time when I am justified in jettisoning the old beliefs in light of the newer ones. This is not what usually happens, but it happens often enough to bear notice. The process I have in mind shows up nicely when one justifiably abandons a previously well-supported and impressive scientific theory (perhaps, but not necessarily, in favor of another) in the face of accumulated anomalies. Originally, one is justified in rejecting each of the anomalies as misleading (as illusions, distortions, or inaccurate observations) in light of one's well established theory; however, as the anomalies mount, the case against the original theory builds eventually to the point (at least sometimes) where one is justified in accepting the collection of anomalies as accurate observations and unjustified in continuing to accept the original theory.[59]

How well a particular belief coheres with the other things the person believes, we can now say, is determined by whether it is a member of the maximally coherent subset of what she believes (it doesn't count as cohering at all if it is not), and if it is, whether, and to what extent, it is evidentially supported by other beliefs in that set (the more support it receives the better it coheres). Any belief in the set will at least be permissively justified, and will be more or less positively justified as it receives more or less evidential support from other beliefs in the set. Thus, to say that a belief is justified only if, and then to the extent that, it coheres well with the other things the person believes, is to register the way in which one's justification turns on how one's belief relates evidentially to whatever else one believes.

A full articulation of the coherence theory I've been describing would of course involve developing a theory of what relations count as evidential. And clearly this is not the place to begin that project. But I should emphasize that any plausible theory of justification will require supplementation by an account of evidential relations, since all such theories recognize and rely in some way or other on there being evidential relations that our beliefs might bear to one another.

The extent to which a particular belief is justified, incidentally, does not always vary with the relative coherence of the set of beliefs to which it belongs. A belief does not enjoy an increase in justification simply because the set to which it belongs has increased in coherence. To see why, imagine a person holds some isolated belief—say, that she is feeling pain now—that is consistent with everything else she believes, but not connected (evidentially or inferentially) with them. As things stand, the belief minimally coheres with the person's other beliefs but bears no evidentially relevant connection to them. Suppose that the person then acquires new evidence in support of those other beliefs so that her justification for holding them increases. As long as the isolated belief remains consistent with the new set, it remains justifiably believed. Yet the person's justification for believing it has not changed one bit; an overall increase in the coherence of her beliefs leaves the evidentially isolated belief as it was before. No doubt, truly isolated beliefs are a rarity, but if they are possible then the coherence of one's set of beliefs might increase or decrease without making a difference to one's justification in holding some beliefs (the isolated ones). Even so, because beliefs that are isolated at one point might, with the acquisition of new evidence, be connected with others, isolation should not be confused with insulation. The justifactory status of the currently isolated beliefs will remain, as before and always, dependent upon what else one believes.

Against this background, we can also characterize what it would be for a potential belief to cohere well with what a person actually believes. Whether such a belief would cohere at all with the other beliefs a person holds depends on whether, were the person to believe it, it would then be a member of the (perhaps, in light of the new belief, dramatically different) maximally coherent subset of everything she believes. And how well such a belief would cohere with the others depends on the degree to which the resulting maximally coherent set would be more coherent than its predecessor. If such a belief would cohere with whatever else she believes, then should she believe it, the belief would be justified.[60]

To say, though, that a belief is such that, should one hold it, the belief would be justified, is not to say that one should hold the belief. The Epistemic Imperative requires that we believe only as the evidence allows, it doesn't demand that we believe everything the evidence allows. This means a potential belief that would be justified if held, might, compatible with the Imperative, nonetheless not be believed. What is ruled out as unjustified is believing those things the available evidence, on balance, tells against.[61]

With that earlier discussion in mind, it is perhaps also worth emphasizing that the coherence theory is being advanced here as an account of what it is for a person's belief to be justified, not as an account of what it is for a person to be justified in holding some belief. A belief might belong to the maximally coherent subset of a person's beliefs, and so count as a justified belief, even if the person is not justified in believing it. An account of when a person is justified in believing something that is, in fact, well supported by the evidence available to her will come only when a suitably articulated version of the basing requirement is added to the view. Roughly speaking, though, and according to coherentism, for a person to be justified in holding a belief, she has to believe it *because* it coheres well with her other beliefs (though she needn't believe it coheres).[62]

Some Objections

I can't here do full justice to the range of objections that have been raised to coherentism. However, I would like to indicate the extent to which some of the more common objections miss their mark, at least when it comes to the version of coherentism I am advancing. The objections I have in mind are that coherentism has got to be false because the mere fact that a set of beliefs is coherent is no reason to think they are true; that coherentism is objectionably conservative and inappropriately privileges one's actual beliefs; and that coherentism fails to recognize sufficiently the importance of experience. I will take these objections in order and suggest that each either misunderstands coherentism or underestimates the resources available to it.

Aside from the regress argument, the most common objection to coherentism turns on noticing that for any coherent set of beliefs a person might actually hold, there's another possible set of beliefs that is equally or more coherent.[63] This observation raises two concerns: First, isn't coherentism committed to the obviously false view that the mere coherence of a set of beliefs is reason to think them true; and second, isn't the coherentist consequently unable to account for the fact that we can justifiably reject views we recognize to be more coherent than our own? These concerns are all the more pressing because it looks as if we have exceedingly strong inductive grounds for thinking that any coherent set of beliefs, our own included, is likely to be false.[64]

To respond to these worries we need to distinguish two questions: What is it for a belief to be justified? and What is it that justifies a belief? Coherentism, of the sort I am defending, is addressed to the first question but not the second—a belief is justified if and then to the extent that it coheres well with a person's other beliefs, but it is not *justified by* the fact that it is a member of a coherent set of beliefs. What a person's beliefs are justified by are her other beliefs—or, more accurately, by the facts, as she takes them to be, so far as they provide evidence for her view.

A useful analogy can be found in the expected utility theory of rational choice. According to that theory, a person's choice is rational if and only if, given the available options, the choice maximizes her expected utility. But the fact that the option maximizes her expected utility is not an extra reason for the person to choose it—rather its status as the option that maximizes expected utility is a reflection of (what the theory supposes to be) the reasons the person has for choosing it.[65] Now of course one might have all sorts of objections to this theory, and I don't rest my case for the coherence theory on the acceptability of rational choice theory. Far from it. Still, I do want to suggest that the relation between expected utility and the reasons an agent has for making one choice over another (according to this theory) provides a nice analogue to the relation between relative coherence and the reasons a person has for holding one belief rather than another. As the analogy would have it, the fact that a belief coheres better than do the available alternatives with a person's other beliefs is not an extra reason for the person to hold it—rather its status as the belief that maximizes coherence is a reflection of the reasons the person has for holding it. So thought of, the coherence theory is not committed to saying that the coherence of our beliefs is a reason to think they are true. Instead, what evidence we have for the truth of our beliefs is found in, and only in, what else we believe. This means a coherentist can and should admit that the mere fact that a set of beliefs is coherent provides one with no reason to think they are true, even though, if the beliefs in question are one's own, their relative coherence will reflect the extent to which one's evidence gives one reason to think they are true.

Just as the maximizing theory of rationality doesn't offer substantive reasons for a person to act, so too the coherence theory doesn't offer substantive reasons for a person to believe or not. In both cases, the theories are offered as accurate and informative characterizations of the link between what we value or believe and the rationality or justification of what we do or believe. In each case, the plausibility of the theory depends, of course, on whether it actually captures the conditions under which someone counts as having chosen rationally or believed with justification. While I have my doubts about the theory of rationality on that front, I think the coherence theory of justification does a surprisingly good job.

What, then, does the coherentist say about those situations in which one recognizes that someone else holds a view that is more coherent than is one's own? If justification is a matter of coherence, shouldn't I abandon my beliefs if I discover there is an alternative set of beliefs that is more coherent? The coherentist does have to hold that, if the person's beliefs really are more coherent, then that person has more justification for believing as she does, given her evidence, than one has for one's own view. However, acknowledging this is not yet to say that one has any reason to reject one's views in favor of hers, not least of all because the mere fact that her view is more coherent is no reason to think it true, but also because her evidence, such as it is, might justifiably be rejected by you as misleading, ill informed, or otherwise unacceptable (even if the other person is justified in relying on it).

Often, of course, the alternative coherent views, at least those we take seriously, will be ones that we ourselves see some reason to accept, even if we think on balance the evidence tells against them. To take a moral example: Suppose that concerning various matters I am inclined to think consequentialist considerations are relevant and often decisive. I think, for instance, that when it comes to public policy the fact that one policy would produce more happiness for all than some other policy is a reason to choose it, or I think the fact that some present would ease someone's sorrow is a reason to give it, or whatever. Suppose too, though, that I resist the utilitarian view that some action is right if and only if it produces the greatest happiness for the greatest number, on the grounds that there are some things one cannot legitimately do to another person no matter how much happiness would be produced. In this situation I might well recognize that the utilitarian's position, given her other beliefs, is more coherent than mine. And I may have no single overarching moral principle to propose in place of the utilitarian's. Am I then required to accept utilitarianism? Is a coherentist committed to saying I am? The utilitarian and I share a good number of beliefs concerning the sort of considerations that might be relevant to moral evaluation, and to this extent we both have some grounds for thinking utilitarianism is true. Yet we differ on crucial points; in particular, I think (say) that willful murder is always wrong, no matter what, and that a sadist's pleasures are utterly worthless, and I think the rightness of an act depends as much on why it was performed as on the effects it happens to produce. She believes that I am wrong about these things (and others). I may, of course, be brought around to the utilitarian's view if she offers compelling grounds for seeing my own beliefs as explicable but false. And part of her argument in defense of utilitarianism will reasonably be that the utilitarian view does a good job of accounting for a number of things we both believe, which itself provides some evidence for the principle. Still, and even as I give due weight to the fact that the utilitarian principle captures well a number of considerations, I will justifiably reject it if (but only if) the weight of the evidence provided by what else I believe (some of which she denies) tells on balance against her view.

In the end, whether one is justified in retaining one's original view in light of another depends on whether one's own evidence tells in favor of the other view or not. In the face of (even) coherent alternatives, one justifiably rejects the others, when one does, on the basis of what one justifiably believes.[66] Often, the weight of one's evidence will tell against views one recognizes would be more coherent, and one justifiably rejects them on the grounds that one has reason for thinking them false. Given what else one believes, the alternative views do not after all count as coherent alternatives for you despite their being recognizably coherent when held by others. This means, of course, that had one's initial beliefs been different, had one believed one thing rather than another, one would have justifiably rejected the views that one actually (and with justification) accepts. But this doesn't mean that the fact that one believes as one does is one's reason for rejecting the alternative; rather one's reason is that the alternative clashes with the facts (as you take them to be).

Recognizing the crucial role played by one's actual beliefs naturally raises two more worries about the coherence theory: that it will have objectionably conservative implications and that it inappropriately privileges the beliefs one merely happens to have. The conservativism of the view, however, goes just as far as, but not farther than, the conservativism that comes with allowing that one must base one's beliefs on the available evidence. This inevitable limitation requires acknowledging that throughout our epistemic endeavors we will be appealing to what we believe, because what evidence one has is limited to that provided by one's beliefs (and other relevantly similar cognitive states). We are never able to stand fully apart from those beliefs without then losing all grounds for believing anything at all. Yet this reliance on what we happen to believe has no seriously conservative implications, since those beliefs themselves, especially in light of the new evidence experience and reflection regularly provide, won't stand as fixed points but will instead shift in response to the new evidence (if they are to continue to count as justified).

When it comes to privileging actual beliefs, it is no part of this coherence theory that the mere fact that one believes something, considered alone, provides any reason whatsoever for thinking the belief true; that evidence must come from other things one believes, if it is to come at all. Absent such a background, a person will take the content of her belief to be true, but that is a reflection of what it is for an attitude to count as a belief. And the content of that belief does serve as evidence for other things she might believe, but in relying on that evidence, she is not taking the fact that she believes it to be evidence for something else, rather she is taking what she believes (say, that the coffee is hot, or that willful cruelty is wrong) as her evidence.[67]

Sometimes, though, we do have reason to take the fact that we believe something as reason to believe the belief true. When we do, however, it is always in light of other things we believe about our having the belief—say that we are usually right about this sort of thing, or that it was formed under circumstances that are conducive to the forming of accurate beliefs. Of course, even without these background beliefs concerning the reliability of our belief forming mechanisms, the belief that we believe something will be evidence for a number of things (though not for the truth of the belief). For instance, and trivially, it will be evidence for thinking that we exist. But the evidence it provides for that is independent of the truth of the belief we have a belief concerning. The beliefs we have provide all the evidence available to us at any given time, yet our actual beliefs, on the coherentist view, are not even permissively justified except in light of the other evidence available. Far from treating our actual beliefs as epistemically privileged (in a way that would have the theory collapse into foundationalism) coherentism recognizes them as justified at all only as they relate to the person's other beliefs.

Still, because the coherence theory treats as evidence only what we already believe, it might seem to ignore a crucial impetus for change: experience. On the one hand, the theory may seem unable even to accommodate experiential input and observation. On the other hand, although it might be able to accommodate such input, it may seem not properly to recognize its importance. And surely any adequate theory must acknowledge the role and importance of experience and observation when it comes to the justification of belief.

The first concern, I think, is undercut by the role cognitively spontaneous beliefs are able to play within coherentism. It's true, coherentism doesn't allow experience as relevant to justification unless and until the experience comes into the person's cognitive economy. Yet, especially in its recognition of cognitively spontaneous beliefs, coherentism leaves room for experiences to enter that cognitive economy unbidden, either thanks to the experiences themselves having a cognitive content (in which case it is the content of the experience that serves as evidence) or by their being the content of an appropriate cognitive attitude (in which case it is the fact that such an experience occurred that serves as evidence). At the same time, coherentists can mark off the cognitively spontaneous beliefs that provide observational evidence for other things we believe, by embracing an account of observation according to which any belief formed noninferentially as a direct result of perceptual experience counts as an observation. Of course, which beliefs we justifiably count as having been formed in direct response to perceptual experience will itself depend on what we believe about ourselves and our situation; we can only justifiably distinguish between those spontaneous beliefs that count as observations and those that don't in light of what else we believe. And even when we do justifiably mark that general distinction, we will be justified in treating any particular observation as accurate only in light of what else we believe. Nonetheless, coherentists, no less than foundationalists, are able to recognize these beliefs, and other noninferred beliefs, as a regular source of new evidence that plays a crucial role in determining what we are justified in believing. What is distinctive about coherentism is its claim that the epistemic credentials these beliefs, and all others, enjoy is dependent on the evidential/inferential relations they bear to others. And a belief can bear the appropriate sort of relation to others even if, as it happens, it was caused directly by experience or is concerned directly with experience.

The second concern is encouraged by the thought that the coherence theory is committed to treating a set of beliefs as justified as long as it is coherent, regardless of whether those beliefs have been properly informed by experience. Even if the coherence theory can allow experiential input, the concern is that it treats such input as incidentally important rather than crucial.

The worry can be brought out with an example. Imagine that someone holds an exceedingly coherent set of beliefs, as coherent as any coherentist could demand. But imagine too that because of some neural accident, or a Mad Scientist's mucking about, or God's intervention, her beliefs become insensitive to experience. Her beliefs remain in a coherent stasis, although now they are uninfluenced one way or the other by her accumulating experience. Surely, one is inclined to say, she is no longer justified in holding her beliefs despite their continued coherence, and this shows that, as the foundationalist can hold, the status of our beliefs as justified depends on their being properly responsive to experience and not on their being coherent.[68]

So far, the case is crucially underdescribed. We need to distinguish between: (i) the person whose experiences continue to provide her with evidence that she unfortunately fails to take into account; and (ii) the person who may in a sense continue to have experiences although the link between her experience and her cognitive states is severed in a way that keeps her from acquiring new evidence from those experiences. In the first case, she is clearly unjustified in holding her beliefs precisely for the reasons a coherentist can acknowledge: She violates the basing requirement. Whatever explains her continuing to hold the beliefs she does, it is not the evidence available to her. What she believes may or may not be justified; whether it is depends on whether the evidence provided by her experiences (to which she is unresponsive) tells against them, on balance. But because she doesn't believe as she does because her beliefs cohere well with her evidence, she is not justified in holding those beliefs even on the coherentist's view. In the second case, though, the coherentist will say that the person may in fact be justified in holding her beliefs, though she is in an epistemically sad situation. For in this case she is, by hypothesis, not receiving new evidence from her senses and so her failure to respond to those experiences by changing her beliefs is no reflection on the justification she has for them. To think otherwise is to fall back on the sort of externalism that holds people strictly liable for what they believe even in cases where they have no reason to believe otherwise.[69] Either way, I think the example doesn't support the idea that coherentism ignores the importance of one's being properly responsive to one's experiences.

Nonetheless, coherentism requires experience only to the extent experience (broadly construed) is the source of new evidence. It imposes no specific requirement on the nature of that experience (on either its source or content) nor on how a person must see her views as being related to experience. And its liberalness on these matters may be problematic. There are two plausible claims that together suggest that peoples' beliefs are justified only if they see those beliefs as grounded in their experience. The first is that a person's beliefs are justified only if the supposition that they are true figures as part of the best explanation that person has of her holding the belief. The second is that such an explanation will inevitably, at some point, appeal to that person's experiences. The first claim gets its plausibility from the conviction that we would have reason to rely on our beliefs only if we thought they were responsive to the facts they concern, just as we would have reason to rely on someone else's beliefs only if we thought their beliefs responsive to the facts they concern. The second gets its plausibility from the general conviction that only experience establishes an appropriate link between our beliefs and what they are about.

The first claim goes wrong, in the way the doxastic ascent argument does, if it sees justification as available only to those who have beliefs about their beliefs (to the effect that the truth of the beliefs helps to explain their being held). One might justifiably hold the beliefs one does without even being aware of the beliefs themselves as things that might be explained. Yet for those of us who do have beliefs about our beliefs, it does seem reasonable for us to ask, and to be worried if we can't answer in the appropriate way, the question of why we believe as we do. If we discover our beliefs seem not appropriately sensitive to the facts (as we take them to be) we will normally see that as good grounds for suspecting that our believing as we do in effect violates the basing requirement.[70] So for those who recognize the basing requirement and see the connection between satisfying that requirement and being able to explain their beliefs by appeal to their truth, the requirement will make sense. Others, though, in holding different views, may still be justified in believing as they do.

As for the second claim, whether being appropriately sensitive to the facts involves our views being sensitive to our experiences depends in large part on whether our beliefs concern matters that we believe to be discoverable only through experience. When it comes to morals and mathematics, for instance, the relevance of experience is at least questionable. To the extent we are thorough-going empiricists, though, we will think experience is always crucial, and the demand that we be able to see our beliefs as hooking up in the right way with experience will then be natural. Yet one might intelligibly reject empiricism and, depending on what else one believes, be justified in doing so. Thus, even if empiricism is true, recognizing its truth and living up to the strictures such a recognition would bring, cannot plausibly be seen as conditions on justified belief.

The important thing to notice about both the explanatory requirement and the empiricist assumption is that they represent at most substantive restrictions on what *we* can justifiably believe, given what else we believe. And coherentism can perfectly well acknowledge these restrictions as ones we justifiably believe appropriate; they are more or less justified, according to the coherentist, to the extent to which they are actually supported by the evidence available to those who hold them. All that coherentism denies is that satisfying them represents a necessary condition on justification. On the coherentist's view, even if, on balance, we have reason to reject any belief not properly grounded in experience, other people may, depending on what else they believe, be justified in holding their beliefs even when they have no explanation of them or no explanation of them that links them to experience.

Incidentally, I do think that the truth of our moral beliefs often plays a role in explaining both why we hold them and why we have the experiences we take as evidence for them. Thus we might appeal to the injustice of certain institutions to explain the social unrest we observe; to the value of an activity to explain why it regularly gives rise to satisfaction; to the evilness of a character to explain a person's willingness to act as we learn someone has. Yet these explanations rely on our justifiably believing institutions of that type unjust, or activities of that sort good, or characters of that kind evil; they go through only if, in giving them, we can legitimately invoke other background moral views in accounting for the relation between morality and the experiences we hope to explain. If instead we had to build up, piecemeal, and without recourse to background views, an explanation of moral beliefs relying initially only on certain privileged beliefs (say concerning our sensory experiences) we would, I suspect, never find ourselves having to appeal to the truth of our moral views to explain our holding them. At the same time, though, I suspect as well that were we similarly obliged to explain our nonmoral views in this piecemeal fashion the truth of few of them would figure in an explanation of our holding them.

An important advantage of the coherence theory is that it can make good sense of our legitimately relying in this way on background assumptions, whether moral or not: If these assumptions cohere well with the other things we believe, then when it comes time to show that our particular beliefs, say, some of our moral beliefs, are properly responsive to our experiences, the background assumptions are among the beliefs we may legitimately take into account. If everything comes together appropriately, and the explanations actually go through, we can justifiably believe that our moral beliefs play a role in explaining our experiences. Of course, everything might not come together appropriately; even as we find ourselves initially justified in relying on moral assumptions in trying to explain our experiences, we may discover the explanations are not good. In that case, we need to weigh the justification we have for those beliefs against the recognition that they might be explanatorily impotent. While I think the bulk of the justification we have for our moral beliefs really has nothing to do with their playing an important role in explaining our experiences, I am inclined to think that we would not be justified in believing of some moral principles that they were true, unless we also thought their being true made some difference to, and so contribute to an explanation of, our believing them.[71]

Conclusion

Most of this paper has been given over to articulating and defending a version of the coherence theory of justification. As that theory would have it, a belief is justified if, and then to the extent that, it coheres well with the other things a person believes. And a person is justified in holding some belief if and only if the belief itself is justified and she holds it because it is justified. In various crucial ways the theory differs from most versions of the coherence theory. First of all, rather than dodging the regress argument by embracing a holistic theory of justification, this version meets the argument head on and, with the foundationalist, acknowledges that certain beliefs may serve as suitable regress-stoppers. Unlike foundationalism, however, it insists that these regress-stoppers—the beliefs that count as permissively, but not positively, justified—enjoy no special epistemic privilege and are themselves characterizable only in terms of the evidential connections they bear to other beliefs. When beliefs are permissively justified it is only in light of the relations they bear to other beliefs. Second of all, while it treats the coherence of one's beliefs as a criterion of justification, it treats coherence itself not as a justifying property of those beliefs but rather as a measure of the evidential support the beliefs enjoy. In every case, what evidence a person has for her beliefs is found not in their relative coherence, but in the contents of her other beliefs.

Thus there is in coherentism a built-in commitment to relativism about justification. What a person in fact believes, and so what evidence she happens to have available, is crucial to whether her views are justified, and a belief one person is justified in accepting may be such that others would be justified in rejecting it. The relativism doesn't collapse, of course, into the view that anything one takes to be justified is. The coherentist says a person's belief is justified only if it coheres well with her other beliefs; whether it does is independent of whether she thinks it does (except as such a belief might be countenanced as evidentially related to other things she believes). In any given case, according to coherentism, there is a fact of the matter about whether someone is justified and they, as well as anyone else, might get that fact wrong.

There is as well a deep seated recognition of fallibilism. Not only does a coherentist treat each belief as open to revision in light of others, she recognizes also that even a fully coherent, and so wonderfully justified, set of beliefs might turn out to be false. Justification's link to truth, such as it is, is not provided by coherence itself, but instead by the evidential relations that bind beliefs together into coherent sets. Thus the theory makes good sense of how we can look back on our own earlier beliefs as having been justified and yet now justifiably thought wrong; and it makes good sense out of how we can distinguish among others as between those who are justified in holding their differing (and as we see it false) views and those that aren't.

At the same time, the theory finds a good place for the thought that, while we recognize that any of our beliefs might be wrong, that fact about us and our beliefs doesn't in and of itself count as strong reason to reject our view—certainly not nearly as strong as would be our coming to think we actually had made a mistake (in which case we've got reasons precisely as strong as the support that view has, for changing the view in question). Thus the coherentist responds to the skeptic neither decisively nor simply by deciding not to worry about her challenge, but by advancing a positive view about what sort of evidence the mere possibility of error constitutes. Each suggestion that a person might have made a mistake is appropriately countered, when it can be, by appeal to the evidence available that supports the view. A person might of course be wrong in the positive view she advances—a possibility the skeptic will push—but that fact too tells only so far against the weight of the evidence the person might be able to marshall in defense of her own view. Whether, concerning any particular issue, a person is justified in accepting skepticism will turn (as does the justification for all beliefs) on the weight of the evidence available.

In defending the coherence theory of justification I have, in effect, been offering an extended defense of the particularly epistemic value of the method of reflective equilibrium. The general line of defense is, I hope, pretty clear: The method is valuable because its successful deployment results in our holding justified beliefs. However, the defense remains only partial since it simply assumes that the mutual support sought in using the method corresponds to evidential support. Although I believe it does, I've offered here no argument for thinking so.

In any case, let me turn to the two questions I raised early in the paper: Under what conditions are a person's moral beliefs epistemically justified? and under what conditions are *our* moral beliefs epistemically justified? In answer to the first, I've argued—by defending a version of the coherence theory—that a person's moral beliefs are epistemically justified if, and then to the extent that, they cohere well with the other things she believes. With this answer in mind, it should be clear that an answer to the second question needn't merely repeat the answer to the first, at least when we can say something substantive about the various other things we happen to believe.

As it happens, when we turn our attention to our moral beliefs, most of us find that, on the one hand, we seem to have overwhelmingly good reason for believing certain things (e.g., that deliberate cruelty is wrong, that slavery is unjust, and that courage is valuable, that happiness is important, that justice is appropriately demanded, and that certain considerations are morally relevant, others not); while, on the other hand, we have a substantial number of beliefs about morality as well as about metaphysics and epistemology more generally, that seemingly tell against our having any good reason at all for holding the moral beliefs we do (or any others). Some of our apparently well-supported beliefs, in other words, seem to clash with others. Coherentism councils against taking any of these views as decisive, yet at the same time it encourages seeking out some accommodation by sorting through the various commitments that clash in an attempt to render them at least consistent and preferably more.

To the extent that our moral views can be reconciled with the other things we believe, they will be epistemically justified, and all the more so as they provide evidence for one another. Yet the pressing worries about moral theory are really worries as to whether our moral views will even minimally cohere with the bulk of things we seemingly justifiably believe. In raising metaphysical, epistemological, and psychological worries about the status of our moral claims we are articulating the considerations that seem to stand as, often quite strong, evidence against our moral beliefs. Depending on how strong that evidence is, our moral views, even if they cohere well among themselves, might turn out to be unjustified. This means the coherence theory provides no safe haven for our moral opinions; it won't count them as justified if only they can be made internally consistent and systematically impressive. They will be justified if, but only if, they cohere well with the other things we believe; that is, if, but only if, the weight of all the available evidence tells in their favor. How the evidence weighs is, unfortunately, not at all clear. What is clear, though, is that any account that can succeed in making good sense of our moral views as, by our lights, metaphysically unambitious, epistemically accessible, and psychologically realistic, will straight-away enjoy a huge epistemic advantage. Working out such an account, while essential to the epistemic good standing of our moral beliefs, is not so much a matter of doing epistemology as it is one of doing moral philosophy. Yet, if the coherence theory is right, in doing the moral philosophy, we have good reason to adjust our moral beliefs in light of metaphysical and epistemological concerns. And, to go back to the first point I made in this paper, we have good reason as well to recognize how much of morality is not a matter of belief at all; for that too is part of the evidence we must accommodate.[72]

Notes

1. Presumably, whatever capacities, abilities, and skills, constitute knowing how to be moral would, in principle, find a propositional reflection in a full compendium of moral truths (among which would be included the claim that acting morally requires

having certain capacities, etc.). Yet possession of such a compendium, even if fully grasped and completely justified, may leave one utterly unable, even if willing, to do what one knows is required. And in not knowing how to do what one knows to be required, one would be lacking a pivotal bit of moral knowledge.

2. Later on I will say something about how epistemic justification differs from other sorts of justification. For the time being, however, I will simply assume we all have an intuitive grasp on there being a difference between, say, the moral, the pragmatic, and the epistemic credentials a belief might enjoy. Each set of credentials may, in a perfectly reasonable sense, make it true that the belief is justified, but the sort of justification at issue will change as the relevant credentials shift. My concern will be with epistemic credentials—those that get their point and purchase from a concern with evidence, truth, and knowledge.

3. J. L. Mackie defends this view in *Ethics: Inventing Right and Wrong* (Harmondsworth: Penguin Books Ltd., 1977).

4. For influential defences of what is often called *noncognitivism*, see A. J. Ayer's *Language, Truth and Logic* (New York: Dover, 1952); C. L. Stevenson's *Ethics and Language* (New Haven: Yale University Press, 1944); Simon Blackburn's *Essays in Quasi-Realism* (Oxford: Oxford University Press, 1994); and Allan Gibbard's *Wise Choices, Apt Feelings* (Cambridge: Harvard University Press, 1990).

5. So, for instance, to the extent that an action is successfully justified by appeal to its consequences, then the fact that the action has those consequences is grounds for believing that the action is right or permissible; and to the extent some attitude is successfully justified by appeal to its cause, then the fact that the attitude was caused in the way it was is grounds for believing the attitude appropriate.

6. What I am concerned with here is the justification of belief in general and if moral beliefs don't require justification (because there aren't any) then we can ask equally well what would justify one in thinking there are no moral beliefs.

7. I note here only a natural inclination. One might accept the coherence theory of justification and nonetheless reject the coherence methodology. Aiming directly at some goal is not always the best way of achieving it and it may be that aiming directly at securing a coherent set of beliefs (in the way the coherence methodology recommends) might not be the best way of securing such a set.

8. (Cambridge: Harvard University Press, 1971). Earlier, Nelson Goodman offered a defense of the method's use in determining valid rules of deductive and inductive inference in *Fact, Fiction, and Forecast,* 4th edition (Cambridge: Harvard University Press, 1983), pp. 63–66, originally published in 1955. See Norman Daniels' "Wide Reflective Equilibrium and Theory Acceptance in Ethics," *Journal of Philosophy* (1979), pp. 256–82; and "Reflective Equilibrium and Archimedean Points," *Canadian Journal of Philosophy* (1980), pp. 83–103; for lucid discussion of the method of reflective equilibrium. See also Michael DePaul's *Balance and Refinement* (London: Routledge, 1993) and my "Coherence and Models for Model Theorizing," *Pacific Philosophical Quarterly* (1985), pp. 170–90.

9. This is an empirical claim, of course. In principle, at least, someone might actually settle on an equilibrium that would remain unshaken by further reflection. A huge number of people do actually refuse to change their views in light of further reflection. But I suspect most of these people of dogmatism rather than reflective success.

10. See, for instance, David Lyons' "Nature and Soundness of Contract and Coherence Arguments," in *Reading Rawls,* ed. by Norman Daniels (New York: Basic Books, 1975), pp. 141–67; and Richard Brandt's *A Theory of the Good and the Right* (Oxford: Oxford University Press, 1979), pp. 18–20.

11. To take one example, Sidgwick seems to have accepted a foundationalist theory of justification in ethics and elsewhere, even as he thought of, what was in effect, the method of reflective equilibrium as a useful means of discovering the fundamental principles of morality. These principles are justifiably believed, he thought, not in virtue of their cohering with other things we believe but rather because they are certified by intuition properly deployed. *The Methods of Ethics,* by Henry Sidgwick (London: Macmillan and Co., Limited, 1907), seventh edition.

12. As skeptical as one might be of moral beliefs and the suggestion that some of them might be justified, that skepticism needn't have its source in a rabid skepticism that dismisses the very idea of justified belief. I will assume that the notion of justified belief makes sense, even if no beliefs (moral or otherwise) actually are justified. While this means I will be begging the question against a few skeptical positions, all but the most rabid skepticisms work with some account or other of justified belief to make good their own skeptical position. Most versions of skepticism, though, are advanced as being themselves justified (which means they are committed to at least some beliefs being justified). So it is worth noting that the only skepticisms I will be leaving completely to one side are those that reject out of hand and without offering a justification the very idea of justified belief. (Truth be told, I don't much mind ignoring them.)

13. A person, it seems, might be morally but neither pragmatically nor epistemically justified in holding some belief, or pragmatically but neither morally nor epistemically justified, or epistemically but neither morally nor pragmatically justified. The various different considerations that are relevant to these different evaluations might be such that, in some circumstances, they conflict in their deliverances. Perhaps they might, with suitable specification and elaboration, be shown in fact to coincide. Just such a (partial) coincidence is sought, for instance, by those who offer a pragmatic justification for acting morally. If indeed acting morally were always in our interest, then those actions (including acts of believing) that count as morally justified would be at the same time pragmatically justified (assuming that we are pragmatically justified in doing what is in our interest). Alternatively, such a (partial) coincidence is sought by those who offer a moral defense of believing as one's evidence would allow as well as by those who offer an epistemic defense of believing as morality requires.

14. However, I should note that sometimes our epistemic evaluation of someone's holding of a belief has more to do with whether she has taken due care in collecting evidence and reflected adequately on it, than with whether the evidence she has justifies the belief. Whether these considerations are invoked in determining justification or are instead involved in a distinct notion of epistemic responsibility, is often unclear. To the extent epistemic justification is at issue, though, I suspect that which standards are appropriate for evaluating *due care* and *adequate reflection* will depend on the evidence available to the person being evaluated. If so, then whether or not one is epistemically justified in seeking no further evidence or in limiting reflection depends on whether, for instance, one has grounds for thinking that there is important evidence still to be found or properly appreciated. Yet even if one has no such grounds, and so is not unjustified in holding the belief, one might nonetheless be holding it irresponsibly—if one has a responsibility to seek more evidence or reflect further even in cases where one has no reason to think one has such a responsibility.

15. Even necessary truths are such that a person might come to believe one (say as a result of wishful thinking or testimony one knew better than to trust) in a way that leaves the person unjustified in accepting it.

16. I simply pass over, in this paper, the difficulties facing any attempt to specify exactly what it would be for a person's beliefs to be based *in the appropriate way* on her evidence. I pass over as well the complications that are induced by a person's

beliefs always being only *more or less* based on her evidence; a number of other factors are inevitably required in order for one to form or maintain a belief at all. To what extent one's belief needs to be based on one's evidence in order to satisfy the basing requirement is, at best, difficult to say.

17. See the *Groundwork of the Metaphysics of Morals* (New York: Harper & Row, 1964), trans. by H. J. Paton, p. 65.

18. How far the parallel can be pushed, I'm not sure. I certainly don't want to defend the Epistemic Imperative as a synthetic a priori truth (but then I wouldn't want to defend the Categorical Imperative as one either). Regardless, in both cases there's some plausibility in thinking the two imperatives cash out appealing conceptions of justification. Hume advocates something like the epistemic imperative, when he observes that "A wise man, therefore, proportions his belief to the evidence." See *Enquiry Concerning Human Understanding,* ed. by L. A. Selby-Bigge, revised by P. H. Nidditch (Oxford: Oxford University Press, 1975), p. 110.

19. *ibid.,* p. 88.

20. She might even be both morally and pragmatically justified in holding such beliefs if, for instance, she is within her rights to believe as she does and her so believing is to her advantage (as it may well be if she is surrounded by others who share her convictions).

21. Suppose some people are epistemically justified in holding an immoral view, are they then morally culpable for the evil they do on the basis of those beliefs? The answer to this turns crucially on whether (and if so, how) the standards of moral responsibility are sensitive to peoples' epistemological situation. If the boundaries of moral responsibility are set in part by what one could justifiably believe, then it might well be that a person who acts immorally on the basis of epistemically well-justified, but morally objectionable, views is not responsible for what she does. Ignorance is, in the absence of negligence, a reasonable moral excuse. And whether one has been negligent depends (I am inclined to think) on whether one had reason to think acting differently was important.

22. Someone might resist the "only if" in this formulation arguing that a liberal minded foundationalist could say just that one way (among others) for a belief to be justified is for it to be either foundational or inferentially supported by foundational beliefs. I opt for the stronger formulation of foundationalism because the main argument for foundationalism—the regress argument (which I discuss later in the paper)—turns on the "only if" clause when it assumes that no beliefs would be justified in the absence of some noninferentially justified beliefs. Other arguments might be appealed to, though, and they might require only the weaker formulation of foundationalism. In fact, the chapters by Audi and Sinnott-Armstrong in this collection work with he weaker definition of foundationalism. Even these weaker foundationalisms, though, accept the view, rejected by coherentism, that some beliefs are epistemically privileged independently of the inferential/evidential relations they bear to other beliefs.

23. See William Alston's "Two Types of Foundationalism," in the *Journal of Philosophy* 73 (1976), pp. 165–85.

24. Two metaphors have dominated characterizations of the two theories: the metaphor of a pyramid to capture foundationalism and that of a raft at sea to capture coherentism. But both are grossly misleading. The pyramid metaphor is misleading since the arguments for foundationalism alone do not support any particular view of how the structure of justified belief will be shaped (other than by requiring some sort of hierarchy). The raft metaphor is less misleading, I suppose, because it does capture nicely the idea that, on a coherentist's view (but also on the foundationalist's view)

things are going better to the extent the raft holds together and better still as the various pieces initially merely lashed together become well secured. But usually the point of the raft analogy is that coherentism allows that, at any particular time, any piece of the raft is liable to replacement. A foundationalist, too, though, might consistently grant that every belief is in principle liable to replacement—foundationalism doesn't require infallibilism—even as it is committed to saying that there must be on board at least some beliefs of a certain privileged kind. See Ernest Sosa's "The Raft and the Pyramid: Coherence versus Foundations in the Theory of Knowledge," in *Midwest Studies,* vol 5. (Minneapolis: University of Minnesota Press, 1980), pp. 3–25.

25. See David Hume's *A Treatise of Human Nature,* 2nd edition (Oxford: Oxford University Press, 1978), p. 469.

26. Most self-described intuitionists fall into this group. See H. A. Prichard's *Moral Obligation* (Oxford: Oxford University Press, 1949); G. E. Moore's *Principia Ethica* (Cambridge: Cambridge University Press, 1903); and W. D. Ross' *The Right and the Good* (Oxford: Oxford University Press, 1930). Sidgwick, however, falls squarely in the next group. See *The Methods of Ethics, op. cit.* More recently, the analogy with perception has been stressed by, for instance, John McDowell in "Value and Secondary Qualities," *Morality and Objectivity,* ed. by Ted Honderich (London: Routledge and Kegan Paul, 1985), pp. 110–29; Mark Platts in "Moral Reality," in *Ways of Meaning* (London: Routledge and Kegan Paul, 1979), pp. 243–63; Jonathan Dancy in *Moral Reasons* (Oxford: Blackwell, 1993); and David McNaughton in *Moral Vision* (Oxford: Blackwell, 1988). Despite their reliance on the perceptual model, however, each of these more recent works adopts epistemological views that lean towards coherentism.

27. Compatible with this crucial difference, coherentism may have a great deal in common with foundationalism. It might, for instance, recognize different classes of belief (even as it rejects the suggestion that any class is epistemically privileged), or embrace the same inferential principles, or even allow that justified beliefs take on, for instance, a pyramid structure.

28. Although foundationalism and coherentism, as I have characterized them, are mutually exclusive, they clearly don't exhaust the possibilities. Someone might well reject foundationalism's commitment to an epistemically privileged class of beliefs and yet resist coherentism's positive account of justification in terms of coherence. One might hold, for instance, that one's beliefs are justified if they are reliable indicators of the facts they concern, or, alternatively, if they are the product of a reliable belief-forming mechanism. In neither case would their justification turn on their cohering with one's other beliefs, except to the extent the relevant sort of reliability is related to coherence.

29. Here again the familiar suggestions emerge: An inferential relation might count as appropriate only if it is deductive, or inductive, or explanatory.

30. And of course that one belief rather than another might be prompted directly by an experience will almost surely be a reflection of what else one believes and will in any case be available in the first place only thanks to one having the conceptual repertoire one does.

31. Clearly, when it comes to working out the details of the basing requirement, coherentists need to make sense of how it is that a justified, though uninferred, belief might still be such as to be held because it is justified. And this might look to be especially tricky for a coherentist since the belief's status as justified is supposed to depend on its inferential relations to other beliefs. Here, though, what the coherentist maintains is that such a belief appropriately depends on its being justified as long as it would not have been held had it not borne the right relations. (In whichever way

this gets worked out, it will have to take account of the complications mentioned and sidestepped in note #16.)

32. Aristotle, *Posterior Analytics,* 72a25–73a20.

33. A powerful skeptical position in ethics, for instance, embraces foundationalism as an account of justification, mobilizes the "is"/"ought" distinction to show that if our moral views have a foundation that foundation must be provided by some of our moral beliefs, and then maintains that none of our moral beliefs will do the job.

34. The collection of arguments I run through find their source in Wilfrid Sellars' "Empiricism and the Philosophy of Mind," although there the discussion is in terms of knowledge, not justification, and it unfolds without making explicit appeal to the basing requirement. See *Science, Perception and Reality* (London: Routledge and Kegan Paul, 1963), pp. 127–96, esp. sec. 36. Laurence BonJour, in *The Structure of Empirical Knowledge* (Cambridge: Harvard University Press, 1985); and David Brink, in *Moral Realism and the Foundations of Ethics* (Cambridge: Cambridge University Press, 1989), both offer clear expressions of this argument.

35. In these two examples I am just picking up on one sort of reason one might have for thinking one's belief justified. Alternative suggestions come with different accounts of what would need to be true of a belief for it to serve appropriately as grounds for believing anything else. The variety of suggestions here is as plentiful as the variety of accounts foundationalists have offered for treating one class of beliefs or another as epistemically privileged.

36. A great deal might be packed into what is required in order for a person's beliefs to be appropriately sensitive to her evidence. It might be, for example, that she must be able to offer reasons for her view, or be able and willing to change her view in light of new evidence, or be able to re-evaluate the value of old evidence in light of new. I don't know whether any of these additional requirements are actually appropriate. What I am suggesting, though, is that self-consciousness of oneself as a believer is not required, whatever else is.

37. They might hold, for instance, that when beliefs are based on certain noncognitive states—e.g., perceptual or introspectable states—those states justify the beliefs. See Anthony Quinton's *The Nature of Things* (London: Routledge & Kegan Paul, 1973); and John Pollock's *Contemporary Theories of Knowledge* (Totowa, NJ: Rowman and Littlefield, 1986).

38. But only a version since, as will become clear, the sort of coherentism I defend counts as an externalist theory of justification even though it embraces an internalist account of reasons.

39. In what follows I will use "belief" loosely enough to cover a whole slew of cognitive states that have propositional content. The distinctions I thus cover over may well be important, of course, in other contexts where one might contrast belief with, for instance, experience on the grounds that belief is active and reflectively-sensitive, whereas experience is passive and receptive. If the distinction were to be drawn in that way, I am committed to saying that the contents of experience and of belief are of a piece (and both are conceptual) at least to the extent the experiences are supposed to provide reasons for believing. See John McDowell's *Mind and World* (Cambridge: Harvard University Press, 1994).

40. By embracing this sort of internalism, I am taking a stand on a controversial issue and merely rehearsing fairly familiar arguments. A satisfying discussion of the issues would take more space than I can give it here. Still, in the end, I believe the familiar arguments do carry the day. For an in-depth attack on internalism, though, see Frederick Schmitt's *Knowledge and Belief* (London: Routledge, 1992).

41. This will be true when a person has no reason not to hold it or when, if she has such a reason, it is at least balanced by some reason she has for holding it.

42. Clearly there are two other possible readings: (i) one belief provides (permissive) justification for another only if it is, itself, (permissively) justified; and (ii) one belief provides (permissive) justification for another only if it is, itself, (positively) justified. The first of these is weaker even than the weak reading defended in what follows, and would in any case be irrelevant to establishing that we ever have positive reason to believe as we do; and the second would, like the strong reading rejected in what follows, make an appeal to permissive justification useless when it comes to stopping the regress.

43. A foundationalist might conceivably maintain that the epistemically privileged beliefs can provide positive support for themselves. This may be the hopeful idea behind holding that a belief might be *self*-evident. But then a foundationalist needs to make sense of the idea that a belief (that is, the content of a belief) can provide evidence for that very belief. And she needs to do this in a way that doesn't entail that all beliefs provide this kind of support for themselves. (So she can't simply say, for example, that what justifies *her belief that she seems to see blue* is that *she seems to see blue,* which at first might sound plausible, since every *belief that p* could then be justified by *p,* for any p.) The most likely candidates for status as self-evident are presumably beliefs that have analytic truths as their content, yet even they seem only sometimes justifiably believed. Whether a person is positively justified in holding such beliefs seems to depend on why she is holding them, on whether, for instance, she recognizes them to be analytic or accepts them on good authority or has some other reason to think they are true.

44. Although permissively justified beliefs can serve to stop the regress, presumably only positively justified beliefs enjoy the sort of support that knowledge is usually thought to presuppose. In any case, a belief that is *merely* permissively justified will be a belief one has, on balance, no reason to believe—it enjoys no positive justification.

45. Whether these cases are ultimately intelligible is open to question. It's arguable (but I think not true) that the beliefs we are able to attribute to two people so differently situated must always be different. If so, then the supposition that they share beliefs can't be sustained. What matters, though, is not so much whether these represent real possibilities; what matters is that, were they possible, we would normally count the people involved as being equally justified, though not equally well-situated epistemically.

46. G. E. Moore articulates this idea as he spells out what it would be for something to exhibit *organic unity.* See *Principia Ethica, ibid.*

47. Given the definition of positive justification and the rejection of externalism about a person's reasons for believing, no belief will count as positively justified when considered in isolation. Interestingly, though, someone inclined to accept foundationalism, who will then treat some beliefs as positively justified even when considered in isolation from other beliefs, can, and I think should, grant that beliefs to the effect that there are the proper relations among one's beliefs actually enhances the privileged beliefs' justificatory status.

48. If this suggestion is to be worked out in a way that is compatible with the version of internalism I've defended, the justification enhancing role of evidential relations cannot be that of giving a person more reason to believe as she does (since the presence of the relation may be something about which she has no beliefs even when it holds).

49. See Kant's *Groundwork of the Metaphysics of Morals, ibid.,* pp. 61–62.

50. Incidentally, even if the relations themselves are seen as being valuable, the value they have might itself be conditional on their relating real evidence. Thus, while

the relations will presumably be characterized in terms that allow them to stand among propositions (whether believed or not), the evidential value of these relations might depend upon the status of those propositions as evidence—which status they will have, I've argued, only as they become the content of the relevant person's beliefs.

51. Although misleading in some ways, the Bayesian principle of conditionalization, and the phenomenon of the "swamping of priors," may nonetheless provide a suggestive model for the link between evidential relations and truth that I have in mind. Loosely characterized, here's the phenomenon: given certain assumptions concerning the structure and availability of probability estimates, it can be shown that people who start with even wildly different beliefs (priors) concerning, for instance, the fairness of some coin (each thinking it biased, but in opposite ways) will, given enough information about the results of repeated coin tosses, come to the same view concerning the probability that it will come up heads on the next toss, as long as they revise their beliefs according to the principle of conditionalization; and this will be true (almost) no matter what probabilities they originally assigned. Moreover, the view they will then share will be an accurate view, if the information they receive about successive coin tosses is accurate and bountiful enough.

52. Just as foundationalism admits of both skeptical and anti-skeptical strands, so too does coherentism: a skeptical coherentist holds, in effect, that there are no evidential relations that might hold among our beliefs. Thus, on this view, coherentism gives the right account of what it would take for our beliefs to be positively justified, but none of them have what it takes—an evidential relation to our other beliefs.

53. Lewis Carroll uses his own regress argument to establish this in "What The Tortoise Said to Achilles," *Mind* 4 (1895), pp. 278–80.

54. How well, and whether, a belief coheres with the others a person holds will depend, in part, on what alternatives are available to her. Before Newton came on the scene, people were justified in believing things about the workings of the world that later they would have been unjustified in accepting in light of the evidence and options available. So we might say, a bit more precisely, that a belief is justified only if, and then to the extent that, it coheres *better than does any competitor belief* with the other things the person believes (where two beliefs will compete with one another if either might, but both can't, be held by the person in question).

55. Although here I will be characterizing the coherence of a set of beliefs, the same considerations of evidential consistency, connectedness, and comprehensiveness, will serve to characterize the relative coherence of sets of propositions directly. So, for instance, a set of propositions that constitute a theory will count as minimally coherent if appropriately consistent, and then as more than minimally coherent as the theory is connected and comprehensive.

56. The evidential consistency requirement insists on both more and less than would a requirement that demanded logical consistency from the contents of the beliefs in the set. It demands more because a set that contained only logically consistent beliefs would nonetheless fall short of evidential consistency if the evidence provided by some of the beliefs, on balance, told against one of the beliefs. It demands less because a set that contained logically inconsistent beliefs that were equally well supported by the evidence provided by the other beliefs would count as evidentially consistent (and so minimally coherent). For arguments against requiring logical consistency, see Richard Foley's "Justified Inconsistent Beliefs," in *American Philosophical Quarterly* (1979), pp. 247–57.

57. I don't suppose that there is any algorithm for determining the relative contributions connectedness and comprehensiveness make to the over-all coherence of a set.

It would be a mistake, though, to think that connectedness and comprehensiveness will never compete. While any belief that increases the connectedness of an evidentially consistent set will likewise increase comprehensiveness, and any belief that increases comprehensiveness in such a set will at worst make no difference to connectedness, when it comes to comparing one coherent set with another, we may be faced with one that's more connected but less comprehensive than another and sometimes, at least, comprehensiveness may win out over connectedness or vice versa.

58. There's no worry about a tie here since if two subsets are evidentially consistent and equally coherent, the set that includes all the beliefs in each that can be combined without losing evidential consistency will be more coherent than either. Of course, the larger set may contain logically inconsistent beliefs that enjoy evidential support to the same degree, so that the total weight of the evidence provided by beliefs in the set does not, on balance, tell against either. In that case, the inconsistent beliefs will be justified but ònly permissively so. When we recognize the inconsistency, the fact that the beliefs are inconsistent will certainly provide evidence against accepting both and may constitute grounds for agnosticism. Yet recognizing the inconsistency provides evidence against both equally, and thus leaves the balance unchanged. We will then have positive—in fact conclusive—reason for thinking the inconsistent beliefs are not all true, which means justifiably holding them will be possible only if we can believe each separately without believing their conjunction. This isn't quite the same as saying, though, that we ought to give up one or the other of the beliefs—we might have no positive reason for giving up any one of them, although we have positive reason for looking for some reason.

59. The same case will build, of course, even without the unjustified beliefs as long as corresponding justified beliefs to the effect that anomalies had emerged are taken on board as the unjustified beliefs are rejected. When the case these beliefs provide has become formidable, it will be because the best explanation of all the apparent illusions, seeming distortions, and ostensibly inaccurate observations is that they are nothing of the sort and that the old theory is false.

60. Nice complications emerge when we consider situations in which the person herself is considering various things she might believe, each of which would cohere well with the other things she believes. In that case, which belief would be justified will depend on which of the options would cohere *better* with the other things she believes (including her beliefs concerning which of the options is more justified), and, having considered the options, believing one that coheres less well, but still well, with her beliefs, would presumably be unjustified.

61. Whether a person's evidence will tell against some of her current beliefs, when it provides stronger support for some other potential beliefs, will depend on whether the person is aware of those options that would cohere well with what else she believes.

62. Suppose that a person holds some belief that does cohere well with her other beliefs. Yet suppose also that she believes something stupid (and unjustified) from which she self–consciously inferred the belief? Is she justified in believing it? That depends: Would she have held the belief even if it hadn't cohered well with the other things she believes? If so, then the fact that the belief was justified doesn't explain her holding it and her holding it is not justified. If not, then the fact that the belief was justified does explain her holding it and her holding it is justified. What then should we say in face of the explicit and yet unjustified and non-justifying reason she offers for her belief? I think we should say that she was justified in holding it given her evidence though mistaken about why. What if she falsely believes of the belief that it doesn't cohere with the other things she believes? Well, if she also believes the

coherence theory, then her belief that the belief doesn't cohere with her other beliefs will be, for her, a reason to reject it—yet it is just one reason among many and that reason may still be overridden by the other reasons she has in virtue of which it counts as actually cohering better than alternatives.

63. Although there are some complications here: Merely taking the original set and negating the content of all the beliefs may give one an equally consistent set of propositions, but that procedure will often leave one with a much less coherent set of potential beliefs because the negation of an explanatory principle does not always explain the negation of the set of claims that was originally explained. Still I think it reasonable to allow that suitable competitor sets can always be constructed, even if not by any simple procedure.

64. In "Coherence and Models for Moral Theorizing," *op. cit.,* I raise this objection to the all too common practice, in moral theory, of treating the fact that one theory is more coherent than another as an independent reason to think the theory true.

65. A person may, of course, be wrong in the probabilities she associates with various outcomes, or the value she attributes to those outcomes. Expected utility often differs from actual utility. Yet, according to this theory, so far as the rationality of her choice is concerned, it is rational if given those views the choice she makes maximizes expected utility.

66. Here the analogy with decision theory may be helpful again. We might well recognize another person as making a choice, from among the same options we face, that maximizes her expected utility, and (if only we could make good sense of interpersonal utility comparisons) we might recognize too that given her expectations and values, the option she takes has a greater expected utility for her than our best option has for us. Nonetheless, that provides us with no reason whatsoever to embrace the option she rationally chooses. We might of course take the fact that she has the expectations or values she does as evidence that ours are misguided, and if so, we will have reason to change ours, but often enough we have good reason to think what she expects or values is irrelevant.

67. Just as the theory of rational choice is not committed to saying that the fact that something advances one's own interests need be a reason a person has for acting, since people's preferences may all be other-directed, so too the coherence theory is not committed to saying that the fact that one believes something need be a reason a person has for believing, since people's beliefs may all have as their content things other than their own beliefs. Now in fact we can expect people to be interested in their own interests and to have beliefs concerning their beliefs, but these interests and beliefs constitute only a fraction of the interests and beliefs a person usually has and neither the maximizing theory of rationality nor the coherence theory of justification gives them any special weight or importance.

68. See Alvin Plantinga's *Warrant: The Current Debate* (Oxford: Oxford University Press, 1993).

69. We may need yet a third case: It may be that the person has actually had her beliefs "frozen" so that she is not simply insensitive to the beliefs she forms on the basis of experience, nor simply cognitively cut off from her experiences. In this case, I think the most reasonable thing to say is that she is no longer believing anything. But if we still count her as believing, she will still fail the basing requirement because, once her beliefs are "frozen," what explains her holding of them is no longer her evidence but the fact that they are now unchangeable.

70. Of course, even in our own case, we often find ourselves with beliefs we take to be justified despite our inability to offer any respectable explanation of why we

hold them, but lacking such an explanation is conspicuously different from having positive reason for thinking the beliefs are insensitive to the relevant facts.

71. For discussion of these issues, see Gilbert Harman's *The Nature of Morality* (New York: Oxford University Press, 1977); and Nicholas Sturgeon's "Moral Explanations," in *Morality, Reason and Truth* (Totowa, NJ: Rowman and Allanheld, 1985), ed. by David Copp and David Zimmerman, pp. 49–78; as well as my "Moral Theory and Explanatory Impotence," *Midwest Studies* XII, ed. by Peter French *et al.* (University of Minnesota Press, 1988), pp. 433–57, and "Normative Explanations," *Philosophical Perspectives* VII, ed. by James Tomberlin (1992), pp. 55–72.

72. Shorter versions of this paper were given at Dartmouth College, the University of North Carolina at Chapel Hill, and the 1995 Pacific Division Meetings of the American Philosophical Association. For helpful discussions and comments on earlier versions of this paper I am grateful to Louise Antony, Robert Audi, Simon Blackurn, Malia Brink, Michael Gill, Dan Hunter, Andrew Johnson, William Lycan, Joan McCord, Sean McKeever, Elijah Millgram, Bijan Parsia, Wayne Riggs, Harriet Sayre-McCord, and especially Walter Sinnott-Armstrong and Stephen Darwall.

6

Foundationalism and Coherentism in Ethics

R. M. Hare

When Kant called his most-read ethical book *Groundwork* (or *Foundations*) *of the Metaphysic of Morals,* was he enrolling himself as an ethical foundationalist? Simply to ask this question is to raise another, of what it is to be a foundationalist? It is clear that in the view of many moral philosophers and others it is a bad thing to be; but, apart from this pejorative content, does it have any other? I shall try to illuminate this question by first giving a caricature of the kind of foundationalism that its enemies are attacking. This picture I shall call 'Cartesian foundationalism', without implying any disrespect for Descartes, and without even claiming that he held such a view (though he has often been accused of holding it). It is not my intention to offer any scholarly exegesis either of Descartes, or of Kant, or of any other historical figure, though I shall draw on some of their ideas.

After pointing out some obvious and well canvassed faults in Cartesian foundationalism,[1] I shall go on to explain again where it goes wrong.[2] My only reason for reviving these old arguments is that since then they have been forgotten. I shall then outline a procedure for moral reasoning which escapes these faults, on the lines already suggested in *Freedom and Reason* (chapters 6–9) chs. 6ff. and more fully worked out in *Moral Thinking.*[3] This method has some claim to be called foundationalist in a different sense, which is perhaps in accordance with Kant's aims. It can also claim to be in a sense coherentist, thus breaking down the supposed opposition between foundationalism and coherentism, about which much has been written. For sources, I can refer readers to Mark Timmons' helpful paper.[4]

After that, I shall introduce perhaps my only new point. This is, that in the attempt to reconcile foundationalism and coherentism, the dispute between which has dogged epistemology, *moral* epistemology has a big advantage over most other kinds of epistemology. This advantage derives from the fact that moral statements have a *prescriptive* element in their meaning. That this should be thought an advantage will surprise many people; for it is generally held that, if moral statements were prescriptive, this would put an obstacle in the way of a satisfactory moral epistemology.

I aim to show that the boot is on the other foot: moral epistemology, just because moral statements are prescriptive, can overcome the chief obstacle to success in general epistemology. It is the fact that in general epistemology (in philosophy of science for example) we are after a way of establishing *facts,* that makes it so difficult to achieve success. Moral epistemology, which is after something different, namely rationally acceptable prescriptions, can overcome this obstacle. Whether general epistemology can learn a lesson in this respect from moral epistemology is a question I shall leave for others.

I proceed now to my caricature of Cartesian foundationalism. This is supposed to operate by a kind of inference that I have called, adapting Bosanquet's term, *linear inference.*[5] The idea is that, since all inference is from premisses, we proceed by deriving desired conclusions from premisses, and these in turn from further or higher premisses, until we reach a 'foundation', which has to be indubitable or self-evident (otherwise the process would have to go on for ever). I leave it to those who do not like mixed metaphors to decide whether the foundation is at the top or the bottom of this structure—the *angularis fundamentum lapis* is also the headstone in the corner. In what follows I shall adopt the terminology which puts the foundations at the top.

The belief that underlies this procedure is that linear inference is the only possible kind of inference. I do not wish to deny that there *is* this kind of inference, with which we are familiar from the logic books. It is, indeed, an essential part of any logical structure. But such structures do not have to be exclusively linear. They do not have to consist entirely of a single straight (or even crooked) line of inferences, starting from some hopefully indubitable first premiss and ending with the conclusions we want to reach. As we shall see, there is an alternative kind of structure.

As is well known, the weakness of such a Cartesian structure is that the supposedly indubitable first premiss turns out not after all to be indubitable. Usually the trouble is that, interpreted in one way, it is indubitable (maybe because it is analytically true) but then does not entail the conclusions we want to draw from it; but, if it is made, by a different interpretation, substantial enough to entail the conclusions, it can be doubted. Ever since philosophy began people have been trying to find first premisses which are both indubitable and substantial, but nobody has succeeded. All the claimed successes have turned out to be conjuring tricks. This encourages us to think that nobody ever will succeed.

Is there an alternative structure? Both Quine and Popper have suggested that there is.[6] My own design would be something like this: we could have in it trains of inference of the linear sort, but no attempt would be made to anchor them at either end. That is, the logical links between the elements of the inferences would be firm; but the ends of the trains of inference would be floating. Confining ourselves for now to moral reasoning: at the top end of these trains of inference would be moral principles of some universal sort; and at the bottom end would be singular prescriptions for actions by ourselves and others. In between would be general prescriptions of lesser degrees of generality, and also factual statements about the situations in which they had to be applied.

It is crucially important to distinguish here between the terms 'universal', whose opposite is 'singular'; and 'general', whose opposite is 'specific'.[7] The two propositions 'One ought never to tell lies' and 'One ought never to tell lies to one's children' are both equally universal, but the first is more general, i.e. less specific, than the second.

For now I shall take it that the factual statements that we need really are factual, containing no prescriptive element in their meaning, and that they can be established by the ordinary fact-finding procedures. As we shall see, things are not really so easy; the weakness, if there is a weakness, in our proposed structure is that it relies on a secure way of establishing facts (ordinary facts)—a secure way that general epistemology has so far not supplied. But to supply it is not the business of the moral philosopher; so I shall leave this difficulty until later, and even then not try to overcome it.

Assuming that the facts about situations in which we make moral statements are firm, how does my proposed structure of reasoning look? At the top there are universal moral principles, and these, as I said, are floating, not fixed. So there is, as yet, no problem about how to fix them. At the bottom there are singular prescriptions for action. These too are floating. But, given that the facts are firm, and the logic secure (as it often is not, when in the hands of philosophical conjurers), there is no play or 'give' in between the top and the bottom. There cannot be, because logic keeps the joints tight.

What logic is this? It is the logic of the moral concepts, which I have elaborated elsewhere.[8] Its main features are the prescriptivity and universalizability of moral statements. A statement is prescriptive if and only if, in conjunction if necessary with purely factual statements, it entails at least one imperative committing anyone to whom the prescription is given, and who assents to it, to action. 'Entails' here is used in the following sense: a speech act 'p' entails a speech act 'q' if and only if 'p' is logically inconsistent with the negation of 'q': anyone who affirms 'p' but negates 'q' is contradicting himself. It is important to notice that the notion of inconsistency is not applicable only to speech acts which can be true or false; 'Go' is inconsistent with 'Do not go': someone who said 'Go and do not go' would be contradicting himself.[9]

A statement is universalizable if and only if it commits anyone who assents to it, on pain of inconsistency, to accepting that there is a universal principle which holds, and which applies equally to any situation exactly similar in its universal properties. It is in these senses that moral statements, like other normative statements, are in their central uses prescriptive and universalizable. These formulations are crude, but will suffice for the present argument[10] They have the consequence that one cannot without self-contradiction say that someone ought to do something in a situation, but that a precisely similar person in a precisely similar situation ought not to do it; and that if one assents to a moral statement used prescriptively,[11] one is prescribing actions in accordance with it, and, if one is the person called upon by it to act, will so act. If it is some other person who is called upon to act, one is prescribing that *he* (or she) so act.

These purely logical features of moral statements have the consequence that if we accept a set of universal moral principles, and accept that the facts of a situation are as they are, then we cannot avoid assenting, at the bottom end of the structure, to a set of singular prescriptions for actions. To refuse to assent to these would be to involve ourselves in self-contradiction. We might try to escape these consequences by interpreting our moral statements, some-where in the structure, as not, or not fully, prescriptive; and this is a common manoeuvre.[12] But if we retain the prescriptivity of our moral statements, we are constrained to assent to the prescriptive conclusions if we assent to the premises. If we do not want to assent to the conclusions, we have to alter the premises; and if we do not want to do that, we have to put up with the conclusions.

Let us illustrate this with a simple and familiar example.[13] I have a moral principle that one ought never to lie. I am in a situation in which if I do not lie an innocent person will be killed. If I stick to my principle I shall have to refrain from lying, because the inference is firm from the principle to the singular prescriptive moral statement that I ought not to lie, and if I assent to this, as I must, I shall not lie. There are various complications and subter-fuges which have been suggested to deal with this dilemma, but we can ignore them as not affecting the main argument.

In such a dilemma, if I am to be allowed to tell the lie, I shall have to modify my universal principle, by admitting an exception to it for situations like my present one. The principle will thus become for me less general, though still as universal as it was.[14] This is what a sensible and rational moral thinker who follows the method of reasoning to be explained later will do. It illustrates what I meant by saying that the top end of the structure of moral reasoning is floating.

Suppose, on the other hand, that the effect of not telling the lie would be, not the death of an innocent person, but a financial loss to myself. In that case, if I am a person of principle, I may stick to the universal principle which forbids me to lie, and so tell the truth. This entails the abandonment of a prescription to lie in this situation—a prescription to which I am very much inclined to assent, because I do not want to lose the money. Why would I stick to my principle? It is likely to be because I know that I have to universalize my prescription (or permission) if I say that I ought to lie (or that it is all right to lie); and that if I do this, I shall be prescribing (or permitting) that *other people* lie to me in similar circumstances, which I do not want. So I settle for the universal principle that one ought not to lie (at least in circum-stances just like this), because *on the whole* I prefer this principle to any modification of it to cover these circumstances. This illustrates what I meant when I said that the bottom end of the structure also was floating.

Real-life examples are likely to be a great deal more complex than this crude familiar one. But they will retain the feature that, in order to have a consistent set of moral principles, factual statements and singular prescriptions, we shall have to make adjustments to one end of the structure or the other, or both.

We may compare this procedure with those that we find in Popper's and Quine's accounts of scientific method, although these differ from each other.[15] I do not agree with Quine's attack on the use of the analytic-synthetic distinction.[16] But I can accept his rejection of the attempt to verify observational data piecemeal. He says that science has to confront the world as a whole. This is because no reports of particular observations are independent of theory; they are all, as it is said, theory-laden. My own proposed structure is holistic in the same way. On the scheme I am suggesting, the structure of our moral principles and particular moral judgements has to confront the world in which we live, and our lives in it, as a whole. Because of universalizability, even particular moral judgements involve moral principles; they are principle-laden.

Popper holds that we have to form scientific hypotheses and test them against particular data. In my proposed scheme, we put up candidate moral principles and test them against the prescriptions that we are prepared to accept for particular cases. I drew attention to this analogy between science and morals, and between my theory and Popper's, in *Freedom and Reason* (pp. 87–90); but it needs further explanation.

An apparent difficulty with applying a Popperian scheme to morals is that, whereas in science the particular data of observation are hard facts, in morals what occupy the same place are prescriptions. It might therefore be asked how they could verify or falsify anything. Are they not *ad lib.*? The investigation of this problem takes us to the very root of moral philosophy. But before that, it is worth pointing out that according to Quine (following Duhem) there are no such hard facts, because any statement of fact has to rely on some theoretical assumptions (for example, that our instruments work in accordance with reliable laws). We shall come back, but only briefly, to this deep-seated problem in general epistemology.

Leaving that aside for the moment, let us ask by what morality is constrained, if not, as science is, by the facts of observation. The answer is that it is constrained, as Kant saw, by what we can *will*. Prescriptivity thus turns out to be, not an obstacle to objectivity, but the key to it. But this needs to be understood, and is often misunderstood, because Kant himself is unclear. When he tells us that we are to act only on that maxim through which we can will that it should become a universal law, what does he mean by 'can'?

Commentators have made heavy weather of this question; and they have some excuse, because Kant has more than one explanation of what he means. But, looked at in terms of our proposed structure, the question turns out to be not so difficult to answer. Suppose that, in Kant's own example,[17] I am tempted to make a lying promise (i.e. a promise that I have no intention of fulfilling), in order to secure some financial gain. I can certainly will to do this as a singular prescription. But can I will it as a universal law? If not, what is it that prevents me? It is, that I cannot will that such a lying promise should be made to me in identical circumstances; and if I cannot do that, I cannot universalize my proposed maxim.

Suppose, now, that I am trying to find a set of universal moral principles with which to confront my own and other people's moral lives as a whole. That I cannot will this singular prescription, that someone should make such a lying promise to me, prevents my willing the universal principle that *anyone* should make such a promise when it is to his advantage. I have set out the details of this kind of argument, and answers to some difficulties, elsewhere;[18] here I am only trying to place it within the general structure. There are several awkward characters who are often trotted out as objections to this scheme: the acratic or weak-willed person[19]; the satanist and the nihilist[20]; the fanatic and the amoralist.[21] But the objections can be answered, although there is no space for it here.

Why cannot I will that anyone should make such a lying promise to me? Kant believed the will to be free and autonomous, so it ought to be able to will *anything*. It is at least likely that I *shall* not will my own loss; but *can* I not? I can certainly will a particular loss in return for some greater gain. I can even will a particular loss to myself in return for a greater gain to somebody else, if I am not too selfish. This is where it becomes so important to remember that we are confronting our morality with the moral life as a whole. Can I, at least if rational, accept a complete set of moral principles that would allow me, if I were in the positions of all the other people affected, to suffer more in sum than I should suffer under some other set of principles? Do I not necessarily, if I am rational, and am required, if thinking morally, to universalize my maxims, opt for a set of principles that does the best for me in all these roles taken together? If I necessarily, if rational, opt for such a set, does this not entail that I *cannot* rationally opt for any other?

This may explain how the will can be both free and constrained by reason. The argument is only summarized here.[22] If it is right, then the 'can' in Kant's 'Act only on that maxim through which you can ...' is explained. It means, or *should* mean, 'can if rationally universalizing'. And to universalize one's maxims is a logical requirement for moral thinking.

We can now see the advantage that moral epistemology has over other kinds of epistemology, which are trying to find a way of establishing facts. The will, as Kant saw, is determined by nothing except 'the fitness of its maxims for its own making of universal law'.[23] It does not need to establish hard facts, except in so far as these are needed in order to *apply* universal principles or laws to particular situations. What it does need is to choose moral principles or laws that it can rationally accept; but this it can do. 'The dignity of man consists precisely in his capacity to make universal law, although only on condition of being himself also subject to the law he makes.'[24]

However, because facts (ordinary not moral facts) are needed for the application of moral principles, moral thinking will always be dependent on some way of establishing them. It is thus dependent on a reliable *general* epistemology, which does not yet exist. If it were the case that we had no reliable way of establishing the ordinary facts which are needed in order to apply moral principles to actual situations, moral thinking could indeed say what we ought to do *if* the facts were such and such; but it could not say what we ought to do, period.

I shall not, however, try to deal with this problem, but shall merely take it that, as most people think, we can establish the facts of our situations with enough assurance to base moral judgements upon them, given our moral principles. That is, I shall assume that the problems raised by sceptics in general epistemology have a solution, though we do not know yet what the solution is. At least if scepticism about ordinary non-moral facts can be answered, *moral* scepticism should no longer be a particular worry. The problem of scepticism about ordinary facts is to some extent an academic one (though of fundamental importance), because ordinary people, in contrast to philosophers, are not in general troubled by it.

It is now time to ask whether the kind of structure of moral epistemology that I have been sketching is a kind of foundationalism or a kind of coherentism. It should be apparent by now that this contrast is too simple. The structure certainly looks coherentist. And it is certainly not foundationalist in the Cartesian sense, because it does not rely on indubitable first premisses. Yet those (e.g., Bernard Williams) who do not like the structure sometimes call it foundationalist, as if this were enough to give the dog a bad name.[25] To this it can be replied, as I did in my reply to Williams, that the bad name attaches to Cartesian foundationalism and not to the Kantian kind which I have espoused.[26] Kant, if I understand him rightly, thought that he could provide a groundwork or foundation for the metaphysic of morals by exhibiting its logical structure; and that is what I also have been trying to do.

We do not need to quarrel about the distinction between metaphysics and logic. This is firstly because it is not a viable distinction if 'logic' is taken in any but the narrowest sense; Carnap thought that what was worth while in metaphysics could be reduced to logic, and Bradley thought that logic if pursued in any depth turned into metaphysics.

And secondly, Kant himself says that in the first two chapters of his *Groundwork* he has been 'developing the concept of morality as generally in vogue' that is, it is for him a conceptual or in a broad sense logical enquiry.[27] That is what the metaphysic *of morals* is for him; he implies in the same passage that the problem discussed in his next and last chapter is one 'whose solution lies no longer within the bounds of a metaphysic of morals'. I shall likewise take it that, although there is much more to be done, the logical structure of moral thinking can be elucidated by 'developing the concept of morality as generally in vogue'.

My claim then is that the kind of structure I have been sketching is both coherentist and foundationalist, but foundationalist in a Kantian not a Cartesian sense. That is, it does not rest on an allegedly indubitable first premiss, but rather on an understanding of the logical properties of the moral concepts. *Any* viable account of moral reasoning has to rely on this; the only philosophers who can do without it are those who think that moral reasoning either is unnecessary, or does not need a logic to govern it.

It may be opportune to add to this essay a coda to explain the relation between the Kantian foundationalism that I have said is consistent with coherentism, and the utilitarianism that I have also advocated as the foundation, in a related sense, of morality. The relations in general between Kantianism and utilitarianism are discussed in "Could Kant Have Been a Utilitarian?".[28] I there show that, contrary to what is commonly thought, there is no inconsistency between carefully formulated versions of the two kinds of theory. But confining ourselves for now to the question of foundationalism, we have to answer the objection that any utilitarian has to have an indubitable foundation or supreme principle for his moral system, namely the principle of utility itself, however formulated. A simple formulation would be Mill's, that 'actions are right in proportion as they tend to promote happiness, wrong in proportion as they tend to produce the reverse of happiness.'[29] This is indeed a foundation of morality for Mill, and he tries (unsuccessfully in the eyes of most commentators) to show that it is indubitable.

It is important to understand that no such 'principle of utility' is needed in a utilitarian theory, and that there is none in my own. A principle of utility purports to be a substantial, normative, prescriptive moral principle which is somehow known to hold, and which is the supreme principle or ground of morality, so that all moral questions can be decided by appeal to it. If one accepts such a principle as the ground of all subordinate principles, but itself not requiring any ground, one is clearly in danger of becoming a Cartesian foundationalist. This danger has to be avoided by anyone who also wants to be, like Kant, a coherentist, as I do.

I avoid it by not having a principle of utility. In its place I have a *method* of moral reasoning, determined by the logic of the moral concepts. This method leads, indeed, to the same moral conclusions as a traditional utilitarian would seek to reach by the application of his principle of utility. But the conclusions are reached, not by linear inference from a first principle, but by the kind of coherentist reasoning outlined above. We have to find a coherent set of moral principles and other judgements which we can accept in the light of the known facts. It has been my contention that rational thinkers will agree on a unique set. The 'principle of utility' is therefore superfluous.

To understand this, it is necessary to realize that moral thinking takes place on at least two levels, the intuitive and the critical.[30] The intuitive level is that at which we operate most of the time in our day-to-day life, when we are not faced with conflicting duties. At this level we can follow our intuitions.

Intuitionists think that we need never do more than this; but the frequent occurrence of moral conflicts shows how superficial such a view is. In cases of conflict, we have to scrutinize our intuitions by critical thinking, in order to satisfy ourselves as to what are the right intuitions to have, and thus settle the moral conflict.

There will indeed be, in a two-level utilitarian system such as I have advocated, something that looks at first sight like a principle of utility. This will be one of the many principles acknowledged at the intuitive level of morality, namely that which prescribes what W. D. Ross called the duty of beneficence, coupled perhaps with what he called a duty of non-maleficence.[31] These are for Ross prima facie intuitive principles; and most moralists will want to include them in their systems. They are not foundations, in the sense of indubitable first principles, of morality, and have no place in pure critical thinking (the higher level of moral thinking). This higher level will determine that they are principles we should cultivate for use at the intuitive level, because their general acceptance in our society is conducive to states of affairs that we can universally and rationally prescribe. These are, indeed, the same states of affairs as a principle of utility would bid us bring about, because they are such as we can will for ourselves, were we in the situations of all those affected, and thus can will universally. But it will determine this, not by appeal to a principle of utility, but by the method of moral reasoning described above, using the logical properties of universalizability and prescriptivity. These intuitive prima facie principles are defeasible, and can be overridden by other principles (of justice, for example) in cases of conflict. So there is no foundationalism here.

In passing I must mention that the existence in a moral system of the principles of beneficence and non-maleficence will have an important consequence, that where one of the other principles (justice is again an example) cannot be followed without infringing beneficence, there will always be a moral conflict between prima facie principles (in this case justice and beneficence). For example, it may be impossible to do the best for all concerned, treated impartially, without infringing distributive justice. To settle such a conflict it may be necessary to do some critical thinking, in which the principles of justice and beneficence cannot themselves be appealed to. This shows that they are not foundational principles.

The upshot is that a utilitarian system does need principles of beneficence and non-maleficence at the intuitive level, but does not need a principle of utility as a foundation. It needs a logic of moral reasoning, established not by moral intuitions, but by the methods of philosophical logic, which appeal to our understanding of the moral words.

Notes

1. Already noticed in R. M. Hare, *The Language of Morals* (Oxford: Oxford University Press, 1952), 38–44.

2. See Hare, *Freedom and Reason* (Oxford: Oxford University Press, 1963), 87–90.

3. Hare, *Moral Thinking* (Oxford: Oxford University Press, 1981).

4. Mark Timmons, "Foundationalism and the Structure of Ethical Justification," *Ethics* 97 (1987), 595–609.

5. B. Bosanquet, *Implication and Linear Inference* (London: Macmillan, 1920). See also R. M. Hare, *Freedom and Reason,* pp. 87–90.

6. W. V. O. Quine, "Two Dogmas of Empiricism," *Philosophical Review* 60 (1951). Cited from his *From a Logical Point of View* (Cambridge: Harvard University Press, 1953) pp. 20–46. See for example, Sir Karl Popper, "Philosophy of Science: A Personal Report," in C. A. Mace, ed., *British Philosophy in Mid-Century* (London: Allen and Unwin, 1957).

7. Hare, "Principles," *Proceedings of the Aristotelean Society* 73 (1972). Reprinted in R. M. Hare, *Essays in Ethical Theory* (Oxford: Oxford University Press, 1989).

8. See Hare, *Freedom and Reason,* and *Moral Thinking.*

9. On this see Hare, *The Language of Morals,* pp. 24–27.

10. I have explained the notions more fully in *Moral Thinking,* p. 21, and refs.

11. There are also other uses; see ibid., p. 22.

12. See Hare, *Freedom and Reason,* p. 99.

13. Immanuel Kant, "On a Supposed Right to Lie from Benevolent Motives" (1797), A301 = VIII 426. Translated in T. K. Abbott, *Kant's Critique of Practical Reason and Other Works on the Theory of Ethics* (London: Longmans, 1923).

14. See Hare, "Principles."

15. Popper, "Philosophy of Science"; and Quine, "Two Dogmas of Empiricism," p. 42.

16. See Hare, "Why Moral Language?" in P. Pettit et al., eds., *Metaphysics and Morality* (Oxford: Oxford University Press, 1987). Cited from Hare, *Essays on Religion and Education* (Oxford: Oxford University Press, 1992), p. 203. Also see Allan Sidelle, *Necessity, Essence, and Individuation* (Ithaca: Cornell University Press, 1985), chap. 5.

17. Kant, *Groundwork for the Metaphysics of Morals,* BA67–68 = 429–30.

18. Hare, *Moral Thinking,* chapters 6–7.

19. Hare, "Weakness of Will," in L. Becker, ed., *Encyclopedia of Ethics* (New York: Garland, 1992).

20. See "Satanism and Nihilism" in Hare, *Essays on Religion and Education,* pp. 98–112.

21. Hare, *Moral Thinking,* chapters 10–11.

22. Ibid., chapter 6.

23. Kant, *Groundwork,* BA88 = 441.

24. Ibid., BA87 = 440.

25. For example, Bernard Williams, "The Structure of Hare's Theory," in D. Seanor and N. Fotion, eds., *Hare and Critics* (Oxford: Oxford University Press, 1988), 194.

26. Ibid., pp. 291–2.

27. Kant, *Groundwork,* BA95 = 445; see also BA87 = 440.

28. Hare, "Could Kant Have Been a Utilitarian?" *Utilitas* 5 (1993), 1–16. Also in J. Dancy, ed., *Kant and Critique* (Dordrecht: Kluwer, 1993).

29. John Stuart Mill, *Utilitarianism* (1861), chapter 2.

30. Hare, *Moral Thinking,* chapters 2–3.

31. W. D. Ross, *The Right and the Good* (Oxford: Oxford University Press, 1930), 26.

7

Science as a Basis for Moral Theory

Richard B. Brandt

A problem that has vexed philosophers from the very beginning is how to determine the truth or justification of normative beliefs, especially whether a certain kind of action is *morally wrong* or *morally permissible.*

One possible solution to the problem is to the effect that statements containing such normative words can, in view of their *meanings,* be logically deduced from statements that manifestly can be appraised by the methods of empirical science. For example, "is morally right" has been construed to mean "will contribute maximally to the happiness of sentient creatures."[1] Again, "is morally wrong" has been construed to mean the same as "would be disapproved of by any person who was factually omniscient, impartial, devoid of emotions toward particular persons, but otherwise a normal person."[2] If ethical terms meant what these writers suggest, then ethical statements could be confirmed by the methods of empirical science. We can call these theories that ethical statements can be properly construed as identical in meaning with some statement that manifestly can be appraised by science, forms of "old line naturalism."

Since the work of the philosopher G. E. Moore in 1903, such old-line naturalism has largely disappeared. Moore pointed out that the proposed "naturalistic" definitions (at least mostly) do not mean the same as the original ethical statements. For example, we can believe that a certain action will maximize human benefit, but wonder, contrary to Bentham, whether it is right, perhaps on the ground that it would produce unjust inequalities in the well-being of persons. Or, "good for a person" can be construed as meaning "is wanted by the person," but it is clear that many things a person can want may not be good for him or her. And the same for at least almost *all* such definitions that have been proposed: the ethical terms mean one thing and the definitions another, as we can see from the fact that one can, in virtually all cases, *doubt* whether the ethical predicate applies whenever the definition applies and hence the normative term just does not *mean the same* as the proposed definition. (This objection does not apply to proposals including a normative term in the definition: such as that some action is "wrong" means it is "*fittingly* disapproved of," as A. C. Ewing suggested.) Consequently, the truth of an ethical statement can hardly be determined by appraising the truth of some synonymous statement that can be tested by the methods of empirical science.

So how are we supposed to decide whether any ethical statement is true? One answer to this question is that we can know such things just by thinking about them. For instance, it has been pointed out that we can know some synthetic statements to be true just by taking thought. Thus we can know, just by thinking, that anything that is a cube has twelve edges or that, if anything is red in color, it will resemble in color anything orange more closely than anything that is yellow.[3] So a person might ask: If we can know these things just by thinking about them, may we not equally know the truth of ethical judgments just by thinking about them? Some philosophers think we can.[4]

But there has developed wide skepticism about whether the power of reason, or "intuition" as it is sometimes called, can provide any such knowledge. One might ask what is the difference between ethical statements, about which there is this doubt, and the statements listed the truth of which we can ascertain just by thinking. This could be hard to say, although a careful phenomenology of ethical judgments (see below) might provide a clue. But there is one clear difference: There is no disagreement among educated people about the statements listed as ones we can appraise just by taking thought. But educated people do differ sharply about moral statements. For instance, some people think that if you have made a promise there is some obligation to keep it—"A promise is a promise"—whereas others have thought that there is an obligation to keep a promise only if breach of it would be harmful to the promisee in some way. Moreover, there are wide divergences of opinion about the morality of abortion, capital punishment, and many other things. And these disagreements do not arise just from divergences about relevant facts. Furthermore, not only are there these disagreements: there are disagreements that occur among educated philosophers, indeed specialists in moral philosophy. Given that this is the case, can we seriously say that we can know the truth of an ethical statement just by taking thought? It looks as if reliance on reason, or taking thought, is not a satisfactory avenue to truth of ethical statements.

Is there some more convincing way to show how to know the truth of normative statements, or at least their "justification," if we mean by "justification," as I think we should, some showing, free from factual error and conceptual confusion, that will *recommend* a relevant moral stance to every person—convince him of it—given he is thoughtful and factually informed?[5] I shall try to provide a justification along this line.

One thing we must do, to bring about such a justification, is first of all to get a clear conception of the state of mind of a person who accepts some type of normative statement, and then to show that such a state of mind must (or, alternatively, could not) exist in a person who is fully apprised of facts which can be known by empirical science. I will try to provide a satisfactory proposal for execution of these tasks, for the case of morality, in what follows.

Beliefs About What Is Morally Right or Wrong

We often hear it said that "morality requires. . . ." I take it that what this means is that "sound or defensible moral beliefs require that. . . ." To appraise such thoughts we need first to define what is a "moral belief."

When we speak of a person's "moral beliefs," presumably we should be referring to whatever state of mind a person is *expressing* when he affirms that some action is "morally wrong," "morally required," "morally good," and so on. The main traditional view about this has been *cognitivist:* that moral statements affirm that some action has the property of being morally right or wrong in some unanalyzable sense, a property it has independently of anyone's thoughts or attitudes about the matter; and that a true moral judgment is one that affirms a proposition corresponding to this real state of affairs.

There is, however, another main, but noncognitivist, explanation of "moral beliefs' a *motivational* one. This view, held roughly by David Hume and John Stuart Mill, and widely held today (e.g., roughly, by R. M. Hare), is that the phrase "*A is morally wrong*" *expresses a syndrome* in the mind of the speaker: roughly that he has a strong aversion to anyone (including her or himself) doing things like *A* in certain circumstances (so an aversion to actions of a *given type*), and if he or she infringes this without an excuse he or she will feel guilt or remorse,[6] and if he or she knows someone else has done so without an excuse he or she will feel indignation (anger), coolness, or something of the sort toward that person.

This formulation may suggest that moral statements are primarily a device for condemning persons who harm others (the talk of indignation). But "morally wrong" can also express quite different disapproving attitudes, for example, if one says that incest is "revolting" (H. Rashdall) or that masturbation is "degrading" (Kant). In these cases it is not clear that any *indignation* (anger) toward offenders is expressed, although doubtless some kind of disapproval is. "Conscience" is most notorious for its "pricks": discomfort when an agent does something contrary to his moral standards. But a speaker's moral code of conscience can also be expressed in such judgments as that some action "*is morally good*" (such as in statements recognizing "acts of supererogation," acts producing good for others at cost to the agent and when not required to avoid condemnation as being morally wrong), which express admiration or gratitude for the agent. (In this case, the appraised agent may properly feel pride or self-satisfaction.) Thus we should not limit morality to judgments of some kind of condemnation, but recognize the opposite—judgments in praise; nor should we limit conscience to guilt feelings, but allow it feelings of pride and satisfaction. We must avoid taking "conscience" or "moral code" in an unduly narrow sense.

This conception of morality and conscience is not just a very recent one. In fact, there are very early documentary indications of these in what seems likely to be this very sense: inscriptions over the dead Pharaohs and the Hebrew Ten Commandments (Exodus 20:3–17), which are all rather humanitarian documents, all proscribing violence (except in war); usury; deception especially in court proceedings; theft; dishonest measures; adultery; and calling for kindness to children and the poor, and respect for father and mother. Much the same might be said for the writings of the Greek Hesiod (eighth century B.C.) In contrast, the Homeric corpus *possibly* permits a so-called morality in which shame takes the place of guilt/remorse, and concern for reputation the place of "moral motivation." This, however, is controversial. There is contrary evidence: the adultery of Paris and Helen was condemned even by Hector; Hector was rebuked for not revering the corpse of Sarpedon; Achilles was condemned for treating Hector's body as he did; Eumaeus the peasant was praised as "noble" for preventing his dog from attacking the disguised Ulysses; and there was general disapproval of "hubris" (overweening pride). So even Homeric Greek morality did not praise only the competitive virtues—martial ability and valor—but also had a humanitarian side, so seeming more like the other moralities just mentioned.[7]

The Appraisal of Moralities

Is there anything that can be said in appraisal of these moralities? Some writers seem very doubtful that much can be done. In a monumental work. Edward Westermarck detailed an enormous number of differences among the moralities of different societies: permitting or requiring or condemning killing (of parents, children, the sick, women, fetuses, and slaves), blood revenge, dueling, charity, hospitality, subjection of wives, slavery, property, regard for good faith, suicide, marriage, adultery, regard for animals, and cannibalism.[8] He thought many variations were a result of differences of external conditions: hardship, economic circumstances, numerical proportion of men to women. His summary leaves the impression of a lot of moral views, different from each other, but none distinctively defensible. He hardly touches, moreover, on an important question: How far can all these variations be traced to differences in the *conception* of the act in question?

This question was addressed some years ago by two psychologists, Karl Duncker[9] and Solomon Asch,[10] who contended that such variations are only apparent: that when we hold fixed the 'meaning' of an action for a person, the moral appraisals are uniformly roughly the same. (This was in line with a Gestalt tradition in psychology.) For instance, Duncker affirmed that whereas charging interest was prohibited in the Middle Ages but is taken for granted today, in the Middle Ages loans were used mostly for personal consumption, and today they are used mostly for investment. (One might wonder about credit card purchases!) The question is important because, if the thesis is correct, all *moral disputes* can be resolved by science and conceptual clarity, by *ascertaining what is the correct description* of some projected action. If that were granted, it would be one step toward showing some sort of objectivity in moral beliefs.

The Duncker-Asch view is defended by some contemporary philosophers. For example, David Wiggins says we can expect convergence in most moral judgements by "people of a certain culture who have what it takes to understand a certain sort of judgment." Then he says, "What really matters . . . is only that the judgment should represent an answer to a question asked with respect to a given place and time, that the question should have a sense fixed by reference to the historical context and circumstances of that place and time, and that the answer should be better than all competing answers to that question, *so understood.*" So Wiggins seems to think that there need not be disagreement among persons who intimately understand a situation being judged.[11] As for objections from the psychological theory of the learning of moral attitudes, he says these overlook the fact that moral tutoring is itself "a response to something that is simply there (there to be found by anyone, or by anyone who is sufficiently attuned to what bears upon the matter)," and goes on to doubt "whether one can imagine a psychological theorist's dispensing entirely with value properties not just in the case of non-standard reactions but in every case."[12]

It is not easy to ascertain whether these theses affirming uniformity of moral appraisals are true. But they are difficult to believe. Consider the treatment of animals. In some parts of South America, according to a verbal report from the anthropologist Ralph Linton, a chicken is (was) plucked before it is killed, on the theory that makes for a more succulent dish. Hopi children are (were) notorious for their (permitted by parents) maltreatment of small animals. We need not go so far afield: hunters, trappers, and fishermen among ourselves are not known to take care to avoid inflicting pain on the animals they kill. Most of us will disapprove of all these things. Moreover, the theses are difficult to reconcile with what we know about changes in social moralities, say, when two cultures are in contact. The effect of this may arise not from the dominant culture providing a new picture of the behavior being appraised morally, but simply because it is thought to represent a more civilized way of thinking. The same occurs if some prestigious figure such as a chief is baptized and accepts Christian values. H. G. Barnett showed that this process is accelerated if some individuals in the recipient group are frustrated and motivated to identify with the dominant group.[13] E. Z. Vogt made a study of the values of Navaho veterans. He found the tendency to be receptive to white values was influenced by extensive connections with older and more conservative relatives, especially the father, the extent of contact with the white world and its friendliness toward Indians, and the utility of traditional beliefs in resolving psychological problems, for example, the belief in witchcraft.[14] All these changes seem to be independent of changes in the conception of the acts being appraised.

Other changes are the result of internal dynamics, which may operate in this same way. For instance, the introduction of the contraceptive pill, which (doubtless partly because of a change in the expectation of pregnancy) fostered an increase of sexual activity, hence conflict with accepted norms, and eventually a large change in the accepted norms themselves.

Is all this consistent with the Duncker-Asch defense of the objectivity of moral judgments on the ground that moral appraisals are in fact always the same when the judges have identical conceptions of the action being appraised? No—not only are there often conflicting appraisals of actions apparently understood in the same way, but there have been changes in widely accepted moral norms, apparently without any (or at least much) change in the *conception* of the behavior.

A Defense by Appeal to Science

Various contemporary philosophers, who do not defend the Asch-Duncker line of *uniformity* of moral appraisals, take the line of claiming that moral judgments can be supported by a kind of essentially scientific reasoning—like the justification of belief in electrons for the reason that the electron theory provides an *explanation* of the data of observation. So essentially they say that if one accepts the soundness of scientific reasoning, one must also accept properly supported moral principles. Nicholas Sturgeon, for example, thinks that the *wrongness* of children pouring gasoline on a cat and setting it afire is established essentially in the same way as we establish the existence of electrons. Because, he thinks, the assumption of wrongness is essential to the *causal explanation* of observers of such an act taking it to be wrong, despite the fact that there is an alternative explanation—that the response of the observers was a result of their observation plus their moral attitudes, either native or imbued by parents. (The latter explanation manifestly fits psychological knowledge better.) Sturgeon, however, is not satisfied with this. He says that "if a particular assumption [here of the wrongness of the act] is completely irrelevant to the explanation of a certain fact [the belief that it is wrong], then the fact [belief of wrongness] would have obtained, and we could have explained it as well, even if the assumption had been false."[15] Thus, if children are burning a cat and if the (assumed) wrongness of this is causally irrelevant to observers' belief that what the children are doing is wrong, then the fact that the children are burning the cat, plus the empathy and/or moral attitudes of the observers, cannot explain the beliefs; for that, we have to take into account the act's actual wrongness. To this we should retort: Why so? We know enough about the psychology of moral disapproval to see that observation of the treatment of the cat is sufficient to produce the disapproval in normal observers. Thus it appears that Sturgeon's argument is ineffective.

Some other contemporary writers take a quite different line, holding that there is an *evidential* basis for moral judgments comparable to observation in science: in the former, our "spontaneous beliefs" (=moral intuitions) just as in science there is a basis in sensory stimulation.[16] But one must wonder whether the set of "spontaneous moral beliefs" has a status in relation to the allegedly supported moral beliefs such that the parallel with observations in science can go through, so that these spontaneous moral beliefs support a general moral theory in the way observations in science support explanatory theories. It is true that if we observe a bank official making a denigrating remark to a female underling, or observe boys maltreating a cat, there is (seems to be) a rush of angry feeling, culminating in an unfavorable moral judgment. That is a fact, so there *is* a "spontaneous belief." Moreover, there may be a multitude of such facts, maybe one for every case of our disapproving strongly of some action. So there might be feelings of *disapproval* toward any couple having sex outside of marriage, although perhaps not a rush of *angry feeling* since no one has been harmed. But exactly how the evidence of these "spontaneous beliefs" is to support general moral beliefs is by no means clear.

The most widely held view about how we may proceed from such experiences to a defensible systematic set of moral principles is that we proceed by appeal to "reflective equilibrium." We start with these experiences, say of angry condemnation, and express the reactions in the language of moral *principles* ("it is prima facie wrong to . . ."). We then collect these various principles along with the principles we *might* (probably) express as a reaction to the posing of hypothetical cases. We then attempt to formulate a *system* of principles, *as far as possible* including the whole set of initial principles, but developed into a coherent set that may exclude some of these. This set of principles might turn out to be somewhat abstract: it might become some form of utilitarian morality, or (possibly as a form of this) it might eventuate in a loose set of independent principles like the "prima facie obligations" advocated by W. D. Ross. It is thought that a set of moral principles arrived at in this way is thereby justified. This way of supporting, or underwriting, moral principles has been convincing to many philosophers.

But it would be a mistake for anyone to think that this procedure for deriving moral principles from basic moral experiences resembles how science supports general scientific principles by appeal to observations. What the scientist does is take his whole set of observations and formulate a set of general principles such that the principles—taken with some other experimentally supported principles—imply that these very observations would be made under the circumstances. In other words, the scientist looks for an *explanatory* theory that implies that the observations would be made under the circumstances. Now it is true that there *can* be an explanatory theory of the basic moral experiences—a psychological theory of learning, motivation, and so on, which implies that the basic moral experiences would occur in the actual circumstances. It is also true that psychologists do in fact have the makings of an explanatory theory that covers the basic moral experiences. But such a theory would not identify some of these experiences as "correct" or *underwrite* any general moral principles in the way the method of reflective equilibrium is supposed to.

I suggest then that, whatever we may think of the method of "reflective equilibrium" as a way of arriving at sound moral principles on the basis of "spontaneous moral beliefs," we ignore the proposals of writers who think that this way of supporting statements that something is "morally wrong" is essentially *identical* with what goes on in natural science in the formulation of explanatory theories. The method of "reflective equilibrium" is not the same as the kind of reasoning we find in the natural sciences.

A Possible Alternative Defense

Is there then no alternative, seriously scientific support we can give for normative generalizations? Let us agree with child psychologists that a child's "morality" mostly comes, although doubtless *partly* from native empathy/sympathy, from scolding or punishment by parents, the resulting negative feelings becoming associated with acts of a certain sort, especially in the presence of explanations of why such an action should not be done.[17] But this kind of conditioning of a child's morality is often regarded as less important than the tendency to imitate, especially parental behavior. This may be imitation of specific actions, like picking up a phone and dialing, but also of more general traits: motives, attitudes, and values. All this, of course, may be gratifying to the parents, who reward the child for it. This process is emphasized by "social learning theory," which stresses the importance of "models" of all kinds, including the mass media and television.[18] There have been various suggestions for why a child should be motivated to imitate an admired figure: that he wants competence and thinks he can gain it in this way; or he feels anxious in the absence of a parent and can make himself feel better by becoming a kind of parent-substitute.

But *changes* in a person's moral commitments, which manifestly do occur, can hardly come from imitation of or tuition by *parents,* the older generation. So we must allow that the adolescent's standards at a given time are doubtless an amalgam with diverse sources: the educational system, Supreme Court decisions, and so on. A famous study of Bennington College students some years ago showed that students rapidly changed their attitudes toward liberalism, from the negative attitudes they had formed at home to more favorable views which they attributed both to the faculty and other students at the school. It was found that receptivity to change depended on the student's success in college, the absence of strong family ties, motivation to achieve position in the college community, and intellectual energy—incidentally not what they had learned in classes.[19] A retest twenty-five years later showed these new attitudes still to be firm. So changes in a person's moral commitments can be produced in a variety of ways.

So far, then, the psychology of moral development, both individual and social, seems to leave room for variety, and certainly does not point to some one type of morality as the kind thoughtful and factually informed persons would necessarily have.

But is there no other line of reflection that might be more helpful in evaluating a person's morality? I think there is. But what is it?

One possibility is to show persons that if they were factually fully informed they would *want* a certain sort of moral system *for the whole society* in which they expect to live. (This "system" would include variations for specific groups like physicians and lawyers, appropriate for their various interactions with others.) If persons all *want* a certain sort of system, in this sense, for their society, they will presumably be *somewhat* favorably disposed to embody it in themselves and to recommend it to others, although I make no attempt to outline the psychology leading from the former to the latter. (Of course, a person might want a certain type of system for society generally, but want exceptions for himself.)

But how can we show a person that, if he were fully informed, he would want and support a certain form of morality for his society? Well, we can draw a loan on the general psychological theory of motivation: that a person will *do* something, here support a certain system of morality, only if he thinks so doing will likely produce *a state of affairs* he *wants*. Thus he will support a certain social *moral code* only if he can see how its existence will likely produce a state of affairs he wants. So we must consider to what desires of his we can appeal in order to render the likely effects of a certain social moral code attractive to him. Can we find such desires?

One desire that is especially important for recommending a social moral system is that of *empathic/sympathetic altruism*. This emphasis goes back to David Hume and Francis Hutcheson. But the conception has been developed by the psychologist Martin Hoffman in a series of articles, primarily on the basis of observation of young children.[20] He uses *empathy* to refer to an affective reaction, particularly distress, *appropriate* to the situation of another, not just mimicking the emotion the target expresses, facially or otherwise. This empathic distress will support helpful or protective behavior on the part of the child, and may explain the disapproval we feel of the bank official's demeaning criticism of an underling, even if we have never been *taught* that such behavior is morally out of bounds and the disapproval is no residue of parental scolding/punishment.

Why there should be a disposition to experience empathic altruism is a question. Probably the theory of evolution is the best explanation, because it can explain why a gene-stream with this phenotypical expression would be selected, since in early society such a widespread disposition would contribute to the survival of the society. But there is another possibility.[21] This is that small babies cry when in pain, and then by conditioning the sound of a cry (by any other child) comes to be itself aversive. (Note how adults feel sad when they see someone cry.) By more conditioning, a representation of the unhappy internal states of another may also become aversive. Whichever the right explanation turns out to be, young children do regularly show sympathetic responses to the ills of others. If this is the fact, then there is a basis for thinking that a person's preference for a social moral system would be affected by this basic (probably native) aversion to others being in distress.

According to Martin Hoffman, the most successful form of moral teaching is by "induction": a parent showing a child that a specific kind of behavior is likely to be helpful/harmful to others, for example, telling lies, breaking promises, discriminating on the basis of race or sex. So the motivations of a child's morality could well be requirements on behavior that result from connecting his empathic/sympathetic altruism to various types of action.

Of course, empathy/sympathy hardly explains the objection to incest, the prohibition of extramarital sex, and the condemnation of suicide, attitudes that are seemingly rather widespread. What it does explain is moral objection to acts, social rules, and so on, that clearly have an unfavorable impact on individuals' well-being.

Aside from appeals to empathy/sympathy, how else can we recommend a social moral system to a person? One further thing we can do is rely on a parallel with criminal and tort laws. A thoughtful person will presumably want these laws, in some form or another, because of the protections they give: against forms of injury, taking of property, attacks on status, frustration of major sources of happiness, and so on. People do not want to be assaulted, raped, kidnapped, killed, have major ambitions frustrated, or undergo even threats of these. The law protects against some of these things—and a certain kind of morality can do the same, only *more broadly.* So, if people understand this, we can count on their wanting a social *moral* system that provides these protections: against being harmed, in person, property, or status, or having major ambitions frustrated or even threatened, indeed any kind of personal impact they do not like.

But the social moral system people will want, out of self-interest, may not reach as far as we would like. Which specific deficits might a critic point out as areas a morality backed by interest in self-protection will not reach? Well, it may not inspire desire for a social morality protecting animals. Protection of human beings does not cover protection of all animals. There may also be a problem about racism, since if one belongs to a favored race he has no motivation for protection against the disadvantages of belonging to a disfavored race. However these things may be, it is true that a moral code one might not want out of self-interest one might well want in view of one's sympathetic altruism. And, if Hoffman is right that this trait is nearly universal, we can count on being able to recommend a humanitarian (and nonspeciesist) morality to nearly everyone. But how strong this recommendation might be is not so clear: How strong is the motive of empathic altruism in most people? Is it strong enough to compete successfully with the agent's selfish motivations, say to make money or get prestige?

What set of moral principles can be recommended in one of these ways? If we take the appeal to empathic altruism as having serious weight, then possibly some principles we might classify as a form of utilitarian morality, if we define a utilitarian morality as one the main features of which are designed to enhance the average[22] good, or well-being, of sentient creatures generally. But what more specific kind of morality would this be? In the first place it must contain a number of specific requirements or prohibitions, in the form of motivations, dispositions to feel remorse, and so on, rather like W. D. Ross's list of prima facie duties, but much more numerous, rather like commonsense morality—and these all chosen and supported by showing that people being motivated in these ways would have the effect of enhancing the well-being of sentient creatures. The code cannot consist of only a rule so unspecific as just, always, to do what will likely be most socially beneficial; such a vague commandment would not provide other people with specific expectations about what moral people will do, thereby making rational planning rather difficult. Rather, an acceptable form of morality will contain more specific rules, such as prohibition of dishonest dealing, and a requirement to keep promises. Ideally the prohibitions in such a moral code will be of sufficient *strength* to overcome normal temptations to act otherwise—else what would be the point? It is true that some prohibitions (like "Don't lie," "Don't injure anyone") may also give *conflicting* directives, and when they do, we may ask what, if we adopt this general program, moral persons are to do. Doubtless ideally the rules should be taught by tutors (=parents?) with a specific degree of weight, so that in conflict it would be clear which is the strongest. But so much fine-tuning is probably too much to expect in such a motivational moral code. When there is such conflict, it seems that moral reflection must go rather like the law, which refers such decisions to judgments of appellate courts, these then deciding which interpretation would be the most socially beneficial precedent, and one that leaves the law an organic whole. So, the answer to our question what to do is that the *individual agent* must *think:* decide which obligation is stronger on the same basis as that I suggested be used to recommend a moral system as a whole—long-range social benefit, all costs and benefits taken into account, in view of desire for protection and empathy/ sympathy.

This necessity may be worrisome, since it opens the door to defective predictability regarding what people will do. But we need not worry too much: as Berkeley pointed out long ago, in his ground-breaking defense of a kind of "rule-utilitarianism," there are some practical (moral) propositions that do "to right reason evidently appear to have a necessary connexion with the Universal well-being included in" them and are "to be looked upon as enjoined by the will of God." These "are well known to mankind, and suggested and inculcated by conscience."[23] His view was that, at least in the case of the major prohibitions to be taught, it can be *manifest* that their teaching and prevalence will be roughly beneficial to society, at least as compared with no such teaching. Thus we may hold that divergences will concern mostly allowable exceptions in special circumstances, or the relative weight of principles where there is conflict, that must be matters of agent-judgment and of some uncertainty. Fortunately, the moral rules that will optimally govern the main business of society will, we may think along with Berkeley, not be controversial, so that normally one person can reliably predict what another will do in a certain situation, provided this other person is a "moral" person. The main rules of morality—not those requiring agent-judgment—can be publicly known. So a main pragmatic criticism (that it makes prediction of behavior difficult) raised against the simple act-utilitarian theory is to a degree applicable to the present theory, but only to a minor extent. I see no reason why this amount of possible disagreement should be a pragmatic obstacle to the acceptance of the general proposal.

We should notice that this kind of moral code will surely contain general prohibitions of injury to others and an injunction to give aid to those in distress. Moreover, such a system will surely permit or even enjoin behavior otherwise prohibited by its basic, *normally* optimal, rules, when omission of such behavior would be disastrously harmful or would prevent important goods.[24] Such flexibility, from permission to break from the normally optimific rules in special circumstances, is important for societies in which there is only partial compliance (and partial compliance is surely very frequent), especially when the noncompliance is a result of disagreement about moral principles, for instance in a society that practices racial discrimination. Here persons not following the local code but rather the *normally optimal* code might cause a great deal of harm. In this type of case it might be better for the basic rules to be amended, by adopting a compromise *disjunctive* item in the code that it would be beneficial for everyone to have, like the one we reach for in cases where keeping a promise would be very harmful. The rule might be: "Do not try to kill anyone, unless you are a soldier engaged in combat, in which case you may defend yourself." Here the harm of following the standard rule is avoided, since the amended rule permits not following the normally optimific rule in a very special kind of case; and the effect will be that the rule as a whole will maximize benefit either where there is full compliance or, as a result of the requirement about what one may do if one does not follow the normally optimific rule, where compliance is only partial. So an optimal morality may contain disjunctive clauses. My suggestion is that all cases apparently beset by difficulty because of partial compliance can be satisfactorily handled in this way. It is true that such disjunctive rules may get internalized only in mature persons.

This conception of an optimal morality can be applied in two contexts: first, as fixing what is the right thing to do if the present "institutions" of society are accepted just as social facts, not subject to moral criticism; and second, as reforming criticism of the system of existing institutions. Thus a philosopher, in his role as reforming critic of institutions, will presumably wish to comment about the implications of the various principles he is teaching for the institutions of his society, in the light of the effects there are likely to be if the institutions are modified in one way or another, to conform to his possible moral principles: say, rules about how corporations should be run in a capitalist society, tax laws, how public officers are selected and the powers they should have, whether marriage with all its rights and duties should be made available to couples of the same sex, and so on. When no change in institutions seems called for by justifiable moral principles, the existing institutions will serve as a background for identifying the specific optimal moral code.

The foregoing depiction of a possible "optimal" moral code will be criticized by various contemporary philosophers on the ground that it pays too little attention to the "separateness" of persons. It seems to suppose that a moral code should be approved in view of supporting a gain in the average general well-being, even if the "gain" consists in small increments to the well-being of many persons, paid for by very large losses to a few. So it is questioned whether a moral system should require one person to make a sacrifice for the benefit of someone else, when the sacrificer is in no way compensated for what he loses. (This is different from intrapersonal exchanges, such as sacrificing a good at one time for the sake of a greater total good later, which is acceptable because it is one and the same person who gains and loses, but at different times.) A rather contrary view is supported by other philosophers (who also are opposed to a utilitarian theory): they think that it is *justified* to impose a greater burden on the superrich to prevent harm to the destitute. They may say in defense of this that persons at the bottom end are already much worse off than others, so that an additional good is more *important* to them.

Roughly this last view is defended, in a systematic way, by T. M. Scanlon, in a view he calls "contractualist." He says that an act is "wrong if its performance under the circumstances would be disallowed by any system of rules for the general regulation of behavior which *no one* could *reasonably* reject as a basis for informed, unforced general agreement."[25] This means that a moral system is to be rejected if just one person can reasonably reject it, and "reasonable" rejection by a person can occur if the moral system makes him worse off than others and indeed quite badly off, provided there is no other system that would make him better off without making others equally badly or even worse off. Thus he rejects the utilitarian view which is said to balance the *considerable* suffering of some by the relatively small suffering of a great many. This objection has some intuitive appeal. But it is itself subject to two serious intuitive objections: First, that what can be done to *relieve the worst off* might achieve *less benefit* (at the same cost) than what can be done to help the *slightly less badly off.* Are we bound to confer a trivial benefit on the person worst off, in contrast to a big benefit for someone slightly better off? Second, suppose there are many persons with a slightly lesser complaint, and they would be substantially helped by a program that would not help the worst off. Is it obvious that we should pass them by in order to help the worst off? It is true that a great many trivial benefits seem not as morally demanding as one very serious hardship, but in the absence of a program for comparing help to the nearly as badly off, Scanlon's simple plan is not very convincing.[26]

In any case, it is not clear that the kind of "utilitarian morality" I have outlined would have the suggested implications about distributions of the good, for it surely may be held that the long-term public well-being is more assured by people's consciences being especially sensitive to serious suffering. So why should the theory imply that many trivial gains can outweigh serious losses to a few? Whether they should is a serious problem, but the implications of the type of "utilitarian" morality I have outlined (and which Berkeley had in mind) for *distributive justice* must be more complex than Scanlon suggests they would be.

There are various other moral problems about which "contractualism" seems to give no special guidance: for example, where the issue is not a choice between agreeing to a system that would make one very badly off although an alternative system would make others equally badly or even worse off—a rather special situation. The kind of "utilitarian" morality I have outlined offers guidance about many other types of problem situation—say, sexual freedom generally, abortion, retributivism in the criminal law, speaking the truth. It gives us a clue how to decide these and many other issues, but at least some of them seem to be outside the specific scope of Scanlon's contractualist theory—although he, on occasion, has suggested that his theory is close to a form of rule- or motive-utilitarianism.[27]

Notes

1. Jeremy Bentham, *An Introduction to the Principles of Morals and Legislation* (Oxford: Clarendon Press, 1876), 3–4.

2. Roderick Firth, "Ethical absolutism and the ideal observer," *Philosophy and Phenomenological Research* 12 (1952).

3. C. H. Langford, "Moore's notion of analysis," in P. A. Schilpp, ed., *The Philosophy of G. E. Moore* (Evanston, Ill.: Northwestern University, 1942), 319–42.

4. See, for instance, John Finnis, *Natural Law and Natural Rights* (Oxford: Clarendon Press, 1980); and Robert Audi, "Intuitionism, Pluralism, and the Foundations of Ethics," in this volume.

5. For a defense of this view of "justification," see my *A Theory of the Good and the Right* (Oxford: Clarendon Press, 1979), chapter 10.

6. Should we include "shame"? Gabriella Taylor views shame as primarily "a self-directed adverse judgment of the person" in which awareness of the appraisal of an audience plays a causal role. See her *Pride, Shame, and Guilt* (Oxford, Clarendon Press, 1985). I incline to include shame partly because "I felt ashamed of myself" is not very different from "I felt remorse," partly because of doubts about how sharply that is different from guilt/remorse, say in a society like the Japanese, often classified as a "shame-society." Bernard Williams offers an interesting and provocative discussion in *Shame and Necessity* (Berkeley: University of California Press, 1993), chapter 4.

7. See Michael Gagarin, "Morality in Homer," *Classical Philology* 82 (1987), 287–306; and reply by A. W. H. Adkins, "Gagarin and the 'Morality' of Homer," ibid., 311–22. Also A. A. Long, "Morals and Values in Homer," *Journal of Hellenic Studies* 90 (1970), 121–39. See also Bernard Williams, *Shame and Necessity*, chapter 4.

8. Edward Westermarck, *The Origin and Development of the Moral Ideas* (London: Macmillan, 1906).

9. "Ethical relativity?" vol. 48 *Mind* (1939), pp. 39–56.

10. *Social Psychology* (Englewood Cliffs, N.J.: Prentice-Hall, 1952), chapters 11–14.

11. David Wiggins, *Needs, Values, Truth* (Oxford: Basil Blackwell, 1992), 162.

12. Ibid., pp. 159, 162.

13. "Personal Conflicts and Culture Change," *Social Forces* 20 (1941), 160–71. See also A. M. Padilla, *Acculturation: Theories, Models, and Some New Findings* (Boulder, Colo.: Westview Press, 1980).

14. "Navaho Veterans: A Study of Changing Values," *Papers of the Peabody Museum* (Harvard University) 41, no 1 (1951).

15. "Moral explanations," in G. Sayre-McCord, *Essays on Moral Realism* (Ithaca: Cornell University Press, 1988), 241, 245.

16. W. G. Lycan, "Moral Facts and Moral Knowledge," in *Southern Journal of Philosophy* 24, Supplement (1986: Spindel Conference).

17. For a survey of evidence on the effects of reward/punishment, see P. H. Mussen, J. J. Conger, Jerome Kagan, and Aletha Huston, *Child Development and Personality* (New York: Harper & Row, 1984), especially 174–75, 388–91.

18. See Albert Bandura, "Social Cognitive Theory of Moral Thought and Action," in W. M. Kurtines and J. L. Gewirtz, eds., *Moral Behavior and Development* (Hillsdale, N.J.: Lawrence Erlbaum, 1988), volume 1. Also Martin Hoffman, "Moral Development," in M. H. Bornstein and M. E. Lamb, *Developmental Psychology: An Advanced Textbook* (Hillsdale, N.J.: Lawrence Erlbaum, 1984).

19. T. M. Newcomb, *Personality and Social Change* (New York: Dryden Press, 1943); T. M. Newcomb, L. E. Koenig, and C. Morris, *Persistence and Change: Bennington College and Its Students after Twenty-five Years* (New York: Wiley, 1969).

20. See his "Development of Prosocial Motivation: Empathy and Guilt,"in N. Eisenberg, ed., *The Development of Prosocial Behavior* (New York: Academic Press, 1982), 281–313; "Is Altruism Part of Human Nature?" *Journal of Personality and Social Psychology"* 40 (1981), pp. 121–37; "Empathy and Justice in Society," *Social Science Research* 3 (1989), 283–311.

21. See R. B. Brandt, "The Psychology of Benevolence and Its Implications for Philosophy," *Journal of Philosophy* 78 (1976), 429–53.

22. *Average* is inserted to avoid questions as to whether some things should be done to increase the total good by increasing the size of the population.

23. George Berkeley, *Passive Obedience* (1712), reprinted in *Berkeley,* ed. M. W. Calkins (New York: Charles Scribner's Sons, 1929), 436.

24. J. S. Mill wrote, at the end of chapter 5 of *Utilitarianism:* "Particular cases may occur in which some other social duty is so important as to overrule any one of the general maxims of justice. Thus, to save a life it may be not only allowable, but a duty, to steal or take by force the necessary food or medicine, or to kidnap and compel to officiate the only qualified medical practitioner."

25. In "Contractualism and Utilitarianism," in A. K. Sen and B. Williams, eds., *Utilitarianism and Beyond* (Cambridge: Cambridge University Press, 1982), 110.

26. The problem is discussed lucidly and at length by David Brink, "The Separateness of Persons, Distributive Norms, and Moral Theory," in R. G. Grey and C. W. Morris, eds., *Value, Welfare, and Morality* (Cambridge: Cambridge University Press, 1993), chapter 13.

27. See his "Contractualism and Utilitarianism" 110, 120.

8

A Contractarian Account
of Moral Justification

Christopher W. Morris

Contractarianism

We may think of contractarianism generally as a family of views that seek to justify morality or political institutions by reference to rational agre ...ent. We are, according to this tradition, to think of morality or legitimate states as objects of some sort of "social contract." Until recently it was widely thought that the contractarian tradition was dead. In the last three decades all this has changed. The contractarian tradition has been revived and expanded in a variety of ways. It might even be said that it has never been more alive in moral and political thought. In the fifties and early sixties, works by John Harsanyi, John Rawls, and James Buchanan and Gordon Tullock initiated the contractarian revival. In the seventies and eighties, David Gauthier developed his contractarian "morals by agreement."[1]

In this essay I shall survey the contractarian tradition and distinguish some of the different camps and strands, mentioning some of the most common and, to many, powerful criticisms that have been made against particular contractarian theories. My main object, however, is to present the outlines of a particular contractarian account of moral justification, and to make apparent the ways in which contractarian moral theory may be understood as a response to some classical worries about moral knowledge.

The Contractarian Tradition: Distinctions and Contrasts

The contractarian tradition, as I suggested, is a family of views that seeks to justify morality or political institutions by reference to rational agreement. The general idea is that a morality or a form of political organization (e.g., a state) is to be justified by being shown to be the outcome of the rational agreement of the individuals over whom it has authority. This general idea may take many different forms, and we need to distinguish between different sorts of contractarian theory, as well as between different purposes to which it may be put.

Contractarianism may be moral or political or both. *Moral contractarianism,* we shall say, is the attempt to justify morality, or part of morality (e.g., justice), by reference to agreement. *Political contractarianism* is a normative (usually, albeit not necessarily moral) theory of political institutions (e.g., the state, law). Hobbes, Locke, and Rousseau are usually thought of as political contractarians, transforming a late medieval tradition of political thought that sought the basis for political rule in agreement between ruler and ruled. But while Locke explicitly invokes a noncontractarian, natural law conception of morality, Hobbes and Rousseau can be understood to be moral as well as political contractarians.[2] And some have found contractarian elements in Hume's account of justice and property.[3]

In some ways, moral contractarianism, at least with regard to justice, is the older tradition. It appears to have been a view defended by many of the Greek "Sophists," and it is best known to contemporary philosophers through Plato's Glaucon, who challenges Socrates to rebut the common understanding of justice:

> They say that to do wrong is naturally good, to be wronged is bad, but the suffering of injury so far exceeds in badness the good of inflicting it that when men have done wrong to each other and suffered it, and have a taste for both, those who are unable to avoid the latter and practice the former decide that it is profitable to come to an agreement with each other neither to inflict injury nor to suffer it. As a result they begin to make laws and covenants, and the law's commands they call lawful and just. This, they say, is the origin and essence of justice; it stands between the best and the worst, the best thing to do wrong without paying the penalty and the worst to be wronged without the power of revenge. The just is the mean between the two.[4]

The central idea of moral contractarianism may also be found in Epicurus, who asserts justice to be "a pledge of mutual advantage to restrain men from harming one another and save them from being harmed ... a kind of compact."[5] Our concern in this essay is primarily with moral contractarianism.

Most contractarians are normative theorists; that is, they seek to *evaluate* or to *justify* moral or social practices—hence our general characterization of contractarianism as *justificatory.* Some contractarians, however— for instance, James Buchanan—appear to be as interested in the explanation of the emergence of norms as in their evaluation.[6] And for others—Hume (on justice) and Harman,[7] for instance—the evaluative and the explanatory may not be easily separated. Nonetheless, we might distinguish between *evaluative* and *explanatory* contractarianism. The former, insofar as it is distinct, will be our main concern; an adequate treatment of the issues raised by explanatory contractarianism, belonging more to the theory of social explanation than to moral or political philosophy, is beyond the scope of this essay.

The contemporary revival of (evaluative) moral contractarianism is due in part to a debate initiated by Harsanyi and Rawls in the fifties. Harsanyi was interested in developing a conception of social welfare (that is, a social welfare function) that would not be subject to the methodological criticisms of fellow economists and decision theorists. He proposed that judgments regarding social welfare be modeled as judgments that we would make in complete ignorance of our actual relative position in society. Assuming that one would, in this situation, have an equal chance of assuming any particular position enables one to understand the hypothetical choice as one involving (what decision theorists call) *risk*.[8] Given the assumption of equal probability, Harsanyi derives from certain axioms a form of utilitarianism. The foundational argument, however, is contractarian in a manner: moral principles are derived from hypothetical rational choice.

In his classic paper, "Justice as Fairness," and later in his influential book, *A Theory of Justice,* Rawls develops a basically contractarian account of justice, understood as a virtue of social institutions. His

> aim is to present a conception of justice which generalizes and carries to a higher level of abstraction the familiar theory of the social contract as found, say, in Locke, Rousseau, and Kant. In order to do this we are not to think of the original contract as one to enter a particular society or to set up a particular form of government. Rather, the guiding idea is that the principles of justice for the basic structure of society are the object of the original agreement. They are the principles that free and rational persons concerned to further their own interests would accept in an initial position of equality as defining the fundamental terms of their association. These principles are to regulate all further agreements; they specify the kinds of social cooperation that can be entered into and the forms of government that can be established.

Justice, then, consists of those principles that rational people would propose and acknowledge, with limited knowledge, behind "a veil of ignorance," as appropriate for the adjudication of disputes that arise in a society or system of practices.[9] Taking issue with Harsanyi's utilitarianism, Rawls argues that two distinctively nonutilitarian principles would be chosen in "the original position."

The debate between Harsanyi and Rawls may be understood to be one regarding the nature and content of basic moral principles, the disagreement being that Harsanyi's argument favors a type of utilitarianism, Rawls's argument his famous two principles of justice. While the main issues between them concern questions about rational choice under (complete) uncertainty,[10] we may think of their common contractarianism as a method for adjudicating between their two conceptions of the demands of morality. Contractarianism here is a type of *decision procedure,* a method for determining the nature and content of fundamental moral or political principles. David Gauthier also views contractarian theory in this way, frequently invoking Rawls's remark, "The theory of justice is a part, perhaps the most significant part, of the theory of rational choice."[11] Gauthier favors different principles than either Harsanyi or Rawls. The quarrel between these three contractarians, then, may be understood in part to be one regarding the nature and content of the principles that would be chosen, under specified ideal conditions, by rational people.[12] The three disagree as well about the "ideal conditions" that should frame the choice of moral principles, so the quarrel between them is not merely a seemingly technical one about rational choice. Rather, it reflects complex disagreements about the nature and purpose of contractarian moral theory.

We may think, then, of contractarianism as a decision or discovery procedure; we are to determine what morality (or the polity) asks of us by ascertaining what we would agree to under certain conditions. Rawls's remark about understanding moral or political theory as part of the theory of rational choice, however, suggests another possible aim or purpose of contractarianism, one that is explicit in Gauthier's writings, as well as in much of late medieval and early modern political contractarianism. If the theory of rational choice instructs as to how it is rational to choose or to act, and if moral theory is part of rational choice theory, then moral theory also determines how it is rational to choose or to act. On this view, moral theory provides agents with reasons for action. Specifically, the fact that certain principles or practices are determined by rational agreement is a reason for accepting and abiding by them. We contrast, then, contractarianism as *a decision or discovery procedure for moral theory* and contractarianism as *a particular attempt to provide reasons for the acceptance of and compliance with morality.*

It is important, if one wishes to understand the differences between the various forms of contemporary contractarianism, to see that these aims are not the same. Both aims may be understood to presuppose a view of morality or of political society as a cooperative venture for mutual advantage, to use another of Rawls's useful phases.[13] But mutual advantage and cooperation can signify several different things. One might think, as Harsanyi and Rawls do, that the outcome of hypothetical rational agreement determines the nature and content of fundamental moral principles, without thinking that agents are necessarily provided thereby with reasons for action. Compliance may be another matter, because agreement will not always suffice to ensure that individuals in certain situations have reason to act in accord with mutually advantageous principles. Specifically, what has been called the "free-rider problem"—the temptation of rational agents in certain situations to take advantage of the cooperative behavior of others—remains.[14] By contrast, other theorists think that rational agreement can provide reasons for compliance; this seems to have been the view of Hobbes in his answer to the Foole, and it certainly is the view of Gauthier.[15] The two aims of contractarianism are independent, and one does not entail the other. Gauthier would espouse both aims. Harsanyi and Rawls, as mentioned, would use contractarian agreement only as a discovery procedure.

Justification, with regard to normative[16] matters, may be thought to address two different, although related, concerns. We might wish to know what morality (or the law) asks of us; we might also want to know what reasons, if any, do we have to do what is asked of us. The two questions often are not distinguished, but we shall need to in order to understand the difference between these two uses of contractarian theory. The first addresses concerns about our knowledge of the content of morality, the second about our reasons for action. Both concerns may reflect skeptical doubts, but they are worries about different aspects of morality. The two different forms of moral skepticism correspond to what Walter Sinnott-Armstrong calls "moral knowledge skepticism" ("no moral belief or claim can be known to be true") and "practical moral skepticism" ("there is not always a reason to be moral").[17]

Having discussed the aims of contractarianism, we move now to a consideration of the *nature* of the rational agreement that is at the center of contractarianism, where a number of distinctions need to be made. First, we must distinguish between *actual* and *hypothetical* agreement. Most contemporary contractarians suppose the agreement that founds morality or political society to be hypothetical; certainly we are not to imagine that people actually gather and contract. While Hobbes and Rousseau may be best interpreted as hypothetical contractarians, some classical political thinkers understood the agreement between ruler and ruled to be actual. This may be as one would expect from a modern political tradition that finds its origins in the compacts and oaths that princes and lords made with or to kings and emperors. However, a distinction between explicit and tacit forms of (actual) agreement was often made, as it seemed evident that some, if not most, people could not be understood to have explicitly agreed.[18]

A social contract, whatever it is, is a type of agreement. As just noted, it may be actual or hypothetical. However, agreement here is ambiguous, which leads us to another important distinction between types of contractarian theories. Agreement may be a species of *consent* or something else—for example, merely evidence of advantage (in a sense to be explained). It is hard to see how hypothetical agreement could count as genuine consent. Actual agreement will normally so count, barring certain conditions (e.g., coercion or duress, lack of relevant information), but hypothetical consent doesn't engage the will in the requisite manner.[19] Hypothetical agreement, however, can be, just like actual consent, evidence of advantage. While there are often reasons to agree to something (actually or hypothetically) other than those of advantage, the fact of (actual or hypothetical) agreement offers some reason to think that what was agreed to was *believed* to be advantageous. Suppose one of the constraints on a hypothetical agreement is adequate information; then the fact of informed agreement would be evidence that what was agreed to *was* advantageous. If we suppose further that the parties making the agreement are self-interested, then we have evidence for the agreement being mutually beneficial, where "benefit" here is to be understood more narrowly than "advantage" to cover self-regarding desires and ends. The main distinction, between agreement as consent and agreement as advantage, is important, for many criticisms of contractarianism, especially of political forms, apply only if agreement is understood to be a form of consent, and consequently, only if agreement is actual.[20]

We normally count an act as one of consent only if certain conditions obtain. According to most philosophers, agreement will constitute consent—or "consent" will obligate—only given certain background *moral* conditions that define and limit agreement.[21] Without taking a stand on the difficult matter of whether consent can be understood nonmorally, we shall introduce another distinction regarding contractarian agreement, one relevant to our exposition of the forms of this tradition. In political theory, an obvious distinction between Hobbes and Locke is that for the latter contractarian agreement is morally constrained (by natural law), whereas for the former it is not, or so his theory is often read. That is, for Locke consent can generate obligations only if the constraints imposed by the laws of nature are respected, which is to say only if certain moral constraints are not violated. For Hobbes, at least on this familiar reading, there are no *moral* conditions that constrain the sort of consent that can create obligations. Rawls has made it clear that his theory is to be understood as one where agreement is morally constrained.[22] By contrast, Buchanan and Gauthier's theories are morally unconstrained forms of contractarianism.[23] As the examples show, this distinction applies equally to moral as to political forms of the theory: Gauthier's theory is primarily a moral theory. So contractarian agreement may be morally constrained (e.g., Rawls) or unconstrained (e.g., Gauthier). It cannot be claimed of the former, however, that agreement is the ground of all of morality, insofar as it presupposes moral constraints that are prior to and independent of agreement.[24]

We may ask generally about the *scope* of the agreement that is to generate moral norms: who are the parties to the agreement? The simple answer, offered by many contractarians, is: all those who are to be bound by the norms, namely, all those who find themselves in "the circumstances of justice" in question. For these contractarians, *the circumstances of justice* are the conditions that give rise to the particular virtue of justice. They include two sorts of conditions: (1) rough equality of physical and mental powers, vulnerability to attack, moderate scarcity, and (2) consciousness of the latter, and awareness of conflict as well as of some identity of interest. Moderate scarcity is relative to preferences and is understood to include variability of supply, thus allowing the possibility of mutually beneficial cooperation. People presumably find themselves most of the time in the circumstance of justice, that is, in situations where cooperative, constrained behavior is mutually beneficial, given their preferences.[25] Many objections to contractarianism stem from the limited scope of moral norms that appears to be entailed by this doctrine of the circumstances of justice.[26]

We contrasted contractarianism as *a decision or discovery procedure for moral theory* and as *a particular attempt to provide reasons for the acceptance of and compliance with moral constraints.* The sort of contractarian theory I shall propose seeks to achieve both ends. It is not uncommon for those seeking to rationalize morality in this way to be *moral internalists*—to assume that moral requirements provide their subjects with reasons for action.[27] If someone is morally obligated to do something, then he or she has a reason to do so.

Moral internalism has often been rejected because (as formulated) it implies that if one lacks the relevant reason, then one lacks the obligation in question. It is not clear, however, that philosophers interested in finding reasons to be moral should worry about this consequence.

What sorts of reasons are provided by our duties? Trivially, our moral duties provide us with *moral* reasons for action.[28] But this is uninformative. They also, on the internalist's view, provide us with reasons *simpliciter*. Moral reasons in this sense are simply reasons provided by morality. Such reasons are not special sorts of reasons by virtue of being moral, though morality does, in the view of many, provide us with special sorts of reasons. We return to these issues later in the essay (see also the Appendix).

The Attractions of Contractarianism

Contractarianism is, in some respects at least, an attractive or plausible theory, or so we may suppose, given its popularity in contemporary moral and political thought. The possible advantages, theoretical and practical, of the approach to morals and politics may be numerous. First of all, recalling one of our distinctions, contractarianism may offer a decision or discovery procedure for ethics and political theory. The content of (part of) morality or of the demands of the political community may be determined by asking what we would agree to under certain conditions. Such a procedure, it may be argued, makes certain perennial disputes about ethics and politics more tractable. Here contractarianism offers a response to what Walter Sinnott-Armstrong characterizes as skepticism about moral knowledge.

Second, referring to the other half of the distinction just recalled, contractarianism, understood as an attempt to provide reasons for compliance, proposes an answer to the familiar questions, "Why be moral?" and "Why obey the law?" This is to address practical moral skepticism in Sinnott-Armstrong's sense.

Third, the answers contractarianism provides to questions regarding the nature and content of morality and of the demands of the political community do not, it is sometimes claimed, presuppose very demanding conceptions of reason or value. Certainly, some of the normative properties postulated by certain alternative accounts—moral realism[29]—may be eschewed. It may be thus thought that contractarianism has distinct metaphysical advantages.[30] Given the complexity of the debate over moral realism, it is not easy to determine if contractarianism offers clear advantages here. It seems more important to stress that contractarianism, as I shall suggest below, may be equally compatible with a number of different positions on the nature of value and of normative properties.

Of course, these advantages do not belong to all versions of contractarianism, as should already be clear from our various distinctions and early discussion. Contractarians, such as Harsanyi and Rawls, who restrict their interest to be determination of the content and nature of moral principles, cannot claim to have resolved puzzles about reasons to be moral. And theorists, such as Gauthier, who find themselves rejecting the orthodox understanding of rationality as straightforward utility maximization, cannot claim to have adopted the least controversial contemporary conception of practical reason. But the possible general advantages of contractarianism as an approach to the theory of morality should be clear.

A brief word should be said also about the availability of the theory, as it may be thought that it is wedded to particular conceptions of value, rationality, and motivation. Specifically, it is sometimes said that the approach is available only insofar as one takes a subjectivist view of value, an instrumentalist conception of reason, and a (largely) self-interested understanding of humans.[31] But this, as I argue later, need not be. Contractarianism is available to nonsubjectivists, noninstrumentalists, and certainly to those who reject self-interested conceptions of people.

Some Criticisms

Criticisms of the contractarian tradition abound. A problem with the formulation and assessment of these, however, has been that it has not always been clear which variant they target. With the distinctions drawn in the first section, this task should be somewhat simpler. I shall enumerate, very briefly, some of the standard worries.

One common criticism of moral contractarianism, traceable to Hume, is that it begs the question. Sometimes the argument is flat-footed: if contractarians reach moral conclusions, they must have implicitly introduced moral premises. The more serious versions of this criticism purport to discover moral elements in the contractarian argument. My particular response to such claims is simple: if genuine moral elements are found in a particular contractarian construction, then that is reason to reject it. If moral elements are found in *all* such constructions, then, barring some alternative account, that is evidence for moral skepticism.

In recent years the most frequent criticism made of contractarian theories is that their implications are counterintuitive. Typically, this criticism takes one of two forms, owing to the structure of contractarianism. One, as contractarianism would have us derive our moral principles and norms from rational agreement, these will reflect whatever determines that agreement. If the parties are unequal in some (independently) objectionable way, the outcome—that is, the principles or norms—will also be (independently) objectionable. Different contractarian theories address this worry differently, some imposing moral or nonmoral constraints on the differences between parties that may be taken into consideration in the basic agreement, others constraining agreement by modeling the original position as one of uncertainty or risk. Rawls, for instance, imposes "a veil of ignorance" preventing parties to the agreement from knowing their identities; Harsanyi would have us suppose that we could be any one of the people in society and that, given that we have no knowledge of the relevant likelihoods, we should assume that there is an equal chance that we are any one particular individual. The desired effect of these devices is to filter out the apparently objectionable features of the preagreement position. If we do not know who we are, or what positions we might occupy, then the agreement should not reflect these features or be unduly biased in various ways. Other contractarians (e.g., Gauthier) however, do not think that there are independent standards for determining what outcomes of agreement are objectionable and do not impose any of these devices on choice in the original position.

The second form typically taken by the accusation of counterintuitiveness is due to the manner in which contractarianism determines *scope*. According to this tradition, moral principles—or at least principles of justice—bind only those who are parties to the basic agreement. The question, then, is who is a member of this original agreement? Many theories slide over this important question. One answer tacitly given is all rational persons. Another is all rational persons in the circumstances of justice (see above). We must distinguish two questions of scope: determining the set of individuals who have duties, and determining the set of individuals (or entities) to whom duties are owed. If we think of *moral standing* as the state of being owed (some) moral consideration, then we may reformulate these criticisms as follows: contractarianism is objectionable either because it does not recognize the moral standing of some individuals (e.g., the infirm and helpless, nonhumans) or it wrongly accords different individuals different degrees of moral standing (e.g., children, fetuses).[32]

Critics, however, have not generally noted one of the most interesting, and possibly objectionable, features of the manner in which contractarian theories are led to understand moral standing. Insofar as these theories generate moral relations between individuals from agreement in the circumstances of justice, then, assuming a certain degree of variety in the conditions in which people find themselves, moral relations between people are likely to be multifaceted and overlapping. (See notes 18 and 26.) That is, moral standing is likely to be a pairwise or many-place relation, binding different people to each other in different ways. This contrasts with the implicit univocal understanding in the contemporary literature, where it is tacitly assumed that moral standing is like citizenship as this is now understood—namely, a single, equivalent state that does not permit differentiation of status.[33] Contractarianism, however, may call this assumption into question.

Contractarian Justification

Let me now offer an account of moral justification. Let us first distinguish between different moral justifications. Justification, we might think, is contextual in the sense that the sort of justification required is determined by the context in question. For we may agree with Rawls when he notes that "justification is argument addressed to those who disagree with us, or to ourselves when we are of two minds."[34] Sometimes we ask someone to justify some act ("What entitles you to do that?") or some claim ("What gives you a right to this?"). Many ordinary requests for moral justifications do not require appeal to anything but commonly accepted norms or values. If the person in question cites some commonly accepted rule or principle, or gives some other satisfactory moral account, the story is closed. Some have imagined that is all there is to justification in moral contexts. To justify something morally, they may say, is always to appeal to some moral principle or norm or ideal; nothing more need be done.[35]

It seems clear that there are other sorts of justifications that may be called for in some contexts, especially those when the doubts giving rise to the call for justification are deep. "How do we know that this is the relevant norm, or that this principle is binding?" Or, we might ask, "Where does this principle come from? What is its basis?" We might also go on to ask similar questions of the initial answers given to these queries: "What justifies you in taking such and such as a good justification in these contexts?" Much of moral philosophy consists of questions such as these.

I am not sure how to distinguish these different sorts of questions concerning justification; there does not seem to be any particular distinguishing marks setting some apart from others. Rather, it just appears that in some contexts the questioners' doubts or worries are set to rest sooner than in others. It may not matter that we distinguish neatly different sorts of calls for justification. Our interests here are in questions regarding justification that are not quickly or easily answered. These are the sorts of questions typically asked by people who have some reason to be skeptical of (certain) moral claims, either because of doubts specific to particular moral claims or because of doubts about morality itself. My "contractarian account of justification" is intended to address these sorts of global or skeptical worries.

I shall, then, propose a general contractarian account of justification. The account will be incomplete, as I shall explain. It should, however, be sufficiently complete to enable us to consider contractarian approaches to the issues under consideration and to see what is distinctive and promising about this tradition's response to various skeptical doubts about morality. The account will be formulated in terms of norms, though nothing should turn on this.[36] And I shall talk about making or accepting particular moral judgments without distinguishing between realist and antirealist accounts;[37] my account is meant to be open to realist as well as to (most) antirealist accounts of moral language.

I shall present the (partial) account in stages. I shall say that a moral judgment p is justified if:

(1) There is a norm N which is justified and which, given the relevant facts, implies p.

A norm N is justified if:

(2) All bound by N have (sufficient) reason to endorse it, and
(3) All bound by N have (sufficient) reason to comply with it, conditional on the expected compliance of others.

Condition 3 is a requirement of moral internalism; as such it is controversial and some contractarians (and other moral theorists) may not accept it. The compliance required by this condition is conditional on the expected compliance of others, and this will distinguish the account from many others.

Conditions 1–3 state general requirements for the justification of moral judgments; there is, as of yet, nothing particularly contractarian about them. The contractarian element of my account is introduced as support for 2. Condition 2 is true if:

(2.1) N would be the object of a rational, nonmoral, hypothetical collective choice of all bound by N.

We may think of this as the contractarian or social contract condition.[38]

Condition 3, as I said, is an internalist requirement. As N will often require action contrary to one's preferences, the truth of 3 is dependent on the truth of a view of practical reason according to which we may have (sufficient) reason to act counterpreferentially or against the balance of reasons.[39] An account of this sort is an important part of Gauthier's contractarian theory, but several noncontractarians defend theories of practical rationality that would support 3.[40] We shall return to this matter later. (An account is sketched in the Appendix.) I shall say, then, that condition 3 is true only if:

(3.1) Practical reason allows for counterpreferential choice or acting against the balance of reasons.

If conditions 1–3 are satisfied for some judgment p, then p is justified. I assume at the outset that p is a *moral* judgment, but this will need to be established if we are to claim that 1–3 provide an account of *moral* justification. Reason must be offered for identifying judgments like p and norms like N as moral. The case for understanding p and N as moral is complicated and rather controversial, so it is best to postpone discussion for the moment.

The account is incomplete in a number of ways; it is merely a partial account, as I shall explain in a moment. Let me briefly explicate the different parts of the story. The contractarian condition (2.1) introduces rational, nonmoral, hypothetical collective choice as part of the justification for norms such as N. In keeping with the sort of contractarian theory I wish to propose and some of the distinctions I made earlier, I emphasize that the hypothetical choice process described by 2.1 is heuristic, a process of discovery. It is not to be understood as consensual or promissory.[41]

A particular moral judgment p is justified, then, if several conditions obtain. There must be some norm N that implies p when certain facts obtain (condition 1). This norm must have certain properties (conditions 2 and 3); most importantly, for our purposes, it must be the object of a hypothetical rational agreement (condition 2.1). For example, suppose that I make a judgment regarding the keeping of a promise or the refraining from defrauding others: "you ought to keep that promise"; "it would be wrong for me to take the money." Presumably there are norms that imply these judgments in the circumstances: "promises should be kept"; "fraud is wrong."[42] Suppose that these norms bind everyone in the situation and that all would benefit from the object in question, that is, the keeping of promises and the absence of fraud. Then these norms would be the object of the rational hypothetical choice of agents selecting rules for governing their interactions. For the consequences of general respect of these norms are better for each than what may be expected from the absence of these norms. A norm that exempted some people would be more advantageous to those people, but it would not typically be the object of hypothetical rational agreement of all concerned, absent some benefit to all.[43] Lastly, norms and judgments such as these give me reasons for action, at least if practical rationality allows for what I have called counter-preferential choice (condition 3.1; see appendix).

What if some would not benefit from a norm prohibiting fraud or from some norm ruling out various harms to others? Then these norms would not secure *their* hypothetical agreement (condition 2.1). This means that these persons would not be bound by the norms; they would, as it were, be outside of the moral framework established by contractarian rational agreement. This is a feature of this type of contractarianism that many moral philosophers have found objectionable.[44] We shall return to the objection later. For now let us note that various norms, such as those mentioned above, may be forthcoming from an account such as ours, but their *scope* is likely to be more limited than we ordinarily assume.

This account is incomplete, as I mentioned. It is formulated as a simple conditional, leaving open the possibility that other ways of justifying particular moral judgments exist. If, as Rawls claims, "justification is argument addressed to those who disagree with us, or to ourselves when we are of two minds," then there may be justifications that terminate in particular norms or ideals, without requiring additional appeals. We may, as I mentioned earlier, contrast such "ordinary" requests for justification with the less easily provided requests for justifications characteristic of philosophical ethics. But there is another reason. Particular norms may be imperfect and allow for improvement. Given that compliance is conditional on the expected compliance of others (condition 3), the norms that are justified in any particular situation may not be best. That is, there may be other norms available that promise greater benefits if only people can coordinate their behavior around these. For instance, norms of *vendetta* or norms requiring dueling for European aristocrats may have been, after a time, mutually disadvantageous to the parties involved; they may have preferred not having the relevant institutions or practices and instead having alternative ways of resolving disputes.[45] Similarly, it might be preferable for us to have norms that give more weight to the prevention of harms and less weight to compensation of victims than do present norms. Our general propensity to weight more heavily small likelihoods of great disasters than greater chances of smaller losses is reflected in some of our norms, and there may be room for improvement here.[46] We may need, then, an account of the improvement of norms or introduction of new norms.[47]

We need to say something about what motivates an account such as ours; specifically, we need to talk about the justifications for the crucial contractarian condition (2.1). But we should explicate the account further and discuss some other issues before proceeding to a general defense.

Note that conditions 1–3 (including 2.1 and 3.1), as I have stated them, are nonmoral. This is crucial to the sort of contractarian account I wish to defend. I shall reply below to some skeptical doubts concerning this claim, but let me first be clear as to what I am asserting. These conditions are, it is claimed, nonmoral. This is *not* to assert that they are non*normative,* for conditions 2 and 3 are meant to be normative; they are claims about what is rational. There is no question, then, of attempting to derive moral conclusions from nonnormative premises. It is just that they are not *moral* conditions. This is essential to the sort of account I propose, which is meant to provide us with reasons to be moral. I can think of no other way of providing reasons to be moral that is not question-begging.[48] As I mentioned earlier, I am methodologically committed to removing any moral element that may have been introduced into this (or another) condition, and, if this cannot be done, to skepticism regarding (this part of) morality.

We can now see how this type of contractarian story addresses the skeptical problems about justification that motivate much of moral philosophy. Consider the following worry: If someone is justified in accepting a particular moral judgment *p,* then he or she has some reasons for accepting *p.* Whatever those reasons are, they must themselves be justified in order to justify that person's acceptance of *p.* These reasons, then, are to be justified by prior reasons. *The latter* must be justified by an additional set of reasons, and so on. A possible and (to epistemologists) familiar regress looms.

Let us now distinguish between two skeptical worries, each of which threatens to generate a different regress. There may be a *general* skeptical worry concerning the sum total of our reasons, including moral and nonmoral ones. And there may be a *narrow* skeptical worry involving (merely) our moral reasons. My contractarian account addresses only the second, narrow worry. The manner in which it proposes to resolve it is very simple. The acceptance of *moral* judgments is ultimately to be based on *nonmoral* (albeit normative) considerations. Thus, it is crucial for this account that conditions 1–3 not be moral.

This justificatory strategy may appear to be foundationalist. Certainly, some of the classical contractarians (e.g., Hobbes), interested in refuting skeptical doubts about morality (or the state's authority), seemed to be foundationalist either about morality or about knowledge generally. Foundationalism we may think of as roughly the view that judgments or beliefs are to be justified in relation to more basic judgments or beliefs themselves in need of no justification (call these *basic*). Foundationalist accounts of knowledge or of justification are composed of different elements: a claim that there are some basic judgments in terms of which other judgments are to be justified, and a claim about the self-justifying or self-evident nature of the former. Many foundationalists have claimed that the basic judgments must be certain, indubitable, or incorrigible, though there are now many versions of fallible foundationalism. Foundationalist accounts typically are hierarchical and pre-suppose an epistemic ordering of judgments. Justification is understood to be hierarchical in the sense that something is justified by appeal to some other element that is more basic and epistemically prior. Elsewhere I have distinguished two types of moral foundational theories.[49] One, "simple moral foundationalism," justifies moral judgments in terms of basic *moral* judgments (or facts); the other, "reductive moral foundationalism," interprets the relevant set of basic judgments (or facts) to be *nonmoral*. Our contractarian account, then, may be a species of reductive moral foundationalism.

If we take claims about the self-justifying nature of the basic judgments to be essential for foundationalism, then ours is not foundationalist. I make no such claims. I leave open the option of adopting whatever account holds true of the epistemic status of nonmoral judgments (nonnormative and normative).[50] But we might not regard claims about the self-justifying nature of the basic judgments to be essential. The affinities my contractarianism may have with foundationalism have little to do with what I say about the alleged "foundations," but with a hierarchical conception of justification and the presupposed order of epistemic priority. I appear to suppose that moral justification is in terms of something prior, namely, the (nonmoral) rational. And this, it may be claimed, makes this approach in some respect foundational.

I do assert that the rational is epistemically prior to the moral (but see some of my reservations below about our understanding of "the moral"). Depending on our analysis of the priority relation, this may suffice to make the approach foundational, at least in one respect. But I am not sure that the notion of epistemic priority I need to suppose is strong enough to make this comparison informative. All I suppose is that if we wish to give reasons why we should act morally, we need an account of the moral that shows how we could (and typically do) have nonmoral reasons to do what is required of us. And to generate such an account we must, for the purposes of this inquiry, accord a priority to the nonmoral over the moral. Whether this sort of inquiry and the sorts of presuppositions it requires prevent us from adopting a non-foundationalist—for example, coherentist account of justification generally (moral and nonmoral)—is a question that I should think is left open by my approach. Coherentism about knowledge generally does not rule out the possibility that some of our judgments are to be justified in relation to certain other judgments, even though these are justified in relation to yet others. In this sense my contractarianism may not have any particularly deep or interesting affinities with foundationalist approaches to knowledge or justification.[51]

Consider the following possibility: We justify (the set of) our moral judgments, *P*, in relation to some of our nonmoral judgments, *Q* (e.g., our judgments regarding rationality and value). The latter, in turn, are justified by reference to (sets of) other judgments, *R*, *S*, and *T* (or some combination of these):

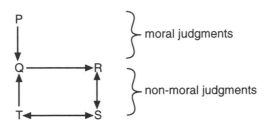

The possibility illustrated above is one where there is no (set of) judgment(s) that is not to be justified in relation to (some) other (set of) judgment(s). But this does not entail that *any* (set of) judgment(s) must be justified in relation to *any* other (set of) judgment(s).

Motivation and Some Replies to Objections

What motivates this sort of contractarianism? What is it that drives this sort of account? I phrase the question this way in order to stress that many proponents of this sort of theory are, as it were, "in the grips of a picture" and cannot see any alternative justification for morality. It is not just that this account seems (to proponents) superior to others; it is that all others fail and that it is hard to see how there could be an alternative. This is not to say that there are no positive reasons in favor of contractarianism. It is merely to stress that the approach is understood by many of its proponents as the only serious alternative to moral skepticism. Indeed, what upsets some critics is its closeness to skepticism.

I wish to set aside immediately two possible grounds for contractarianism. As I said earlier, it is often claimed that contractarianism, or at least the variety that I am defending, presupposes either a self-interested view of humans or a subjective account of value (or both).[52] Some suppose that contractarianism find values "queer" much in the way that J. L. Mackie did.[53] Contractarians need assume none of these views, as I shall suggest presently and as I have argued elsewhere.[54]

Contractarianism, as I understand it, is motivated by two principal assumptions: (1) a claim about the prevalence of value-driven conflict in human affairs, and (2) skepticism about "a right reason constituted by nature," to use Hobbes's words. These assumptions, especially the first, are much weaker than one might expect. The first assumption is the claim that there is considerable conflict caused by different values. If people are (relatively) self-interested, then this will give rise to value-driven conflict. But self-interestedness is not necessary. Suppose that all value is agent-relative—that is, value from particular perspectives.[55] Then there will be value-driven conflict. Suppose that some but not all value is agent-neutral, then it is possible—depending on the type of agent-neutral value—that there will be considerable value-driven conflict. The agent-relativity of all (or most of) value is sufficient to generate conflict. Self-interestedness is not necessary. On most accounts, if values are "subjective" in the sense of being mere expressions of our desires or preferences, then they are agent-relative.[56] But, again, subjectivism is not necessary for agent-relativity. Nonsubjectivists may adopt agent-relative conceptions of value.[57]

What is necessary for the sort of contractarianism I am defending is the existence of considerable value-driven conflict between persons. When conjoined with the second assumption, the stage is set for the contractarian's case. The second assumption is the "want of a right reason constituted by nature," at least with regard to justice. The norms and ideals typically associated with justice, as well as some associated with benevolence, are not knowable by reason; that is, absent conventions establishing norms, individual reason cannot ascertain the existence of moral norms (of justice). Contractarian justice is a substitute for natural justice. As I mentioned earlier, the basic idea is found in Antiphon, Glaucon, and Epicurus. I quote the best-known modern proponent of the view:

> Therefore, as when there is a controversy in an account, the parties must by
> their own accord set up for right reason the reason of some arbitrator to
> whose sentence they will both stand, or their controversy must either come
> to blows or be undecided, for want of a right reason constituted by nature,
> so it is in all debates of what kind soever.[58]

The absence of right reason regarding justice does not, it is important to understand, entail a subjective account of value. Skepticism about natural justice is perfectly compatible with rationalism about value and other virtues.[59]

Suppose that these two assumptions are true. And suppose that humans typically find themselves in "the circumstances of justice." That is, they find themselves in situations where all may be better off if all abide by certain constraints—for example, refrain from predatory activity, engage in mutual aid. But they individually lack a reason so to restrain themselves in the absence of a guarantee of like restraint on the part of others.[60] The type of conflict involved here, then, is not straightforwardly solvable by ordinary rational means. If agents merely act on the balance of reasons, or straightforwardly maximize expected utility, they will often fail to achieve mutually preferred outcomes. (Consider what are often referred to as "collective action problems," e.g., providing public goods such as clean air, reducing traffic congestion.) If they are able to coordinate on certain norms (e.g., those to which it would be rational to agree hypothetically), and if they can count on one another abiding by these norms, then they can achieve these mutually preferable outcomes.

Morality, or at least justice, on this view, is a conventional standard which provides a means whereby rational agents in the circumstances of justice can improve their condition. Virtually everyone accepts the conventionality of many of our norms (e.g., various norms governing property, liability, politeness). Contractarians "merely" extend this to all norms of justice. Conventional or "artificial" justice is a type of "indirect strategy" aiming to bring about mutually advantageous improvements in people's lives.[61]

One of the main ways of objecting to this sort of account has been to question whether N or p, justified in this manner, are genuine moral norms or judgments. For, it is often said, the moral is not "reducible" to the nonmoral. Admittedly, the term "moral" may be used in various different ways, with considerable variability. So I shall not reply to this objection by resort to analysis. Moreover, I am not entirely clear as to how the moral and the nonmoral are to be delimited. My concern is, in any case, with a certain part of the moral, namely what traditionally falls under the virtue of justice. The account I propose is not designed to work for virtues such as temperance or courage. This said, the exclusionary account I give in the appendix of the reasons provided by our duties is meant to go some way toward addressing the concerns of some of those who worry about "reductionism," as I shall suggest.

What reasons do we have to count norms and judgments thus justified as moral? What evidence do we have for this in some particular case? Earlier I supposed that norms prohibiting fraud or requiring respect for promises could be supported by contractarianism, albeit with less than universal scope. Similarly, we may suppose that prohibitions of theft and killing, requirements of mutual aid, and the like will also be generated by our framework. Are these norms moral, then? The most important reason for identifying them as such is that they resemble standard moral directives in various ways. They have similar or identical contents ("don't kill the innocent"; "theft is wrong"; "keep your promises"), presumably with the same sorts of defeating conditions. They have a certain bindingness which we characteristically associate with moral directives. This feature is captured in my account by the exclusionary nature of the reasons provided by moral judgments (see the appendix). They constrain our behavior (or our intentions or desires) in certain ways. Additionally, they function much like ordinary moral directives. They assist us in deciding what to do in certain kinds of problems, guide our action, and the like. They provide solutions to what I call cooperation dilemmas, for example, collective action problems, like those representable by the Prisoners' Dilemma.[62]

In classical Greek philosophy it is often held that a necessary condition of something's being a virtue is that it be beneficial to the person whose virtue it is. Condition 2.1 establishes that N is a mutually advantageous norm. If we accept this requirement on virtues, then 2.1 establishes a necessary condition for norms being moral.[63] It is, of course, characteristic of much of modern moral philosophy to reject this condition on moral virtues. So contractarianism's ability to satisfy it may not impress many contemporary moralists. One of my purposes in bringing up the point is to remind us how conceptions of the moral may differ and thus to blunt the contemporary criticism that contractarian justice does not (fully) capture "morality."[64]

Some contractarians have insisted on *impartiality* as a defining characteristic of moral judgments.[65] Accordingly, we can determine whether certain norms and judgments are moral depending on their impartiality. It is important to distinguish two different uses of impartiality as a condition of the moral. One way is to use a construction (e.g., hypothetical agreement) as an *expression* of impartiality. This would be one reading of Rawls's contractarianism: "the contract device illuminates the basic ideas of morality as impartiality."[66] The second way is to understand impartiality to be a *characteristic* of moral judgments, such that no judgment can be moral if it is not impartial. This is Gauthier's approach; his theory seeks to generate rational constraints on individual behavior "that, being impartial, satisfy the traditional understanding of morality."[67] Impartiality here is not an independent moral value. It is merely a characteristic of moral judgments, and thus a condition to be satisfied if we are to identify certain judgments as moral.

The first use of impartiality is not available to the sort of contractarian theory I have been supporting, as it presupposes the existence of a prior, independent moral value. It is not clear, however, that one should want to use impartiality in the second way. For one, it is not entirely clear what impartiality is.[68] And different accounts may have different implications.[69] I propose, then, not to make use of impartiality in either of these two ways.

For these reasons we may agree that norms and judgments such as those I have mentioned are moral. But some will remain unconvinced, thinking that something essential to moral judgment has been omitted. The contractarian may decide at this point that it is not important whether these norms and judgments are moral. What is important is that they provide agents with reasons to constrain their behavior so as to bring about mutually preferable states of affairs. The contractarian, faced with a critic who demands an account of the moral that severs all connection between justice and prior ends, may simply give up the project of accounting for the moral and offer a substitute, namely, an enriched account of practical reason which will enable people to cooperate in important ways.[70] If this can be accomplished, that may be sufficient—or all that we can hope for. This would be, of course, to embrace a type of moral skepticism, at least with regard to our reasons to be moral ("practical moral skepticism"). To be able to reject this skeptical objection, establishing that the norms and judgments justified by conditions 1–3 are moral is crucial.

The critic may change tack and insist, correctly, that not all of our ordinary duties will be derivable from such an account. For instance, the requirements of contractarian benevolence or justice may be less onerous on this view than utilitarians or some egalitarians have supposed. More significantly, we may turn out to have no duties whatever to some individuals to whom we ordinarily think ourselves bound. Contractarianism is an ethic of reciprocity, and those with little or nothing to contribute may not end up being parties to the determining conventions. This issue is much more complicated than these brief remarks and the discussions in the literature usually suggest. For instance, many, if not most, of the examples often cited to make this point are mistaken.[71] Nevertheless, the general theoretical point is surely right: not all commonly thought (today) to have moral standing will have standing on this sort of account. I do not wish to dispute this general claim, even if many examples fail (e.g., children, the infirm) to make the point. The question then is, what follows?

Most contemporary moral theorists conclude from these implications that the account is flawed and should be rejected. Any theoretical position that conflicts this starkly with some of "our fundamental moral intuitions" must be mistaken. This type of reaction may be foundationalist—"our basic moral intuitions" may have a certain privileged status—but it need not be. A coherence methodology could give the same result. But I do not see how such a response is available to someone who wishes, as I do, to inquire into the basis of morality in our reasons for action. For such an inquiry, this line of response is question-begging.

The contractarian project I have sketched *is* revisionist in its implications. It is doubtful that it will reveal all of our "intuitively" accepted moral directives to be justified.[72] But this is what we should expect. Some of our ordinary moral judgments undoubtedly reflect the historical influence, for instance, of religious traditions we no longer accept.[73] Most people appear to think that incest *per se* is morally wrong, yet no contemporary moral theory supports that claim. Some revision seems inevitable. So we should not be surprised to discover that some of our "moral intuitions" are groundless.

Appendix on Reasons

Moral reasons, on the internalist's view, provide us with reasons *simpliciter.* Some will allow that the reasons provided by our duties need not be special in any way; they may simply be reasons that we add to the other reasons favoring or opposing a particular act. Suppose we act rationally insofar as we act "on the balance of reasons"; if the weight of reasons favors acting in one way rather than another, then we act rationally if we so act. On this view, we are to weigh all considerations favoring or opposing a particular course of action and to act according to the most weighty considerations.[74] If the reasons provided by our duties are merely reasons to be added to others favoring or opposing a particular act, then we are to weigh the former along with the latter. On some versions of this sort of account, moral reasons are especially weighty (or "heavy") reasons, so that they usually determine the outcome of deliberation.

I reject this sort of account and insist that moral reasons be special in a certain manner; they are to be understood as *preemptive* reasons in a particular sense. It is widely thought that moral reasons in some way preempt other reasons. They are not merely to be added to other reasons and weighed in the balance with these. Moral reasons are stronger than the reasons they defeat, but the relation of "strength" here needs to be understood so as not to allow comparisons of weight. Preemptive reasons in this sense I shall understand using Joseph Raz's notion of an "exclusionary reason."

Some reasons are first-order reasons to act (or to refrain from acting); other reasons are second-order reasons to act (or to refrain from acting) for a reason. An *exclusionary reason* is a second-order reason to refrain from acting for a reason. The directive "Do this because I say so," were it authoritative, would provide second-order reasons; the directive "Do this because he said so" or "Don't do this out of devotion to her" would provide exclusionary reasons.[75] A moral reason, on this view, includes an exclusionary reason. Moral reasons would have us act in a particular way and refrain from acting differently for other reasons.[76] On this view, the reasons provided by obligations are reasons to do the obligatory act and second-order reasons not to act on (otherwise valid) reasons to do something else. The reasons provided by our duties, then, are not simply added to our other reasons and weighed along with these; to the contrary, our duties give us reasons that bypass normal considerations of weight. In effect, the exclusionary reasons provided by our moral duties are reasons to disregard the balance of reasons.[77] Suppose the weight of reasons favors doing some act A, but we have promised to act otherwise. Our promise, on this view, provides us with a reason so to act and a reason not to act on the (balance of) reasons favoring A.[78]

This account of practical rationality, although central to the contractarian theory I favor, is not crucial to much of I have claimed; many contractarian accounts of morality do not assume any such conception of moral reasons. It plays, however, an important role in some of my answers to some of the criticisms made against contractarianism. And it is crucial in defense of my condition 3. Nevertheless, it cannot be said to be specifically contractarian, and some may wish to do without it.

Notes

I am grateful to many participants in the Dartmouth Conference on Moral Epistemology for helpful comments and criticisms of an earlier version of this essay. I should like especially to thank Geoffrey Sayre-McCord, Stefan Sencerz, Mark Timmons, and William Tolhurst for their suggestions in conversation, and Malia Brink and Walter Sinnott-Armstrong for exceptionally useful written comments. I am grateful as well to David Brink for written comments on a final draft of this paper; some of these I address in a new essay, "Justice, Reasons, and Moral Standings" (unpublished).

1. John Harsanyi, "Cardinal Utility in Welfare Economics and the Theory of Risk Taking," *Journal of Political Economy* 61 (1953), 434–35; and "Cardinal Welfare, Individualistic Ethics, and Interpersonal Comparisons of Utility," *Journal of Political Economy* 63 (1955), 309–21; John Rawls, "Justice as Fairness," *Philosophical Review* 57 (1958), 164–94, and *A Theory of Justice* (Cambridge, Mass.: Harvard University Press, 1971); James Buchanan and Gordon Tullock, *The Calculus of Consent* (Ann Arbor, Mich.: University of Michigan Press, 1962); David Gauthier, *Morals by Agreement* (Oxford: Clarendon Press, 1986), and *Moral Dealing* (Ithaca and London: Cornell University Press, 1990).

2. Thomas Hobbes, *Leviathan* (1651); John Locke, *Second Treatise of Government* (1690); and Jean-Jacques Rousseau, *Of the Social Contract (1762)*. (Specific editions of classical works will not be cited unless necessary.)

3. Rawls, *Theory*, pp. 32–33; Gauthier, "David Hume, Contractarian," reprinted in *Moral Dealing*, pp. 45–79; and J. L. Mackie, *Hume's Moral Theory* (London: Routledge & Kegan Paul, 1980). The relevant texts of Hume are *A Treatise of Human Nature* (1740) and *An Enquiry Concerning the Principles of Morals* (1752).

4. *Republic* 358e2–359b1 (G. M. A. Grube, trans. Indianapolis: Hackett, 1974). Antiphon apparently claimed that "Justice consists in not transgressing the laws of the city in which one dwells. The best way of combining one's own interests and the demands of justice is to act according to justice when there are witnesses but according to nature when one is alone and unobserved. For the authority of the laws is imposed artificially, but the authority of nature is intrinsically binding. The former is established by common consent." *The Presocratics,* ed. P. Wheelwright, (New York: Odyssey Press, 1966), 259.

5. "Principle Doctrines," paragraph 31, *The Stoic and Epicurean Philosophers,* ed. W. Oates, (New York: Random House, 1940), 37.

6. Jean Hampton, "The Contractarian Explanation of the State," in *Midwest Studies in Philosophy XV,* ed. P. French, T. Uehling, and H. Wettstein (Notre Dame, Ind.: University of Notre Dame Press, 1990), 344–71. The phrase "emergence of norms" is the title of a book by Edna Ullmann-Margalit (Oxford: Clarendon Press, 1977).

7. "Moral Relativism Defended," *Philosophical Review* 84 (1975), 3–22; *The Nature of Morality* (Oxford: Oxford University Press, 1977); "Relativistic Ethics: Morality as Politics," *Midwest Studies in Philosophy* III, ed. P. French, T. Uehling, and H. Wettstein (Morris, Minn.: University of Minnesota Press, 1978), 109–21.

8. A decision or choice problem is one in conditions of *certainty* when the agent associates a unique outcome with each act or alternative. By contrast, if each act is associated with a number of possible outcomes and if a probability can be assigned to each possibility, then the context of choice is one of *risk.* When probabilities cannot be assigned, or where they are not meaningful, the choice problem is said to be one of *uncertainty* or *complete ignorance,* though this is somewhat controversial. Some decision theorists such as Harsanyi wish to understand apparent uncertainty (in this sense) to be a kind of risk by claiming that a particular assignment of probabilities is rational in these contexts—namely, equal probabilities. The issues are rather complex, having to do with difficult questions about the nature of probability and with the best way of combining information about value or preference with probabilities.

9. The veil of ignorance "ensures that no one is advantaged or disadvantaged in the choice of principles by the outcome of natural chance or the contingency of social circumstances. Since all are similarly situated and no one is able to design principles to favor his particular condition, the principles of justice are the result of a fair agreement or bargain." *Theory*, pp. 11, 12.

10. Rawls rejects Harsanyi's view that an assignment of equal probabilities is rational in contexts of uncertainty or ignorance.

11. *Theory*, p. 16.

12. It must be noted that Rawls now disowns his remark about the theory of justice being part of rational choice theory. It remains, however, an apt characterization of Harsanyi and Gauthier's views.

13. *Theory*, p. 4.

14. What I have called the free-rider problem should not be confused with another compliance problem, that of *assurance*: the temptation not to cooperate when one

believes that others will not cooperate. The free-rider problem occurs when agents are disposed not to cooperate (even) when assured of the cooperation of others. For this way of distinguishing the problems, see David Schmidtz, *The Limits of Government: An Essay on the Public Goods Argument* (Boulder, Colo.: Westview Press, 1991), 56.

15. "Three against Justice: The Foole, the Sensible Knave, and the Lydian Sheperd," in *Moral Dealing,* 129–49.

16. The normative and the moral should not be understood as coextensive. The former is more general than the latter; in addition to moral and political norms, there are standards of evaluation and conduct for scientific inquiry, aesthetic appreciation, rational action, etiquette, and so on. The term "normative" is used throughout in this broad way.

17. See Sinnott-Armstrong's essay in this volume.

18. Some theorists will imagine agreements between the relevant individuals to involve all the parties simultaneously. Others, by contrast, will think of agreements as essentially "pairwise," involving only small sets of people at any one time. The norms that emerge may be "universal" or "dyadic"; they may bind all individuals in an area or merely particular pairs or small groups. (I borrow the universal/dyadic distinction from Russell Hardin, *One For All: The Logic of Group Conflict* [Princeton, N.J.: Princeton University Press, 1995].) On this second view, a large group of individuals may be bound together by a series of agreements, none of which by itself connects everyone. Robert Nozick's model of the emergence of states is something like this. See *Anarchy, State, and Utopia* (New York: Basic Books, 1974), Part I. And insofar as Harman may be understood as a contractarian thinker, his account of moral conventions will be like this.

Returning to our earlier distinction between evaluative and explanatory social contract theory, it is interesting to note that actual contractarianism can easily have both explanatory and evaluative features: the actual conventions that bind one may serve both to explain and to evaluate behavior.

19. "Theories of hypothetical consent discuss not consent but cognitive agreement. It is the essence of consent that its actuality changes the normative situation. One may ask what one would have had to do had one consented. But this is in no way relevant to what one has to do given that one did not. What one would have believed in certain circumstances is equally immaterial to what one should now believe. But that one should have believed something in a hypothetical situation may and often is used as part of an argument to establish what one should now believe." Joseph Raz, *The Morality of Freedom* (Oxford: Clarendon Press, 1986), 81 n.

20. Ronald Dworkin famously argues that "a hypothetical contract is not simply a pale form of an actual contract; it is no contract at all." "Justice and Rights," in *Taking Rights Seriously* (Cambridge, Mass.: Harvard University Press, 1977), 151. It is not clear, however, that his arguments work against hypothetical agreements that are meant to be purely heuristic and to have, by themselves, no independent normative force.

21. See Raz, *Morality,* p. 84.

22. Rawls, *Theory,* p. 585.

23. The qualification to be added is that Gauthier's theory is not normally unconstrained in the same manner that Buchanan's is. For in the later versions of his theory, that is, in *Morals by Agreement,* Gauthier adopts a two stage account of agreement (inspired by Buchanan's similar account), but argues that the second stage is constrained by moral principles that emerge from rational interaction in the first. However, the

constraints that Gauthier defends—a "Lockean proviso" and a set of rights regarding appropriation—are conventional, not natural. See Morris, "Natural Rights and Public Goods," in *The Restraint of Liberty, Bowling Green Studies in Applied Philosophy* VII, ed. T. Attig, D. Callen, and J. Gray (Bowling Green, Ohio: Bowling Green State University, 1985), 102–17.

24. Contrasting "Kantian contractarianism" (e.g., Rawls) with "Hobbesian" versions (e.g., Gauthier), Will Kymlicka claims that the former "is simply an expression of prior moral commitments. . . . The ultimate evaluation of Kantian contractarianism depends, therefore, on one's commitments to the ideals of moral equality and natural duty that underlie it." "The Social Contract Tradition," in *A Companion to Ethics,* ed. P. Singer (Oxford: Blackwell Reference, 1991), 194.

25. See Hume, *Treatise,* Book III, Part II, Section II, and *Enquiry,* Section III, Part I; H. L. A. Hart, *The Concept of Law* (Oxford: Clarendon Press, 1961), 189–95; Rawls, *Theory,* pp. 126–28. The doctrine of the circumstances of justice is implicit in Hobbes's account in *Leviathan,* as well as in the thought of various proto-contractarians and moral conventionalists.

The assumption of internalism—moral requirements provide their subjects with reasons for action (see below)—seems to entail that in the absence of certain conditions, the above circumstances, there is no virtue of justice. That is, outside of the circumstances of justice, individuals have no reason to constrain their behavior in accordance with the normal requirements of justice.

26. Here it may be important to determine whether for the set of individuals in the circumstances of justice, agreement is universal and simultaneous or pairwise and sequential (or pairwise and simultaneous). (See note 18.) Are we to imagine the agreement to take place amongst all agents (in the circumstances of justice) at one time? Or might we not understand it to take place amongst pairs, or small groups, of individuals, perhaps sequentially? The normal procedure is to model the agreement in the first manner, as one involving a simultaneous choice amongst all agents. But Gauthier's conventionalist argument for constraints on his (second stage) agreement, as well as Nozick's "invisible hand" derivation of a state from pairwise agreements, suggest that the agreement need not be unanimous and simultaneous.

27. See W. D. Falk, "'Ought' and Motivation," reprinted in *The Collected Papers of W. D. Falk* (Ithaca and London: Cornell University Press, 1986), 21–41. The internalism/externalism distinction is usually formulated in terms of motivation, but it may be preferable to make it in terms of reasons, leaving aside the question of the relation between motivation and reasons.

28. Similarly—and equally trivial—our legal duties provide us with legal reasons for action.

29. See the chapter by Peter Railton. Ontological "economy" is often cited by antirealists as a comparative advantage of their theories. For a representative antirealist, see the chapter by Simon Blackburn.

30. James Rachels thinks that one of the main attractions of contractarianism is to resolve certain worries about "moral facts." "Morality is not merely a matter of customs or feelings; it has an objective basis. But the [social contract] theory does not need to postulate any special kinds of 'facts' to explain that basis. Morality is the set of rules that rational people would agree to accept for their mutual benefit. We can determine what those rules are by rational investigation and then determine whether a particular act is morally acceptable by seeing whether it conforms to the rules. Once this is understood, the old worries about moral 'objectivity' simply vanish." *Elements of Moral Philosophy* (New York: Random House, 1986), 131.

31. Leslie Green, for instance, characterizes contractarianism in terms of instrumental reason and subjective value. See *The Authority of the State* (Oxford: Clarendon Press, 1988), 124. In conversation especially, I have found these associations commonplace.

32. Issues about scope are considerably more complicated than may be suggested here. For instance, we may need to distinguish between *being owed duties* and *being protected by duties* (owed to third parties or owed to no one in particular). Some of the relevant distinctions are developed in my "Moral Standing and Rational-Choice Contractarianism," in *Contractarianism and Rational Choice,* ed. P. Vallentyne (Cambridge: Cambridge University Press, 1991), 76–95.

33. Fundamental equality of status for Christians and many other theists may be guaranteed by our being all children of God.

34. Rawls goes on to add, "Being designed to reconcile by reason, justification proceeds from what all parties to the discussion hold in common." (Rawls, *Theory,* p. 580). It is not clear that the contextuality of justification entails that the standards to which one must appeal are ones held in common.

35. For a developed "contextualist" account of moral justification, see the chapter by Mark Timmons.

36. It may be possible to restate it in terms of *values.* See Allan Gibbard, *Wise Choices, Apt Feelings: A Theory of Normative Judgment* (Cambridge, Mass.: Harvard University Press, 1990). 87 n2.

37. According to realists accepting the judgment that *p* involves thinking *p* to be true; many antirealists will deny *p* a truth-value and construe "accepting" to be the expression of a type of endorsement. Again, see the chapters by Railton and Blackburn. See also Gibbard, *Wise Choices.*

38. The stress on agreement (between different people) introduces a social element and differentiates this sort of theory from individual choice theories like those of Harsanyi, Rawls, and Brandt. For the latter see Brandt, *A Theory of the Good and the Right* (Oxford: Clarendon Press, 1979) and his chapter in this volume. A "society-based" moral theory such as David Copp's also introduces a social element but without contractarian agreement. See *Morality, Normativity, and Society* (New York: Oxford University Press, 1995). The differences between our contractarianism and the society-based approach are nicely laid out in Copp's chapter in this volume.

39. "Preferences" here should be understood broadly to include desires, needs, interests, or values, or whatever goes into determining "the balance of reasons," the set of considerations directly favoring or opposing some contemplated course of action. "Preference" is thus something of a technical term in these contexts, and it should not be supposed that preferences reflect desires or whims.

40. See Joseph Raz, *Practical Reason and Norms,* 2d ed. (Princeton, N.J.: Princeton University Press, 1990 [originally published in 1975]), chapter 1 and postscript; Michael Robins, *Intending, Promising, and Moral Autonomy* (Cambridge: Cambridge University Press, 1984); and Michael E. Bratman, *Intentions, Plans, and Practical Reason* (Cambridge, Mass.: Harvard University Press, 1987). See also Edward F. McClennen, *Rationality and Dynamic Choice* (Cambridge: Cambridge University Press, 1990); and Peter Danielson, *Artificial Morality* (London and New York: Routledge, 1992).

41. See notes 19 and 20.

42. The "implication" relation between norms, facts, and judgments is a matter of some controversy. As may be evident from these formulations, norms have a variety of implicit conditions, and it is rarely possible to state all of these explicitly.

43. A norm that exempted persons occupying special roles might be beneficial to all. For instance, norms of truth-telling may be thought so to exempt politicians, medical care providers, or parents in certain circumstances. Of course, persons occupying such roles may have to satisfy higher standards. The possibility and nature of such norms is a basic question in professional and political ethics. See Alan H. Goldman, *The Moral Foundations of Professional Ethics* (Totowa, N.J.: Rowman & Littlefield, 1980).

44. See the chapters by Copp and Sinnott-Armstrong.

45. See the illuminating discussion of these practices in Hardin, *One For All,* chapter 4.

46. For brief, accessible surveys of some of the odd but characteristic human patterns of reasoning and valuation, see Shaun Hargreaves Heap, et al., *The Theory of Choice* (Oxford: Blackwell, 1992), chapters 3–4; and Robyn M. Dawes, *Rational Choice in an Uncertain World* (New York: Harcourt Brace Jovanovitch College Publishers, 1988).

47. Additionally, our talk of moral norms and judgments must be broadened to bring in moral dispositions and moral ideals and values.

48. Kant's approach to the foundations of morality may be understood to seek reasons to be moral that do not beg the question in the manner I claim is objectionable. If it is successful (which I do not think it to be), then it would show that one need not follow the strategy I am defending.

49. "Foundationalism in Ethics," in *Ethics: Foundations, Problems, and Applications,* ed. E. Morscher and R. Stranziger (Vienna: Hölder-Pichler-Temsky, 1981), 134–36. See also "The Relation between Self-Interest and Justice in Contractarian Ethics," *Social Philosophy & Policy* 5, no. 2 (Spring 1988), 131–133.

50. Dale Jamieson calls this sort of account "derivationism" and mentions Gauthier and Brandt as examplars: they "seek to derive a moral theory from what they regard as more fundamental considerations concerning rationality. . . . Though Brandt and Gauthier are derivationists, they are not foundationalists. For they do not claim that the beliefs from which their theories are derived are self-evident or self-justifying." "Method and Moral Theory," in *A Companion to Ethics,* 482.

51. See the chapters by Geoffrey Sayre-McCord and Walter Sinnott-Armstrong. For a coherentist attack on Hobbesian political contractarianism and on preference theories respectively, see Arthur Ripstein, "Foundationalism in Political Theory," *Philosophy & Public Affairs,* 16, no. 2 (Spring 1987), 115–37; and "Preference," in *Value, Welfare, and Morality,* ed. R. G. Frey and C. Morris (Cambridge: Cambridge University Press, 1993), 93–111.

52. See note 31.

53. See *Ethics: Inventing Right and Wrong* (Harmondsworth: Penguin, 1977). Will Kymlicka, recognizing that what he calls Kantian contractarianism presupposes a prior commitment to the values of equality and of natural duty, claims that "to the Hobbesian, these ideals have no foundation. Kantian contractarianism claims to express Moral Truths, but Hobbesians deny that there are any moral truths to express. Talk of natural moral duties is 'queer,' for these alleged moral values are not visible or testable." "The Social Contract Tradition," p. 194. For the view that contractarians of our sort have trouble with normativity generally, see Jean Hampton, "Hobbes and Ethical Naturalism," in *Philosophical Perspectives,* volume 6, ed. J. Tomberlin (Altascadero, Calif.: Ridgeview Publishing, 1992), 333–54.

54. See "Self-Interest and Justice in Contractarian Ethics" and "Agent-Relative Value, Justice and the Availability of Contractarianism" (unpublished).

55. The ultimate value of *x* is *agent-relative* insofar as *x* has value from particular perspectives, those of the particular valuers *to* whom *x* is valuable. By contrast, *x* has *agent-neutral* value insofar as *x* is valuable, necessarily, from the perspective of all, or rather, of any valuer. An agent-relative value *could* but need not be a value from the perspective of all.

Suppose that the value of *x* provides *reasons*. Then agent-relative values provide reasons only to some, namely those *to* whom *x* is valuable; agent-neutral value, by contrast necessarily provides all agents with reasons. A value *to* A need not be a value *for* A, that is, a self-interested or self-regarding value. In other words, the preposition "to" is used to indicate the self as subject, the preposition "for" the self as object.

56. Value "subjectivism" in this sense is not to be confused with meta-ethical (or "meta-normative") expressivism or antirealism.

57. See Eric Mack, "Agent-Relativity of Value, Deontic Restraints, and Self-Ownership," in *Value, Welfare, and Morality*, pp. 209–32. In her attack on the notion of "a good state of affairs," Philippa Foot suggests that "perhaps no such *shared ends* appear in the foundations of ethics, where we may rather find individual ends and rational compromises between those who have them." "Utilitarianism and the Virtues," *Mind* 94, 374 (April 1985), 209.

58. *Leviathan*, ed. E. Curley (Indianapolis Ind.: Hackett Publishing, 1994 [1651]), chapter 5, 23.

59. Plato's worries about justice in the *Republic* are an illustration of this. See also Philippa Foot's worries, quoted below in note 63.

60. In the absence of an account of practical reason that allows agents to commit themselves to act against the balance of reasons, people face an additional problem: they will often lack a reason to restrain themselves *even if* guaranteed the restraint of others (the free-rider problem). (See note 14.) The plausibility of a contractarian account of justice diminishes, in my view, in the absence of some such account of rationality. Many contractarians, however, may differ with me here. See the Appendix.

61. R. M. Hare's well-known "two levels of moral thinking" is another type of indirect strategy. See *Moral Thinking: Its Levels, Method, and Point* (Oxford: Clarendon Press, 1981), chapters 2–3. See also L. W. Sumner, *The Moral Foundations of Rights* (Oxford: Clarendon Press, 1987), 181–98, 207–8.

62. It is notoriously hard to distinguish moral norms from norms of etiquette. (If gratitude is a moral virtue, and if the norm prescribing writing a thank-you letter after receiving a present is a norm of etiquette, the distinction is hard to draw. Triviality will not suffice to distinguish the two domains, as many particular moral directives may be comparatively trivial.) Similarly, in many religious cultures, it is very hard to distinguish moral and religious norms and ideals. But it is not clear that we need always sharply to distinguish these.

63. It is this feature of a virtue that creates a problem for justice. Foot asked "how, on our theory, can justice be a virtue and injustice a vice, since it will surely be difficult to show that any man whatsoever must need to be just as he needs the use of his hands and eyes, or needs prudence, courage and temperance?" Famously, she goes on to suggest that if this question "cannot be answered, then justice can no longer be recommended, as a virtue." "Moral Beliefs," in *Virtues and Vices* (Berkeley and Los Angeles: University of California Press, 1978 [originally published in 1959]), 125. Were one to abandon moral internalism (as Foot now has), then presumably one would also reject this condition on something being a virtue.

64. David Copp argues that contractarianism at best provides an account of sophisticated rational choice, extended to cover certain sorts of problems; it is not, for him,

an account of the moral. See the discussion of this chapter in this volume. This complaint is a major theme in Jean Hampton's recent papers on contractarian moral theory (see earlier references).

65. Gauthier, *Moral by Agreement.*

66. "The Social Contract Tradition," p. 193. Kymlicka immediately adds, "even if it cannot help defend those ideas." See also Jean Hampton, "Two Faces of Contractarian Thought," in *Contractarianism and Rational Choice,* pp. 31–55; and Allen Buchanan, "Justice and Reciprocity versus Subject-Centered Justice," *Philosophy & Public Affairs* 19, no. 3 (Summer 1990), 227–52.

67. *Morals by Agreement,* p. 6. He notes that he "does not assume that there must be such impartial and rational constraints. . . . We claim to demonstrate that there are rational constraints, and that these constraints are impartial. We *then* identify morality with these demonstrated constraints" (emphasis added).

68. *Morals by Agreement* is surprisingly unclear on this matter.

69. James Rachels claims that the "basic idea" of impartiality is "that each individual's interests are equally important. . . . We must acknowledge that other people's welfare is just as important as our own." Later he claims that "the requirement of impartiality, then, is at bottom nothing more than a proscription against arbitrariness in dealing with people; it is a rule that forbids us from treating one person differently from another *when there is no good reason to do so." Elements of Moral Philosophy,* pp. 9–10. The first characterization seems more substantive than the second, which is rather formal.

70. This is Copp's conclusion about contractarianism.

71. Or so I claim in "Moral Standing in Rational Choice Contractarianism." See also "Self-Interest and Justice in Contractarian Theory," and "Punishment and Loss of Moral Standing," *Canadian Journal of Philosophy* 21, no. 1 (March 1991), 53–79.

72. Gauthier recognizes that "no doubt there will be differences, perhaps significant, between the impartial and rational constraints supported by our argument, and the morality leaned from parents and peers, priests and teachers." *Morals by Agreement,* p. 6.

73. See, for instance, Margaret Urban Walker's chapter in this volume.

74. The influential utility maximization conception of practical rationality is a species of the general balance of reasons view. The *expected* utility maximization conception is a specification for contexts, of *risk,* where some way of assigning weights to probabilities is needed. The balance of reasons view, as I understand it, need not presuppose that all reasons (or values) are comparable; however, *maximization,* understood in a technical sense, does presuppose full comparability (or completeness).

75. See *Practical Reason and Norms,* chapter 1, as well as *The Morality of Freedom* (Oxford: Clarendon Press, 1986), chapters 2–3. Raz's account of exclusionary reasons may be considered part of a revisionist conception of practical rationality insofar as it allows for reasons that would have one refrain from acting on the balance of reasons. There are other revisionists accounts with which I am sympathetic (e.g., Gauthier's theory of "constrained maximization" and McClennen's "resolute choice"). (References provided in note 40.) These other theories would have us eschew standard maximizing reasoning in some interpersonal and intrapersonal contexts. Famously—or infamously, depending on one's position on these issues—Gauthier and McClennen argue that in some one-shot Prisoners' Dilemmas, it is rational *not* to select the dominant strategy. My selection of Raz's account is due in part to its greater accessibility.

76. These are "protected reasons." Raz, "Legitimate Authority," in *The Authority of Law* (Oxford: Clarendon Press, 1979), 18.

77. "[E]xclusionary reasons exclude by kind and not by weight. . . . Their impact is not to change the balance of reasons but to exclude action on the balance of reasons." The notion of exclusionary reasons Raz uses to understand the concept of legal and political authority, and specifically the difference between an order and a request: "Valid orders are not necessarily more weighty or important reasons than valid requests. . . . The difference is not in importance but in mode of operation." "Legitimate Authority," pp. 22, 23.

78. This account, it is important to understand, does not make promissory obligations absolute or indefeasible. A particular promise may be overridden. If it is, then some other second-order reason defeats the original exclusionary reason.

9

Moral Knowledge in Society-Centered Moral Theory

David Copp

We like to think that we have moral knowledge. For example, we think we know that slavery is wrong. If we do know this, however, then, of course, it must be *true* that slavery is wrong. Yet the judgment that slavery is wrong expresses an evaluation of slavery rather than a mere description of it. It is *normative.* And it is difficult to understand how this judgment could express a truth, given its normativity.

In holding that slavery was *widespread,* we hold up a mirror to the world, as it were, and reflect in our thought this fact about the world. If our thought is true, it accurately reflects something in history. In holding that slavery is *wrong,* however, we hold slavery up to our judgment and evaluation, we do not simply hold up the mirror of our thought to an aspect of the world and aim to reflect the world in our thought. The *wrongness* of slavery does not seem to be something there in the slavery that we are simply aiming to represent accurately when we hold that slavery is wrong. There seems to be no question of our thought being an accurate reflection of anything in the world. If not, then there is no question of its being true, for the truth of a proposition is a matter of its accurately representing the world.[1]

The challenge, then, is to explain how moral truth is possible, given that moral claims are normative, that they are "action-guiding," "practical," or "evaluative." There is not, unfortunately, a generally accepted theory that explains what makes a claim normative. The idea is basically that a normative proposition is essentially relevant to action or choice, because of its content.[2] But it is not immediately clear how to explain this, and we will do well enough for present purposes if we can classify a variety of central examples as normative or nonnormative, even if there are some other examples we are not certain how to classify.

Consider, then, the following examples. Ordinary nonmoral empirical claims, mathematical propositions, and scientific theories are not normative. For instance, the claims that the cat is in the window and that earthquakes sometimes occur in Los Angeles are not normative. But moral claims, many epistemological claims, and many claims in aesthetics are normative. So the following are normative claims: It is morally wrong to lie; we are justified to believe that the sun will rise tomorrow; it would be vile to wear an orange shirt with yellow trousers.

If the problem of moral knowledge is due to the normativity of moral claims, there is a similar problem about our knowledge of normative claims of other kinds. There is not a special problem about moral knowledge. But we need to begin somewhere, and the issue I want to address in this paper is the possibility of moral knowledge.

I therefore assume that we know a great variety of things about the world. There is room to debate how to account for such knowledge, but we do not need to have settled these debates about nonmoral knowledge in order to address the problem of moral knowledge. The problem about moral knowledge takes the same shape, regardless of which position one takes on these larger background epistemological issues.

I also assume that some normative claims are true. For example, I assume it is true that many of our beliefs are justified. Since, on the account I have given, the problem of moral knowledge arises because of the normativity of moral claims, I am simplifying our problem greatly by assuming certain normative claims in epistemology are true. Otherwise, however, we would need to address quite general issues about normative knowledge before we could address issues about moral knowledge. Indeed the claim to know anything at all is one that, at least arguably, entails a normative epistemological claim: the claim to be justified in one's belief, or perhaps, the claim not to have violated any epistemic norms in believing as one does. If we do not assume that some normative claims are true, we could not assume that we know anything at all.

The problem I want to tackle, however, is to explain how we can have moral knowledge. The problem has two parts: The first is to explain what propositions we express when we make moral claims in a way that accounts for the normativity of the claims. The second is to explain how we could be in a position to have knowledge that some such propositions are true. Of course, the second problem may be trivial, once we have a satisfactory account of moral propositions, but that remains to be seen.

Moral Propositions

Some philosophers hold that insofar as moral claims are normative, they do not express propositions; that is, they think, the normative content expressed by a moral claim is not a statement that could be literally true or false. In making moral claims, we do not describe or represent the world as being one way rather than another. Rather, we express our moral attitudes, our acceptance of certain norms, or our prescriptions for the world.[3] In a roughly similar way, crying may express sorrow; it does not describe sorrow or express any true or false proposition about sorrow.

To be sure, the claim that it was wrong of Alan to sell Bill into slavery does express the proposition that Alan sold Bill. However, its normative content is the claim that Alan's action was wrong, and this claim, these philosophers would hold, does not describe what Alan did. Rather, a person who makes this claim thereby expresses an attitude toward what Alan did, namely, her moral disapproval of what he did, or perhaps her acceptance of a norm that prohibits what he did.

This view is often called "antidescriptivism." Another common name for it is "noncognitivism." It is one way to attempt to account for the normativity of moral claims in a theory of what is expressed when a person makes a moral claim.

If antidescriptivism were correct, moral knowledge simply would not be possible. The idea that we could *know* that slavery is wrong, or even *believe* it, would be as nonsensical, if taken literally, as the idea that we could know or believe the imperative "Abolish slavery!" For again, to know something, it must be true, and propositions are the things that have truth value. Of course, it is *grammatical* to say we believe and know that slavery is wrong. But antidescriptivism implies that it nevertheless *makes no sense* to claim that we have such beliefs or such knowledge, at least not if we take the claims literally.

I shall assume, however, that moral claims do express propositions. This assumption is supported in part by my earlier assumption that some normative epistemological claims are true. I assume, for example, that it is true that we are justified in believing the sun will rise tomorrow. If so, then this claim about our being justified expresses a proposition even though it is normative. That is, *some* normative claims express propositions. It would therefore be puzzling if the normativity of moral claims meant that *they* do not express propositions.

The assumption that moral claims express propositions is supported as well by considerations of intuitiveness and simplicity. It is common sense to think that we have moral beliefs. For instance, I believe that slavery is wrong. If moral claims did not express propositions, however, it could not be that I believe this, except perhaps in some attenuated sense different from the sense in which it is true that I believe slavery used to be widespread. But consider the following sentence: "I believe that slavery used to be widespread and also that it was wrong." Intuitively, the term "believe" is not equivocal in this sentence. But if moral claims did not express propositions, *believe* would be equivocal in this sentence in the way *beat* is equivocal in "Yesterday I beat John in tennis and also some eggs in a bowl."[4] This and a variety of other considerations illustrate the intuitive implausibility of antidescriptivism.

The fundamental idea of antidescriptivism is that insofar as moral claims are normative, they are expressive of attitudes rather than descriptive of the world. In his chapter in this volume, Simon Blackburn argues that this underlying idea is compatible with the thesis that moral claims are literally true or false. (It would follow that they express propositions.) His argument depends on a minimalist or "disquotational" account of truth according to which, for a sentence *s,* the claim that *s* is *true* is equivalent to the claim that *s.* For example, the claim that it is true that slavery is wrong is equivalent to the claim that slavery is wrong. On this view, the claim that slavery is wrong can straightforwardly be said to be true by anyone who would claim that slavery is wrong. I said before that we face the challenge of explaining how moral truth is possible. On Blackburn's view, the "challenge" is trivial.

A full discussion of the disquotational theory is well beyond the scope of this essay. But there is a problem with Blackburn's combination of the disquotational theory with antidescriptivism. It is a truism, guaranteed by our concept of truth, that a claim is true only if it is accurate to the facts. For example, if it is true that slavery was once widespread, then the claim that slavery was once widespread is accurate to the facts. This truism is not something an antidescriptivist can easily accept, however, if he also accepts the disquotational theory.

The antidescriptivist holds that normative moral claims are not straightforwardly descriptive of the world; that is, they do not represent or describe any facts as being a certain way. If moral claims do not represent any facts, however, then, at least insofar as they are normative, they cannot be accurate to any facts. The disquotational theorist insists that moral claims can nevertheless be true, even though they are normative. If so, however, then moral claims may be true even if they are not accurate to the facts. This is quite implausible. It would mean holding that it may be true that slavery is wrong even if the claim that slavery is wrong is not accurate to the facts.[5]

As I said, I shall assume that moral claims express propositions, that they are literally true or false. I reject antidescriptivism or noncognitivism. This leaves us, however, with the first of the problems I mentioned before, the problem of explaining the content of moral propositions in a way that accounts for their normativity.

Moral Propositions and Moral Standards

Let me introduce the idea of a *standard.* Rules and norms are examples of standards. A standard is expressible by means of an imperative. For example, there is a standard that calls on us to brush our teeth after every meal; it is expressed by the imperative, "Brush your teeth after every meal." A standard could be quite arbitrary. Consider, "Pull a tooth after every meal."

The idea of a standard should not be difficult, for we do have the idea that imperatives express something. Imperatives have "content," or "meaning" even though they do not express propositions, even though they do not express things that could be true or false. Imperatives express standards, I say.

We hold that slavery is wrong, and there is a corresponding standard, which could be expressed by an imperative prohibiting slavery.[6] Indeed, we speak intuitively of moral norms and moral rules. We would express such norms and rules using imperatives; hence, they are standards in my sense of the word.

There are, then, standards that correspond to moral claims that we take to be true, in the way the standard prohibiting slavery, or calling for there not to be slavery, corresponds to the claim that slavery is wrong. Similarly, however, there are standards that correspond to moral claims that we take to be false, such as a standard calling for the existence of slavery. But we think that the standard calling for there not to be slavery is authoritative or justified in a way that any standard calling for the existence of slavery is not. For since we think slavery is *wrong,* we must think that a standard prohibiting slavery is relevantly *authoritative* or *justified.* I do not mean that it has been justified *by* anyone, or that someone has *given* it authority, but that it has a *status* in virtue of which it may be true that slavery is wrong.

This idea is at the root of the theory I will present. In the central cases, I propose, a moral proposition is true only if a related moral standard is justified. For example, slavery is wrong only if a standard prohibiting slavery, or calling for it not to exist, is appropriately justified.[7] Indeed, I propose more generally that in the central cases a normative proposition is true only if some corresponding standard has an appropriate status or standing. I call this the "standard-based theory" of normative judgment. It says, for example, that propositions of law are true only if corresponding legal standards have an appropriate standing in the local legal system.

What I have said so far begins to account for "positive" and unconditional normative propositions, which are the central cases. I call them the "paradigmatic" normative propositions. They are true only if a relevant standard has a relevant standing. But what I have said does not account for certain normative propositions in which a paradigmatic proposition is embedded, such as the proposition that if swimming is wrong, it will disappear from the world. This proposition could be true even though swimming is not wrong, and so it could be true even though no justified moral standard prohibits swimming. Propositions of this kind are "nonparadigmatic"; it is not a necessary condition of their truth that some corresponding standard have a relevant standing. Some paradigmatic normative proposition is embedded in each nonparadigmatic proposition; in the example, the proposition that swimming is wrong is embedded in the conditional that if swimming is wrong, it will disappear.[8] I will ignore nonparadigmatic normative propositions in most of what follows.

The standard-based theory is intended to explain the normativity of normative claims. A claim is normative just in case it expresses a normative proposition. Leaving aside the nonparadigmatic cases, a proposition is normative just in case it entails (nontrivially) the existence of a standard that is appropriately justified or has an appropriate standing.[9] Standards call for certain things to be done or to be chosen. This is what accounts for the normativity of these propositions. According to the standard-based theory, a (paradigmatic) normative proposition is essentially relevant to action or choice because it entails (nontrivially) the existence of a standard with an appropriate status that calls for action or choice.[10]

There are different kinds of normative propositions, including moral propositions, propositions of law, and certain epistemological propositions. The standard-based theory leaves us with a key question regarding each of these kinds: What standing must the corresponding standards have as a condition of the truth of propositions of that kind? This question is a substantive theoretical one. It is not a question that can be settled by conceptual analysis alone, nor is it a question that is settled by the standard-based theory alone. In the moral case, the key question is this: What status must a moral standard have, in order for a moral proposition to be true?

Each meta-ethical theory can be construed as implying an answer to this question, as I will briefly illustrate, before giving my own answer. Of course, few theories have been constructed with the aim of answering the question, for the standard-based theory is not widely accepted. The fact that it can nevertheless help us to organize the space of meta-ethical theory is one thing that recommends it.

A Brief Catalogue of Theories of Moral Justification

Suppose we had an account of the conditions under which a moral standard would be justified. Given the standard-based theory, we could then explain both the normative content of paradigmatic moral propositions and the nature of moral properties. The standard-based theory says that if slavery is wrong, it is prohibited by a justified moral standard. This suggests that the proposition that slavery is wrong is a proposition about slavery's (at least) being prohibited by a justified moral standard. It also suggests that the property of being wrong is the property of (at least) being prohibited by a justified moral standard. If we had a theory of justified moral standards, we could use it to explain the nature of moral properties and the content of moral propositions involving those properties.

A number of familiar moral theories can be construed as making proposals about the conditions under which moral standards would be relevantly justified. I will briefly describe three.

Each of us benefits from the fact that the local culture has a moral component, and we benefit if the people we deal with in our society adhere to a moral code. Plainly, the currency of some moral codes in the culture would serve each of us better than would the currency of others. Richard Brandt has proposed, in effect, that the code that is justified relative to *me* is the code that *I* would be rational to choose for my society. And in general, a moral standard is justified relative to a person just in case the standard is a part of a moral code which she would be rational to choose for currency in her society.[11]

Despite the individualistic nature of this approach, Brandt suggests in places that moral propositions are propositions about the standards *every* person in a relevant society would support for currency in the society, if he were fully informed and rational; a moral proposition is true only if the corresponding standard is a part of a moral code that everyone in a society would be rational to choose for currency in the society.[12] Call this the "unanimity interpretation."

Unfortunately, as Brandt has conceded, there is no guarantee that the moral system justified in his sense relative to one person is the same as the system justified relative to a second person, even if they belong to the same society.[13] As I shall say, "rational unanimity" is not guaranteed. For example, suppose that Stanley and Stella are the parents of a small child. Stanley's system might call for child-care duties to be performed by the female parent, and Stella's system might call for child-care duties to be performed by the male parent. Given this, the unanimity reading says that neither parent has any obligation to take care of their child since no standard concerned with child care would be justified relative to everyone in the society. Each parent may do everything required of her, given the system justified relative to the society, and yet neither of them may contribute anything to the care of their child.

It may seem that Brandt could solve this problem if he did not demand unanimity. Moral propositions could be interpreted as propositions about standards that *some* relevant person would support for her society if she were fully informed and rational. On this individualistic interpretation, a moral proposition is true only if the corresponding standard is a part of a moral code that the relevant person would be rational to choose for currency in her society.[14]

Unfortunately, if we apply this individualistic reading to the case of Stanley and Stella, Brandt's theory now implies that Stanley has no obligation to take care of their child, given the moral system justified relative to him, and Stella has no obligation to take care of their child, given the moral system justified relative to her.

On both the unanimity and the individualistic interpretations, therefore, the fact that rational unanimity is not guaranteed can lead to a troubling result for Brandt's theory. The example of Stanley and Stella illustrates one important benefit for everyone in a society if (nearly) everyone in the society subscribes to (largely) the same moral standards. The benefit is that people are able to coordinate their behavior, to cooperate, and to anticipate how other people will respond to them, in interacting with them. Brandt realizes this, of course, for in his approach, we consider which moral code to support for the society as a whole. Yet we consider this one by one; Brandt's theory is fundamentally individualistic. Because of this, different codes might qualify as justified relative to different persons even if all persons need a common code in order to live together successfully in their common society. In the example of Stanley and Stella, it is likely that each parent wants their child to be cared for. A compromise might call on the parents to share the responsibility of caring for their children. Each may be rational to prefer that all subscribe to some such compromise moral code rather than the code justified for him in Brandt's scheme. In such a situation, it seems more plausible to take the compromise code to be relevantly justified.

This is the insight behind contractarian theories. There is a tension between two ideas, each of which is accepted by contractarians. First, the point of morality is to enable groups of persons to get along together. But second, a moral code is binding on a person only if he would be rational to subscribe to it and comply with it. The tension is due to the fact that there is no guarantee that everyone in a group would be rational to subscribe to and comply with the same moral code if each of them evaluated moral codes without paying attention to the reasoning of the others. The contractarian solution is to propose that the justified code relative to a group is the code that would be agreed to as a result of rational bargaining among the members, provided that every member would be rational to subscribe to it and comply with it. Christopher Morris defends an approach of this kind in his chapter in this volume, and David Gauthier has also proposed a theory of this kind.[15]

Given this account of justified moral standards, the standard-based theory tells us the following: A moral proposition is true only if the corresponding standard is such that (a) it is part of the moral code that everyone in a relevant group would rationally agree to accept as the code for the group, as a result of rational bargaining, and (b) everyone in the group would be rational to comply with it and to subscribe to it.

Nothing guarantees that such a group is an entire society. Of course, a contractarian could stipulate that a relevant group must be an entire society, but nothing in contractarianism makes this a natural stipulation. For Gauthier, a relevant group would be a group of persons that find cooperation to be mutually beneficial. This could be a small part of a society, a group that is able to exercise power over the rest of the society and exploit it. And the standards that qualify as justified by the contractarian test, if any, could be ones that the exploiters are rational to subscribe to and comply with because doing so enables them to cooperate efficiently in exploiting the society as a whole, as if it were a natural resource. I do not find this a persuasive account of morality. It seems, rather, to be an account of a sophisticated extension of the theory of rational choice to cases where each member of a group with shared interests can benefit from a strategy of committing himself to certain standards for interactions with others in the group.[16]

One might think that an adequate account of morality must show that justified moral standards are binding on all moral agents, without exception. This traditional idea would be accepted by Kantians, as well as by many others whose thinking has been influenced by Kant. And Kantians share with contractarians the idea that compliance with a standard must be rational, if the standard is binding on a person. The combination of these ideas suggest the position that a moral standard is justified just in case every rational agent would comply with it. Call this the "Kantian thesis."[17]

To avoid circularity, however, a Kantian theory would need a "morally neutral" conception of rational agency. Obviously I cannot explore all the possibilities. But I am doubtful that there is a plausible construal of rational agency that is morally neutral and that also makes plausible the Kantian thesis.

For example, one might construe rational agency as self-interested agency. It seems highly implausible, however, that a justified moral standard is such that, necessarily, every (well-informed) strictly self-interested agent would comply with it. Moreover, the fact that some self-interested agent might not comply with a standard calling for loyalty or honesty seems no objection whatever to the claim that the standard is morally authoritative or justified.

Given the standard-based theory, the notion of rational agency as such is not morally neutral. A rational agent is an agent who is responsive to reasons, and an agent who is responsive to reasons is responsive to justified standards that call on her to do things. These would include justified moral standards. Indeed, the way I apply the standard-based theory, the proposition that a person has a reason to do something is exactly the proposition that a justified standard calls on her to do the thing. The proposition that a person has a *moral* reason to do something is the proposition that a justified *moral* standard calls on her to do it. Hence, on the standard-based theory, one cannot explain the idea of a justified moral standard by invoking the idea of a rational agent as such because the idea of rational agency is explained partly by reference to the idea of a justified moral standard.

This has been a very brief discussion of alternatives to my own view. Let me nevertheless forge ahead.

Society-Centered Justification

I cannot hope to do much more than introduce the main idea of the approach I favor, together with some of the reasons that persuade me of its plausibility. I have developed the approach in more detail elsewhere.[18]

The central idea of society-centered theory is expressed by the following thesis, which I call the "justification thesis":

> A moral code is justified in relation to a society just in case the society would be rationally required to select the code to serve in it as the social moral code, in preference to any alternative.

In a fuller account, this thesis would need various qualifications, two of which I will discuss below, but, for now, let me ignore the qualifications.

I have been using the term "justified" to do duty for whatever status moral standards must have as a necessary condition of the truth of corresponding (paradigmatic) moral propositions. I now claim that the justification thesis explains this status. That is, standards that are part of a code justified in the sense given by the justification thesis are justified in the way that they must be as a necessary condition of the truth of corresponding moral propositions.

Call this claim the "linkage thesis," for it links society-centered theory with the standard-based theory in an account of the truth conditions of moral propositions.

Many things need to be explained before it can be clear why I believe the justification thesis and what I mean by it. I need to introduce a notion of rationality that is morally neutral in the sense I used before. And I need to say more about moral propositions before I can motivate and explain the linkage thesis. I will return to the linkage thesis in a later section. Let me begin by explaining the idea of a social moral code and the idea of subscription to a standard.

By a "social moral code" I mean a system of moral standards that is shared among the members of a society, that is socially enforced, and that is transmitted from generation to generation with the culture. A social moral code has currency in a society in the sense that the members of the society generally subscribe morally to the standards in the code.

A person's moral standards play a distinctive role in her psychology; they are standards to which she takes a complex attitude I call "moral subscription." This is not simply a matter of accepting or endorsing a standard. For if a standard is among a person's moral standards, if the person "subscribes morally" to the standard, as I say, then she intends to conform to it, and to support conformity to it. She tends to have a favorable attitude toward those in her society who comply with it and to have an unfavorable attitude toward those who fail to comply. A person who subscribes morally to a standard wants it to have currency in her society; that is, she wants it to be generally so, in her society, that people have these intentions, desires, and attitudes regarding the standard; she wants the standard to be included in the social moral code of her society. Subscribing morally to a standard is, then, a complex of attitudes toward it that is reflected in a person's intentions, desires, and attitudes toward herself and others in her society. A person's "moral code" is the set of standards she subscribes to in this way.

Now, I think it is common sense that a society needs a social moral code; that is, a society needs it to be the case that there is, among its members, a shared system of moral standards which plays this complex role in the psychology of its members, and which is socially enforced and culturally transmitted. A society needs an efficient way to reduce the harmfulness of conflict among its members and to give its members the security they need in order to cooperate successfully. And the currency of a moral code is, I believe, the most efficient way to achieve these ends. Other things equal, a society with a social moral code would experience less conflict, and less harmful conflict among its members, and more cooperation among them, and its members would be more successful at meeting their own needs and pursuing their values, than would be the case if the society did not have a social moral code.

A legal system can supplement a shared moral code, but cannot replace morality. For although coercion and self-interest can do some of the work in bringing about compliance with law, it is doubtful that they can do all of the work. Some people must enforce the legal rules and operate the system, and it is unlikely that they could be motivated solely by self-interest. It is also doubtful that they could sustain the system if everyone in the society were motivated solely by coercion and self-interest. It would be much better, from the point of view of the society as a whole, if people widely subscribed to a background moral requirement to comply with law.

I hold then, and I believe it is common sense, that a society needs a social moral code. With a social moral code, a society does better than it otherwise could at meeting its need to have cooperative interaction, and to avoid harmful conflict, among its members. Furthermore, I believe, it is common sense that some moral codes would better serve the needs of society than others. The better codes are the ones whose currency would better enable a society to meet its needs.

Given differences in the circumstances of societies, moreover, the code that would best serve the needs of one society might be different from the code that would best serve the needs of another society. A society facing an epidemic might need the currency of a prohibition of certain kinds of behavior where, in the absence of the epidemic, it would have had no need of the prohibition. Intuitively, the prohibition would have a kind of justification in the face of the epidemic that it would lack in the absence of the epidemic.

Society-centered moral theory is a development of these ideas. To begin, I think that we have a reason to pursue satisfaction of our basic needs. By a basic need, I mean a fundamental need the status of which, as something needed by a person, does not depend on the person's happening to have a desire that the thing is a means to satisfying. Food and water are examples of things for which we have a basic need in this sense. Societies also have reason to pursue satisfaction of their basic needs, including their need to have cooperative interaction, and to avoid harmful conflict, among their members. Hence, the fact that the currency of some given moral code would better serve the (basic) needs of a society than would the currency of some other code means that the society has reason to prefer the first code. And I want to claim that the code that would best serve its needs, the code whose currency it has reason to prefer over that of any other code, is the code that is justified relative to that society.[19] Hence the justification thesis. And according to the linkage thesis, as I said, a code that is so justified is justified in a sense that underwrites the truth of corresponding moral propositions.

I now must explain some of the ideas that I have been taking as given, such as the idea of a society, the idea of a society's making a choice, and the idea that the rational choice for a society is the one that would best serve its needs.

Societies and Rational Societal Choice

Unfortunately, the idea of a society is readily misunderstood because of a common tendency to think that any fairly large group of people can be counted as a society. In the sense I have in mind, however, societies are quite large multigenerational groups that are somewhat socially independent and self-sufficient in much the way and to the degree that the populations of states such as Mexico or Germany are socially independent and self-sufficient. Leon Mayhew says that a society is usually characterized as "a relatively independent or self-sufficient population characterized by internal organization, territoriality, cultural distinctiveness and sexual recruitment."[20] A more detailed and precise account would take up more space than I have.[21]

The metaphysics of this should not be a problem. A suit of clothes is simply various articles of clothing that are suitably related to one another, and a family is simply various persons who are relevantly related to one another. Similarly, a society is simply a population of persons who stand in certain characteristic complex relations to one another.

Some readers may doubt that it makes sense to think of a society as making a choice. But it surely makes sense to think of a couple as making a choice. We all know of many couples that decided to get married, to have a family, and so on. There is nothing mysterious about this. It is enough if the two people in the couple reach an agreement or form a consensus about what to do. Similarly, a discussion group can make a choice if its members can reach a consensus about what to discuss. There does not appear to be any number of members such that a discussion group with more than that number of members can discuss things but cannot choose what to discuss. It seems, then, that groups can make choices. Societies may be too large and diverse, and communication among their members may be too sporadic, for them actually to reach a consensus on anything very important, but there appears to be no theoretical barrier to a society's making a choice. This is possible, at least in principle.

Recall that applying the justification thesis requires evaluating a hypothetical societal choice, not an actual one. The issue raised by the thesis is whether a society *would* be rational to choose a given moral code to serve as its social moral code. Notice too that the issue is whether a *society* would be rational to choose a given code. This is different from the issue of whether each member of the society would be rational to choose the code. A society may be rational to choose something from its perspective even if some of its members would not be rational to choose it from their perspectives. This point will be explained in what follows.

I have said that a society's choice is rational when it best meets the society's (basic) needs. This is a simplification of a more complex view. Yet we do in general have reason to satisfy our basic needs. To be sure, our options can be assessed from a variety of standpoints, using a variety of standards. But I have in mind here assessments of an agent's options from the standpoint of the agent himself. Such assessments are sometimes said to concern "self-interested rationality," although I prefer the more neutral label, "self-grounded rationality." From his own standpoint, I think, any agent has reason to choose what would best satisfy his basic needs.

Of course, I cannot hope to defend this claim adequately here.[22] A full defense of it would require a full explanation of what is meant by a basic need as well as an explanation of why, as I would claim, we have reason to satisfy our basic needs even if we would prefer to do otherwise. The issues here are difficult, but I think the basic idea is intuitively plausible.

It may be difficult to give a philosophical analysis of the concept of a basic need, yet I believe the concept is a familiar and a viable one. We need food and water, for example. These are basic needs of the sort at issue here. And although different philosophers would give different accounts of the relation between reasons and needs, I believe most would agree that each of us has a reason from his own standpoint, or a self-grounded reason, to pursue the satisfaction of basic needs. Each of us has a reason to seek food and water, for example. Moreover, I believe most would agree that a person has a reason to satisfy his basic needs even if he doesn't want to eat or to drink and even if he wants something else that he cannot have unless he does not eat or drink. This much agreement may be sufficient for my purposes.

Those who disagree can interpret the justification thesis in terms of their own preferred account of self-grounded rationality, extended to the case of societies. Some may think, for example, that self-grounded rationality is simply a matter of satisfying one's preferences. On this view, the rational choice for a society would be the choice that best satisfies the society's preferences, which would presumably be understood as some aggregate of the preferences of its members. Given this, the justification thesis implies that a moral code is justified relative to a society just in case, roughly, the currency of the code in the society would best satisfy the society's preferences.

I believe, however, that if we imagine a society making a choice, then the rational choice for the society, considered as such, is the option that would best serve its basic needs. Its choosing would consist in its members reaching a consensus on a given option. The rationality of such a consensus, assessed from the standpoint of the society considered as a whole, would depend on how well the option would serve the society's needs.[23]

What then does a society need? First, it needs to ensure its physical integrity, to ensure that the population it is continues to exist. Second, it needs cooperative integrity, to ensure that there continues to be a system of cooperation among its members. This requires that it ensure internal social harmony. Third, a society needs peaceful and cooperative relationships with neighboring societies.

To meet all of these needs, a society needs, among other things, to ensure that at least the bulk of its members are able to meet their basic needs as humans and persons. In most circumstances, moreover, it can best meet its needs by ensuring that *all* members are able to meet their basic needs with rough equality. There may be extreme circumstances in which a society cannot meet everyone's basic needs, or cannot equally meet everyone's basic needs. And a society may need to deter some individuals from antisocial behavior by threatening punishments through a legal system. But leaving aside issues of punishment and deterrence, and leaving aside extreme circumstances, a society best meets its needs by ensuring that its members are able to meet their needs with rough equality. This is the default case, although as I said, extreme circumstances may dictate otherwise. In the absence of a special reason connected to its needs, there is no reason from the standpoint of the society to favor one group over another. And people are more likely than otherwise to contribute willingly and well to the overall flourishing of the society when they have been able to meet their needs. So, I believe, a society does best to ensure that everyone is able to meet her basic needs.

Given these claims, the justification thesis implies that a justified moral code would be such that its currency in a society would best contribute to the society's meeting the needs I have described. The currency of the code would promote the physical and cooperative integrity of the society, by promoting internal social harmony and the ability of each member to meet her basic needs, other things being equal, and it would promote peaceful and cooperative relationships with neighboring societies.

Societies are alike in having these basic needs, and justified moral codes are alike in being such that their currency would enable the relevant society to meet these needs. Differences in circumstances can make for differences in how these basic needs are best met. But when combined with my views about reason and needs and about the needs of societies, the justification thesis implies that there will be a deep similarity among the moral codes justified relative to different societies.

An Amendment: Overlapping Societies

I said above that the justification thesis needs to be amended in various ways. To simplify matters, I am here going to discuss only two of the necessary amendments. The first is intended to deal with overlapping societies and the second, which I discuss in the next section, is intended to deal with cases where no single moral code would be best for a society.

The overlap problem is due to the fact that societies can overlap, and one society can be contained within another. People can therefore belong to more than one society. If society *S* overlaps society *S'*, the unamended justification thesis leaves open the possibility that different moral codes are justified relative to *S* and *S'*. And it could turn out that a person belonging to both societies faces a standard justified relative to *S* which calls on him to do *A* and a standard justified relative to *S'* which calls on him *not* to do *A*.

For example, Inuit society is contained within the larger North American society. Given the extreme circumstances faced by the traditional Inuit society some decades ago, it may be that it would have best served the needs of that society if the social moral code required elderly people to sacrifice their lives to save their families from starvation during especially dangerous weather conditions when food was scarce. It presumably would not have served the needs of the larger North American society for its social moral code to include such a requirement. Suppose, however, that the moral code justified relative to the larger society included a prohibition on suicide. This would mean that a person could be required to sacrifice herself by the justified Inuit code but prohibited from sacrificing herself by the justified code of the larger society.

In cases of nesting, there is a society that contains the smaller societies nested within it. In cases of overlap, there is a population that is the mereological sum of the overlapping smaller societies; I will deem this population to be a society for present purposes, with the result that cases of overlap can be treated in the same way as cases of nesting. In cases of nesting or overlap, other things being equal, I want to say that if the code that best serves the needs of the smaller society includes a standard that cannot be complied with by someone in the smaller society except by failing to comply with a standard justified relative to the larger society, then the former standard is not justified all things considered. That is, the code that is justified relative to the smaller society is the code that best meets the needs of that society without conflicting with the code justified relative to the larger society. The code that best meets the needs of the smaller society is to be amended in a minimal way to avoid conflict with the code justified relative to the larger society. In the case of the Inuit, for example, the elderly would be required to sacrifice themselves for their family provided that, as seems likely, the code justified relative to the larger society did not *prohibit* such sacrifices. If, contrary to fact, it did prohibit such sacrifices, then the elderly would actually be wrong to sacrifice themselves.

This amendment meshes with the characteristic idea of society-centered theory, which is, we could say, to give priority to societies over less inclusive groups. Suppose that the needs of a certain group would be best served if its members subscribed to a given moral code. It might be a group of entrepreneurs, a group of professors, or a criminal gang. It might be the group of white residents of South Africa. The code might require the members of the group to promote the interests of the group. I would not want to say on this basis alone that the group's code is justified. I would not want to say on this basis that the members of the group do nothing morally wrong if they promote the interests of the group. Whether the members do something wrong depends on the content of the moral code whose currency in the society as a whole would best serve the needs of the entire society. In this sense, society-centered theory gives priority to societies over less inclusive groups. The amendment I am proposing here extends this priority to larger societies over societies included within them.

This amendment ensures even greater similarity among the moral codes justified relative to different societies than is already ensured by the fact that societies have the same basic needs. I believe that most societies overlap with other societies or are contained within other societies. Indeed, I believe that, in the modern world, there is a global society, embracing all the peoples of the earth. This is an optimistic belief, but if it is true, then the amendment enforces a fundamental kind of coherence among justified moral codes.

An Amendment: Ties

I believe it is quite unlikely that several moral codes would be exactly equally well suited to enabling a society to meet its needs. But whether or not it is likely, it is theoretically possible for several moral codes to be "tied" in this way in relation to a society. The society would have to choose among the tied codes, but none of the codes would be the best code, and so none would be the code that the society is rationally required to choose. Hence, according to the unamended justification thesis, none of the codes would qualify as justified.

Codes that are tied could have some standards in common. If so, then I want to say that these standards qualify as justified. Let the justification thesis be understood to imply this. Unfortunately, codes that are tied might have no standards in common.

If several codes are tied for best relative to a society, then, given my position, the society would be rationally required to choose *among* the codes. Moreover, if one of the tied codes already had currency in the society, it would be reasonable to count it as justified. The fact that it already is the social moral code would give it the edge if the social costs of changing the moral culture were taken into account. I therefore propose that "choice breaks ties." This proposal gives a preference to the moral status quo, but only in cases where there is no alternative that the society is rationally required to choose instead of the status quo.

Suppose, however, that we have a tie in a case where the existing moral code of a society is not among the best moral codes the society could choose. The possibility of ties in cases of this kind suggests the possibility of indeterminacy in morality. Certain kinds of indeterminacy may be reasonable to expect, however.

Suppose, for example, that a given society needs the currency of a code that calls for everyone to be enabled to meet her basic needs; yet suppose that several different codes of this kind are equally eligible to serve as the society's social moral code. Code C attributes a right to each person to be enabled to meet her needs and therefore entitles people to complain on their own behalf if they are denied the ability to meet their needs; code C' postulates a requirement of justice that people be enabled to meet their needs, but it does not imply that there is a right to be enabled to meet one's needs.[24] Assume that codes C and C' are tied for best. In this case, the society would be rationally required to choose between the codes; let us say that the disjunction of C and C' would be justified. There would not be a right to be enabled to meet one's needs, and there would not be a requirement of justice that everyone be enabled to meet her needs. The choice between these ways of conceptualizing matters would be underdetermined. Yet there would be a moral flaw in the society if people were not enabled to meet their needs.

The Linkage Thesis

The important issue for our purposes is this: In what sense must a moral standard be justified as a condition of the truth of a corresponding moral proposition? According to the linkage thesis, society-centered theory gives the answer to this question: A moral standard is justified in the sense that it must be, as a necessary condition of the truth of a corresponding (paradigmatic) moral proposition, just in case it is included in the moral code that a relevant society would be rationally required to select as its social moral code.[25]

The linkage thesis is supported by a number of intuitions. First, moral nihilism is the position that there are no moral truths—that there are no true (paradigmatic) moral propositions. Nihilism seems intuitively untenable, given the intuition we discussed before that a society needs to have a social moral code. The linkage thesis explains this intuitive connection between the latter intuition and the falsity of nihilism. According to the view I have developed, the fact that a society needs a social moral code means that the society would be rational to select a code to serve as its social moral code. Given the justification thesis (and ignoring the possibility of ties), it follows that some moral code is justified relative to the society. And given the linkage thesis and the standard-based theory, it follows that the nihilist has no reason to deny that there are true moral propositions. For the key necessary condition of there being true moral propositions is satisfied—namely, certain moral standards are relevantly justified.

A second intuition that supports the linkage thesis is the idea shared by many of us that the function of morality is to make society possible. Contractarians seem to share this intuition, for they typically stress the advantages that a shared morality brings to society. But contractarianism is essentially individualistic. It gives each member of society a rational veto over the content of morality; that is, if some member would not be rational to agree to certain standards for the society, or if he would not be rational to comply with them, they do not qualify as justified in relation to the society. The analogous contractarian view about debating rules for a legislature would imply that each member of a legislature has a rational veto over the content of its rules; that is, if some member would not be rational to agree to certain rules, or if he would not be rational to comply with them, they are not justified for the legislature. A member who found it in his interest to insist on a rule that permitted filibustering would be able to say that no rule that would prohibit filibustering is justified. It would be natural to reply that the function of debating rules is to facilitate debates in the legislature, and that a rule that permitted filibustering is therefore unacceptable and unjustified. Similarly, I maintain, it is natural to object to moral contractarianism that the function of morality is to make things go well in society. Because of this, a moral standard may be justified even if some member who is pursuing his interests would find it rational to refuse to agree to it, or to fail to comply with it.

Now, the idea that the function of the heart is to pump blood is at least in part the idea that the primary standard for evaluating a heart is on the basis of how well it pumps blood. A heart that pumps well is functioning well; it is a good one. Similarly, the idea that the function of a moral code is to make society possible is the idea that the primary criterion for evaluating a moral code is on the basis of how well it serves society. And since the needs of a society are the things it must have in order to continue to exist and to thrive, it is a small step to conclude that the primary criterion for evaluating a moral code is on the basis of how well it serves the needs of society.

Consider the standards in a code that serves well the needs of a society. I will now argue that corresponding moral propositions must then be true insofar as they are normative. For example, if a standard that rules out slavery is one of the standards in a code that meets the primary functional criterion for evaluating moral codes, then any plausible theory must imply that it is true that slavery is morally ruled out. Otherwise true moral propositions would entail that certain standards are justified, and these standards might be different from the standards that meet the primary criterion for evaluating moral codes. The former would meet a truth-conduciveness criterion of evaluation while the latter would meet the primary functional criterion of evaluation for moral codes. This would be a very untidy result in a theory of moral truth and moral belief. It would mean that a person complying with, and making moral judgments in accord with, a moral code that met the functional criterion for evaluating moral codes might be acting otherwise than he truly ought to act and might be making moral judgments that are not true. There would be a tension between the goal of having true moral beliefs, and complying with the corresponding standards, and the goal of complying with moral standards that are the best moral standards. Hence, the intuition that the function of morality is to make society possible leads to the linkage thesis, given the usual norms for the construction of theories.

Relativism and Moral Truth

I have been using the term "justified" in the phrase "justified moral standard" to do duty for whatever status moral standards must have in order for corresponding paradigmatic moral propositions to be true. The linkage thesis says that the status a moral standard can have of being justified is a relation to a society. In particular, it is the status of being included in the moral code that the society would be rationally required to select as its social moral code. And given my arguments, this status is the property, roughly, of being included in the moral code the currency of which would best serve the society's needs.

Given this, the linkage thesis implies that moral propositions are relational. For it implies that if a moral proposition is true, then there is a relevant society and a corresponding standard such that the standard is included in the moral code justified with respect to the society. And, of course, it implies that the code is justified in the sense that the society would be rational to select the code as its social moral code. Hence, for example, if slavery is wrong, it is wrong in relation to a society where the justified moral code prohibits slavery.

It would be compatible with this to hold that slavery is wrong in relation to every society. Indeed, since all societies have the same basic needs, and since the rationality of a society's selecting a code to serve as its social moral code turns on how well the code would serve the needs of the society, one society's justified moral code is likely to be similar in a fundamental way to every other society's justified moral code. But this is not guaranteed. And it remains that moral propositions are relational in logical form.

The fact that moral propositions are in this way relational to a society is not normally explicit in the sentences we use to express them. We normally would say simply, "Slavery is wrong." Moreover, most people who have moral beliefs, and so most competent speakers of the language, do not realize that moral propositions are relational to a society. But these points are no objection to what I am saying, as I will explain.

A person who believes slavery is wrong would be expected to understand it to follow that slavery is ruled out by the authoritative moral standards. She would realize that "Slavery is wrong" attributes a characteristic or a property to slavery, but she may have no idea that this property is a relation to a society. A person would need more than linguistic competence to realize that moral propositions are relational to a society in the way I have been explaining. Similarly, a person may believe that Moose Jaw is located to the north without realizing that her belief involves relating Moose Jaw and her location to the north pole. She would realize that "Moose Jaw is to the north" normally expresses a proposition that relates Moose Jaw to her own location, but she may have no idea that it also relates Moose Jaw and her own location to the north pole. More than linguistic competence would be needed to realize this.

In the "default" case, a person who says, "Moose Jaw is to the north" expresses a proposition that relates Moose Jaw to her own location. But specific features of the context may change the reference to some other location. For example, if the conversation is about Big Beaver, she may express the proposition that Moose Jaw is to the north of Big Beaver by saying "Moose Jaw is to the north."

Similarly, when a speaker expresses a moral proposition, she does not normally refer overtly to any society. She says, "Slavery is wrong." The context determines which society is at issue. In the default case, I propose, the society at issue is the one that embraces all the people at issue in the context. Or to be more exact, the relevant society is the smallest society that includes the person making the claim as well as all the people in the person's intended audience and all the people otherwise referred to in the context. Specific features of the context may change the reference to a different society from the default society.

For example, if Reagan and Nixon are discussing slavery in the nineteenth-century United States, and Nixon says, "Slavery is wrong," then in the default case Nixon has expressed the proposition that slavery is wrong relative to American society. If Thatcher joins the conversation, however, and Nixon says again, "Slavery is wrong," then in the default case he has expressed the proposition that slavery is wrong relative to the society that embraces both the English population and the American population. Suppose he says instead, "I don't know about England, Mrs. Thatcher, but slavery was wrong in this society." In this case, his explicit reference to a society would signal a departure from the default case. Suppose Thatcher replies, "Slavery can never be justified, no matter what." In this case, she may mean to express a proposition to the effect that there is no society relative to which slavery is acceptable.

In the default case, one does not need to make explicit the reference to one's society. Hence, a person who does make explicit the reference to her society, by saying, for example, "Slavery is wrong in this society," implies conversationally that he does not mean to say what he could say with greater economy simply by uttering the words, "Slavery is wrong." In many contexts, to say "Slavery is wrong in this society" would be to qualify one's condemnation of slavery. It would be to imply that there may be societies in which slavery is not wrong, something which is not implied in the default case where one says simply, "Slavery is wrong." In other contexts, to say "Slavery is wrong in this society" would be to imply that one does not intend to express a normative moral proposition at all. It would be to imply a sociological proposition to the effect that slavery is considered wrong by people in this society, or that a condemnation of slavery is part of this society's moral code.[26]

Moral Knowledge

The society-centered theory I have introduced here takes the first step toward explaining how moral knowledge is possible. It gives an account of the content of the propositions we express when we make moral claims, and it thereby explains the content of moral facts. I believe it accounts better than any alternative for the normativity of moral facts. Although some of the details are less important than others, the theory is best evaluated as a whole.

The problem of accounting for moral knowledge has two parts. We are still left with the second part, which is to explain how we could be in a position to know that some moral propositions are true. I assume that knowledge consists of, as I shall say, *reliably justified true beliefs.*[27] I still need to account for the possibility of reliably justified moral belief.

The truth of a person's moral belief does not guarantee that the person is justified in believing it. It may be true that capital punishment is unjust; a standard prohibiting capital punishment may be justified in the way I have explained. Yet an American who believes dogmatically that capital punishment is unjust, despite the widespread belief in American society that it is morally appropriate, may not be justified in his belief. In general, a person is not justified in believing a proposition about which (otherwise) reasonable people have raised doubts unless he has dismissed the doubts in a way that is reasonable according to epistemic standards that he justifiably accepts. A person who dogmatically sticks with a belief that is widely rejected has not reasonably assessed the reasons to doubt his belief, and so he is not justified in this belief. This reasoning accounts for the fact that, as I believe, people living today in modern societies are not justified in believing that God exists unless they have dealt reasonably with atheistic doubt.

Most of us are justified in a variety of our beliefs. In the standard case, we are taught something, and we accept what we are taught. In the absence of a reason to doubt what we have been taught, we are not at fault to believe it, and we are justified in believing it. This reasoning accounts for the fact that, as I believe, most Europeans in medieval times were justified in believing that God exists. Similarly, people are justified in their moral beliefs in the standard case where no reasons have been given for them to doubt their beliefs.

There are, then, two types of cases in which people may be justified in their moral beliefs. The first is the standard case, and the second is the critical case, where doubts have been raised but have been reasonably dismissed. These are cases where people are justified to base their moral reasoning on their moral intuitions, either without questioning them, in the standard case, or, in the critical case, without going beyond answering specific doubts about them in a reasonable and limited way. For example, we may be justified to base our reasoning on our intuition that capital punishment is impermissible provided we have reasonable answers to the objections of reasonable people who disagree with us. In these cases, moral reasoning can be described as a process leading toward a "local reflective equilibrium."[28]

A person's moral belief may be true even if the explanation of his believing what he does has little or nothing to do with the fact that his belief is true. In this case, even if the person is justified in his belief, it may be entirely fortuitous that his belief is true, and so we should not count it as a case of moral knowledge. We should not count it as "reliably justified."

Consider examples of scientific knowledge, such as our knowledge that lightning is an electrical discharge. You believe this, and I believe both that you are most likely justified in believing it and that you likely know it. This is an example of the standard case of justified belief, for, I imagine, you believe this about lightning simply on the basis of what you have read. You are unaware of any reason to doubt it. You know it because what you have read about lightning was produced by a system of research, education, and publication that is responsive to the truth in such matters, and reliable in getting at the truth. Because I believe this, I think your belief about lightning is a bit of scientific knowledge.

Our moral beliefs are produced by a system of education and training that may or may not be reliable in producing true moral beliefs. If the social moral code in our society is justified, if it is a code that the society would be rational to choose, if, that is, its currency would best serve the society's needs, then the moral beliefs we have as a result of learning the moral culture of our society are likely to be true, by and large. In such a case, there is a connection between moral culture and moral truth, for learning and subscribing to the moral culture tends to produce true moral beliefs. In this kind of case, if a person is justified in his moral beliefs, either in the standard way or the critical way, his beliefs are reliably justified. Hence, if his beliefs are true, they qualify as pieces of moral knowledge.[29]

There may also be cases in which, although a social moral code is not entirely justified, it is close enough to being justified that the moral beliefs that tend to be produced in a person who subscribes to the code tend on the whole to be true. We may have moral knowledge in cases of this kind as well.

A person may try to work from first principles, to discover the moral code that is justified relative to her society by developing a theory of societal needs and a sociology of the meeting of societal needs through moral culture. She would need to resolve difficult philosophical and empirical issues before she could make real progress in this way. But we are not required to be moral explorers of this kind in order to have moral knowledge any more than we must be astronomers in order to know anything about meteors. We are not even required to understand that justified moral standards are the ones whose currency in the moral culture would best contribute to the meeting of societal needs. This is a bit of specialized philosophical theory that most of us cannot be expected to know. Unlike such arcane theory, moral knowledge is readily available, or it would be, if our society were well-ordered by a justified moral culture.

Notes

I benefitted from the helpful comments of those who participated in the conference on moral epistemology that was held at Dartmouth College in September 1994. I am especially grateful to Malia Brink, Christopher Morris, Geoffrey Sayre-McCord, and Walter Sinnott-Armstrong for their detailed written comments.

1. I use the term "proposition" to speak of the things that have truth values.

2. This cannot serve as a definition, for some nonnormative proportions are relevant to action or choice because of their content. Consider, for example, the proposition that if you do not obey him, Smith will destroy the thing you most prize. This seems to be "relevant" to your choice of whether to obey Smith because of its content, and it may be "essentially" relevant, yet it is nonnormative. Normative propositions are relevant to action and choice in a characteristic way yet to be explained.

3. R. M. Hare, *The Language of Morals* (Oxford: Clarendon Press, 1952); and, more recently, *Moral Thinking: Its Levels, Method and Point* (Oxford: Clarendon Press, 1981); Allan Gibbard, *Wise Choices, Apt Feelings: A Theory of Normative Judgment* (Cambridge, Mass.: Harvard University Press, 1990). Simon Blackburn has defended a similar, "expressivist" view in chapter 6 of his book, *Spreading the Word: Groundings in the Philosophy of Language* (Oxford: Clarendon Press, 1984). See Blackburn's chapter in this volume.

4. I am indebted to Jeffrey C. King for helpful discussion of this point.

5. The disquotational theorist might reply that, on his view, the claim that slavery is wrong *is* accurate to the facts, if it is true. In effect, this reply proposes a disquotational account of facts, and it appears thereby to rule out the thesis that moral claims are not straightforwardly descriptive of facts. If so, it precludes the disquotational theorist from accepting antidescriptivism as it is usually understood. Hartry Field discusses some of these issues and defends a disquotational account. See his "Disquotational Truth and Factually Defective Discourse," *The Philosophical Review* 103 (1994), 405–52.

6. By an "imperative," I mean a sentence in the imperative mood. I take it that the following are examples: "Abolish slavery" and "There is not to be slavery."

7. It is not in general a sufficient condition for the truth of a moral proposition that a corresponding standard be appropriately justified. Consider, for example, the proposition that it was wrong of Alan to sell Bill into slavery. The existence of a justified prohibition of selling persons into slavery is necessary for the truth of this

proposition, but it obviously is not sufficient. For the existence of such a standard does not entail that Alan sold Bill into slavery.

8. The propositions that slavery is wrong and that kindness is a virtue are paradigmatic. But the proposition that it is not the case that slavery is wrong, and the proposition that if slavery is wrong, it will disappear from the world are not, for they may be true even if there are no standards with a relevant justification or standing. These are examples of nonparadigmatic normative propositions. Nonparadigmatic normative propositions result from performing certain logical or semantic operations on a paradigmatic normative proposition. For example, if *p* is a paradigmatic moral proposition, then the following are moral propositions that are nonparadigmatic: *it is not the case that p, it is possible that p,* and *if p is the case, I am a monkey's uncle.*

9. I say "nontrivially" to avoid a technical problem. John Fischer and J. G. Bennett reminded me of the problem.

10. Nonparadigmatic propositions are normative in an extended or derivative sense. They embed a proposition that is normative in the sense explained in the text.

11. In his chapter in this volume, Brandt talks of "evaluating a person's morality" by showing that, if she were fully informed, she would support a certain form of morality for her society. See Richard B. Brandt, *A Theory of the Good and the Right* (Oxford: Oxford University Press, 1979), 179–95. Also, Richard B. Brandt, "The Explanation of Moral Language," in David Copp and David Zimmerman, eds., *Morality, Reason, and Truth* (Totowa, N.J.: Rowman and Allanheld, 1984), 117–18.

12. For example, in his chapter in this volume, Brandt talks about showing "persons" that if they were fully informed, they would support a certain sort of moral system for their society. In *A Theory of the Good and the Right,* Brandt suggests that a justified code is one that all fully rational persons would tend to support for a given society if they expected to live in it. (See pp. 179–95.)

13. Richard B. Brandt, *A Theory of the Good and the Right,* pp. 188, 194.

14. In *A Theory of the Good and the Right,* Brandt says that the idea that a justified code is one that *all* fully rational persons would tend to support for their society is a "simplifying first approximation." The root idea is individualistic. (See pp. 188, 194.)

15. David Gauthier, *Morals by Agreement* (Oxford: Oxford University Press, 1986).

16. I have discussed Gauthier's views in some detail in "Contractarianism and Moral Skepticism," in Peter Vallentyne, ed., *Contractarianism and Rational Choice: Essays on Gauthier* (Cambridge: Cambridge University Press, 1990), 196–228.

17. Kant defends this thesis, in effect, in the third section of the *Grounding of the Metaphysics of Morals* where he aims to show that every rational agent is bound by the moral law. I discuss Kant's argument in "The 'Possibility' of a Categorical Imperative: Kant's *Groundwork,* Part III," *Philosophical Perspectives,* volume 6: "Ethics" (1992), 261–84.

18. In my book, *Morality, Normativity, and Society* (New York: Oxford University Press, 1995).

19. This sentence involves a simplification of my views about rational choice.

20. Leon H. Mayhew, "Society," in David L. Sills, ed., *International Encyclopedia of the Social Sciences* (New York: Crowell, Collier and MacMillian Inc., 1968), volume 14, 577.

21. For details, see chapter 7 of my *Morality, Normativity, and Society.* I am grateful to Christopher Morris for helping me with this passage.

22. See chapter 8 of my *Morality, Normativity, and Society.* In this paper, I ignore the fact that an agent's values are relevant to the rationality of his choices. An agent's

(mere) preferences are also relevant, although they cannot trump his needs or his values.

23. We might also be interested in the rationality of the choices of the persons who are party to the consensus, which would depend partly on how their choices serve their needs. And we might be interested in the rationality of the process leading to the consensus, which would depend partly on the cogency of the reasoning and the accuracy of the beliefs that led to the consensus.

24. For purposes of illustration, I am assuming certain things about rights and justice that may be controversial. I cannot discuss these matters in detail here.

25. The phrase "included in," would need some explication in a fuller account. For example, the standard, *Do not lie to Jones,* follows (nontrivially) from the standard, *Do not lie.* If the latter is included in a moral code, then I want to say the former is also included in it. Suppose it would be a lie, in the present context, if I said, "It was blue." Given this, the standard, *Do not lie,* implies the standard, *Do not say "It was blue" in this context.* In this case, I want to say that if the former is included in a justified moral code, the latter is included as well. And so on.

26. Paul Grice developed theory of implications of this kind, which he called "conversational implications." See Grice, *Studies in the Way of Words* (Cambridge, Mass.: Harvard University Press, 1989), 22–40.

27. I therefore adopt a version of "reliabilism." One of the first to propose reliabilism was Alvin I. Goldman, in "What is Justified Belief?" in George S. Pappas, ed., *Justification and Knowledge* (Dordrecht, Holland: D. Reidel, 1979), 1–23. I do not adhere to the details of Goldman's account.

28. John Rawls introduced the term "reflective equilibrium" in his *A Theory of Justice* (Cambridge, Mass.: Harvard University Press, 1971). Norman Daniels discussed a notion of "wide" equilibrium in "Wide Reflective Equilibrium and Theory Acceptance in Ethics," *The Journal of Philosophy* 76 (1979), 256–82.

29. This is so even if he does not *know* that his beliefs are reliably justified. One can know without knowing that he knows.

10

Feminist Skepticism, Authority, and Transparency

Margaret Urban Walker

No "problem of skepticism" looms in feminist ethics. Yet feminist ethics is deeply, relentlessly skeptical. It is skeptical about the ways moral thought and practice interlace with social understandings that do not see or treat all "kinds" of people as similarly whole, worthy, respectable, free, rational, or even human. It is skeptical about whose experiences and judgments are taken as definitive or representative of moral thinking, whose self-images and motivations are normative for moral personhood, and whose presumed entitlements and liabilities set the standards for moral responsibilities. Unsurprisingly, feminists suspect it has not been women's moral experiences, moral self-images, and senses of responsibility that have been the benchmark.

Feminist philosophers turn skeptical eyes on typical conventions and claims of moral philosophy, especially on the substance and structure of prominent contemporary moral theories. Claims that "the" moral point of view is characterized by universality, impartiality, impersonality, or disinterested objectivity have been analyzed as expressions of particular social positions and prerogatives, rather than as necessary truths about a timeless human condition. Poses of reflective transcendence and unproblematic authority to define "our" intuitions (or interests, or sense of justice) are part of the manner of moral philosophy as an intellectual practice and genre of writing. Feminist philosophers question whether such poses are responsible and whether such authority is earned. Some have expressed skepticism about the enterprise of philosophical ethics itself. A feminist moral epistemology must be able to explain how this sort of skepticism is possible, and why it is important to understanding the nature and justification of moral judgment and practice.

There are as many possible feminist moral epistemologies as there are compatible combinations of an ethic, an epistemology, and a particular version of feminist theory. In fact, there are many different ethical views feminists

267

endorse. Alison Jaggar notes that there are "feminist Aristotelians, Humeans, utilitarians, existentialists, and contract theorists as well as 'carers,' 'maternal thinkers,' 'womanists,' and 'spinsters'."[1] Yet Jaggar correctly suggests that any ethics that is recognizably feminist will be committed to two assumptions: "that the subordination of women is morally wrong and that the moral experience of women is worthy of respect."[2] A feminist moral epistemology should be able to account for the availability and nonarbitrariness of these assumptions in a way consistent with the skepticism about received moral judgments, practices, and theories already mentioned.

Because of the actual diversity of feminist views in and about ethics, I make no claim to present either a definitive or a representative view of feminist ethics or its moral epistemology. What I shall do is to focus on a body of work in ethics by feminist philosophers which begins from the kind of skepticism mentioned. This feminist ethics does not take for granted received moral thinking and moral philosophy's formulations of it; it assumes that these need to be examined for effects of, and on, the distribution of powers by gender.[3]

This examination leads from skepticism about the typical content and form of philosophically dominant moral theories to questions about the epistemic and moral authority these theories embody and represent. Feminist epistemology provides a view of knowledge that makes sense of this skepticism about authority and representation. On this view, knowledge is socially and historically *situated* and *communal.* I will appeal to the results of feminist critique of ethics and to this critical social epistemology to construct the outlines of a moral epistemology that serves what I call an *expressive-collaborative conception* of morality. This conception of morality and its epistemology support the defining commitments of feminist ethics as well as the skeptical momentum that drives it, but render the implications of feminist criticism general. In concluding I will return to skeptical problems, which are no longer one, and not always the same.

Feminist Ethics: Skepticism of Content, Form, and Practice

Feminist ethics is the outgrowth of contemporary feminist political movement in the United States and other Western European democracies from the 1960s onward.[4] It is part of a larger project of feminist theory that "attempts to account for gender inequality in the socially constructed relationship between power—the political—on the one hand and the knowledge of truth and reality—the epistemological—on the other."[5] While feminist ethics focuses on the role of moral conceptions in expressing and reinforcing the distribution of powers by *gender,* it contributes to an ethics set to challenge social domination, exploitation, and marginalization of many kinds.

Western Anglo-European philosophical ethics as a cultural tradition and product has been until just recently almost entirely a product of some men's—and almost no women's—thinking. Historically, the societies producing these ethics have also typically excluded women (and many men) from the publicly authoritative forums for the expression and endorsement of moral values and ideals (political offices, religious hierarchies, policy institutions, higher education, mass media). Almost every canonized philosopher up to the twentieth century has explicitly held that women are lesser, defective, or incompetent moral (and epistemic) agents. The historical facts put in question authoritative representations of "our" moral life. Are these representations really representative? Of what? Of whom?

Feminist ethical critique argues that authoritative representations of morality, for example those in the canonical and contemporary works of the Western tradition of philosophy, are marked by *gender and other bias.* Neither by nor about women, this ethics is not *for* women either. It distorts or fails to reflect responsibilities, social positions, and moral self-images that form the lives of many women in a society where gender pervasively structures social life. At the same time, a tradition and practice of ethics that expresses the dominance of privileged groups may not be by, about, or for many men either.

Feminist ethics particularly targets for criticism modern moral theories, those neo-Kantian, utilitarian, rights, and contract theories that dominate discussion both in public arenas and in the journals and textbooks, classrooms and conferences of contemporary Anglo-American academic ethics. While proponents of these views see them as sharply divided over fundamental moral issues, feminist critics see them differently. They see similar preoccupations, images, and assumptions among these modern theories of morality, and a suspicious convergence of these with activities, roles, social contexts, opportunities, and character ideals associated with (at least privileged) men in our society, or with norms of masculinity that apply to them.

A great deal of feminist criticism alleges gender bias in the *content* of such theories. Preoccupation with equality and autonomy, uniformity and impartiality, rules and reciprocity fits voluntary bargaining relations of nonintimate equals, or contractual and institutional relations among peers in contexts of impersonal or public interaction. It ignores the often unchosen, discretionary responsibilities of those who care for particular others, often dependent and vulnerable, in intimate, domestic, or familial—"private"—contexts. It slights relations of interdependence centered on bonds of affection and loyalty whose specific histories set varying terms of obligation and responsibility. It obscures the particularity of moral actors and relations by emphasizing universality, sameness, and repeatability, excluding or regimenting emotional experience. Ignoring or slighting continuing relationships of intimacy and care, these views feature abstract problem solving to the neglect of responsive attention to actual others. Yet women's traditionally assigned (or permitted) responsibilities—paid and unpaid—center on forms of caring labor in both private and public spheres. These works sustain intimate, domestic, and other personal relations, and tend to the comfort and nurturance, bodily safety, nourishment, and cleanliness of others.[6]

Worse than being incomplete or lopsided, however, these moral theories mystify social reality. For the community of freely contracting peers or mutually respecting reciprocators could not exist without the extensive and required labors of the care-givers, whose physical and emotional work cannot be recognized or valued in the moral terms these theories set. As Kathryn Morgan puts it, these theories effect the "invisibility of women's moral domains."[7] But it is not only women who thus disappear. Joan Tronto correctly broadens the point: socially vital caring, maintenance, and support activities are not only gendered, but "raced" and "classed," as "questions that have traditionally informed the lives of women, and servants, slaves, and workers, have not informed the philosophical tradition or political theory."[8] Tronto's diagnosis is that "questions we find interesting about moral life parallel the distribution of political power in our society."[9] But not all interests are equally authoritative in society (or philosophy), and whether our interests are represented depends upon who "we" are.

While most feminist criticism has gone to the content of dominant moral theories, these theories are not only alike in what they are about; they also share a quite specific *form*. This form projects a logic of abstraction, generalization, and uniformity as the normal form of moral consideration. I call the underlying conception of morality a *theoretical-juridical model,* and the theories this model requires *codelike* theories.

The regnant type of moral theory in contemporary ethics is a *codifiable* (and usually *compact*) set of moral *formulas* (or procedures for selecting formulas) that can be applied by *any* agent to a situation to yield a justified and determinate *action-guiding* judgment. The formulas or procedures (if there are more than one) are typically seen as rules or principles at a high level of generality. Application of these formulas is typically seen as something like deduction or instantiation. The formulas and their applications yield the same for all agents indifferently. These formulas model what the morally competent agent does or should know, however implicitly.[10]

The picture of morality as a *compact, impersonally action-guiding code within an agent* results from a powerfully restrictive set of assumptions about what morality is. It is assumed that morality is essentially *knowledge,* or that philosophers can reflectively extract a core of knowledge specific and essential to morality; that the core of moral knowledge is essentially *theoretical,* of an explicitly statable, highly general, and systematically unified type; and that this pure theoretical core of moral knowledge is essentially *action-guiding,* so that when brought to bear on incidental "nonmoral" information about a situation at hand, it tells "the" agent what to do. Theoretical-juridical moral philosophy sets itself the task of (largely reflective) construction, testing, and refinement of codelike theories that exhibit the core of properly moral knowledge.

Emphasis on the application of general formulas to determine judgments in particular cases projects a stylized and reductive logic of moral judgment. Moral consideration presses toward abstraction; only when superfluous detail has been cleared away can cases be sorted into broad types that figure into the formulas or principles that unify the moral field. This serves to guarantee uniformity in judgment and action both across cases and across agents. This view gives priority to achieving sameness and repeatability by regimenting moral consideration into fixed paths. This moral logic is aptly called an "administrative" or "procedural" one. It envisions the impartial application of set policies to all, and best describes participants in a structured game or institution, or administrators and judges disposing of cases in accord with existing rules or laws.

The normal form of moral consideration prescribed might be described as *evasive* in most interpersonal situations, and *bureaucratic* or *authoritarian* in social or institutional ones. It puts unilateral decision, formulaic responses, and repeatable categorial uniformities where flexible appreciation and communicative interaction might be. In actual interpersonal relations, it models the vantage point of the more powerful vis-à-vis the less, or the equally powerful and confidently like-minded vis-à-vis each other. Moral thought so structured is vaunted in influential literatures of moral psychology and philosophy as embodying the maturely objective or impartial view, freed from inappropriate particular interests or partialities. It actually embodies a highly selective view appropriate to certain kinds of relationships and interactions in certain public, competitive, or institutional venues. These are traditionally contexts of male participation and authority, and symbolically associated with masculinity as well, or more precisely, with the masculinity of men otherwise privileged.

A tide of objections to and defections from the project of codelike theory has swelled in the last quarter-century. Not only feminists but Aristotelians, Humeans, communitarians, contemporary casuists, pragmatists, historicists, Wittgensteinians, and others find the assumptions and constructions of this kind of moral theorizing descriptively or normatively inadequate. So clear is this schism in late twentieth-century moral philosophy that talk of "antitheory" in ethics is now familiar. Some feminist criticisms overlap with these others, but there is a difference.

Feminist ethics has pursued questions about *authority, credibility,* and *representation* in moral life and in the *practice* of moral theorizing itself. Its scrutiny of contemporary moral theory (and the social norms and ideals it reflects) does not conclude simply that modern (or other) moral philosophy rests on (philosophical) mistakes. Instead, feminist ethics finds that philosophical and cultural figurations of moral agency, knowledge, and judgment portray, in abstract and idealized form, actual social positions and relations, or views from specific social locations. When these partial and positioned representations of moral life are put forward *authoritatively* as truths about "human" interest, "our" intuitions, "rational" behavior, or "the" moral agent, they uncritically reproduce the represented positions and locations as *normative,* that is, as the central or standard (if not the only) case.

When this happens, the specific, partial, and situated character of these views and positions disappears. At the same time, experiences of those otherwise situated appear as "different" or problematic; often, perspectives from other locations do not appear at all. Not everyone, however, can authoritatively define moral life. To have the social, intellectual, or moral authority to perform this feat, one must already be on the advantaged side of some practices of privilege and uneven distributions of power and responsibilities in the community in which one does it. To be able to uncritically reproduce one's specific position as the norm both *exercises* one's privilege and *reinforces* it.

In the practice of theory, especially in a social world with highly specialized institutions of knowledge production and a high valuation of expertise, this is done under the mantle of epistemic authority, of those most entitled to speak because they are most likely to know. What is required to confront this self-reinforcing exercise of authority in moral theorizing goes beyond counterexamples, refutations, and counterarguments that stay within those same practices. What is required is critical examination *of* those practices, of the *positions to know* and *means of knowing* moral life that these practices assume and construct, and of the conditions that in turn make these positions and means possible. Critical examination of positions to know and means of knowing may support but can also defeat or circumscribe the *credibility* of claims and claimants.

Moral theorizing itself is a specific practice of intellectual authority. Kathryn Addelson reminds philosophers that theirs is a professional status, politically won and politically maintained. Like social workers and religious leaders, teachers and scholars of ethics have powers to legitimize and even to enforce certain constructions of moral life. Presenting these as "discoveries" conceals the production and reproduction of these forms in social interactions, including the socially authorized interactions of teaching, lecturing, and theory-making. Unless moral philosophers become politically self-conscious and more inclined toward the empirical study of morality as a tissue of interactions, Addelson warns, they may simply uncritically enshrine existing "gender, age, class, and race divisions" in their analysis.[11] Cheshire Calhoun argues that this can happen simply by the repetition of patterns of emphasis or exclusion within authoritative discourses on ethics. These produce "ideologies of the moral life"—standard assumptions about moral agency, motivation, or knowledge—that are not logically presupposed or implied by particular theories, but are presupposed in making sense of what is talked about and what is passed over.[12]

In addition to repetition and exclusion of themes and topics, the discursive conventions of moral philosophy—its canonical styles of presentation, standard tropes, methods of argument, framing of problems—favor certain understandings over others. Standard conventions of moral philosophy include absence of the second person and plural in depictions of deliberation (while often invoking an unproblematic "we" in entering moral intuitions); neglecting collaborative and communicative ways of formulating moral problems and arriving at resolutions; regimenting moral reasoning into formats of deductive argument; relying on schematic examples in which the few "morally relevant" factors have already been selected and in which social-political context is effaced; omitting narratives that explore prior histories and possible or actual sequels to moral "solutions." Moral philosophers learn these conventions in learning what moral philosophy is; we repeat them and enforce them in instructing our students in what moral thinking "is."

The discursive and expressive resources in which we make moral judgments and explain moral life to ourselves—what I call below the "moral medium"—

are crucially important. But distributions of social power and authority make some people's uses and interpretations of these resources more effective than others. In considering what representations this medium permits and encourages, we should ask: what actual community of moral responsibility do these representations purport to represent, and whom do they actually represent? What communicative strategies do they support, and who is in a position (concretely, socially) to deploy them? In what forms of activity will they have (or fail to have) applications, and who is permitted these activities or served by them? Who is in a position to transmit and enforce the rules that constrain them?

These questions are foreign to most contemporary moral philosophy, even to most of it critical of the project of codelike theory. In philosophy, these questions violate a disciplinary self-image formed around the picture of a disinterested search for core moral truth by a process of reflection subject to timeless criteria of precision, clarity, and consistency. Few philosophers today will defend a vision of the Good, supersensible intuition of moral properties or truths, or pure practical reason. Yet the notion of a pure core of moral knowledge, available to individual reflection, lives on.

The assumption of a pure core of properly moral knowledge that reflective thought might reveal and a compact code might articulate, permits moral philosophers to bypass the interlacing of moral vocabularies and practices with other historically specific beliefs and social practices. It also shields from view the historical, cultural, and social location of the moral philosopher, and of moral philosophy itself as a practice of authority sustained by particular institutions and arrangements. The purity of properly moral knowledge, the reflective purity of moral philosophy, and the moral philosopher's pose of objective (even "scientific") disinterest are mutually supporting constructs. Feminist ethics challenges a reflective method that is all too apt to reflect the moral experience of someone in particular.

Feminist criticism of the form and content of ethics finally goes to questions about the *authority to represent* moral life. First it targets the ways gender bias renders moral theories substantively inadequate to, or distorting of, much of the matter of social life. Feminist critics further hold that the form canonical for moral theories models the viewpoint, and assumes the prerogatives and preoccupations, of those relatively privileged by power and status. Finally, feminist criticism reinserts the activity of moral theorizing itself into its actual social situation as a specific practice of intellectual authority with significant powers to define for all of us what may seem obvious, acceptable, or comprehensible only to some of us.

Different Voices, Critical Epistemology

In a century of moral philosophy in which epistemological anxieties and skeptical threats drive discussion in ethics to issues of justification in and of morality, moral philosophers are typically casual about their own positions to know.

Feminist philosophers, on the contrary, have been forced to confront the assumptions and effects of such poses, not only by a critical examination of the philosophical tradition and discipline, but by their own attempts at constructing feminist ethics.

The idea that there is a "woman's voice" or a fund of "women's experience" which is ignored or distorted in mainstream theorizing, and which can serve as a touchstone of corrective or reconstructive feminist theorizing, has had very great appeal.[13] Yet claims to theorize "women's" experiences, or to represent what "women's" voices say, have foundered on the same epistemological challenge feminists direct at nonfeminist views. Not all women recognize the voice or experience theorized as theirs, for reasons that are not idiosyncratic in a society where gender always interacts with other powerful social divisions of labor, opportunity, and recognition. Feminist ethics and feminist theory have been the scene of struggles and negotiations over who is representing whom, why, and with what authority. Feminists continue to learn in hard ways that claims to represent are weighty and dangerous, often not only epistemically dubious but morally indefensible.[14]

At the same time, contests over credibility and authority within feminist theorizing, and between feminist and nonfeminist theorizing, provide instructive examples for a critical epistemology. They expose aspects of the production of knowledge within communities pushed to examine the links between their epistemic practices and their configurations of social authority and privilege. Here both the products and the process of feminist ethics get light from recent work in feminist epistemology.

The key idea is that knowledge is "an intersubjective product constructed within communal practices of acknowledgement, correction, and critique" of claims to know.[15] As Lynn Nelson puts it, "none of us knows (or could) what no one else could. However singular experience may be, what we know on the basis of that experience has been made possible and is compatible with the standards and knowledge of one or more communities of which we are members."[16] On this view, all would-be knowers are *situated* in (typically multiple, overlapping) epistemic *communities* (i.e. groups that share and maintain the resources for the acquisition and legitimation of knowledge). These resources include languages and other symbolisms, and accepted methods, procedures, instruments, and technologies (sometimes specialized and technical); but also social interactions that structure, interpret, qualify, and disqualify evidence and reasoning in the context of specific relations and practices of cognitive authority.

Of particular concern to feminist epistemologists are background assumptions working alongside or loaded into the cognitive instruments and practices of communities of inquiry. These assumptions may be cultural commonplaces (including stereotypical ones about gender or race), theoretical or disciplinary assumptions that supply the frame within which creditable work is done (established paradigms, well-confirmed theories), or beliefs that seem obvious to, and interests that make sense for, people with certain similar kinds of experiences. These are the things that will typically not need stating or proving *within* a community or inquiry; indeed, "unreflective acceptance of such assumptions can come to define what it is to be a member of such a community."[17]

Traditional norms of objectivity, allied to a conception of knowledge as something individuals have or do, aim to eliminate bias due to *individual* values and interests that differ *within* a community. But requirements that might weed out idiosyncratic ("subjective") bias don't touch the problem of concerns, values, interests, or assumptions *shared* by all members, or by the members with most authority, in a particular community. Similarity of cultural outlook and social experience, as well as similarity of education and training, among members of an epistemic community protects the invisibility or inviolability of these assumptions. As Louise Antony puts it: "The more homogeneous an epistemic ommunity, the more objective it is likely to regard itself, and if its inquiries are relatively self-contained, the more likely it is to be viewed as objective by those outside the community."[18]

Because of this "objectivity effect," the constitution of epistemic communities and the interrelations of their members become crucial. Norms of sound epistemic practice must be applied to the practices, relations, and background assumptions within communities. Sandra Harding calls this demand on knowledge claims *strong objectivity*. Strong objectivity requires an epistemic community to engage in *self-reflexive* scrutiny, rendering more transparent the discourses, instruments, processes, and relations of authority by which it produces what it claims to be knowledge. Strong objectivity requires publicly recognized standards and forums which institutionalize and reward evaluation and criticism of knowledge claims. It requires examination of processes and relations of cognitive authority, which must not cloak cultural, political, or economic dominance or suppress relevant criticism from diverse viewpoints. It requires critical techniques for exposing the powers and limits of the discourses and instruments that enable us to know, and needs conceptual and empirical analyses of biases and saliencies and the specific ways they make possible what we know and what we cannot or do not.[19] "Power-sensitive conversation," in Donna Haraway's words, is the practice of objectivity that "allows us to become answerable for what we learn how to see."[20]

This epistemology is a "naturalized" one, taking actual processes and determinants of human cognition and inquiry as its subject. It sees theories of knowledge as interdependent with, and subject to, the same sorts of confirmation or reconsideration as whatever else we (suppose we) know. Something this epistemology supposes we *do* know is that prevalent or authoritative assumptions will shape the direction, practice, interpretation, and results of inquiry, and that social powers can render some people's views and assumptions arbitrarily prevalent or undeservedly authoritative in contexts of inquiry as elsewhere. So this epistemology needs both an understanding of the *actual* production of knowledges communities credit and *normative* standards (at least, necessary conditions) for *good* epistemic practice.

Normative standards of epistemic practice will require self-reflexive strategies of criticism that are historically informed and politically sensitive; they will endorse social and institutional relations that support effective critical strategies. We know things, and can come to know more, about the history and politics of unreliable theorizing and the kinds of epistemic community that shelter it. It is what we already know about this that suggests both the need for, and the specific nature of, the normative standards that this epistemology must include. Accurate accounts of individuals' epistemic responsibility in the context of their social communities are part of what this epistemology needs.[21] But the communally sustained practices of inquiry that allow knowers to be judged responsible and their claims credible is what this epistemology must render explicit, and the reliability of these shared practices is what it must assess. So this naturalized epistemology is a *normative epistemology of knowledge produced by communities,* whose epistemic practices will be intertwined with—formed or deformed by—their other ones. Naomi Scheman says its proponents qualify as realists "if by realism we mean the recognition that the world may not be the way anyone (or any group, however powerful) thinks it is."[22]

Now, what might a feminist *moral* epistemology that reaps results of feminist ethical critique and critical epistemology look like? This is an interesting and complex instance in which to examine the basis of representative claims and the authority of claimants to enter them. For representative claims here are not just "about" moral life, they are *part* of it.

An Expressive-Collaborative Model and Its Epistemology

Certain ideas about the nature of moral understanding are conspicuous in feminist writings on ethics. Responsive attention to particular people in actual relationships, rich context and narrative form in moral thinking, communication as a means of moral deliberation are recurrent themes. Rather less is said in feminist ethics about "what to do" than one might expect; rather a lot is said about paying the right kinds of attention to people and things, about preserving trust and mutual intelligibility.[23]

These are ingredients of a moral epistemology that is particularist and interpersonal. As elements of a feminist moral epistemology they need to be placed within a social view of moral knowledge that explains the possibility and credibility of the criticisms of ethics feminists have made. But to view moral knowledge as a communal product and process is to think of *morality itself* in a different way than the theoretical-juridical conception assumes. I call this different way an *expressive-collaborative model* of morality.

The expressive-collaborative model looks at moral life as a continuing negotiation *among* people, a socially situated practice of *mutually* allotting, assuming, or deflecting responsibilities of important kinds, and understanding the implications of doing so. Like other philosophical constructions of moral life, this representation functions both descriptively and normatively. Descriptively, it aims to reveal what morality "is"—what kinds of interactions go on that can be recognized as moral ones. Normatively, it aims to suggest some important things morality is "for"—what in human lives depends on there being such practices (or known or imagined alternatives to them), and how these practices can go better or worse.

Like all such constructions, this one is a creature of its specific historical time and social place. If the theoretical-juridical conception reflects, for example, interests and problems of an emerging (later maturing) class of citizen-peers assuming authority in the context of political and economic modernization, so will a social scene many now call "postmodern" invite other attempts to think the history and future of its moral circumstances. The descriptive and critical tasks of this alternative conception are shaped by pressures on existing relations of authority, and interests in new forms of social recognition and participation, among other things.

The theoretical-juridical model pictured morality as an individually action-guiding system within a person. The expressive-collaborative conception pictures morality as a *socially embodied* medium of understanding, adjustment, and accounting *among* persons in certain terms, especially those defining people's identities, relationships, and values. This medium includes varied resources. There are shared vocabularies and grammars of moral discourse that give us things we can say, and an understanding of when to say them ('kind,' 'ungrateful,' 'fair,' 'wrong,' 'irresponsible,' 'promise,' 'honor,' 'lie,' etc.). There are commonly recognized moral exemplars and paradigmatic moral judgments that show and teach the accepted sayings of such things; we learn the kinds of things "any of us" will recognize as a lie or a kindness, assessments "any of us" would make, like the wrongness of inflicting unnecessary or undeserved suffering. There are formats of moral deliberation and argument that give recognized ways to enter reasons and to weigh, elaborate, or disqualify them, such as generalization arguments, reversibility tests, appeals to empathy, consequences, consistency, self-respect, and more. There are standard forms of imputation ("You knew the consequences" or "That was deliberately cruel") and excuse ("I couldn't have known" or "I thought she was dangerous") along with their occasions, limits, and implications ("He's only a child"; "You should have thought it over"; "Now you'll have to set things right").

These resources are starting points for the continuing construction and definition of the moral dimensions of a particular form of social life. The practices of interpersonal responsibility they make possible will mesh and blend with other practices characteristic of that social life. Yet these resources, their authorship, and their continuing usefulness and acceptability will also be contestable and renegotiable, like other social practices, within the very processes they frame. Morality on this view is *constructive:* the materials for the definition of responsibilities and the resolution of problems are given, but exactly how to go on with them, how to make them work in particular cases, and where and how to extend or modify them, may not be.

The theoretical-juridical model is powerfully shaped by the assumption that the point of morality is action guidance; moral judgments are to tell us what to do. The expressive-collaborative view reminds us that seeing what to do is *one* exercise of moral understanding, and action-guiding judgments (in the usual sense) *one* kind of application of the language of morals. Morality provides as well for knowing and explaining who we and others are as expressed in our values, commitments, and responses. It permits us to know for what and to whom we will have to account when we have done or failed to do something, and what makes sense as a moral reason or excuse. It serves to reckon failures and derelictions, to understand what can be repaired and what compensated, to assess the costs of choices in morality's own currencies of integrity and appropriate trust. It forms and articulates reactive attitudes of blame, indignation, shame, forgiveness, remorse, gratitude, contempt, and others, measuring the appropriateness of what we feel and the tractability of mutual misunderstandings. Morality informs choice, but what distinguishes it is the ways it does so. It does so by means of assessments that render us accountable to each other in certain terms. These terms provide for our *mutual intelligibility* as *agents of value,* beings capable of considered choices and responsive to mutually recognizable goods, and so responsible for ourselves and to others for the moral sense our lives make.

This progressive and mutual moral accounting is a cultural practice already there that we learn from others. We arrive at any situation of moral assessment with moral concepts, maxims, deliberative strategies, and intuitive convictions shared, even if incompletely, with some others. So too we come with sensibilities, emotional responses, and senses of relevance and seriousness shaped by a history of interactions in some personal and political environment, and by our places in that. By accounting to each other through this moral medium, we acknowledge each other as agents of value. At the same time we renew and refine the moral medium itself, keeping it alive as we keep our identities as moral persons afloat within it.

So mutual moral understanding both presupposes and seeks a continuing common life. It requires a presumption in favor of accounting to others and trying to go on in shared terms. This presumption may be defeated in specific cases. We may come to lack enough common, mutually acceptable moral terms to go on with some others, we may lock up or fall out severely over their meaning and application, or we may fail to find them in the first place. These too are cases of moral understanding; the importance of some of them I return to in the following section.

In order to say something about the epistemology of this view of morality, I make the simplifying assumption for now that a moral community is identified by its members' familiarity with and similar understanding of roughly the same media of moral understanding. What is it, now, that these members know?

On theoretical-juridical approaches, moral agents must master that logic of generalization and abstraction that guarantees uniform judgment on relevantly similar cases by subsumption under covering principles. The problem of justification on this approach goes to the principles or procedures the theory comprises. Claims that such principles are self-evident, or can be compellingly supported by broader background theories of human nature or practical reasoning seem increasingly implausible, for good reasons, to many contemporary philosophers. A "reflective equilibrium" approach, which seeks the best fit between some set of moral principles and our best considered or most firmly entrenched judgments, is widely perceived as more promising.

Reflective equilibrium offers not demonstrable or incorrigible foundations but "reasonably reliable agreement"—coherence—between "our" intuitive judgments about particular cases and those principles we can recognize as "the premises of their derivation."[24] This incorporates the theoretical-juridical understanding of the relation of judgment to theory, without promising unimpeachable foundations for either: theory and intuitive judgments are to be mutually supporting in the completed view. But precisely for this reason there is a curiosity in the role of (what are now commonly called) "intuitions"—those moral judgments or generalizations that seem obviously or compellingly right to us—on this view. They are seen at once as the *data* for the construction of moral theory (on analogy with scientific theory selection), and as assumptions that are *negotiable* (revisable, or dispensable) in the course of working out what "we" think morally. "We" (theorizers of ethics?) get to prune and adjust the data going in, selecting the "best-considered" ones to set the balance for reflective equilibrium. Further, we may decide to disqualify some of these data if they impede a particular state of epistemic equilibrium that we prefer (out of the many possible ones that will always be available).

But there are no principled procedures for disqualifying moral data short of the moral theories that the data are supposed to constrain. The curiosity lies in the kind and degree of discretion "we" are seen as exercising, not only in fitting theory to data, but in *fitting data to theory*. If moral intuitions are really "datal" they cannot be negotiable in this way; if intuitive judgments that are to anchor principles are negotiable, morality is not science and "we" are not constructing "theory." But then what are "we" doing here, and why? And who are "we" who enter into the quest for reflective equilibrium, with the discretionary power to decide which of our judgments are well considered, and which will stay and which go?

An expressive-collaborative view makes different sense of this. It drops the dubious image of moral science seeking the covering laws that explain the outputs of an idealized internalized system. It supplies instead the picture of morality as social negotiation in real time, where members of a community of roughly or largely shared moral belief try to refine understanding, extend consensus, and eliminate conflict among themselves. "We" are the members of some actual moral community, motivated by the aim of going on together, preserving or building self- and mutual understanding in moral terms. We will try not only to harmonize our individual practices of moral judgment with the standing moral beliefs we each avow but to harmonize judgment and actions among us. In doing so we seek equilibrium between people as well as within them.

Moral *equilibrium* is created through shared moral understandings, and creates mutual intelligibility. In it, we know what to expect and what is expected of us morally; how to understand and express ourselves morally in ways that others will, or at least can, understand; not just what to do but what it means, and hence what we can be understood to mean by it. Moral equilibrium is *reflective* to the extent that we are capable of making it and its conditions and consequences the subject of explicit attention and consideration between us. Mutual equilibria (just as individual ones) may become unstable under reflection, or may be unmasked as merely apparent. A system of complementary gender roles, for example, may support a shared understanding between spouses of their different responsibilities in family life, under a presumption of reciprocity and respect. But a wife's depression, labor department statistics on patterns of sex-segmentation in the workforce, or sociological studies of relations between power and earned income in marriage, might reveal to one or both that this arrangement is something other than it had seemed. A dominantly heterosexual community may move from a punitive or denying attitude to greater acceptance of and tolerance toward same-sex erotic relations. Those who enjoy same-sex relations may be relieved to suffer less or to live less guardedly, but may find "tolerance" infuriatingly inferior to respect, and "acceptance" a demeaning concession that presupposes unfortunate but blameless deviance. Moral equilibria coordinate beliefs, perceptions, expressions, judgments, actions, and responses. Where present, they may not be fully shared; and they may not be present where they are perceived to be. Some may be sustained or sustainable only under exclusion, concealment, or coercion. This is one key to where the issue of justification goes on this conception.

On an expressive-collaborative view moral agents must learn a logic of interpersonal acknowledgement[25] in moral terms. Because people and their relationships are not uniform and situations are not necessarily repeatable, moral consideration on this view presses toward enrichment of detail and amplification of context. Because negotiation of our lives in moral terms is a continuing process, new situations must be mapped onto past understandings and projected into future possibilities. The greater part of moral reasoning will thus be *analogical* and *narrative.*

Analogies test how like or unlike new cases are to familiar or decided ones. Narratives are stories that show how a situation comes to be the particular problem it is, and that explore imaginatively the continuations that might resolve that problem and what they mean for the parties involved. Analogical and narrative reasoning is inductive, and so indefinitely open to the impact of fresh information. These patterns of moral thinking provide for *flexibility,* rather than uniformity, in adapting existing values to, and honoring standing commitments in, cases at hand. What is at stake in moral understandings is the preservation of integrity, sustainable responsibilities, valued relationships, and certain moral values themselves.

The skills on which these understandings rely are many and varied, and not necessarily specific to morality. Skills of perception are shaped by learning what to notice and how to attend to it; discursive skills by learning how to describe things and what it makes sense to say; skills of responding appropriately in feeling and behavior by learning where feelings fit and what counts as expressing them. The moral epistemology of this view encompasses close description of and critical reflection on all such skills as belong to a particular form of moral life, the trainings that teach them, the kinds of human relations that make them possible, and the kinds of values and relationships they support in turn.

Since many of these perceptive, discursive, and responsive skills are not unique to moral competence, the field for moral epistemology potentially includes every kind of cognition, sensitivity, and aptitude we need to get around competently in any social-moral surround. There is *no pure core of moral knowledge*, much less one to which access might be gained by pure reflection. For present purposes, I limit my discussion to two features of moral thinking that bear directly on the matter of moral justification: *intuitions*—the basic stuff of it—and *narrative*—the characteristic form.

Contemporary moral philosophy is rife with appeal to "intuitions," usually in the role of data for moral theory. Here intuitions are seen as presumptive *outputs* of idealized capacity or *endpoints* of reconstructed moral derivations, and so are served up either as confirming instances of theories that yield them, or counterexamples to theories that fail to yield them or that yield their contraries or contradictories. Most attention is paid to *what* intuitions "we" are claimed to have. Little is paid to the representative status of the claims made in invoking them—that intuitions are characteristically spoken of as "ours" or as something "we" think. Yet the latter is important for the authority these ready responses carry, and rightly so.

It is tempting to defend the authority intuitions are presumed to carry for us by appeal to their "compelling" character; the view that intuitions are "self-evident," at least upon proper reflective survey, mounts this defense.[26] The expressive-collaborative view turns this around: the authority of these moral claims rests on the reason they strike *us* as compelling. What philosophers sometimes describe as our apparently immediate (noninferential) awareness of *their* truth is, more simply, *our* unhesitating inclination to believe and say these things, either ongoing or in certain circumstances.

This is in turn explained by the fact that such moral claims are ones we have learned from, and been taught by, others to say; or ones we have learned are unlikely (or significantly less likely than some others) to be contested by those to whom we presume ourselves accountable. Those moral claims will be "intuitive" that we have learned to make in common with others who have received a like moral training or inhabit "our" moral world. Indeed, the ability to enter just these (sorts of) claims appropriately—that is, unhesitatingly, either ongoing or in specific circumstances—is a condition of being morally competent in the eyes of the training community and one's moral cohorts. One's own moral authority derives from the authority of these judgments as the bases or *starting points* of a particular form of shared moral life. Anyone who does not share enough of, or important enough ones of, these starting points is either a morally incompetent one of us, or just not one of us at all; not, that is, our cohort in the practices of mutual intelligibility that the moral resources of a community make possible.

Intuitive judgments are relatively fixed starting points and continuing reference points of understanding, reasoning, and discussion; they are simply the judgments most commonly, and so usually initially, taken for correct. From these socially shared bases for moral thinking, deliberation and debate often *goes forward,* occasionally by simple deduction, but often by analogical and narrative elaboration. Some intuitive judgments are generalizations that define standard connections between some moral concepts and other moral and nonmoral concepts. ("Breaking promises is wrong"; "True friends are there when you need them"; "All human beings have dignity and moral worth.") Some intuitive judgments are particular, and function as if perceptual. These we learn to make in learning moral vocabularies through which to report states of affairs directly in (thick) moral terms; absent special or unnoticed circumstances "this" is a lie, "this" cruelty, "this" arrogance.

Many moral judgments are *simply* intuitive in these ways. Many others are *mediated* by intuitive ones. The intuitive ones serve as *markers* of the moral relevance of certain features and *guides* to the typical moral weight of certain acts or outcomes, but require to be linked to particular situations by connecting tissues of analogy and narrative. In some cases moral judgments result from generalizations standardly understood, applied to cases uncontroversially perceived. In these cases we get instances that conform to the deductivist ideal of the theoretical-juridical view. ("Breaking promises is wrong; this would be promise-breaking; so, this would be wrong.") But these are not the only cases, and perhaps not the most common ones. Below, I return to the social reality of a moral community that corresponds to the assumption that *all* moral judgment is like this, or should be.

Perfectly common cases of moral judgment may embody complex interactions of moral perceptions and generalizations, typically mediated by analogies and narratives. Where mediating links are arguable because not matter of course (questionable analogies, borderline cases, unfamiliar perceptions), or where different mediating links are possible (alternative analogies, diverging narratives, competing perceptions), moral perplexity and disagreement can emerge from shared and relatively clear starting points.

Still, intuitive starting points *themselves* may be called into question; they may be modified, relinquished, or replaced, for they are *not better* than relatively fixed and common assumptions, not better than where, in fact, we tend to begin. One way intuitive starting points may come into question is when they are found to lead in application to intractable conflicts or untenable or unintelligible moral positions of, or within, a moral community. Their continuing authority depends not on higher-order beliefs from which they may be derived, but on the *character of the common life* they lead us to. The question is whether existing intuitions continue to furnish the standing terms for a negotiation of that life that supports reflective equilibrium among us. This is the form of justification appropriate to them.

The view of morality as progressive mutual acknowledgment and adjustment uses the notion of a *narrative* structure of moral understanding twice over. To say moral thinking is narrative in pattern is, first, a way of seeing how morally relevant information is selected and organized *within* particular episodes of deliberation. The idea is that a story is the basic form of representation for moral problems. We need to know who the parties are, how they understand themselves and each other, what terms of relationship have brought them to this morally problematic point, and perhaps what social or institutional frames shape their options.

Lovers and strangers, kin and citizens, co-workers and spouses are not bound by all (even if they are by some) of the same commitments and responsibilities. Nor do similar commitments always imply the same demands; actual histories of marriages, friendships, or family or citizen relations may create specific (reasonable) expectations and so set distinct terms of responsibility. Values—fairness, loyalty, kindness, respect—are expressible in various ways: expressions that are appropriate to certain relations, settings, and histories make little sense (or the wrong kind) for others. The mutual fairness of X's and Y's shared child-care arrangements is apt to require different measures than the fairness of a medical school's admission policies, the division of a parent's estate among children, or a national system of health-care delivery.

Narrative also captures the way resolution of a moral problem itself takes the form of a *passage,* a transition that links past moral lives (individual, interpersonal, and collective) to future ones in a way not completely or necessarily determined by where things started, and open to different continuations that may affect what the resolution means. If moral life is an ongoing work of sustaining or reshaping our understanding of what values mean, and how we hold ourselves and others accountable for being guided by them, even matter-of-course moral decisions acknowledge an existing history of such understandings and express a presumption that the same understandings continue to hold. In hard moral cases, the resolution of a quandary or conflict constructs an understanding not available before or modifies an existing one; either way, what certain values mean or what certain commitments or relationships demand is newly configured with implications for future moral thought and choice. In this way there form continuing stories of individual and shared moral lives.

The theoretical-juridical picture of applying principles to cases is modeled on the deductive relation of validity that holds between some premises and a conclusion when that conclusion is true if the premises are. This relation either holds or it does not; when it holds, it holds under the impact of all further additions of information. In narratives, however, what comes later means what it does in part because of what preceded it, whereas what came earlier may come to look very different depending on what happens later. Determining responsibilities in the concrete usually involves grasping histories of trust, expectation, and agreement that make particular relationships morally demanding in particular ways. And knowing what general norms or values mean in current situations requires appreciating how these have previously been applied and interpreted within individual and social histories. Narrative constructions allow us to take thought backward in these ways, and then forward to explore the costs and consequences of moral choices for individuals and between them.

Resolutions of moral problems—whether in action or understanding—are more or less acceptable depending on how they sustain or alter the integrity of the parties, the terms of their relationships, and in some cases the meaning of moral (and other) values that are at stake. Moral resolutions are "more or less acceptable" to the parties and the communities they rely on for the conservation of the means of mutual moral understanding. This is why the resolution of a moral problem may be less like the solution to a puzzle or the answer to a question than like the outcome of a negotiation. This does not mean that anything settled on is right, nor that a resolution is right only if everyone can settle on it. A narrative view can be as committed as another to holding that certain things are really better or worse for people, certain responsibilities inescapable, or certain requirements obligating.

The narrative approach is about the forms through which commitments and perceptions are invoked to allow people to make and justify such judgments, as well as to dispute or repudiate them. These commitments and perceptions can be expressed in no other way than by their embodiment and preservation in the moral trainings, discourses, institutions, judgments, and practices of the community that claims to honor them. What that community can in turn claim justifies these commitments and perceptions is the habitability and acceptability of the common life to which they lead.

Authority, Transparency, and Feminist Skepticism

Moral understandings and their enabling stories have to make sense to and stand up within some moral community. Ideally, moral accounts must make sense to those *by* whom, *to* whom, and (except in special cases of immature or diminished agency) *about* whom they are given. This requires that we share with others a moral medium and familiarity with the social terrain of interactions, roles, and relationships to which it belongs.

Earlier I simplified the discussion of intuitions and narratives by assuming that members of a moral community share a similar grasp of roughly the same media of moral understanding. But even in very homogeneous communities this will be an idealization, as variations in moral instruction, familiarity of applications, and individual sensibilities and experiences create differences. In social or political communities that inherit diverse religious and moral traditions, or are unhomogenous, divided, or stratified by socially marked differences with consequences for experiences and opportunities, much of social life will not be unproblematically common, and moral understandings, intuitive and constructive, are likely at best to overlap.

From the perspective of an expressive-collaborative view, the deductivist picture of moral reasoning at the heart of a theoretical-juridical approach idealizes a *closed* moral community: similar moral judgments are made by everybody, because equivalent moral generalizations are applied alike by everybody to cases that are perceived alike by everybody. In such a community the moral terms are given and their applications are set. This kind of closure on moral understanding could be approximated in an actual community only to the degree that moral authority in that community is locked up, unanimous, and perfectly consistent, and social life so homogeneous that divergent personal and social experiences do not challenge standing terms or their applications. I doubt this is a possible social world, even a "hypertraditional" or authoritarian one. It is, in any case, not our social or moral world, in which we go on under conditions of imperfect understanding, conflict among and within ourselves, and diverse perceptions from different social positions which include dramatic inequities in material and discursive resources.

Imperfect understandings, conflicting judgments, or incomprehension are obviously problems for moral equilibrium; they are potentially occasions for interpersonal breaches, social fractures, and individual or group violence. But they are also opportunities. They can propel rethinking and the search for mediating ideas or reconciling procedures within (or between) communities; they can challenge superficiality, complacency, or mere parochialism of moral views. Whether they go one way or another depends on the moral and non-moral interests of contending parties, and no doubt on many contingencies that individuals may not be able to cognize, much less control.

Here I attend to one familiar kind of case: a de facto social community, with many nonmoral interests in and practical necessities of going on as such, and with many overlapping moral understandings already in play. Such a community has motive and opportunity to continue its moral form of life, but also to experience conflicts within it and challenges to it. This kind of familiar setting—ours—houses moral traditions, terms, and trainings that overlap and diverge at various points.

Yet because this society is segmented and stratified by many forms of privilege and disadvantage, not everyone is comparably situated in the continuing negotiation of moral life. Not all intuitions, interpretations, and narrative constructions carry the same authority, or carry authority in the same places. Divisions, instabilities, conflicts of authority, and diverse experiences of social reality provide occasions and materials for critical, and possibly transformative, moral thinking of one kind.

Moral terms and assumptions already in place and carrying authority for "our" moral life may be found to render some of us mute or invisible, our moral positions incoherent or inexpressible, our standing as moral agents compromised or unacknowledged, in some personal and public venues of "shared" life. These moral terms may then be challenged by appealing to or inventing others. Standard applications of moral concepts may be reconfigured around existing social realities or by the pressure of new or newly visible social practices. It is this kind of critical possibility that is realized in feminist ethics, and supported by its social and critical epistemology. Social change that responds to critical possibilities may be incomplete, uneven, or co-opted in unintended ways; it may also be simply unavailable. I return to this important point below.

Feminist skepticism about authoritative representations of morality questions closures of moral discourse around images, ideals, social prerogatives, roles, and viewpoints on social reality that reflect the privileged social positions of some men. The positions reflected in these ideals and norms are not only those of sex privilege; those with access to these positions (or the hope of it) are (almost invariably) men whose privilege is never only that of being men, but of being men with a lot of other privileges.

Still, while being a man has not been sufficient qualification for exercising many of the most coveted forms of agency and power in Western society, being a woman has historically routinely been sufficient disqualification for it. Because of this, feminist criticism of ethics is in one way unabashedly partisan: it aims to enter claims of and on behalf of *women* as full moral agents, for this is what women in the Western tradition have rarely been acknowledged to be. In doing so, however, it poses a *completely general question* about the moral terms set for our common life: where do these come from, and what (or whose) authority and experiences do they represent? It is a richly illustrative instance of a kind of criticism that draws power from what Bernard Williams calls the aspiration toward "transparency" in moral life.

Williams describes this as a "hope for truthfulness" in the ethical thought and practice of society, specifically, that "the working of its ethical institutions should not depend on members of the community misunderstanding how they work."[27] Sabina Lovibond similarly invokes the ideal of "a community whose members understood their own form of life and yet were not embarrassed by it."[28] There are many kinds of misunderstanding possible, and only certain forms of embarrassment available, in given forms of moral life. Feminist ethics works with what is to hand in ours.

Feminist ethics pursues transparency by making visible gendered arrangements that underlie existing moral understandings, and the gendered structures of authority that produce and circulate these understandings. In doing so it magnifies embarrassing double binds of modern morality. One is that its "official" conceptions of moral agency, judgment, and responsibility devalue or disqualify *other* forms of agency, judgment, and responsibility that make the official ones possible in actual social life. Another is that purportedly universal norms defining moral personhood, rationality, autonomy, and objectivity are constructed in ways that depend on these *not* being universally accessible positions or statuses under actual conditions.

In both cases the authoritative conceptions can claim to be representations of something only if they admit their partiality or exclusivity: they represent features of the actual positions of some of us, not all of us. But to own up to their partiality and exclusivity is to lose the kind of authority they claim, for they are supposed to represent universal norms of "our" moral life. Feminists conduct a purposeful exercise in reflective disequilibrium, forcing a collapse of credibility under conditions of transparency, of making some conditions and consequences of moral thought and practice reflectively available for explicit attention.

The ideal of transparency is at once a moral and epistemic one; and not a timeless, placeless condition of the acceptability of moral life, but itself the product of a particular moral and philosophical tradition. So is western feminism. The demands for transparency embodied in feminist ethics are of specifically democratic, participatory, and emancipatory kinds, squarely founded on moral and political ideals of modern Western social thought. The feminist exercise is embarrassing precisely because it exploits a tradition—its own—in which values of representation, consent, self-determination, respect, equality, and freedom are common currency. The authority of these values can be used to put into question the value—the credibility—of authorities and their claims.

There are, however, social conditions for this kind of criticism to emerge. Certain degrees of "disarticulation"—the coming apart—of authority or authorities, or of the fit between existing ways of judging and changed or novel social practices, opens critical space within moral understandings that could otherwise go on as before. When members of groups historically or systematically disqualified from epistemic or moral authority begin to occupy positions that carry it, for example, new judgments and new means of judging are likely to result. This kind of change depends in turn on many other changes.[29]

This is a reminder to philosophers. Whether the question "Is X (really) good (right, best)?" *is* an "open" one is not a purely conceptual matter. Diverse kinds of social, economic, technological, and discursive conditions make available real or imagined alternatives to what and how we think now. Possibilities of critical and speculative thought inhere in real social spaces in real time; how much space there is for this, as well as who can enter it, is determined in many ways. These possibilities are not made available *simply* by thinking, nor should anyone assume their nature and availability is obvious from just any "reflective" vantage point. The demand for transparency, interpreted within a democratic and participatory ethos, is a powerful wedge in this regard; it can be used to invite report and reflection on moral life from many points of view within it, and even outside it. These may become further materials for moral theorizing that doesn't forget that it, too, is a practice intertwined with others. As an epistemic practice, it is answerable to strong objectivity, which includes rendering transparent the relations of authority by which it produces or represents moral knowledge.

Feminist Skepticism and That Other Skepticism

The standard "problem of skepticism" threatens us with there being no knowledge, because propositional justifications of knowledge-claims will either terminate arbitrarily, curve back into a circle, or infinitely regress. The naturalized, but social and reflexively critical, epistemology favored by many feminists, locates the problem differently. Its problem of justification is a problem about *people's claims* to knowledge and their *credibility* in entering those claims. And if knowledge is embodied in communities of inquiry upon which individual knowers depend, anyone's credibility must implicate the credibility of others. The problem of justification becomes: who knows? This problem of knowledge is no philosopher's artifact. Anyone recognizes it who asks, "Whom should I believe?" or "Whom can I trust to know?" or even, "This is what we believe, but is it right?" It is finally, on one end, a question about the instruments and practices of inquiry and relations of authority by which *communities* produce and legitimate their claims to knowledge; on the other, it is about the lives that can be organized around the knowledge claimed. It is about the reliability of the former, and the habitability of the latter.

Moral justification among us appeals to the available languages of morals in their mutually recognized applications. One *can* push the question of justification farther; one can ask for the provenance of these moral means, and the relative worth of alternatives to them, or to the lives they furnish. Or, at least *sometimes, some* of us can. The social conditions for the exercise of critical moral imagination must be there; and those who would open these questions and make them stick must have, or must struggle for, a certain degree of credibility. Not all the logical space of moral justification or criticism is already available, because not all possible social spaces are. And neither the space nor the right to enter it is available at will. No endless regress looms. When questions of justification do arise, answers to them can only back up so far as there are some standing terms of justification and practices of appraisal that give those terms sense. Any actual regress that questions the reliability of our authoritative practices and the credibility of our authorities is then quickly pushed forward again to questions about the lives we are willing to live. These matters are hardly arbitrary, as the stakes here include mutual recognition, cooperation, and shared enjoyment of many goods, or deception, misery, oppression, and violence. In both the backward and forward movement of moral thought there may be contests over who "we" are. Preserving coherence is a powerful constraint in the case of moral understanding, as elsewhere, but what has to cohere is not just a body of belief but a set of social arrangements and the ability of a community of people to make a certain kind of shareable sense of themselves within it.

Feminist ethics presses on both the illegitimacy of some forms and applications of authoritative moral discourse, and on the possibilities for moral life under broadened conditions of mutual candor and acknowledgment. It does not need to say that existing morality is worthless, evil, or corrupt in pointing out that moral authority that is based on, and in turn reproduces sex and other privilege, is unearned and inconsistent. It only needs to show that it *is* unearned or inconsistent, and arguably not for the best, for women and for many men. To show this, it needs to appeal to some of the existing terms, to use some of "the same instruments on the same boat, but on a little visited and basic part of its structure."[30] Under the impacts of social, economic, technological, and discursive changes we sometimes find we are not (quite) in the same boat; we then use old instruments to fashion new ones. Sometimes old tools are transformed in (and by) "the hands of those who were never meant to touch them."[31]

The questions and possibilities raised by feminist ethics are only some of those that might be raised about the habitability and worth of our moral forms of life. Moral and epistemic authority matter particularly to feminism because of the historic denial of them to women. But problems about them, about who has them, and why, can be recognized by anyone, and they matter to everyone. Feminist skepticism visits those parts of our knowledge of morality and politics that house the politics and morality of our knowledge.

Notes

Thanks to the following people who read and provided comments on earlier drafts of this essay: Malia Brink, Marilyn Friedman, Christopher Gowans, John Greco, Alison Jaggar, Diana Meyers, Hilde Nelson, Jim Nelson, and Walter Sinnott-Armstrong. Special thanks to Susan Walsh, who provided perfect work space when I was in transit and at sea. Brief portions of this paper are adapted or excerpted from "Moral Understandings: Alternative 'Epistemology' for a Feminist Ethics," *Hypatia* 4 (1989), 15–28; "Feminism, Ethics, and the Question of Theory," *Hypatia* 7(1992), 23–38; and "Keeping Moral Space Open: New Images of Ethics Consulting," *Hastings Center Report* 23 (1993), 33–40.

1. Alison Jaggar, "Feminist Ethics: Projects, Problems, Prospects," in Claudia Card, ed., *Feminist Ethics* (Lawrence, Kans.: University Press of Kansas, 1991), 88.
2. Ibid., p. 95.
3. I do not discuss here recent work that puts nonfeminist moral frameworks to feminist uses, for example: Marcia L. Homiak, "Feminism and Aristotle's Rational Idea," Barbara Herman, "Could It Be Worth Thinking About Kant on Sex and Marriage?," and Jean Hampton, "Feminist Contractarianism," all in Louise Antony and Charlotte Witt, ed., *A Mind of One's Own* (Boulder, Colo.: Westview Press, 1993); Onora O'Neill, "Justice, Gender, and International Boundaries," (Kantian) and Martha Nussbaum's comment (Aristotelian) in Martha Nussbaum and Amartya Sen, ed., *The Quality of Life* (Oxford: Oxford University Press, 1993); and Susan Miller Okin, *Justice, Gender, and the Family* (New York: Basic Books, 1989) (contractarian).
4. Jaggar, "Feminist Ethics" is the best compact summary of sources and directions of feminist ethics. Rosemary Tong, *Feminine and Feminist Ethics* (Belmont, Calif.: Wadsworth Publishing, 1993) provides an overview. Collections include Card, *Feminist Ethics,* Lorraine Code, Sheila Mullett, and Christine Overall, ed., *Feminist Perspectives: Philosophical Essays on Method and Morals* (Toronto: University of Toronto Press, 1988); Eve Browning Cole and Susan Coultrap-McQuin, ed., *Explorations in Feminist Ethics: Theory and Practice* (Bloomington: Indiana University Press, 1992); Marsha Hanen and Kai Nielsen, ed., *Science, Morality and Feminist Theory* (Calgary: University of Calgary Press, 1987); and Eva Kittay and Diana Meyers, ed., *Women and Moral Theory* (Totowa, N.J.: Rowman and Littlefield, 1987).
5. Catharine MacKinnon, *Feminism Unmodified* (Cambridge, Mass.: Harvard University Press, 1987), 147. Recent theory on gender is extensive. On the crucial insight that gender is about hierarchical power relations, not about "differences," see MacKinnon, especially chapter 2. On how the powers gender distributes differ among and between men and women otherwise differently placed in society (by race, class, etc.), see references in note 14, below. On gender as a set of norms that produce what they purport to regulate, see Judith Butler, *Gender Trouble* (New York: Routledge, 1990). On social and textual constructions of gender in and outside feminism, see Donna Haraway, "Gender for a Marxist Dictionary: The Sexual Politics of a Word" in *Simians, Cyborgs, and Women* (New York: Routledge, 1991). Alison Jaggar, *Feminist*

Politics and Human Nature (Totowa, N.J.: Rowman and Allanheld, 1983) provides thorough analysis of gender in the structure of liberal, Marxist, and some feminist political frameworks. Iris Young, *Justice and the Politics of Difference* (Princeton, N.J.: Princeton University Press, 1990), explores interactions of gender with other systems of privilege.

6. Many of these critiques are found in debates surrounding an "ethic of care"; for references, see note 13. In addition, see Annette Baier, "Trust and Anti-Trust," *Ethics* 96 (1986), 321–60, and "The Need For More Than Justice," in Hanen and Nielsen; Seyla Benhabib, "The Generalized and The Concrete Other," in Kittay and Meyers; Lorraine Code, "Second Persons," in *What Can She Know?* (Ithaca: Cornell University Press, 1991); Robin Dillon, "Care and Respect," in Cole and Coultrap-McQuin; Diana ʻMeyers, *Self, Society, and Personal Choice* (New York: Columbia University Press, 1989) on autonomy and masculine character ideals; Iris Young, "The Ideal of Impartiality and the Civic Public," in *Justice and the Politics of Difference.*

7. Kathryn Morgan, "Women and Moral Madness," in Hanen and Nielsen, p. 220.

8. Joan Tronto, *Moral Boundaries: A Political Argument for an Ethic of Care* (New York: Routledge, 1993), 3.

9. Ibid., p. 61.

10. I discuss this model in "Feminism, Ethics, and the Question of Theory," *Hypatia* 7 (1992), 23–38. Compare Annette Baier on the "tightly systematic" form of theory in "What Do Women Want in a Moral Theory?," *Nous* 19 (1985), 53–63; and Rita Manning on "the textbook picture," with deductivist and inductivist, foundationalist and relativist versions in *Speaking from the Heart* (Lanham, Md.: Rowman and Littlefield, 1992), 4–5.

11. Kathryn Addelson, "Moral Passages," in *Impure Thoughts* (Philadelphia: Temple University Press, 1991), 104–5.

12. Cheshire Calhoun, "Justice, Care, Gender Bias," *Journal of Philosophy* 85 (1988), 451–63.

13. Psychologist Carol Gilligan's *In a Different Voice* (Cambridge, Mass.: Harvard University Press, 1982) is the best-known source of such a view. Mary Jeanne Larrabee, ed., *An Ethic of Care* (New York: Routledge, 1993) collects both psychological and philosophical literature in response to Gilligan. For creative and systematic developments of care ethics, see Nel Noddings, *Caring* (Berkeley and Los Angeles: University of California Press, 1984); Sara Ruddick, *Maternal Thinking* (New York: Ballantine Books, 1984); Virginia Held, *Feminist Morality* (Chicago: University of Chicago Press, 1993); Rita Manning, *Speaking from the Heart;* and Joan Tronto, *Moral Boundaries.* Critical responses to Gilligan or care ethics include Jean Grimshaw, *Philosophy and Feminist Thinking* (Minneapolis: University of Minnesota Press, 1986), chapters 7 and 8; Barbara Houston, "Rescuing Womanly Virtues: Some Dangers of Moral Reclamation," in Hanen and Nielsen; Sarah Lucia Hoagland, "Some Thoughts About 'Caring' " and Michele Moody-Adams, "Gender and the Complexity of Moral Voices," in Card; and Marilyn Friedman, *What Are Friends For?* (Ithaca: Cornell University Press, 1993), Part 2. On race and class concerns see Sandra Harding, "The Curious Coincidence of Feminine and African Moralities," in Kittay and Meyers, and Carol Stack, "The Culture of Gender: Women and Men of Color," in Larabee.

14. A compelling and artful statement of the problem is Maria Lugones and Elizabeth Spelman, "Have We Got a Theory For You! Feminist Theory, Cultural Imperialism, and the Demand for 'The Woman's Voice'," *Hypatia,* Special Issue of *Women's Studies International Forum* 6 (1983), 573–81. See also Cherrie Moraga and Gloria Anzuldua, *This Bridge Called My Back* (New York: Kitchen Table Press, 1983);

bell hooks, *Feminist Theory: From Margin to Center* (Boston: South End Press, 1984); Elizabeth V. Spelman, *Inessential Woman* (Boston: Beacon Press, 1988); Gloria Anzuldua, *Making Face, Making Soul* (San Francisco: Aunt Lute Foundation Books, 1990); Patricia Hill Collins, *Black Feminist Thought* (Cambridge, Mass.: Unwin and Hyman, 1990).

15. Lorraine Code, *What Can She Know?*, p. 224.

16. Lynn Hankinson Nelson, "Epistemological Communities," in Linda Alcoff and Elizabeth Potter, ed., *Feminist Epistemologies* (New York: Routledge, 1993), 150.

17. Helen Longino, "Subjects, Power and Knowledge: Description and Prescription in Feminist Philosophies of Science," in Alcoff and Potter, p. 112.

18. Louise Antony, "Quine as Feminist: The Radical Import of Naturalized Epistemology," in Antony and Witt, ed., *A Mind of One's Own*, p. 212.

19. On strong objectivity and on socially marginal standpoints as resources, see Sandra Harding, "Rethinking Standpoint Epistemology: What Is Strong Objectivity?" in Alcoff and Potter. On criteria of objectivity in application to communities, see Longino, "Subjects, Power and Knowledge" in Alcoff and Potter, and "Essential Tensions—Phase Two: Feminist, Philosophical, and Social Studies of Science," in Antony and Witt. On situated knowledge and "material-semiotic" technologies, see Donna Haraway, *Simians, Cyborgs, and Women*. On the need for inquiry into the nature and effects of bias, see Louise Antony, "Quine as Feminist." On complexities of evaluation on a holistic view, see Lynn Nelson, "Epistemological Communities." On empirical study of the social organization of knowledge, and on micronegotiations in epistemic communities, see Kathryn Addelson, "Knowers/Doers and Their Moral Problems," and Elizabeth Potter, "Gender and Epistemic Negotiation," both in Alcoff and Potter.

20. Donna Haraway, "Situated Knowledges," in *Symians, Cyborgs, and Women*, p. 190.

21. Mark Timmons's chapter in this volume offers one such descriptive account.

22. Naomi Scheman, *Engenderings* (New York: Routledge, 1993), 98. See Nelson, "Epistemological Communities" and Antony, "Quine as Feminist" on feminist epistemology as naturalized epistemology.

23. These characteristic themes are found in Gilligan, Whitbeck, Noddings, Ruddick, Held, Manning, Tronto, Baier, and Benhabib (see notes 6 and 13 above); also in Sharon Bishop, "Connections and Guilt," *Hypatia* 2 (1987), 7–23; Marilyn Frye, *The Politics of Reality* (Trumansberg, N.Y.: Crossing Press, 1983); Sara Lucia Hoagland, *Lesbian Ethics* (Palo Alto, Calif.: Institute of Lesbian Studies, 1988); Diana Meyers, *Subjection and Subjectivity* (New York: Routledge, 1994).

24. John Rawls, *A Theory of Justice* (Cambridge, Mass.: Harvard University Press, 1971), 20. Rawls is the original for the reflective equilibrium view, although it is rooted in Sidgwick's approach to rectifying "commonsense morality." Sidgwick in turn thought it was what Aristotle had done.

25. I borrow this signature term from Stanley Cavell. For Cavell's own view, see *The Claim of Reason* (Oxford: Oxford University Press, 1979), Part 3.

26. Robert Audi's chapter in this volume defends a version of this view. Mark Timmons's chapter in this volume argues intuitive judgments are contextually basic. This gives them a structural role similar to the one I give them, at least in many contexts of justification. But Timmons' takes the (apparent) fact that the beliefs in question strike believers as "obvious" and "nonarbitrary" to display a "second-order doxastic commitment." If this means that believers find themselves relieved of justification by other beliefs *because* intuitive beliefs are obvious, this seems to slide back to

the "compellingness" idea about intuitions, whereas if "nonarbitrariness" suggests that believers think there may be something (or a great deal) to be said for holding them, and may be prepared to say it even in "ordinary" contexts, then the idea that intuitions are not in need of justification (from the perspective of the moral community) is not quite right. I don't think Timmons's "phenomenology" is complete, or that the distinction between "ordinary" and other (or between "engaged" and "disengaged") contexts will stand up to a more complete one, even for "the same social group."

27. Bernard Williams, *Ethics and the Limits of Philosophy* (Cambridge: Cambridge University Press, 1985), 101.

28. Sabina Lovibond, *Realism and Imagination in Ethics* (Minneapolis: University of Minnesota Press, 1981), 158.

29. Jana Sawicki, *Disciplining Foucault* (New York: Routledge, 1991), chapter 5, discusses disarticulation of Enlightenment ideals from some practices and rearticulating them in terms of others, within a Foucauldian framework. Patricia Mann, *Micro-Politics: Agency in a Postfeminist Era* (Minneapolis: University of Minnesota, 1994) analyzes the coming apart of liberal conceptions of agency under rapid mutations of certain gendered roles and expectations.

30. Simon Blackburn, *Essays in Quasi-Realism* (Oxford: Oxford University Press, 1993), 51, so characterizes skepticism.

31. Scheman, p. 225.

11

Outline of a Contextualist
Moral Epistemology

Mark Timmons

At the foundation of well-founded belief lies belief that is not founded.
—Ludwig Wittgenstein, *On Certainty*, §253

Why is integrity important and lying bad? I don't know. It just is. I don't want to be bothered by challenging that.
—Interviewee, *Habits of the Heart*[1]

An inquiry, to have that completely satisfactory result called demonstration, has only to start with propositions perfectly free from all actual doubt. If the premises are not in fact doubted at all, they cannot be more satisfactory than they are.
—C. S. Peirce, *Collected Papers*, 5.358

Epistemological contextualism, which has its roots in the writings of pragmatists like Peirce and Dewey and in the later Wittgenstein, is often characterized as an alternative to the more traditional approaches in analytic epistemology. In opposition to both foundationalist and coherentist views about the structure of justification and knowledge, the contextualist claims (in the spirit of the above Wittgenstein quote) that justified belief is ultimately based on beliefs that are not themselves justified. But other so-called contextualist claims, not having to do with structural issues, have gained increasing recognition and discussion by analytic epistemologists in recent years. One such claim (vaguely expressed) is that possession of such epistemic goods as knowledge and justification depends importantly on one's circumstances or "context," including in particular certain facts about one's social group. Unfortunately, "contextualism" and talk of justification and knowledge being sensitive to context are used to cover a variety of themes and theses, some of them fairly uncontroversial, others quite controversial.

My aim here is to articulate and partially defend a moral epistemology that incorporates a number of contextualist themes. More specifically, my plan is this: Because contextualism is perhaps less familiar to moral epistemologists than other epistemological views, but also because of the variety of contextualist themes and theses that have been recently defended, the first section of this chapter will be devoted to sorting out and clarifying the most important of these contextualist ideas. As we shall see, I am interested in defending a version of what I call "structural contextualism" regarding justified moral belief. However, because there is no one notion of justification but many (arguably legitimate) notions, section two of the chapter is devoted to making clear the epistemic notion—a notion of *epistemic responsibility*—that is the focus of my thinking about the justification of moral belief. In the third section, I clarify the main theses of structural contextualism, and then in section four I proceed to elaborate a version of structural contextualism about moral belief. A full defense of contextualism would require that I develop this view in the context of a story about the semantics and associated metaphysics of moral discourse. That project is for another occasion.[2] Here I have the more limited aim of convincing the reader that the version of contextualism I advocate is a promising approach to questions about the justification of moral belief.

Epistemological Contextualism

I'm going to distinguish between what I will call *circumstantial contextualism, normative contextualism,* and *structural contextualism.* The first two theses are roughly analogous to familiar relativist views in ethics. The third represents a response to the infamous regress of justification problem and so rivals foundationalist and coherentist responses to that problem.

Circumstantial Contextualism

One contextualist theme in recent epistemology (applied to the issue of justification), which I will call "circumstantial contextualism," can be expressed this way:

> CC: Whether one has knowledge of, or indeed justifiedly believes, some proposition is partly dependent on certain facts about oneself and certain facts about one's environment.

Now it is uncontroversial that whether or not one knows or justifiedly believes some proposition depends on "internal" (psychological) features of one's circumstances such as evidence one has (whether in the form of other beliefs or certain experiential states), and whether or not one possesses any undermining evidence, and so forth. But many epistemologists have called attention to certain "external" features of one's circumstances that may affect the epistemic status of one's beliefs. Goldman's case of the papier-mâché barns is a well-known example.[3] In that example, one has excellent perceptual evidence that there is a barn in the field though one is unaware of the fact that the surrounding countryside is populated with papier-mâché barn facsimiles. In this case one apparently fails to know that there is a barn in the field because of facts about one's immediate environment representing relevant evidence one does not possess. This is a case in which knowledge is sensitive to one's *physical* environment.

The idea that knowledge and justification depend on facts about one's *social* environment—that epistemic appraisal has a "social dimension"—has been of particular interest in recent epistemology. According to Stewart Cohen and Ernest Sosa, there is an interesting connection between certain social facts—facts about one's community—and requirements relating to the use of an individual's cognitive faculties that nicely illustrates how knowledge and justification can depend on one's social circumstances.

Cohen's contextualism emerges from his study of the conditions under which evidence one *does* possess undermines one's knowledge. He argues first of all that whether or not defeaters one possesses (i.e., beliefs one has that count as evidence against some proposition one believes) undermine one's knowledge of that proposition depends on the reasoning abilities of a normal member of a relevant social group and whether, in particular, the fact that some evidence one possesses is a defeater would be obvious to normal members of that group. Thus, on Cohen's view, one component of knowledge is determined by certain psychological facts about society. But which social group or society serves as the basis for judging the obviousness of defeaters? Cohen's own proposal is that "the standards in effect in a particular context are determined by the normal reasoning powers of the attributor's social group."[4] In light of this social dimension of knowledge, Cohen proposes that ascriptions (and denials) of knowledge are best construed as indexical or context-sensitive: the set of intersubjective standards of obviousness that apply in ascriptions of knowledge can vary from context to context depending on which group counts as the attributor group. The idea that knowledge involves a socially determined level of reasoning ability perhaps also applies to the cognitive faculties of memory and perception.[5] Not only might epistemic requirements for dealing with counterevidence be gauged by certain social facts having to do with cognitive abilities, but other social factors may play a role in knowledge. Sosa, for example, argues that the extent to which members of one's social group possess some bit of information affects one's knowledge. If, for example, most everyone in one's community has information that defeats some true proposition that one otherwise has excellent evidence for believing, then arguably one fails to know. According to Sosa reflection on such cases make it "plausible to conclude that knowledge has a further 'social aspect,' that it cannot depend on one's missing or blinking what is generally known."[6]

Normative Contextualism

Another contextualist claim is that justification (rationality, knowledge) depends on, or is relative to, the social practices and norms of communities of inquirers. Some contextualists like to point out how our knowledge-gathering

practices are social in nature and importantly tethered to the epistemic practices and norms of the members of our group (however talk of "our group"
is to be understood). Construed as a descriptive claim about our epistemic
evaluations this claim is perhaps (with some qualifications) correct since it
amounts to the claim that *as a matter of fact* our epistemic evaluations are
typically made on the basis of ("relative to") the practices and norms generally
accepted and used by a community of inquirers to which we belong. However,
the contextualists I have in mind intend the claim normatively (i.e., as a claim
about the conditions under which one knows, or is justified in holding, some
belief). If we let "context" refer to some community of inquirers and the
relevant evaluative practices and norms they share, then we can formulate a
working characterization of normative contextualism this way:

> NC: A person S is justified at time t in believing some proposition p
> in context C just in case S's holding p at t conforms to the
> relevant set of epistemic practices and norms operative in C.

I am calling particular attention to the idea that there is a social dimension
to epistemic evaluation because the idea that knowledge and justification
depend on one's social group can be taken in two ways. First, as we have seen
with Cohen and Sosa, it can be taken as one feature (or set of features) of one's
circumstances that is relevant for epistemic appraisal. But, as just explained, it
can also be taken as the idea that knowledge and justification *are relative to
the epistemic standards of one's social group or community,* so that whether
or not one has knowledge or is justified in believing some proposition depends
on whether or not one's belief conforms to the epistemic norms of one's
group. The thesis of circumstantial contextualism, then, should not be confused
with normative contextualism. In ethics, it is standard to distinguish between
circumstantial (situational, environmental) relativism and ethical relativism.
The former is analogous to what I am calling circumstantial contextualism
and is often expressed as the general thesis that the rightness and wrongness
of particular actions, practices and so forth depend in part on facts about the
agent's circumstances. So, for instance, whether it would be wrong for an
onlooker to refrain from jumping into the deep end in an effort to save a
drowning child depends (in part) on facts about that person and, in particular,
on whether or not she can swim. Ethical relativism, by contrast, represents a
normative theory which, in perhaps its most common variety, relativizes moral
truth to the moral standards of groups: the moral standards of a group (together
with relevant factual information) determine which particular moral statements are true for members of that group. Now the epistemological analog
of ethical relativism is what I am calling normative contextualism. My point
here is that just as we should not confuse circumstantial relativism in ethics
with normative ethical relativism, so we should not interpret the circumstantial
contextualism of Cohen and Sosa as equivalent to, or entailing, normative
contextualism.[7]

I should mention at this point that it is not my intention to defend some version of normative contextualism over and against nonrelativist epistemological views. As we shall see in the section on justification and epistemic responsibility, it may be legitimate in some contexts and for some purposes to evaluate the epistemic status of an individual's beliefs relative to the epistemic norms of that person's community. But there are contexts in which we intend to make nonrelativized, categorical epistemic evaluations, even if, in doing so, we obviously employ epistemic norms that we accept.

Structural Contextualism

In the last two decades, work in analytic epistemology has been dominated by structural issues relating to justification and knowledge. What is called contextualism is often taken to be a thesis about the *structure of justification* intended as one response to the infamous *regress of justification* problem. That problem gets generated when we notice that some of the propositions that we (presumably) justifiedly believe owe their justification to other beliefs that we accept—such beliefs forming an epistemic chain. But unless these further, justifying beliefs in the chain are themselves justified we only seem to have what we might call *conditional justification:* the original link in the chain is justified *if* the further links are justified. But then how are we to understand the nature of unconditional justification? The two standard options in response to this question are these: 1) *epistemic foundationalism:* the regress stops with beliefs that are somehow noninferentially justified in the sense of not owing their justification to being inferred from, or otherwise grounded on, other beliefs; 2) *epistemic coherentism:* there are no regress stoppers, rather justification is a matter of the interconnectedness of a finite set of beliefs. Contextualism represents a third option: 3) *epistemic contextualism:* the regress ends with beliefs that are not in need of justification in a given context.[8] So what I'm calling structural contextualism may be informally characterized as follows:

SC: Regresses of justification may legitimately terminate with beliefs, which, in the context in question, *are not in need of justification.* Call these latter beliefs, *contextually basic beliefs.*[9]

This admittedly rough formulation at best only conveys the basic structural picture of justification the contextualist favors. For one thing talk about "context" is left unexplained, as is talk about beliefs not needing justification. I save the task of clarifying these crucial notions until I have clarified (in the next section) the specific notion of epistemic appraisal operative in my thinking. However, before going on, note that SC, as formulated, does not *require* that all inferentially justified beliefs be based on contextually basic beliefs, rather it allows that regresses *may* legitimately terminated with such beliefs. This means that the contextualist can allow (strictly speaking) that an individual's justified beliefs may exhibit either a foundationalist or a coherentist structure.[10]

What the contextualist claims is that the contextualist picture represents a realistic and largely accurate picture of the actual structure of an ordinary individual's justified beliefs. And this indeed is what I plan to argue in connection with moral belief.

To conclude, we should recognize three general contextualist theses. I take circumstantial contextualism to be fairly uncontroversial, though epistemologists may disagree over the sorts of circumstantial factors that affect the epistemic status of an individual's beliefs. As we shall see, the moral epistemology that I go on to defend features the importance of one's social circumstances in coming to have justified moral beliefs. Normative contextualism (i.e., epistemological relativism) is quite controversial and should not be confused with circumstantial or structural contextualism. The contextualist moral epistemology I plan to defend is not intended as a version of normative contextualism. Finally, I do plan to defend a version of structural contextualism about justified moral belief, which will occupy most of my attention in what follows.

Justification and Epistemic Responsibility

To set the stage for the version of epistemological contextualism I propose to defend, I first need to specify the notion of epistemic appraisal at work in my thinking. My primary interest here is with questions about the justification of moral belief and not with questions of proving, showing, or demonstrating moral principles. I need to clarify what I mean here, and I also need to say something about how certain terms of epistemic evaluation (such as "justification," "rationality") work. As I will explain, ascriptions of justification (and rationality) are best interpreted as involving certain contextually variable parameters.[11] Getting clear about these matters will allow me to clarify the specific notion of doxastic justification that interests me, the notion of being *epistemically responsible* in what one believes. Let me elaborate.

Preliminary Remarks about Justification

In this paper I am interested in questions about *doxastic justification,* that is, with questions of when someone justifiably holds some token belief, specifically a moral belief.[12] Questions about doxastic justification should be distinguished from questions about the conditions under which some proposition or claim can be proved true, validated, or "justified," apart from anyone believing it—call this *nondoxastic justification.* In ethics, much of the focus has been on nondoxastic justification. I'm here thinking of attempts by moral philosophers to explain what sorts of considerations can be used to prove or show the truth (validity) of moral propositions or claims including especially moral principles. Examples include: Marcus Singer's[13] attempt to prove the Generalization Argument Principle based on an appeal to the logic of moral discourse, Gewirth's[14] attempt to prove the so-called Principle of Generic Consistency based on claims about the nature of rational action, Donagan's[15] attempt to prove a Kantian Respect for Persons Principle based on claims about the nature of practical reasons and the nature of moral agents, Brandt's[16] attempt to justify a version of rule utilitarianism based largely on empirical considerations from cognitive psychology, Rawls's[17] attempt to justify his two principles of justice based on considerations of overall coherence broadly conceived, and Hare's[18] attempt to justify a utilitarian moral principle based on the logic of ethical concepts. Because moral principles are at the heart of normative moral theories, the attempts of these moral philosophers to prove or demonstrate moral principles are concerned with questions of *theory acceptance* in ethics, and not directly concerned with questions of what I am calling doxastic justification.[19] However, even if one takes an antitheory stance in ethics and denies that moral phenomena can be systematized by a single principle or even a small set of principles, the distinction between doxastic and nondoxastic justification can and should be made.[20]

In contemporary epistemology we find a variety of accounts of doxastic justification. In his recent book, Richard Foley points out that ascriptions of rationality should be understood to involve (at least tacitly) reference to (1) a goal or set of goals and (2) a perspective.[21] I am primarily interested in a notion of doxastic justification that can be usefully understood along the lines Foley recommends for rational belief. Whether or not the notion I am interested in is identical to Foley's notion of rational belief, I leave open. What I propose, then, following Foley, is to think of ascriptions of doxastic justification as involving certain contextually variable parameters. Let me briefly comment on two of these parameters, and then I will be able to characterize more precisely the notion doxastic justification featured in my thinking.

First of all, then, evaluations employing talk of justification normally invoke, either explicitly or tacitly, some goal or goals to be promoted in having justified beliefs. Here it is standard to distinguish epistemic goals such as having true beliefs and avoiding false ones, from various nonepistemic goals such as survival. Correspondingly, we distinguish between epistemic justification and nonepistemic justification. Whether some belief is epistemically justified (from some perspective) depends on whether, from within the appropriate perspective, the belief in question apparently[22] promotes the goals of having true beliefs and avoiding false ones. Whether a belief is nonepistemically justified depends on whether the belief apparently promotes or satisfies some nonepistemic goal. In ethics, especially, where debates over whether moral sentences are true or even have truth values are center stage, it is particularly important to distinguish epistemic from nonepistemic justification.

Second, ascriptions of justification presuppose some perspective. Foley characterizes a perspective as a set of beliefs or body of opinion possessed by some actual or imaginary individual or group. Presumably, this body of opinion includes epistemic beliefs that reflect a set of epistemic standards that figure in the perspective in question.[23] There are various epistemic perspectives from which epistemic evaluations proceed; some of the more familiar include: the subjective or egocentric perspective of an individual agent, the intersubjective or sociocentric perspective of some community, the perspective of some group of experts, and the perspective of an ideally knowledgeable observer. The fact that justification talk is perspectival often goes unnoticed since we often do not make explicit the perspective from which such evaluations are made. But the various perspectives operative in our ascriptions of justification and rationality simply reflect various evaluative interests and purposes we have. For instance, when we are interested in understanding some belief held by a particular person (perhaps oneself) on some past occasion, and when in retrospect that belief now seems pretty clearly mistaken, we often are interested in how things looked to the agent on the occasion in question (at least if we are disposed to view the person charitably). Here it is natural to invoke an egocentric perspective and ask whether, given the agent's epistemic perspective at the time, she was justified in holding the belief in question.

However, for certain purposes we might be interested in evaluating an individual relative to the epistemic standards prevalent in her community, in which case our evaluation involves a sociocentric perspective. Still, in other contexts, we have an interest in questions about justification apart from some subjective or intersubjective perspective and the perspective of an ideally knowledgeable spectator—a way of capturing an objective perspective—is appropriate. The most important lesson to learn from all this talk about perspectives is nicely expressed by Foley: "There is no single perspective that is adequate for understanding the entire range of our judgments of rationality. We make such judgments for a variety of purposes and in a variety of contexts, and the kind of judgment we are inclined to make varies with these purposes and contexts."[24]

Obviously, there is much more to be said about these contextually variable parameters of doxastic justification, and some understanding of how they operate will emerge as we proceed. But having said this much, I can now indicate more clearly the focus of my thinking about moral justification.

First, I am interested in the *epistemic appraisal* of individuals's *beliefs*—doxastic epistemic appraisal—where the primary goal involved in such appraisal is the having of true beliefs and the avoiding of false ones. Second, I am particularly interested in the sort of epistemic appraisal that is operative in our everyday, common epistemic appraisals of individuals.[25] The sort of appraisal I have in mind concerns questions about how one might be *epistemically responsible* in the beliefs one holds. Now one illuminating way of evaluating the epistemic responsibility of an agent is to invoke the perspective of what we might call an "epistemically responsible agent" on analogy with the idea of the "reasonable person" standard from Anglo-American law.[26] The idea is to use this model as a basis for investigating the basic epistemic norms (and general epistemic sensibility) that we normally do and should use in evaluating the epistemic status of moral belief. There are two crucial features that this model must have if it is going to serve in this role. First, if it is to have any sort of normative bite and thus be useful as a measure of a person being epistemically responsible in the beliefs she holds, then it must take on the character of an idealization. The epistemically responsible agent is one whose epistemic activities serve as a norm for our epistemic activities: we *ought* to conform to those norms characteristic of the responsible agent. Second, given our interest in characterizing a notion of epistemic justification that is applicable to human beings, we want a notion of epistemic responsibility that is not overly idealized. In short, we want a model of epistemic responsibility that represents a "realistic ideal." With these constraints in mind, let me now proceed to sketch (part of) a model of epistemic responsibility.

Epistemic Responsibility

Broadly speaking, being epistemically responsible has to do with such activities as: (1) gathering evidence, (2) considering and dealing with counterpossibilities, and (3) dealing with internal conflicts of belief. We normally criticize agents whose beliefs are not based on adequate evidence, who have not checked out relevant counterpossibilities to what they believe, and who fail to eliminate certain conflicts of belief. To be epistemically responsible in what one believes, one must not fall below certain standards or norms governing these activities. What do the norms require? More specifically: How much evidence is enough for having a justified belief? Which counterpossibilities must one check? Which conflicts of belief must one eliminate? Since we are interested in the perspective of the responsible epistemic agent, these questions are about the most general epistemic norms characteristic of this representative agent. Limitations of space do not permit a full treatment of these matters here, but we can provide a partial sketch of an epistemically responsible agent that will be sufficient for present purposes by focusing primarily on those epistemic responsibilities and associated norms that have to do with checking counterpossibilities.[27]

Responsibility for checking counterpossibilities to propositions we currently believe (or propositions we are considering) can range from very strict requirements corresponding to a norm requiring persons to check all logically possible counterpossibilities (including the sorts of fanciful skeptical scenarios devised by philosophers) to very lax requirements where, in the limit, there would be a complete freedom from doing any checking at all. In between the extremes is a range of possible norms requiring more or less of an agent. If we begin with the assumption that some sort of "in-between" requirement not only fits actual epistemic practice, but is defensible, then one plausible suggestion for specifying the range of counterpossibilities for which one is epistemically responsible is this:[28]

ER: A person *S* is epistemically responsible in believing some proposition *p* at time *t* only if *S* checks all of those counterpossibilities whose seriousness is indicated by *S*'s background beliefs at *t*.[29]

This is a start, but it will not do as it stands. For one thing, insofar as the epistemically responsible agent is a projection of normal human beings with normal cognitive powers, ER is too strong—it fails to take into consideration normal human powers of for example, inference and memory. Moreover, it ignores those counterpossibilities whose seriousness is implied by information we *ought* to be aware of even if we lack the information in question. Let us proceed to refine ER in light of these remarks.

First of all, in some respects, our model epistemic agent represents an idealization of actual human epistemic practice. So, for instance, our model does idealize away from certain factors that would interfere with or distort the judgment of our epistemically responsible agent. First, the epistemically responsible agent is presumed to always conform his or her beliefs to the relevant set of epistemic norms, just as in the law, the reasonable person "is not to be identified with any ordinary person who might occasionally do unreasonable things; he is a prudent and careful person, who is always up to standard."[30] Second, in characterizing the activities of our model agent, we ignore drunkenness, being drugged, being tired, being distracted, and other such inhibiting factors that would impair the normal judgment of a normal person. Third, our model agent is free from the sorts of pressing emergency situations that would interfere with his or her focusing and reflecting adequately on some proposition or belief whose epistemic status is in question.

However, in other respects, we want our imaginary agent to reflect normal human abilities. Just as in the law, where the representative reasonable person is expected to have cognitive capacities that are "normal" for human beings, our model of a representative epistemic agent should be similarly constituted. We can begin by noting that there are all sorts of deductive inferences that are completely infeasible for normal human beings to perform. And similarly for nondeductive inferences. If some such inferences are impossible for normal humans to make or are, in some looser sense, infeasible, then we should not hold people responsible for counterpossibilities that would require that they make infeasible inferences from their current belief set. We do expect people to make inferences from their current belief set that are humanly feasible—feasible for normal human beings. And here is where empirical considerations yielding theories of deductive and nondeductive *feasibility* as Cherniak[31] calls them, or theories of *obviousness* as Cohen[32] calls them, come into play in helping to set acceptable standards of epistemic care for checking counterpossibilities. Moreover, in setting the level of epistemic responsibility for dealing with counterevidence we expect individuals to be able to recall relevant information from memory, though again, we do not hold people to standards of memory recall that exceed what is feasible for normal human beings. Theories of feasible inference and feasible memory, then, also help to set levels of epistemic responsibility appropriate for normal human beings. For convenience, let us use the expression "obvious counterpossibilities" to refer to those counterpossibilities a normal human being with normal cognitive powers could be expected to recognize. Thus, our original proposal should be revised so that we are required to check some but not all of those counterpossibilities implied by what we believe, where limits on which counterpossibility checking is partly determined by our empirical views about "normal" cognitive capacities.

However, there is more to our understanding of epistemic responsibility for dealing with counterpossibilities. That is, merely checking all of those obvious counterpossibilities whose seriousness is implied by one's current belief set does not mean that one is being epistemically responsible, since (1) one might simply lack certain general information that anyone can be expected to know or (2) be negligent in acquiring evidence that bears on some specific issue or claim. (Here is one place where responsibilities concerning the gathering of evidence characteristic of the epistemically responsible agent come into play.) With regard to general information one ought to have, there are certain things anyone is expected to know, where we are relying in particular on such social phenomena as common experience (e.g., fire burns, water will drown, and countless other bits of information), widely shared educational experiences (e.g., elementary facts about history, physical science, and so forth), and information gathered more informally such as through the media. Again, this general knowledge requirement is reflected in the doctrine of the reasonable person: "there is a minimum standard of knowledge, based upon what is common to the community,"[33] which the reasonable person possesses and thus ordinary agents ought to possess.

With regard to quite special information bearing specifically on some claim or belief, again, what is common to a community normally helps determine the extent of one's responsibility for being aware of that information. A slightly modified example from Austin[34] makes the point clear. If I look out my window and see what I take to be a goldfinch in my front yard, ordinarily I would be justified in believing that there is a goldfinch there. But suppose that stuffed toy goldfinches have become all the rage with children in my neighborhood and everyone is talking about it, though I have been oblivious to this fact. Nothing that I currently believe implies that there is a decent chance that the goldfinch I'm looking at is a toy; however I am subject to fair epistemic criticism because I should have known about the fad. Of course, sometimes information that I ought to acquire is something that is indicated by the beliefs I currently hold, but in this case, the information one ought to have is information possessed by folks in one's immediate community. Thus, as Sosa[35] and others have argued, we are normally held responsible for information representing counterpossibilities that is generally known in our community—ignorance of such information is typically no excuse. This fact about our epistemic practices reflects the importance of the idea that there is a social dimension to epistemic responsibility. In fact, this social dimension plays an important part in the contextualist's picture of epistemic responsibility as we shall see in the next section.

If we let the expression "adequate set of background beliefs" refer to the background beliefs the agent does possess plus any that he ought to possess, we can reformulate ER to reflect the point about socially available information as well as the point about obviousness of counterpossibilities:

ER′: A person *S* is epistemically responsible in believing some proposition *p* at time *t* only if *S* checks all of those obvious counter-

possibilities whose seriousness is indicated by an adequate
set of background beliefs at *t.*

There is much more to be said about this principle and about the notion of
epistemic responsibility generally, but I hope what I have said is clear enough
for our immediate purposes.

Up to this point in this section, I have been engaging in what I take to be
a largely descriptive enterprise of accurately characterizing an important feature of our actual, everyday epistemic evaluations. But I also think that there
is good reason to endorse this norm and other, related norms. I have in mind
a pragmatic rationale that views epistemic norms in terms of their point and
purpose for limited creatures like us. In brief the rationale is this: Given that
we are finite creatures with limited cognitive resources and that we have all
sorts of nonepistemic goals in life, we would expect any genuinely useful
epistemic norms to reflect such facts. We have now explicitly fashioned ER*
so that it reflects our limited cognitive abilities. Moreover, the fact that our
epistemic norms do not normally require of us that we devote inordinate
amounts of time to checking our claims and beliefs for possible error, rather
they require only that we expend a "reasonable" amount of time doing so,
reflects the fact that we are not purely intellectual beings whose only concern
is with having an interesting stock of true beliefs.[36] Life is short and there are
other things to do. Given the need for some epistemic norms, but given what
we are like (including limitations), norms like ER* seem to be the very sort
of norms we would want and expect to be operative in everyday life. So, once
we think about norms in these broadly pragmatic terms, we can see that the
sorts of norms we do tend to use are ones for which there is a good rationale.

Finally, before leaving this section, I want to raise a question that is directly
related to what follows. First, a bit of terminology. As I am using the term,
epistemic responsibility is a broader notion than the notion of justified belief.
For an individual to be positively epistemically justified in believing some
proposition is for one to have positive (undefeated) sufficient reasons or
grounds for that proposition. Being epistemically responsible in holding a
belief does not necessarily require that one be justified in holding the belief.
So, in light of our characterization of epistemic responsibility, we might ask
whether one is always required to have justifying reasons for all of the beliefs
one holds, and holds without being epistemically irresponsible. Perhaps in
some contexts at least, certain beliefs that one is not irresponsible in holding,
and which play an epistemic role in the justification of other beliefs, do not
themselves *need* justification. Whether or not there are cases like this will
depend on the epistemic norms and practices characteristic of our epistemically
responsible agent. It might be the case, after all, that in some contexts, we
are epistemically responsible in holding certain beliefs that can serve as a
basis for holding other beliefs, even if we do not have justifying reasons for
the justifying beliefs in question.

In fact I do think this is the case and that the sort of pragmatic rationale
just sketched in defense of ER* can be extended to explain why our epistemic

practices are this way. In brief—given such facts as that we have nonepistemic goals, that we are not able to remember everything we have learned, and that any intellectual endeavor takes time, we simply should not spend time investigating and gathering evidence for all of our beliefs; in fact we could not possibly do so. We have no choice but to rely on all sorts of beliefs, skills, and abilities we do have when we engage in any intellectual pursuit. Reflection on our finitary predicament, then, makes it plausible to suppose that one is epistemically responsible in holding a belief unless there are concrete reasons for suspicion. (Recall Peirce's methodological remark quoted in the third epigraph.)[37] And this allows that one may be responsible in believing some proposition even if one no longer has, or indeed, has never had, positive evidence of a sort that would serve as justifying reasons for the proposition in question. The idea that one may be epistemically responsible in holding certain beliefs without needing justification is central to what I have been calling structural contextualism. Let us consider that thesis in more detail.

More on Structural Contextualism

Having partially sketched a notion of epistemic responsibility that is the basis for the sort of epistemic evaluation I am interested in describing, I want to return to structural contextualism for purposes of clarifying that thesis. Recall that according to structural contextualism, certain beliefs, at least in certain contexts, do not need justification although they may provide one with justifying reasons for holding other beliefs. Let us take a closer look at the claim that certain beliefs, at least in certain contexts, may not need justification.

As I am understanding the basic structural contextualist thesis, it is comprised of three basic tenets: (1) One may be epistemically responsible in holding certain beliefs at some time t even though one has no justifying evidence or justifying reasons for holding those beliefs at t. (2) Such beliefs may serve as an epistemic basis for being justified in holding other beliefs. (3) Which beliefs need justification depends crucially on certain facts about one's social circumstances—one's social context. Let us take these one by one.

1. The thesis that it is possible for someone to be epistemically responsible in holding a belief without justification is one way to express what has come to be called *epistemic conservatism*. The epistemic conservative claims that mere doxastic commitment may be enough to create some degree of epistemic respectability for certain beliefs. There are two basic versions of this conservative doctrine.[38] According to *first-order conservatism,* epistemic respectability may accrue to a belief as a result of simply holding that belief or, more plausibly, as a result of holding that belief so long as it does not conflict with other beliefs one has. According to *second-order conservatism,* second-order beliefs—beliefs about beliefs—are necessary for creating some degree of epistemic respectability for a first-order belief. So, for example, according to one possible version of second-order conservatism, in order for some level of epistemic respectability to accrue to some belief (for which one has no justi-

fying reasons or evidence), one must not only have the belief, but one must also believe of it that there is something that in some sense makes obvious (e.g., something that justifies or shows true) the belief in question.[39] In short, one must take the belief to be epistemically sound.[40]

This is not the place to launch into an investigation of epistemic conservatism. Jonathan Kvanvig[41] has convincingly argued that versions of first-order conservatism are not defensible but that any fallibilist epistemology needs to recognize a version of second-order conservatism. In the previous section, I offered a tentative and admittedly sketchy defense of conservatism that appeals to our finitary predicament: given limits on our cognitive abilities and limits on our time, it makes sense that our epistemic practices do not always require of believers that they have evidence or justifying reasons for everything they responsibly believe. As we shall see in the next section, our epistemic practices regarding moral belief exhibit this same sort of conservatism. So I shall proceed on the assumption that second-order conservatism is correct.

2. The second basic tenet of the structural contextualist—what we might call the thesis of *epistemic adequacy*—claims that beliefs that one is epistemically responsible in holding, but for which one has no justification, are sometimes enough, epistemically speaking, to serve as a basis, or partial basis, for justifiably believing other propositions. Regresses of justification can legitimately terminate with beliefs that one does not have justifying reasons for holding. If I am right, and our actual epistemic practices conform to the thesis of epistemic adequacy, this fact about the thesis provides, I would argue, some presumptive reason in its favor. But again, this thesis, like the thesis of epistemic conservatism, requires more in the way of defense than I can provide here.

3. Finally, whether or not a belief needs to be justified in order to serve as a properly basic belief depends crucially on context and, in particular, on social context. Call this the *social context sensitivity* thesis. Now, the general idea that correct epistemic appraisals are context-sensitive, in the sense of being dependent on one's circumstances, is not exciting and, as we saw in the discussion on justification and epistemic responsibility, not controversial. In general, whether or not an individual is justified (or if not justified then at least epistemically responsible) in holding some belief will depend on certain features of his or her circumstances. What makes contextualism distinctive is the claim that correct epistemic appraisal and, in particular, whether or not one's belief needs justification, depends crucially on one's "social context"—upon certain social facts. We have already noted that certain social facts (e.g., facts about the normal intelligence level of one's social group) importantly affect correct epistemic appraisal, and, again, the fact that the epistemic status of one's beliefs is sensitive to these sorts of social facts is not distinctive of structural contextualism. What the contextualist claims is that facts about the doxastic commitments of one's community are important for epistemic appraisal in general, and for the question of whether or not certain of one's beliefs need justification (on pain of epistemic irresponsibility) in particular. One way of putting this idea with regard to beliefs needing or not needing justification is to say that whether or not one needs justification for

some belief depends (in part) on what one's group will permit one to get away with believing without having a justification.

Of course, there are large and difficult questions looming for the contextualist about this matter of social context sensitivity. Since the contextualist thinks that epistemic evaluation is sensitive to social context, he or she needs to address questions about the sorts of factors that determine the relevant social context for evaluating the epistemic status of an individual's beliefs. We are, after all, members of many groups at any one time, and there are countless ways to individuate groups depending on the purposes at hand. Of course, I seriously doubt that there is an algorithm or completely general and adequate formula that one could use to fix, in a nonarbitrary fashion, the relevant social context in any particular case. Rather, questions about relevant social context are themselves (as you might expect) context sensitive. If this is correct, then we have no choice but to proceed on a case-by-case basis, though doing so does not rule out formulating defeasible generalizations about the sorts of factors that tend to help fix a relevant social group in some specific context.[42]

Before moving on to questions about moral justification, let me relate the main contextualist themes of this section to the notion of epistemic responsibility sketched in the previous section. One is epistemically responsible vis-à-vis some belief one holds only when one has adequately dealt with those (obvious) counterpossibilities whose seriousness is indicated by one's own background beliefs and those indicated by relevant information widely shared by a relevant community. Those cases in which one holds some belief without having a justifying reason for the belief and in which there are no relevant counterpossibilities of the sort just mentioned are candidate cases in which it seems appropriate to say that one is epistemically permitted and hence responsible in holding that belief. But, in light of the distinction between first-order and second-order conservatism, I think we should add the following proviso to our description of contextually basic beliefs: not only should it be the case that there are no relevant counterpossibilities to the belief in question, but the belief in question, to be properly basic, must also be one that the believer and his or her social group takes to be epistemically sound. The implication about contextually basic beliefs is that their status as basic depends crucially on social context and what sorts of epistemic demands one is expected to meet as well as the group's level of epistemic commitment to the belief in question.

Moral Justification in Context

In this section, I want to articulate and partially defend contextualism about the structure of moral belief.[43] My case involves both a descriptive and a normative dimension. First, I am interested in characterizing our actual epistemic practices when it comes to moral belief—in particular, those epistemic practices that bear on being free from or deserving epistemic blame. My descriptive hypothesis is that our epistemic norms, as they apply to moral belief, do not normally require that epistemically responsible agents have justifying reasons for all of their responsibly held moral beliefs. Some moral beliefs, especially those that are partly constitutive of one's moral outlook, serve as a body of very basic moral assumptions which, in ordinary contexts of moral thought and discussion, are not in need of justification. If this descriptive thesis is correct, then it is correct to characterize the structure of moral justification implied by our epistemic norms as contextual. My normative thesis is that there is good reason to reflectively endorse such norms.

In order to make a case for my descriptive claim, my plan is to describe a picture about our practices of justifying moral beliefs that, although it may not represent a complete picture, is quite familiar. The picture I have in mind is to be found in the writings of W. D. Ross. Once we have the picture before us, I want to indicate briefly some reasons for thinking that we often do reason and think about moral matters as the Rossian picture suggests, and then I will elaborate some of the epistemically relevant features that represent what I will call "the ordinary context of moral thought and discussion." What emerges from the picture is a contextualist account of the structure of justification.

A Cue From Ross

I am inclined to think that some of Ross's views about the nature of justification in ethics are correct (at least with regard to a very familiar pattern of justified moral belief), and I use those views to develop a contextualist picture of justification in ethics—a picture or model that seems to gain some support from recent empirical work. The picture I have in mind features moral rules as providing a basis for the justification of particular moral beliefs. And although I do think that rules have *a* role to play in a full story about the justification of moral belief, my version of contextualism is not committed to the claim that moral rules are, in all contexts, necessary in accounting for an individual's moral belief being justified.[44] Thus, the picture to follow is meant only to illustrate my version of ethical contextualism.

Ross, of course, was an ethical foundationalist who advocated a version of ethical pluralism. His specific version of ethical foundationalism involved these two claims: (1) that in ethics, as in mathematics, there are certain "propositions that cannot be proved, but that just as certainly need no proof,"[45] and (2) such propositions are self-evident necessary truths describing nonnatural moral facts and properties that can be known a priori. His ethical pluralism also involved two central claims: (3) There is a plurality of irreducible midlevel generalizations that express prima facie moral obligations. (These are the propositions that need no proof.) (4) In specific cases, these prima facie moral obligations may conflict, and when they do, there is no procedure, rule, or algorithm by which one may adjudicate these conflicts.

I accept (again, tentatively and with some modification) Ross's claims (1), (3), and (4); what I don't accept is the foundationalist epistemology and associated metaphysics of (2). My idea is that we can rework some of Ross's views by stripping away the foundationalist epistemology and nonnaturalist metaphysics, and reinterpret the other claims in light of contextualist epistemology. In fact, claims (1), (3), and (4) represent what I take to be a roughly accurate picture of a good part of the structure of justified moral belief—at least for many people in our culture. Embedded in a contextualist moral epistemology, the structural view involves the following four central claims:

C1: There are a number of irreducible moral generalizations that are defeasible and that we acquire as a result of moral education. In the ordinary context of justification in ethics, these are often epistemically basic.

C2: However, they are contextually basic: they do not represent self-evident moral truths knowable a priori nor do they result from the deliverance of some faculty of moral intuition. Rather, their status as basic is relative to context in a way to be elaborated below.

C3: The contextually basic beliefs provide (along with relevant nonmoral factual beliefs) the justificatory basis for justified belief in other, nonbasic moral propositions. Thus, (ceteris paribus) other, nonbasic moral beliefs are justified if they are appropriately based on some of the contextually basic ones.

C4: However, going from basic moral beliefs—the midlevel moral generalizations—to more specific moral beliefs about particular cases is not always a matter of simply taking the moral generalization together with relevant empirical information and deducing a moral conclusion. In many cases, two or more morally relevant considerations expressed by the basic moral generalizations will be present in a single case, and for these cases we need have no algorithm or ordering system to which we can appeal to adjudicate the conflict. In these cases, moral *judgment* takes over—something that one can do better or worse but something for which we need not have a covering rule that would dictate what, in particular, it is rational to believe. Nevertheless, in ordinary contexts of moral thought and discussion, individuals can be justified in coming to hold certain moral beliefs in cases calling for moral judgment.

Let me elaborate the view.

Tenets C1 and C3 together comprise a very familiar idea about the structure of ethical justification—a view common to both foundationalism and contextualism. Support for these tenets comes from commonsense observation and from empirical work in moral psychology.

So what does available evidence suggest? If we examine actual bits of human moral reasoning, it is plausible to suppose that doxastic justification in ethics rests with epistemically basic beliefs of some sort. We naturally assume that in honestly stating our reasons for holding some moral belief we are expressing the epistemically relevant structure of our moral beliefs. And when people are asked to articulate their reasons for holding some particular moral belief about a specific case, they by and large reason according to the familiar pattern of bringing forth general considerations bearing on the specific case that they take to be morally significant in that case. Such considerations are usually formulated as midlevel moral generalizations like, for example: "Lying is wrong" and "Hurting others is wrong." Moreover, there are two noteworthy features of these mid-level moral generalizations. First, when asked about them, people by and large report that such claims strike them as intuitively *obvious*. Related to this bit of phenomenology is the fact that people treat these generalizations as being *nonarbitrary*. That is, in ordinary contexts, most people are not inclined to take challenges to these beliefs at all seriously—they represent a person's moral bottom line. These facts suggest that many people don't have justifying reasons for these bottom-line moral beliefs.[46] (As I explain below, this does not mean that one can not detach from one's moral beliefs, hold them at arm's length, in order to raise Nietzschean questions about one's own moral outlook. But this does not affect the point I am making here about moral phenomenology or its bearing on contextualism.) I base these remarks on the observations I have made listening to students (who have not been tainted by an introductory course in normative ethics), but also we have the observations reported by, for example, the authors of *Habits of the Heart* as well as empirical research on moral development by, for example, Carol Gilligan.[47]

One of the interviewees featured in *Habits of the Heart* (quoted in the second epigraph), when asked about some of his general moral beliefs that he was using to justify more particular moral beliefs, gave what I suspect would be a pretty typical answer: he was dumbfounded by the question and took his general moral beliefs in question to be obvious. Another sort of response to questions about a person's general moral beliefs is to be found in Gilligan's work. The responses she tended to get from subjects when they were asked to provide a rationale for those general moral beliefs typically used by them to justify more particular moral beliefs were, as Dreyfus and Dreyfus point out, "tautologies and banalities, e.g., that they try to act in such a way as to make the world a better place to live. They might as well say that their highest moral principle is 'do something good.' "[48] My reading of all this (not that it is the only reading) is that in many contexts at least there are moral beliefs—general moral beliefs—that provide the basis for one coming to justifiably hold other moral beliefs, but beliefs for which most ordinary people have no (justifying) reason. In these (rather typical cases), I don't think it is plausible to criticize such agents for being epistemically irresponsible. They have particular moral beliefs that rest for their justification on certain other moral beliefs that represent the core of their moral sensibility. Moreover, they take these beliefs to be obvious and nonarbitrary and so display the relevant sort of second-order doxastic commitment characteristic of what I am calling contextually basic beliefs. There is, of course, much more to say about all this (including the addition of some important qualifications), but my suggestion here is that reflection on these ordinary cases helps reveal something important about our epistemic norms when it comes to moral belief, namely, that in what I am calling "ordinary contexts of moral thought and discussion" one need not have justifying reasons or grounds for certain moral beliefs that play a crucial epistemic role in one being justified in holding other moral beliefs.

Contextually Basic Moral Beliefs

Claim C2 is what distinguishes contextualism about structure from foundation-alism. As we have seen, the contextualist maintains the following two claims.[49] (1) In ordinary contexts of doxastic justification, epistemically basic beliefs *are not in need of justification.* (2) Beliefs that are basic in one context may, in a different context, require justification. What follows is an elaboration of these two claims. In taking up the first claim, we must clarify the notion of *context* (as I use it here). We must also say something about the role of contextually basic beliefs in ordinary contexts of moral thought and discussion.

I will begin by focusing on ordinary, engaged contexts of moral think-ing—contexts in which we bring to bear on some moral question or issue a moral outlook—and I will fill out some of the epistemically important detail of this context. With regard to moral belief, then, an important part of the context when it comes to questions about being justified in holding various moral beliefs involves the role of one's moral outlook. What is a moral outlook?

A moral outlook represents a way of viewing and responding to one's environment from a moral point of view; it is a perspective from which one takes a moral stance. One comes to have a moral outlook through a process of moral education, where some of the more salient features of this process include: (1) developing a sensitivity to various features of one's environment that, according to the particular outlook being taught, are morally relevant and so the basis of moral evaluation; (2) learning to associate various emotional responses with objects of moral evaluation (e.g., learning to have feelings of guilt and resentment toward certain of one's own actions and the actions of others); (3) becoming acquainted with certain *exemplars,* that is, paradigmatic cases of moral or immoral actions, persons, institutions and so forth[50]; (4) learning moral generalizations that encapsulate the most important morally relevant features to which, through training, one develops a sensitivity; and (5) learning basic patterns of moral reasoning (e.g., golden rule/reversibility reasoning as well as learning to reason from moral generalizations to particular cases). As a result of these learning activities, then, one comes to acquire a battery of interrelated skills, beliefs, emotional responses, and so forth that constitute an individual's moral outlook.

Having some particular moral outlook provides (part of) the "context" within which one ordinarily comes to have justified moral beliefs. But notice that in normal cases it is a richly social context—moral education takes place within a certain social environment, normally a large community whose members more or less share certain moral values and beliefs. In what I am calling engaged moral contexts, where one brings one's moral outlook to bear on some specific case calling for a moral response, certain moral beliefs—what I am calling midlevel moral generalizations—often enough play a special justifying role, and it is by seeing how these moral beliefs function in one's moral outlook that we can understand more clearly the epistemic status of those beliefs. Let us then consider the role of midlevel general moral beliefs in a moral outlook.

The five features of a moral outlook represent (at least part of) what we might call "formal" features of a moral outlook; features that characterize any (or most any) moral outlook. But particular moral outlooks differ in content, and one useful way to characterize some *particular* moral outlook, and distinguish it from other moral outlooks, is in terms of those morally relevant features mentioned in (1) and (4). Let us say, then, that those morally relevant features of actions, persons, institutions, and so forth that represent (according to the outlook) the most fundamental morally relevant features of things that are the basis of moral evaluation, are distinctive of that particular moral outlook. Midlevel moral generalizations, as I am understanding them, connect those morally relevant features of things with terms of moral evaluation. Hence, we can say that a set of these midlevel generalizations is (partly) *constitutive* of a particular moral outlook. Thus, in many ordinary, engaged contexts of moral thinking about specific moral questions and issues, these general moral beliefs help structure and organize our moral experience and thought—we think in terms of them. When our focus is on specific issues, they are part of a large body of assumptions that we employ in our thinking. Moreover, such moral beliefs in such contexts are taken for granted: no serious doubts or challenges are considered or taken seriously by the relevant community. Since a large part of being epistemically responsible is a matter of being able to detect and deal with "relevant" challenges, and in the ordinary context of moral justification, challenges to midlevel moral generalizations are not relevant, one's holding such beliefs and basing other, nonbasic beliefs on them is not subject to epistemic criticism and so one is epistemically responsible in holding them without having justifying reasons.

So, if I am right, our actual epistemic norms and practices do not, as a matter of fact, require that individuals have justifying reasons for some of their moral beliefs—moral beliefs that often play a crucial epistemic role when it comes to being inferentially justified in holding specific moral beliefs.

Context Sensitivity

The second feature of contextually basic beliefs to be considered here is the idea that being basic is context-sensitive and so what is basic in one context may not be basic in another. Let us begin by considering different social contexts involving different communities having and inculcating different moral outlooks. Although one would expect that most any two moral outlooks would share many of the same basic moral assumptions (e.g., presumptions against killing humans, theft, and so forth), there may be some differences in the specific moral assumptions that these groups by and large take for granted, as well as the moral weight that is attached to the various morally relevant considerations the rules encapsulate.[51] If so, then one way in which being basic is context-sensitive is simply that different groups may take (some) different moral beliefs for granted. For example, in comparing the basic moral outlook of the Amish culture with the outlooks of many non-Amish Westerners, we see striking differences.[52] The underlying spirit of the Amish moral outlook—what is called *Gelassenheit,* translated as "submission"—puts primary emphasis on the values of submission and obedience to God and community as fundamental for leading a morally proper life. The moral requirement to lead a properly submissive life (which the Amish take as basic and applying to *all* persons) is understood to imply that individual achievement, self-fulfillment, personal recognition, and other manifestations of the modern spirit of individuality are morally perverse. Even if submissiveness and obedience are morally valued by people generally, nevertheless, these values need not and often do not have the sort of fundamental status and importance that they have in the Amish moral outlook. Amish justifications for specific moral beliefs about actions and practices rest with claims to the effect that such and such actions and practices are required (or forbidden) by *Gelassenheit.* So, one rather obvious way in which beliefs that do not need justification are context-sensitive is where talk of different social contexts refers to different communities with differing moral outlooks.

A more interesting possibility to explore is the extent to which our epistemic evaluations might be context-sensitive in a manner that would imply that an individual might be epistemically responsible in holding some moral belief without justification in one context, though not responsible in holding that same belief in a different context—where differences in context here involve different social groups. Of course, over time an individual may come to have a moral outlook whose basic moral assumptions differ markedly from the assumptions of his former moral outlook (perhaps as a result of a radical moral conversion not mediated by argumentation).[53] In some ways, this sort of case is like the one described in the previous paragraph: there are two distinct moral outlooks creating two distinct contexts. But even for an individual whose moral outlook remains relatively unchanged over a period of time, and for whom certain moral beliefs are basic in ordinary, engaged contexts of moral thought and deliberation, there may be special contexts in which those moral beliefs are not basic. One kind of case fitting this description is a context in which one is confronted with skeptical challenges to one's moral outlook—challenges that are aimed at those moral beliefs, which in engaged contexts, are contextually basic. Let me spell out the kind of case I have in mind in a bit more detail.

Let us distinguish between what I have called an engaged context of moral thought and a detached context in which one is not thinking and deliberating entirely from within her or his moral outlook but is instead looking at it from the outside, as it were. Now, in an engaged context of moral thinking, where skeptical challenges to that outlook are not in focus, one is *(ceteris paribus)* epistemically responsible in holding (without justification) those basic moral beliefs and assumptions more or less fundamental to the outlook. However, once skeptical challenges are taken seriously, then the context has been switched (in the sense that the relevant social group or community crucial for epistemic evaluation is the group of skeptics). In this relatively detached context in which, we are supposing, the core moral assumptions of one's moral outlook are being challenged, those ordinarily basic moral beliefs are no longer basic. For example, suppose we are considering skeptical challenges to the deepest aspects of a person's moral outlook, and imagine that this person is confronted by a group of Nietzscheans who argue, in effect, that democratically structured societies produce a false moral conscience and that therefore many of the moral beliefs taken for granted in such societies are mistaken or at least questionable. In such detached contexts, what often seems to happen is that the epistemic norms operative in them differ from those operative in engaged contexts; in particular, in contexts of the former sort, one is not permitted to take for granted the moral beliefs that one may take for granted in contexts of the latter sort. The reason for the difference in epistemic norms governing these contexts is fairly obvious. In engaged contexts, where the point and purpose of the context is (speaking roughly) to negotiate one's way around in a social world, one is not required to have reasons (so I have argued) for certain moral beliefs that are fundamental to the outlook. In detached contexts, where the point and purpose of the context is to examine one's moral outlook in an effort, for example, to detect and correct any cultural or idiosyncratic biases, one is not allowed to take one's core moral beliefs and assumptions as basic.

Cases fitting this general description in which one enters a detached context raise interesting questions about the conditions under which it becomes appropriate or perhaps required to enter such a context as well as questions about the sorts of epistemic norms operative in such contexts. Investigating these matters would require that we consider specific cases in some detail, which we cannot pursue here.

Moral Judgment

We come finally to tenet C4. According to the version of structural contextualism I am articulating, basic moral beliefs often provide the justificatory basis for other, inferentially justified beliefs. Often, talk of inference is taken to be a matter of deductive connections between statements or beliefs. But a realistic account of moral reasoning must, I think, recognize Ross's claim that in many instances, moral reasoning does not follow a simple deductive pattern, in fact, in many instances such reasoning is not governed by rules that dictate what in particular it is rational to believe. Ross's view has been the subject of philosophical dissatisfaction partly because he refused to provide any algorithm or general procedure for arriving at justified moral beliefs in cases where two more morally relevant considerations are present and at least one of them supports one moral evaluation of the action and at least one of the others supports an opposing moral evaluation. The problem is supposed to be that unless there is some general covering rule or procedure that is to be followed in coming to some overall moral evaluation about the action, then any resulting moral judgment on the agent's part will be arbitrary and hence unjustified.

I think Ross is right about how we often *do* reason about moral matters: we work with a handful of irreducible midlevel moral generalizations that cannot be lexically ordered so as to provide a super rule for adjudicating conflicts among the generalizations. Nevertheless, moral thought and deliberation that is not rule-governed in this way often yields moral beliefs that one is justified in holding. For instance, with issues such as abortion (where various relevant considerations pull in opposite moral directions) people reason about the morality of that practice (or specific instances of it) using basically the same stock of general midlevel moral beliefs, even though individuals can differ in their moral assessment of this practice and be justified in their differing individual responses. Moreover, in addition to cases of conflicting moral generalizations, there are many cases in which it is unclear whether or not some moral generalization correctly applies to a particular case. After all, moral generalizations are expressed in terms of such notions as *harm, lying, innocent person,* and so forth, that are vague. Like cases of conflict, these cases of application require that what I am calling *moral judgment* play an important epistemic role in coming to have justified moral beliefs. What we must do, then, is square our moral epistemology with these facts.

There are both philosophical and empirical considerations that support my contention that non-rule-based moral thinking can yield justified moral belief. The main philosophical consideration has to do with the recent work of some philosophers on the notion of rationality. Harold Brown, for instance, has recently criticized what he calls the "traditional" conception of rationality according to which all rational belief is belief according to some rule. Brown persuasively argues that the traditional view involves an impossible ideal implying that even rigorous scientific inquiry must be counted as irrational. What Brown proposes is a new model of rationality, one that makes a place for what he simply calls *judgment:* "the ability to evaluate a situation, assess evidence, and come to a reasonable decision without following rules."[54] So this general model of rationality that assigns a significant epistemic role to judgment comports well with the view that scientific inquiry is rational, and also comports well with the claim that weighing up competing moral considerations and, on the basis of this weighing, making a judgment (which is not a matter of conforming to some specifiable rule) can result in rational or justified belief. I suspect that one of the reasons philosophers have been so unsympathetic to Ross is because they take science as our paradigm of rational inquiry, assume that such inquiry is completely rule-governed, and so conclude that on a view like Ross's, moral thinking has to be epistemically defective. This line of thought is thoroughly undermined by Brown. Indeed, if Brown is right, then the role of moral judgment in coming to have justified moral beliefs is not some isolated and otherwise epistemically queer phenomenon peculiar to moral thinking, but merely an instance of a quite general phenomenon.

The relevant empirical consideration bearing on this issue can be found in the work of the Dreyfus brothers. They argue that moral thinking and judging are activities much like many physical and intellectual activities (they discuss driving a car and playing chess) in that doing them well is a skill that develops through stages. When starting out, a novice chess player is taught to consciously follow rules that, with experience, are no longer consciously entertained, until eventually one can just "see" how to react to the various types of chess positions. Their main point, which they apply to the case of moral reasoning, is that an individual's becoming increasingly adept at some complex activity involves acquiring a skill—coming to *know how* to do something, where one does not consciously rely on rules (which is not to say that rules play no justificatory role at all in coming to have justified moral beliefs about specific cases). But they make a further Rossian point, namely, that adept moral judgment and reasoning in complex cases, where a number of morally relevant considerations come into play, is not grounded in any algorithm or super rule that would rationally determine some outcome. They write:

> [I]f the phenomenology of skillful coping we have presented is right, principles and theories serve only for early stages of learning; no principle or theory "ground" an expert ethical response, any more than in chess there is a theory or rule that explains a master-level move. As we have seen in the case of chess, recognizing that there is no way to ground one's intuitions in an explanation is an important step on the way to acquiring expertise.[55]

The phenomenology of moral thinking that the Dreyfus brothers present supports the Rossian view which emphasizes the role of moral judgment in coming to make reasonable moral decisions, and in coming to have justified moral beliefs.

These remarks about moral judgment comport well with my contextualist moral epistemology. In cases where an expert moral thinker mulls over some issue and comes to a belief about the morality of some action or whatever, he or she is engaged in an activity of weighing and balancing various morally relevant considerations—considerations reflected in his or her general moral beliefs that I have been saying are contextually basic. The moral belief he or she eventually settles on is not dictated by any algorithm she or he has; trained moral judgement is operative here. Nevertheless, the expert is reasoning about the case and can, if asked, state those reasons that, in the end, were decisive. Of course, at bottom, his or her reasons are represented by midlevel moral beliefs. So, after the fact, our expert can provide a justification for his or her belief terminating in his or her midlevel moral beliefs, but there is no covering rule followed dictating that one sort of general moral consideration should trump competing moral considerations in this case. What this reveals about those epistemic norms governing moral belief is that we operate according to epistemic norms some of which permit one to hold moral beliefs, in certain circumstances, on the basis of an exercise of one's moral judgment.[56]

A Brief Rationale

I have been claiming that my contextualist picture is more or less descriptively accurate, at least if we are focused on questions about epistemically responsible moral belief. But even if I am right in my descriptive claim about how our practices work, do we have good reason to endorse our practices? Can we provide a rationale for having norms and practices that are like the one's we have? Here, we turn from descriptive questions to normative ones.

Space does not allow that we pursue methodological issues in any detail, but I shall assume that judging the overall adequacy of an epistemological theory is a matter of that theory's globally cohering with assumptions, views, and theories from common sense and other fields of inquiry. Specifically, there are two dimensions to this sort of holism worth sorting out. First, one would like one's moral epistemology to comport with commonsense assumptions about matters epistemic such as the presumption that many people (at least sometimes) justifiedly believe certain moral propositions. Second, one wants the commitments and implications of one's epistemology to comport with any relevant assumptions, theories, and results from empirical fields such as psychology, biology, and anthropology.[57] Of course, evaluating epistemological theories is a comparative matter. One hopes to show that one's favored epistemological theory does a better job, vis-à-vis any competitors, at satisfying the relevant desiderata.

Though I will not argue the case here, let me just conjecture that my contextualist view comports better than do rival views with such commonsense presumptions as that ordinary persons are often epistemically responsible in many of the moral beliefs they hold. I suspect that these rival epistemological views, whatever virtues they may have, tend to impose epistemic burdens on ordinary believers that would imply that such believers are not generally responsible in many of the moral beliefs they hold.[58] So I think contextualism is more plausible than its rivals with regard to the first desideratum of any moral epistemology.

I also think that my contextualist epistemology comports nicely with certain empirical data about human beings. Specifically, what I have in mind is the sort of pragmatic rationale hinted at above in the second section in defense of an "in-between" requirement governing our responsibility for dealing with counterpossibilities. In connection with the requirement in question I noted that given our "finitary predicament," including the fact that we are beings with limited cognitive resources, limited time, and other, nonepistemic goals, we would expect that the sorts of epistemic norms in everyday operation would impose the sort of "in-between" level of care for checking counterpossibilities we explored earlier. Moreover, viewing epistemic norms from this pragmatic perspective makes sense of the fact that our epistemic norms by and large have an "innocent until proven guilty" bias to them, a conservative leaning that goes to the heart of my contextualism.[59] If this is right, then since there does not seem to be any special reason for supposing that epistemic requirements attaching to moral belief are different in this respect from those attaching to nonmoral beliefs, the sort of pragmatic rationale described earlier applies to the moral cases as well.

Concluding Promissory Note

I have tried to make a case for the plausibility of a contextualist epistemology within the realm of moral belief. After sorting and clarifying various contextualist theses, I proceeded to characterize a model epistemic agent that is appropriate for everyday, epistemic evaluation of ordinary people. On the basis of this model, I proceeded to outline a version of contextualism about the structure of responsible moral belief. Let me close by making a partial list of some tasks that lie ahead if one wants to fully defend this view.

First, there are notions that play a significant role in my view that I have left largely unclarified. For instance, more must be said about the notion of context and how one's so-called social context is determined for specific epistemic evaluations.

Second, I have indicated where some of the key contextualist claims require more defense than I have provided. I suspect, for instance, that more needs to be done by way of supporting the thesis of epistemological conservatism. The same goes for the thesis of epistemic adequacy, according to which nonjustified but responsibly held beliefs can serve as an adequate basis for coming to justifiedly hold other moral beliefs.[60]

Third, there are various questions that come to mind about this sort of view, questions that become the basis for objections: "Does not this view just amount to a version of epistemological relativism (normative contextualism) and so implies that even people with crazy moral beliefs, who have undergone a process of "moral" education, will be epistemically responsible in holding outrageous moral beliefs?" "If the view is not, strictly speaking, a version of relativism, will it not still have the same normative implications as a no-holds-barred version of epistemic relativism?" "Furthermore, even if the view avoids the problems just mentioned, does it not follow that the view is guilty of an unacceptable kind of epistemological dogmatism since the perspective of the model epistemic agent is based on *our* (largely shared) epistemic sensibility, which may not be shared by other groups but which we use to evaluate the beliefs of other groups?"

Finally, as mentioned at the end of the last section, a full defense of a contextualist moral epistemology would require that I show that alternative epistemological views are less plausible than my own. I have only hinted at reasons for making such an assertion.

I am optimistic about responding to the misgivings, filling out the arguments, and filling in the important details. But a more comprehensive attempt must wait for another occasion.[61]

Notes

I wish to thank the audience at the conference on Moral Epistemology (Dartmouth College, September 29–October 2, 1994) for a very helpful discussion of my paper. I am especially indebted to Robert Audi, Denny Bradshaw, Malia Brink, Michael DePaul, Michael Gorr, Mitch Haney, David Henderson, Terry Horgan, Stefan Sencerz, Walter Sinnott-Armstrong, Bill Throop, John Tienson, and Bill Tolhurst for many comments and suggestions on earlier versions of this paper.

1. Interviewee featured in R. N. Bellah, R. Madson, W. M. Sullivan, A. Swindler, and S. M. Tipton, *Habits of the Heart* (New York: Harper & Row, 1985), 6.

2. I develop a view about the semantics and metaphysics of moral discourse in my *Morality Without Foundations* (forthcoming), chapter 4.

3. Alvin Goldman, "Discrimination and Perceptual Knowledge," *Journal of Philosophy* 73 (1976), 771–91.

4. Stewart Cohen, "Knowledge and Context," *Journal of Philosophy* 83 (1986), 579.

5. For instance, it is at least initially plausible to suppose that whether or not a long-forgotten defeater d of evidence e—evidence otherwise adequate for justifiably believing some true proposition p and on the basis of which one currently believes p—undermines one's knowledge of p depends on facts about the normal memory abilities of one's social group. If no normal member of one's group would remember d, then the fact that one used to possess a defeater of e does not undermine one's knowledge of p. See Stewart Cohen, "Knowledge, Context, and Social Standards," *Synthese* 73 (1987), 3–26, for a discussion of the cases of memory and perception.

6. Ernest Sosa, "How Do You Know?" *American Philosophical Quarterly* 11 (1974), 117; cf. Ernest Sosa, "Knowledge in Context: Skepticism in Doubt," *Philosophical Perspectives* 2 (1988), 139–55.

7. Ernest Sosa, *Knowledge in Perspective* (Cambridge: Cambridge University Press, 1991), 10 n. 14, is explicit about this. So we can think of Cohen and Sosa as proposing what they take to be universally correct epistemic principles that imply that the truth of certain specific epistemic appraisals is dependent on facts (including social facts) about one's circumstances.

8. Foundationalists sometimes talk about foundational beliefs not being in need of justification, by which they mean that such beliefs, because they are, for example, "self-justifying," do not need to receive justification from other beliefs. The structural contextualist, however, means something more radical here, namely, there are certain beliefs that, in certain contexts at least, need not have the sort of epistemic status of enjoying positive evidential support (either inherently or from other beliefs and experiences) in order to play a regress-stopping role in the structure of justified belief. For recent defenses of structural contextualism with regard to empirical belief, see David Annis, "A Contextualist Theory of Epistemic Justification," *American Philosophical Quarterly* 15 (1978), 213–19; Michael Williams, "Coherence, Justification and

Truth," *Review of Metaphysics* 34 (1980), 243–72, and David Henderson, "Epistemic Competence and Contextualist Epistemology: Why Contextualism Is Not Just the Poor Person's Coherentism," *Journal of Philosophy* 91 (1994), 627–49.

9. Inferential justification must be distinguished from the process of psychologically inferring one proposition from another. Moreover, such justification does not require any such process of inferring. See Laurence BonJour, *The Structure of Empirical Knowledge* (Cambridge, Mass.: Harvard University Press, 1985), 19–20, for discussion of this point.

10. Of course the contextualist will deny any claim by the foundationalist that having a foundational belief (as the foundationalist conceives of them) is *necessary* for having any justified beliefs at all. And likewise the contextualist will deny any claim by the coherentist that having a maximally coherent set of beliefs is *necessary* for having any justified beliefs at all.

11. Arguably, the same holds for ascriptions of knowledge.

12. It is important to distinguish between what we might call *actual doxastic justification* and *hypothetical doxastic justification*. The former refers to cases where: (1) one has adequate (and undefeated) evidence *e* that justifies the belief that *p,* (2) one believes that *p,* and (3) one believes that *p* on the basis of *e*. Cases in which one is not actually but only hypothetically justified are those cases in which clause (1) holds but either (2) or (3) (or both) fail to hold; given one's evidence or grounds, one would be justified in holding a certain belief were one to base that belief on one's evidence or grounds. I am primarily interested in questions of actual doxastic justification. Some discussion of this distinction can be found in Robert Audi, *Belief, Justification, and Knowledge* (Belmont, Calif.: Wadsworth, 1988), 1–2, though he uses the terms *belief justification* and *situational justification* for what I am calling actual and hypothetical doxastic justification respectively.

13. Marcus G. Singer, *Generalization in Ethics* (New York: Atheneum, 1961).

14. Alan Gewirth, *Reason and Morality* (Chicago: University of Chicago Press, 1978).

15. Alan Donagan, *The Theory of Morality* (Chicago: University of Chicago Press, 1977).

16. Richard B. Brandt, *A Theory of the Good and the Right* (Oxford: Oxford University Press, 1979).

17. John Rawls, *A Theory of Justice* (Cambridge, Mass.: Harvard University Press, 1971).

18. R. M. Hare, *Moral Thinking: Its Levels, Method, and Point* (Oxford: Oxford University Press, 1981).

19. For more on the distinction between questions about doxastic justification and questions about nondoxastic justification in ethics, see Norman Daniels, "Wide Reflective Equilibrium and Theory Acceptance in Ethics," *Journal of Philosophy* 76 (1979), 257 n. 1; David Copp, "Considered Judgments and Moral Justification: Conservatism in Moral Theory," in D. Copp and D. Zimmerman, eds., *Morality, Reason, and Truth* (Totowa, N.J.: Rowman & Littlefield, 1984), 143; and Mark Timmons, "Foundationalism and the Structure of Justification in Ethics" *Ethics* 97 (1987), 598–99.

20. Of course, questions about nondoxastic justification are relevant to questions about doxastic justification at least to this extent: if, for example, moral propositions or claims can be proved, demonstrated, or 'justified' by inferring them from, say, propositions about the nature of human beings, then one way to be doxastically justified in holding various moral beliefs would be to infer them from the relevant set of

(justifiably held) beliefs about the nature of human beings. But this need not be the only way, or even the primary way, in which most ordinary people come to justifiably hold moral beliefs. See, for example, William Tolhurst, "Supervenience, Externalism, and Moral Knowledge," *The Southern Journal of Philosophy* 29, supplementary volume on "Moral Realism" (1986), 43–55, and his example of Amazing Grace.

21. In addition to goals and perspective, Foley, *Working Without a Net* (Oxford: Oxford University Press, 1993), claims that epistemic evaluations are to be understood as also making reference to what he calls a set of resources possessed by the believer. Foley offers this formula, then, for understanding ascriptions of rationality: "It is rational for you to believe _____ because you have resources R and because from perspective P it seems that, given R, believing _____ is an effective way to satisfy goal G" (p. 34).

22. We understand justified belief in terms of *apparently* promoting your goals instead of saying, for example, that they must *in fact* satisfy your goals because even in cases where your beliefs do not satisfy your goals, we want to allow that you can still be justified in holding the belief.

23. This matter is not so clear in Foley. Judging from some perspective involves judging relative to the epistemic standards that partially characterize the perspective in question. Although not explicit about the matter, from what he does say, Foley seems to think that the epistemic standards of a perspective are represented as beliefs (perspectives, after all, are defined as sets of beliefs). I suspect that a better way to construe a perspective would not be simply in terms of beliefs, but we need not get into this issue here.

24. Foley, *Working Without a Net,* p. 14. This implies, of course, that epistemic ascriptions are context sensitive—a claim embraced by epistemological contextualists. However, it will become clear as we proceed that one may grant that epistemic evaluations are contextual in the ways implied by Foley's schema without being the sort of contextualist about structure that I will be defending.

25. Two comments are in order here: First, it is probably too simplistic to suppose that there is a single epistemic goal—having true beliefs and avoiding false ones. Foley, (*Working Without a Net,* p. 19), for example, characterizes a purely epistemic summum bonum as the having of a current system of "accurate and comprehensive" belief. Michael DePaul, *Balance and Refinement: Beyond Coherence Methods of Moral Inquiry* (London and New York: Routledge, 1993), chapter 2, argues that we should recognize that in addition to having true beliefs and avoiding false ones, our epistemic summum bonum includes having a belief system that is both "rational" and "warranted." Out of mere convenience, I shall keep on describing our epistemic goal in the simpler way. Second, given that I am interested in a notion of epistemic justification, I am thus committed to a meta-ethical view that allows for truth to be properly predicated of moral sentences. However, the view about moral truth that I accept is intended to mesh with a metaphysically irrealist stance about moral discourse. For an elaboration of a particular view about moral truth, which construes truth talk as predicated of moral propositions in a *minimalist* spirit, see Terry Horgan and Mark Timmons, "Taking a Moral Stance," forthcoming, and Timmons, *Morality Without Foundations.*

26. It might appear, then, that I am interested in evaluations made from a sociocentric perspective and, in particular, the epistemic perspective of one's group (however I propose to understand talk of "one's group"). In a sense, this is what interests me, but I want to avoid a particular misunderstanding of what I am up to.

First, we need to notice that there are two importantly different types of epistemic evaluation that employ a sociocentric perspective. First, some sociocentric-based evaluations invoke the epistemic perspective of *the believer's* community whatever community that may turn out to be. We might call sociocentric evaluations of this sort *ecumenical* in spirit; they represent a familiar relativist stance in epistemology or what I earlier called normative contextualism. But in other contexts, invoking a sociocentric perspective may be *sectarian* in spirit. That is, for some purposes, we may be interested in epistemically evaluating an agent's belief from the point of view of the *attributor's* epistemic perspective, which, of course, for us includes those epistemic norms that *we* endorse. Now, in focusing on the imaginary perspective of a representative epistemically responsible believer, I am interested in epistemic evaluations that reflect what I take to be *our* most general and widely employed epistemic norms, and so I am interested in evaluations that are sectarian in spirit.

Second, I construe my task as partly descriptive; the epistemic norms employed by the competent epistemic agent are norms that by and large characterize our current epistemic practice. But I also think that the sorts of general epistemic norms I have in mind—norms that ordinarily govern, in a most general way, the epistemically relevant tasks of gathering evidence and checking for counterpossibilities to claims we believe or are entertaining—are norms that stand up to critical scrutiny and thus represent norms that we would want to reflectively endorse. Insofar as they represent norms we would want to reflectively endorse, they represent those norms that we think *should* be used in epistemic evaluation and thus are the basis for nonrelativized, categorical epistemic ascriptions.

27. Actually, responsibilities having to do with gathering evidence seem, for the most part, to derive from responsibilities for dealing with relevant counterpossibilities. Moreover, the sorts of norms governing the elimination of internal inconsistencies are similar in form to those for eliminating counterpossibilities. See C. Cherniak, *Minimal Rationality* (Cambridge, Mass.: The MIT Press, 1986), chapter 1.

28. See Cherniak, *Minimal Rationality*, chapter 5, for a defense of a similar principle that he calls the "special reasons requirement." Much of my discussion of epistemic responsibility is influenced by Cherniak.

29. Talk of "counterpossibilities whose seriousness is indicated by one's current background beliefs" needs clarification. But here I will have to rely on the reader's intuitive understanding of this talk.

30. W. P. Keeton, D. B. Dobbs, R. E. Keeton, and D. G. Owen, *Prosser and Keeton on The Law of Torts,* 5th ed., (St. Paul, Minn.: West Publishing Co., 1984), 175.

31. Cherniak, *Minimal Rationality,* chapter 2.

32. See Cohen, "Knowledge, Context, and Social Standards."

33. Keeton et al., *The Law of Torts,* p. 184.

34. J. L. Austin, *Philosophical Papers,* eds., J. O. Urmson and G. J. Warnock (Oxford: Oxford University Press, 1961), 84.

35. See Sosa, "How Do You Know?" and "Knowledge in Context."

36. Of course, what counts as a "reasonable" amount of time is context-sensitive, and will depend on such factors as how important it is to have correct beliefs about some subject matter on some occasion as well as one's occupation (one's level of care in dealing with counterpossibilities will be higher than normal if one is a member of a special profession whose job it is to gain accurate information about some subject matter).

37. C. S. Peirce, *Collected Papers* (Cambridge, Mass.: Harvard University Press, 1932), 5.358.

38. My discussion of epistemic conservatism, including the distinction between first-order and second-order species of the view follows Jonathan Kvanvig, "Conservatism and Its Virtues," *Synthese* 79 (1989), 153–63.

39. Here I am being intentionally noncommittal about what other requirements (if any) might be involved in a notion of responsible belief for which one has no justification. For example, one might require that someone or other in one's community has justifying reasons for the proposition in question and that the possibility of nonjustified responsible belief reflects one of the ways in which our epistemic practices indicate a kind of division of epistemic labor.

40. Robert Audi suggested to me that the defender of conservatism need not demand that believers possess second-order beliefs, and instead can get by with the requirement that believers be immediately disposed to have the relevant sort of second-order belief. I excuse myself from fussing with the details of an adequate formulation of second-order conservatism.

41. Kvanvig, "Conservatism and Its Virtues."

42. As indicated note 36, one obvious factor that figures importantly in our epistemic evaluations concerns one's special knowledge and skills—knowledge and skills that may or may not be tied to one's occupation. According to the reasonable person doctrine from law as described in Keeton et al., *The Law of Torts,* "Professional persons in general, and those who undertake any work calling for special skill, are required not only to exercise reasonable care in what they do, but also to possess a minimum of special knowledge and ability" (p. 185). This suggests that we rightly expect more of people who have special knowledge or who are members of occupations whose job it is to know more about certain topics.

43. Carl Wellman, *Challenge and Response* (Carbondale, Ill.: Southern Illinois University Press, 1971); Charles Larmore, *Patterns of Moral Complexity* (Cambridge: Cambridge University Press, 1987); and Jeffrey Stout, "On Having a Morality in Common," in *Prospects for a Common Morality,* eds. G. Outka and J. P. Reeder (Princeton, N.J.: Princeton University Press, 1993) profess some version or other of structural contextualism about moral belief. In my "Moral Justification in Context," *The Monist* 76 (1993), 360–78, I defend this view, but do so from an egocentric epistemic perspective, whereas in this paper my focus is on a nonegocentric perspective.

44. So, for example, in specific contexts, the justification of a moral belief may involve an ultimate appeal to moral exemplars, or perhaps instead just an appeal to the particularities of some specific case under scrutiny, and moral rules may play no role at all. I am here thinking of the epistemological views of so-called moral *particularists.* See, for example, Jonathan Dancy, *Moral Reasons* (Oxford and Cambridge, Mass.: Blackwell, 1993), chapters 4–7. My contextualism can allow that the sorts of belief that play a contextually basic role in the justification of moral belief is itself a contextually variable matter.

45. W. D. Ross, *The Right and the Good* (Oxford: Oxford University Press, 1930), 30.

46. As Walter Sinnott-Armstrong pointed out to me, from the fact that people do not take certain challenges seriously does not show that they have no reasons or justification for the belief being challenged; in some cases, we do not take challenges to certain beliefs seriously because of having overwhelming justifying reasons for those beliefs. However, as I go on to explain, I think part of the reason for not taking certain challenges seriously in the case of moral belief is that ordinary people do not have justifying reasons for those beliefs.

47. See Carol Gilligan, *In a Different Voice* (Cambridge, Mass.: Harvard University Press, 1982); "Moral Orientation and Moral Development," in *Women and Moral Theory,* eds. E. F. Kittay and D. T. Meyers (Savage, Md.: Rowman and Littlefield, 1988); and Carol Gilligan, J. V. Ward, J. M. Taylor, and B. Bardige, *Mapping the Moral Domain* (Cambridge, Mass.: Harvard University Press, 1988).

48. Hubert Dreyfus and Stuart E. Dreyfus, "What is Morality? A Phenomenological Account of Ethical Expertise," in *Universalism vs. Communitarianism,* ed. D. Rasmussen (Cambridge, Mass.: The MIT Press, 1990), 252.

49. Here I am just concerned with what I have called the thesis of epistemic conservatism and the thesis of social-context sensitivity. The thesis of epistemic adequacy does not figure in this discussion.

50. Thomas Kuhn, "Second Thoughts on Paradigms," in *The Essential Tension,* ed. Kuhn (Chicago: University of Chicago Press, 1977), uses the term "exemplar" to refer to one of the crucial ingredients involved in what he calls a *disciplinary matrix*—those elements shared by a scientific community that enable them to communicate professionally and arrive at nearly unanimous judgments on scientific questions. As part of a disciplinary matrix, exemplars are "concrete problem solutions accepted by the group as, in a quite usual sense, paradigmatic" (p. 298). Learning a moral outlook involves, I am suggesting, a rough equivalent of learning a disciplinary matrix.

51. Here I skip over important complexities that would need to be considered before we could confidently say that all or most communities share many of the same basic moral assumptions. As Francis Snare, "The Diversity of Morals," *Mind* 89 (1980), 353–69, argues, the scope and importance that certain moral rules have in different cultures signifies real differences in the moral values and associated moral rules of those cultures. So, for example, merely from the fact that two cultures subscribe to *a* prohibition on lying does not mean that they both accept the same moral rule about lying.

52. See Donald G. Kraybill, *The Riddle of Amish Culture* (Baltimore and London: The Johns Hopkins University Press, 1989) for a detailed description of Amish culture.

53. See DePaul, *Balance and Refinement,* pp. 39–48 for a description of such radical moral conversions that result from a "discontinuous" shift in one's moral outlook.

54. Harold Brown, *Rationality* (London and New York: Routledge, 1988), 137. This same theme is stressed by Hilary Putnam, *Reason, Truth and History* (Cambridge: Cambridge University Press, 1981), in connection with explaining the success of science. He points out that attempts to formalize scientific method have not worked and are not going to work, and so we should get over what he calls "method fetishism" in trying to make sense of scientific rationality. Rather, according to Putnam, scientists work with a set of nonalgorithmic, informal "maxims" that require "informal rationality, i.e., intelligence and common sense, to apply" (p. 195).

55. Dreyfus and Dreyfus, "What is Morality?" p. 252.

56. Of course, there is much to say about moral judgment and what makes such judgment *good* judgment even if it is not rule-governed. Space does not permit treatment of this topic here, but the importance of *exemplars* (mentioned above in describing a moral outlook) figures importantly here. Good moral judgment is judgment that one would expect the moral experts to make. This is the sort of story we find in Brown, *Rationality,* and in Dreyfus and Dreyfus, "What is Morality?," which, as the Dreyfus brothers point out, is circular, but (they claim) not viciously so.

57. Here, the claim that descriptive work in the sciences should influence epistemological theorizing represents a so-called naturalized approach to epistemology, one that insists that sound epistemological theorizing must draw on relevant work in the sciences. See, for example, Hilary Kornblith, "Introduction: What Is Naturalistic Epistemology?" in *Naturalizing Epistemology,* 2d ed., ed. Hilary Kornblith (Cambridge, Mass.: Harvard University Press, 1994), 1–14.

58. See Gilbert Harman, *Change in View* (Cambridge, Mass.: The MIT Press, 1986), chapter 2, and "Positive versus Negative Undermining in Belief Revision," in

Naturalizing Epistemology, ed. Kornblith, for this sort of complaint aimed at foundationalism; and see Henderson, "Epistemic Competence and Contextualist Epistemology," for this sort of complaint aimed at coherentism. Henderson's discussion is particularly useful in this connection because he argues that contextualism (with regard to empirical belief) is not just, as he says, a "poor person's coherentism."

59. See Foley, *Working Without a Net,* chapter 3, for discussion of the sort of rationale for the notion of epistemic responsibility I am concerned with here.

60. I thank Stefan Sencerz and Michael DePaul for pressing me on the connection between my notion of responsible belief and the notion of justified belief operative in my thinking. I am afraid I must leave this part of my story for another occasion.

61. I take up these matters in my *Morality Without Foundations,* chapter 5.

12

An Annotated Bibliography
on Moral Epistemology

Mitchell R. Haney

This bibliography aims at aiding those who are beginning to venture into the area of moral epistemology. Therefore, I have selected and annotated a number of works within the field that would help the beginner get a foothold on the various issues and positions involved in the justification of moral claims. In addition, I have organized the selections under a number of important topics within moral epistemology to assist the reader in finding other literature pertinant to their interests. The topics below include: general volumes on moral epistemology, skepticism, several varieties of foundationalism, coherentism, contextualism, feminism, and finally, moral realism and antirealism.

General

Several recent collections bring together a variety of perspectives on moral epistemology:

Copp, David, and Zimmerman, David, eds. *Morality, Reason, and Truth: New Essays on the Foundations of Ethics.* Totowa, N.J.: Rowan and Allanheld, 1985.

Føllesdal, Dagfin, ed. "Justification in Ethics," *The Monist* 76, no. 3 (1993).

Odegard, D., ed. *Ethics and Justification.* Edmonton, Alberta: Academic Printing and Publishing, 1988.

Paul, E.F., F. Miller, Jr., and J. Paul, eds. *Cultural Pluralism and Moral Knowledge.* New York: Cambridge University Press, 1994.

Timmons, Mark, ed. "Spindel Conference 1990: Moral Epistemology." *Southern Journal of Philosophy* 29, supplement (1990). This volume contains an extensive bibliography on moral epistemology from 1971 to 1991.

Skepticism

Classical skepticism is described and endorsed by Sextus Empiricus in his *Outlines of Pyrrhonism* (*Sextus Empiricus,* vol. 1., trans. R. G. Bury, Cambridge: Harvard University Press, 1976). Another classic presentation of both general and moral skepticism can be found in David Hume's *A Treatise of Human Nature* (eds. L.A. Selby-Bigge and P. H. Nidditch. New York: Oxford University Press, 1978). Further developments and challenges to general and moral skepticism can also be found in the following works:

Bambrough, Renford. *Moral Skepticism and Moral Knowledge.* London: Routledge and Kegan Paul, 1979. A general introduction to the questions and proposed solutions revolving around the challenge of moral skepticism.

Brink, David, "Moral Realism and the Skeptical Arguments from Disagreement and Queerness." *Australasian Journal of Philosophy* 62 (1984): 111–25. An essay responding to J. L. Mackie's two arguments supporting ontological moral skepticism (see Mackie below).

Butchvarov, Panayot. *Skepticism in Ethics.* Bloomington: Indiana University Press, 1989. Although the author accepts empirical skepticism with regard to right and wrong, the author replies to the challenges of both epistemological and metaphysical skepticism with regard to goodness in a way similar in spirit to G. E. Moore.

Copp, David. "Moral Skepticism." *Philosophical Studies* 62 (1991): 203–33. This paper contains a defense of a non-argument-based version of epistemological moral skepticism.

———. "Explanation and Justification in Ethics." *Ethics* 100 (1990): 237–58. The author argues that even if moral claims are taken to be explanatory they can still fail to justify moral standards.

Fogelin, Robert J. *Pyrrhonian Reflections on Knowledge and Justification.* New York: Oxford University Press, 1994. Part II of this work develops a neo-Pyrrhonian version of epistemological skepticism, and argues that the best contemporary theories of justification fail to answer the problems posed by the traditional regress argument.

Goldman, Alan. "Skepticism About Goodness and Rightness." *Southern Journal of Philosophy* 29, supplement (1990): 167–84. The author discusses ontological skepticism, and outlines a coherentist version of justification that need not assume moral realism.

Harman, Gilbert. *The Nature of Morality—An Introduction to Ethics.* New York: Oxford University Press, 1977. The author argues that moral claims are explanatorily impotent. Many think that Harman's arguments entail ontological or epistemological skepticism, however, he thinks his version of moral relativism can avoid these conclusions.

Mackie, John Leslie. *Ethics: Inventing Right and Wrong.* New York: Penguin, 1977. In chapter 1, the author defends ontological skepticism based on the arguments from disagreement and queerness.

Russell, Bruce. "Two Forms of Moral Skepticism." *Ethical Theory: Classical and Contemporary Readings,* ed. Louis Pojman. Belmont, Calif.: Wadsworth, 1989. After distinguishing two forms of skepticism—epistemic and practical—the author argues that it is within the bounds of morality to answer epistemic skepticism, but it remains problematic whether or not it can answer practical skepticism.

Singer, Marcus. "Moral Skepticism." *Skepticism and Moral Principles: Modern Ethics in Review,* ed. C. Carter. Evanston, Ill.: New University Press, 1973. This essay presents a typology of moral skepticism and forwards some insightful observations about each type.

Sturgeon, Nicholas. "Moral Explanations," in Copp and Zimmerman, *Morality, Reason, and Truth: New Essays on the Foundations of Ethics.* Totowa, N.J.: Rowan and Allanheld, 1985. Responds to the arguments for moral skepticism derived from Gilbert Harman (see above).

Williams, Bernard. *Ethics and the Limits of Philosophy.* London: Fontana Press, 1985. This monograph contains arguments against abstract moral theorizing as the method for attaining moral justification. The author argues that we have moral knowledge at the level of prereflective moral concepts (e.g., cruelty, gratitude, courage, etc.), but that abstract ethical reflection destroys this knowledge and cannot create or re-create it.

Foundationalism

Foundationalism is one general response to the epistemological skeptic's challenge as it is posed in the regress argument. Here we will focus upon five forms of foundationalism: intuitionism, foundations in science, foundations in language, foundations in rationality, and contractarianism. The classic proponent of foundationalism as a response to skepticism is Rene Descartes in his *Meditations on First Philosophy* (2d rev. ed., New York: Liberal Arts Press, 1968). For more information with regard to foundationalism as a general and moral epistemological position see the following:

Alston, William. *Epistemic Justification: Essays in the Theory of Knowledge.* Ithaca, N.Y.: Cornell University Press, 1989. A collection of the author's essays on epistemology. Part one of the book contains several articles defending foundationalism.

Audi, Robert. *The Structure of Justification.* New York: Cambridge University Press, 1993. A variety of issues in epistemology are discussed in this collection of the author's essays. Part one of this book defends his own view of modest foundationalism, and part three contains his own views on how to respond to skepticism.

Timmons, Mark. "Foundationalism and the Structure of Justification." *Ethics* 97 (1987): 596–609. The author clarifies and distinguishes two types of ethical foundationalism and considers the issues involved in favoring foundationalism generally over nonfoundational alternatives.

Intuitionism

Intuitionism is a species of foundationalism. Since the eighteenth century, intuitionism has been a prominent position in moral epistemology. Some early defenders of intuitionism include: Henry Sidgwick, *The Methods of Ethics* (Chicago: University of Chicago Press, 1962); G. E. Moore, *Principia Ethica* (Buffalo, N.Y.: Prometheus, 1988); W. D. Ross, *The Right and the Good* (Oxford: Oxford University Press, 1930) and *The Foundations of Ethics* (Oxford: Clarendon Press, 1939); and H. A. Prichard, *Moral Obligation* (Oxford: Clarendon Press, 1949). After waning somewhat during the midcentury, intuitionism has begun to re-emerge as a leading response to moral skepticism. Today it is defended most prominently in the work of Robert Audi (e.g., "Ethical Reflectionism," *The Monist* 76, no. 3 (1993): 295–315). A similar view is defended by those who go under the title of moral particularism; such as, Jonathan Dancy, *Moral Reasons* (Cambridge, Mass.: Blackwell, 1993), and Lawrence Blum, *Moral Perception and Particularity* (New York: Cambridge University Press, 1994). However, the particularists reject the generalism of other intuitionists by arguing that moral justification need not and should not be in understood terms of subsuming cases under moral principles or rules. Other classic and contemporary works that discuss and defend intuitionism are:

Audi, Robert. "Moral Epistemology and the Supervenience of Ethical Concepts." *Southern Journal of Philosophy* 29, supplement (1990): 1–24. This essay contains a general overview of various options in moral epistemology, and concludes with arguments for favoring an intuitionist/rationalist position over other competitors.

Dancy, Jonathan. "Ethical Particularism and Morally Relevant Properties." *Mind* 92 (1983): 530–47. Dancy criticizes generalist approaches to the metaphysics and epistemology of morally relevant properties, then argues that particularism is much more successful at dealing with the way morally relevant properties operate in moral reasoning.

Ewing, A. C. *Ethics.* New York: Macmillan, 1947. A classic account of moral intuitionism that abandons the claim that moral intuitions are indubitable.

Hudson, W. D. *Ethical Intuitionism.* New York: St. Martin's Press, 1976. The author provides an historical survey of philosophers who have forwarded intuitionist positions, and then concludes the book with some critical remarks on the general intuitionist position.

McNaughton, David. *Moral Vision: An Introduction to Moral Theory.* Cambridge, Mass.: Blackwell, 1988. An introductory level book that focuses on traditional moral epistemological questions. The author goes on to defend a form of moral particularism.

Sinnott-Armstrong, Walter. "Moral Experience and Justification." *Southern Journal of Philosophy* 29, supplement (1990): 89–96. A critical response to William Tolhurst's "On the Epistemic Value of Moral Experience" (see below).

Tolhurst, William. "On the Epistemic Value of Moral Experience." *Southern Journal of Philosophy* 29, supplement (1990): 67–88. The author argues for the value of moral perception and the emotions for moral knowledge.

Walker, Margaret Urban. "Moral Particularity." *Metaphilosophy* 18 (1987): 171–85. A defense of moral particularism in terms of grounding moral knowledge on individual moral competence.

Foundations in Science

Another form of foundationalism holds that moral principles can be grounded on some nonnormative features of the natural world. Richard Brandt, *A Theory of the Good and the Right* (Oxford: Clarendon Press, 1979), is a leading proponent of this position. He argues that moral principles can be derived from a nonnormative analysis of rationality plus facts about human psychology. The following are works defending and criticizing the project of grounding morality on the findings of science:

Campbell, Richmond. "Sociobiology and the Possibility of Ethical Natural- ism," in David Copp and David Zimmerman, eds., *Morality, Reason, and Truth* Totowa, N.J.: Rowman and Allenheld, 1985. This paper contains a critical yet sympathetic discussion of E. O. Wilson and the implications of sociobiology for moral epistemology (see Wilson below).

Churchland, Paul. "Moral Facts and Moral Knowledge," in *A Neurocomputa- tional Perspective.* Cambridge, Mass.: MIT Press, 1979. This is a short essay relating findings in cognitive science to meta-ethical questions, specifically moral ontology and epistemology.

Clark, Andy. "Connectionism, Moral Cognition, and Collaborative Problem Solving," in Larry May, Marilyn Friedman, and Andy Clark, eds., *Mind and Morals.* Cambridge, Mass.: MIT Press, 1995. The author demonstrates some implications and the value of using findings of cognitive science for understanding moral knowledge.

Flanagan, Owen. *Varieties of Moral Personality: Ethics and Psychological Realism.* Cambridge, Mass.: Harvard University Press, 1991. This book is a thorough defense of the importance of the findings of empirical psychology to ethics.

Hudson, W. D., ed. *The Is/Ought Question: A Collection of Papers on the Central Problem in Moral Philosophy.* London: Macmillan, 1969. Twenty- two essays by leading philosophers on the is/ought problem in ethics. The essays are broken down into four topics: Hume on is/ought, reductions of ought to is, deriving ought from is, and description and evaluation.

Kohlberg, Lawrence. *The Philosophy of Moral Development: Moral Stages and the Idea of Justice.* San Francisco: Harper and Row, 1981. A work in moral psychology focusing on the development of moral thinking. Kohlberg's work has been the focus of much attention in ethics, especially since Carol Gilligan's attacks on his work, which has greatly influenced feminist ethics. (See Gilligan in the section on feminism below.)

Sturgeon, Nicholas. "Brandt's Moral Empiricism." *The Philosophical Review* 91, no. 3 (1982): 389–422. The author criticizes Brandt's account of "reforming definitions" and claims that when it comes to the application of Brandt's method it either begs or ignores substantive moral issues.

Wilson, E. O. *Sociobiology: The New Synthesis.* Oxford: Oxford University Press, 1975. The author argues that moral claims can be justified through grounding them in the findings of sociobiology.

Foundations in Language

R. M. Hare, *The Language of Morals* (Oxford: Clarendon Press, 1952), and others argue that one can ground moral principles in the logic of moral discourse. The following is a list of works that discuss and defend the claim that moral principles can be grounded in the nature of moral language:

Habermas, Jurgen. *Moral Consciousness and Communicative Action,* trans. Christian Lenhart and Shierry Weber Nicholsen. Cambridge, Mass.: MIT Press, 1990. This text forwards an account of moral justification based on the universal acceptance of given norms within a language community.

Benhabib, S., and F. Dallmayr, eds. *The Communicative Action Controversy.* Cambridge, Mass.: MIT Press, 1990. This volume includes articles by Habermas, some of his defenders, and some of his critics.

Hare, R. M. *Essays in Ethical Theory.* Oxford, Clarendon Press, 1989. This work extends Hare's universal prescriptivism into various topics within ethical theory.

———. *Freedom and Reason.* New York: Oxford University Press, 1965. This work argues that a form of utilitarianism is what arises out of an analysis of the logic of moral discourse.

———. *Moral Thinking: Its Levels, Method, and Point.* Oxford: Clarendon Press, 1981. Hare continues in this work his analysis of the logic and structure of moral discourse, and argues that at the critical level of moral thinking the logic of moral discourse justifies a utilitarian methodology.

Seanor, D., and N. Fotion. *Hare and Critics: Essays on "Moral Thinking."* Oxford: Clarendon Press, 1988. A collection of essays on the work of R. M. Hare, with a concluding chapter of Hare's responses.

Foundations in Rationality

Some philosophers, following the lead of Immanuel Kant in his *Groundwork of the Metaphysics of Morals* (trans. H. J. Paton, New York: Harper & Row, 1964) and his *Critique of Practical Reason* (trans. Lewis White Beck, New

York: Macmillan, 1956), have attempted to ground moral principles in either a normative or nonnormative account of rationality or rational action. The following is a list of works defending such an approach to moral justification:

Beyleveld, Deryck. *The Dialectical Necessity of Morality: An Analysis and Defense of Alan Gewirth's Argument to the Principle of General Consistency*. Chicago: Chicago University Press, 1991. This book presents an overview of Gewirth's argument for the principle of general consistency, and contains an encyclopedic account of and responses to a wide variety of criticisms.

Copp, David. "The 'Possibility' of a Categorical Imperative: Kant's Groundwork, Part III." *Philosophical Perspectives* 6, "Ethics" (1992): 261–84. The author argues that Kant's attempt to derive the moral law from practical reason fails, and he argues that other attempts at this type of foundationalism will fail for similar reasons.

Donagan, Alan. *The Theory of Morality*. Chicago: University of Chicago Press, 1977. The author favors a Kantian type of moral justification, and he argues that this theory is grounded in the universality of practical reason; he provides some interesting historical and cultural evidence to support this claim.

Gert, Bernard. *Morality*. New York: Oxford University Press, 1988. The author argues for the position that morality is grounded in impartial rationality.

Gewirth, Alan. *Reason and Morality*. Chicago: University of Chicago Press, 1978. This work attempts to justify a single-principled ethical theory (i.e., the "principle of general consistency") by appealing to certain nonnormative facts of human reason.

Regis, Edward, ed. *Gewirth's Ethical Rationalism*. Chicago: University of Chicago Press, 1984. This volume is a collection of critical articles on Gewirth, including responses by Gewirth.

Contractarianism

Classical contractarianism is formulated and defended as a method for justifying moral principles in Thomas Hobbes's *Leviathan* (trans. R. Tuck, Cambridge: Cambridge University Press, 1991), as well as in Jean Jacques Rousseau, *The Social Contract and Discourses* (trans. G. D. H. Cole, New York: E.P. Dutton, 1947), and John Locke, *Two Treatises of Government* (2d ed., London: Cambridge University Press, 1967). Although a contractarian framework can be used by coherentists in moral epistemology (see Rawls below), contractarianism has also been presented as a form of foundationalism. The following are contemporary works within the contractarian tradition:

Gauthier, David P. *Morals by Agreement*. Oxford: Oxford University Press, 1986. This work forwards a version of the social contract grounded in the actual abilities of human reasoning (making wide use of work in decision theory and economics) whereby moral agreement is grounded in a system that makes no moral assumptions.

Reiman, Jeffrey. *Justice and Modern Moral Philosophy.* New Haven: Yale University Press, 1990. This work sets out to vindicate the social contract procedure as the method for justifying moral claims on the basis of the nature of rationality. This work also contains a nice discussion of the history of the social contract tradition.

Vallentyne, Peter, ed. *Contractarianism and Rational Choice: Essays on David Gauthier's "Morals by Agreement."* New York: Cambridge University Press, 1991. A collection of essays on Gauthier's work. These essays are divided into three topics: Gauthier's contractarianism, his theory of rational choice, and his arguments for the rationality of keeping agreements.

Coherentism

Coherentism gained wider appeal as a response to the regress problem as it became apparent that foundationalist approaches in epistemology continued to suffer from skeptical objections. The following are some works discussing and defending coherentism as a general epistemological approach:

BonJour, Lawrence. *The Structure of Empirical Knowledge.* Cambridge, Mass.: Harvard University Press, 1985. The author offers an articulation and defense of coherentism for empirical knowledge.

Lehrer, Keith. *Knowledge.* Oxford: Clarendon Press, 1974. This work contains a defense of coherentism that differs from that of BonJour.

As a response to moral skepticism, John Rawls, "Outline of a Decision Procedure for Ethics" *(Philosophical Review* 60 (1951): 177–97) and *A Theory of Justice* (Cambridge, Mass.: Belknap Press of Harvard University Press, 1971); and later Norman Daniels, "Wide Reflective Equilibrium and Theory Acceptance in Ethics" (*The Journal of Philosophy* 76 (1979): 256–82) have motivated the use of coherentist methodologies for moral justification. The following are works both criticizing and defending coherentism in ethics:

Brink, David O. *Moral Realism and the Foundations of Ethics.* Cambridge: Cambridge University Press, 1989. In chapter 5, the author defends coherentism as the method of moral justification.

Daniels, Norman. "Reflective Equilibrium and Archimedean Points." *Canadian Journal of Philosophy* 10 (1980): 83–103. A discussion of reflective equilibrium with a focus upon the fact that for it to succeed there must be a set of moral judgments used to constrain our choice of background theories which are different than the judgments that constrain our choice of moral principles.

———. "Two Approaches to Theory Acceptance in Ethics." *Morality, Reason, and Truth,* eds. David Copp and David Zimmerman. Totowa, N.J.: Rowan and Allanheld, 1984: 120–40. A critical discussion of the differences between Rawls's reflective equilibrium approach to theory acceptance and Brandt's empiricism. The author argues that Brandt's empiricism is a form of coherentism.

DePaul, Michael R. *Balance and Refinement: Beyond Coherence Methods of Moral Inquiry.* New York: Routledge, 1993. This work forwards some strong criticisms of traditional ethical coherentism, then forwards a modified view called the method of "balance and refinement," which avoids those criticisms.

Goldman, Alan. *Moral Knowledge.* New York: Routledge, 1988. This work discusses whether or not empirical knowledge is a suitable model for moral knowledge and defends a version of coherentism.

Holmgren, Margaret. "The Wide and Narrow of Reflective Equilibrium." *Canadian Journal of Philosophy* 19 (1989): 43–60. The author argues that wide reflective equilibrium makes no advances over narrow reflective equilibrium when it comes to justifying moral principles; in fact, the author argues that there are good reasons to prefer narrow reflective equilibrium in ethics.

————. "Wide Reflective Equilibrium and Objective Moral Truth." *Metaphilosophy* 18 (1987): 104–24. A discussion of whether or not Rawls's wide reflective equilibrium is independent of epistemology and whether or not it presupposes objective moral truth.

Sayre-McCord, Geoffrey. "Coherence and Models for Moral Theorizing." *Pacific Philosophical Quarterly* 66 (1985): 170–90. This essay contains arguments for a metaphysically conservative account of coherence theory, but he also argues that one ought to be cautious when using coherence methods, because mere coherence belies the attainment of truth.

Sencerz, Stefan. "Moral Intuitions and Justification in Ethics." *Philosophical Studies* 50 (1986): 77–95. The author argues against the use of moral intuitions for the testing of moral principles in reflective equilibrium accounts of moral justification.

Timmons, Mark. "On the Epistemic Status of Considered Moral Judgments." *Southern Journal of Philosophy* 29, supplement (1990): 97–130. This essay contains arguments against realist construals of considered moral judgments (i.e., reflective moral intuitions) based on the fact that the semantic account necessary for such a realist construal is highly implausible.

Contextualism

Philosophers who have inspired or held contextualist responses to the regress argument have included C. S. Peirce, *The Collected Papers of Charles Sanders Peirce* (6 vols., eds. Charles Hartshorne and Paul Weiss. Cambridge, Mass.: Harvard University Press, 1931–35); John Dewey, *The Quest for Certainty* (New York: Minton, Balch, and Company, 1929); and Ludwig Wittgenstein,

On Certainty (eds. G. E. M. Anscombe and G. H. Von Wright. Oxford: Blackwell, 1969). The following are some references to work defending or discussing contextualism as a general epistemological position:

Annis, David. "A Contextualist Theory of Epistemic Justification." *American Philosophical Quarterly* 15 (1978): 213–19. A classic paper defending a general account of contextualism in epistemology.

Moser, Paul. *Empirical Justification.* Dordrecht: Reidel Publishing, 1985. Chapter 2 contains a discussion and criticisms of contextualism as an epistemological position.

Williams, Michael. *Unnatural Doubts: Epistemological Realism and the Basis of Skepticism.* Cambridge, Mass.: Basil Blackwell, 1991. The author presents a thorough discussion of skepticism, and argues for a contextualist response to the skeptic's challenges.

Contextualists in moral epistemology include the following:

Timmons, Mark. "Moral Justification in Context." *The Monist* 76 (1993), 360–78. The author presents contextualism as a structural position in moral epistemology.

Wellman, Carl. *Challenge and Response: Justification in Ethics.* Carbondale, Ill.: Southern Illinois University Press, 1971. This work argues for a model of contextual justification based upon whether an agent can answer all relevant challenges to his or her beliefs in a given context.

Feminism

Feminist philosophy has become a powerful voice in the last thirty years. Along with carving out diverse points of view toward the practice of philosophy generally, feminists have begun to develop many intricate and diverse systems in ethics and meta-ethics. A recent volume contains a set of papers, by leading feminists, on feminist epistemology: *Feminist Epistemologies* (eds. Linda Alcoff and Elizabeth Potter. New York: Routledge, 1993). This volume also includes an extensive bibliography of feminist epistemology. The following are some resources within feminist ethics and epistemology:

Addelson, Kathryn. *Moral Passages: Toward a Collectivist Moral Theory.* New York: Routledge, 1994. The author argues that knowledge and morality are generated in collective actions.

Card, Claudia, ed. *Feminist Ethics.* Lawrence, Kans.: University Press of Kansas, 1991. A collection of papers on trends in feminist ethics.

Code, Lorraine. *What Can She Know? Feminist Theory and the Construction of Knowledge.* Ithaca: Cornell University Press, 1991. The author criticizes traditional epistemology and outlines the criteria that a feminist epistemology must meet in order to capture the epistemology of a women's standpoint.

Gilligan, Carol. *In a Different Voice.* Cambridge: Harvard University Press, 1982. A pivotal work in moral psychology that has had a great impact on ethics in general and feminist ethics in particular. Of particular importance is her articulation of an ethics based on considerations of care as contrasted with ethical systems based on considerations of justice.

Harding, Sandra. *The Science Question in Feminism.* Ithaca: Cornell University Press, 1988. This monograph argues that the aim to achieve a distinctive method of feminist inquiry is misguided, and suggests a different way to pursue the project.

Ruddick, Sara. *Maternal Thinking: Towards a Politics of Peace.* Boston: Beacon Press, 1989. This work contains an elaboration and defense of "maternal thinking" as a distinctive way of knowing the world.

Tronto, Joan. *Moral Boundaries: A Political Argument for an Ethic of Care.* New York: Routledge, 1993. The author contests the association of care with gender, and argues that care is a central activity of human life. As such, traditional political and ethical theories must be reconceived to include the activity of caring.

Walker, Margaret Urban. "Feminism, Ethics, and the Question of Theory." *Hypatia* 7, no. 3 (1992): 23–38. The author explicates various feminist criticisms of ethics, and then outlines her own "expressive-collaborative" conception of morality and ethics.

———. "Moral Understandings: Alternative 'Epistemologies' for a Feminist Ethics." *Hypatia* 4, no. 2 (1989): 15–28. This essay explicates an account of feminist moral epistemology and identifies how it challenges prevailing views.

Moral Realism and Antirealism

Issues in metaphysics and semantics in general, and in particular the debate over realism and antirealism in ethics, have direct bearing upon moral epistemology. The *Southern Journal of Philosophy,* "Spindel Conference 1986: Moral Realism" (24, supplement, 1986), is an excellent collection of essays on this issue and includes an extensive bibliography. Below, however, is a very select set of references to work on this topic:

Blackburn, Simon. *Essays on Quasi-Realism.* New York: Oxford University Press, 1993. This book contains a collection of essays by the author where he presents a view that attempts to bridge the realist/antirealist divide. Section two of the book is devoted to topics in meta-ethics.

Brink, David O. *Moral Realism and the Foundations of Ethics.* Cambridge: Cambridge University Press, 1989. A systematic treatment of the foundations of ethics with a particular emphasis on vindicating moral realism.

Gibbard, Alan. *Wise Choices/Apt Feelings: A Theory of Normative Judgment.* Cambridge, Mass.: Harvard University Press, 1990. With a particular focus on the topic of rationality, the author expands noncognitivist/expressivist accounts of normative judgment into the realms of the rationality of decisions and actions, as well as a continued discussion of its application in the realm of moral judgment.

Horgan, Terry, and Mark Timmons. "New Wave Moral Realism Meets Moral Twin Earth." *The Journal of Philosophical Research,* 16 (1990): 447–65. Also in *Rationality, Morality, and Self-Interest: Essays Honoring Mark Carl Overvold,* ed. John Heil (Lanham, Md.: Rowman & Littlefield, 1993: 115–34). Employing a version of Hilary Putnam's "Twin-Earth" thought experiment, the authors argue that the semantic picture necessary to support naturalistic versions of moral realism is untenable.

Railton, Peter. "Moral Realism." *Philosophical Review* 95 (1986): 163–207. Outlines a naturalistic account of moral properties and argues that they not only play a role in causal explanations but in normative evaluations as well.

Sayre-McCord, Geoffrey, ed. *Essays on Moral Realism.* Ithaca: Cornell University Press, 1988. A collection of essays, both classic and contemporary, on the question of moral realism.

Sinnott-Armstrong, Walter. "Some Problems for Gibbard's Normative Expressivism." *Philosophical Studies* 69 (1993): 297–313. A critical paper on Alan Gibbard's *Wise Choices/Apt Feelings* (see above).

Index